Journal of Pentecostal Theology
Supplement Series
3

Editors
John Christopher Thomas
Rick D. Moore
Steven J. Land

Sheffield Academic Press
Sheffield

On the Cessation

of the Charismata

The Protestant

Polemic on

Postbiblical Miracles

Jon Ruthven

 Sheffield Academic Press

Copyright © 1993 Sheffield Academic Press

Published by Sheffield Academic Press
343 Fulwood Road
Sheffield S10 3BP
England

Typeset by Sheffield Academic Press
and
Printed on acid-free paper in Great Britain
by The Cromwell Press
Melksham, Wiltshire

British Library Catalogue in Publication Data

Ruthven, Jon
    On the Cessation of the Charismata:
    Protestant Polemic on Postbiblical
    Miracles.—(Journal of Pentecostal
    Theology Supplement Series, ISSN
    0966-7393; No. 3)
    I. Title II. Series
    231.7

    ISBN 1-85075-405-5 ✓

29598181

CONTENTS

PREFACE

Perhaps no theological issue among evangelicals provokes more controversy than the role of 'miraculous' spiritual gifts in the contemporary church. A recent *Christianity Today* poll reported that according to their readers two of the ten most important theological issues today concern the cessation and operation of certain gifts of the Holy Spirit. Traditions from within the Reformation and the Scofield *Reference Bible* had produced a broad consensus among evangelicals and fundamentalists (outside of charismatic and Pentecostal believers) that so-called 'extraordinary' or miraculous gifts, such as prophecy, direct divine revelation, healings, miracles and the like, had ceased with the apostles or their writings (this view may be labeled cessationism).

Within the last two decades, however, that consensus has been rapidly eroding. A growing capability in biblical interpretation has weaned these groups from uncritical dependence upon the classic Reformation and Scofieldian traditions. Further, the amazing worldwide growth of the Pentecostal–charismatic movement and the increasing sophistication of its apologists have also prompted a widespread re-evaluation of cessationism.

The purpose of this study is ultimately pastoral: to promote a common and radically biblical understanding of the charismata which may defuse this explosive conflict. Those who claim that miraculous gifts ceased with the end of the apostolic age, and some of those who claim to have experienced these gifts, share an underlying premise about them: that they evidence the divine sanction and status of their bearers. For much of traditional Protestantism, miracles served uniquely to accredit and establish the very foundation of the Christian faith within its first century while for others, contemporary charismatic experiences continue similarly to evidence a higher level of God's Spirit working in one's life.

My study examines this premise (which we may label evidentialism) about the charismata to determine if a philosophical, historical and scriptural investigation would indicate a less divisive role for them.

For example, one might ask, is the traditional Protestant concept of miracle an intelligible notion? Can a miracle serve as 'evidence' of divine sanction to any and all rational observers? Are the New Testament charismata 'miraculous evidence' in this sense? What are their biblically-defined purposes and functions? If the function of the charismata implies their duration, then how long does the New Testament expect the charismata to persist in the church? This study operates on the hope that if satisfactory answers to these questions emerge, then much of the modern conflict over spiritual gifts will be without basis. The intention here is not to preach to the converted or to proselytize, but simply to reframe the questions and propositions which have made the conflict over spiritual gifts so antagonistic. It is also my intention to advance the discussion beyond appeals to personal experience, important though they may be, or to the relatively limited biblical grounding which has characterized the discussion so far, and move toward a more comprehensive examination of the question.

The approach of this study necessarily involves a narrowing of focus: every voice in the debate cannot be heard and examined, though this study attempts to include significant representative viewpoints. For reasons outlined in Chapter 1 I have chosen to work through the significant arguments and presuppositions of the most prominent and representative exponent of cessationism, Benjamin B. Warfield in his *Counterfeit Miracles* (1918). Cessationist arguments—particularly biblical arguments—have advanced since Warfield's work; accordingly this study attempts to interact with these as the occasions arise. But the focus of the study is to evaluate Warfield's work on the basis of his own historical and hermeneutical methodology and to remain as much as possible within the structure of his key work.

I must acknowledge my debt to those who contributed to the project in so many ways: to my teachers throughout the years; to Les Whipp, a primal force in my early education at the University of Nebraska; to those at Central Bible College whose mentoring did not cease at graduation; to those at Trinity Evangelical Divinity School who taught me a deeper appreciation for the precision and power of Scripture; and to those at Marquette University who further confirmed that Christian warmth and intellectual rigor are not incompatible.

A few kind and persistent friends were crucially helpful in bringing this project to light, though they cannot be blamed for its patches of fog and obscurity: Drs Chris Thomas, Ed Neufeld, Larry Hurtado,

Dale Wheeler, Lyle Story and particularly Pat Carey. May God remember this to them for good.

I also acknowledge my debt to my parents, Reverend John Marshall and Beth Ruthven, whose love, zeal, generosity and aggressive faith demonstrated to me the 'power of God unto salvation', and to my parents-in-law, Fred and Dorothy Underhill, whose kindness made so much of this project possible. Finally, I wish to express my love and gratitude to my wife, Pamela, who made 'every surprise a happy one'.

ABBREVIATIONS

ABC	Abingdon Bible Commentary
AB	Anchor Bible
ABD	D.N. Freedman (ed.), *Anchor Bible Dictionary*
ALBO	Analecta lovaniensia biblica et orientalia
AnBib	Analecta biblica
ANQ	*Andover Newton Quarterly*
AQ	*American Quarterly*
ATR	*Anglican Theological Review*
BAGD	W. Bauer, W.F. Arndt, F.W. Gingrich and F.W. Danker, *Greek–English Lexicon of the New Testament*
BDF	F. Blass, A. Debrunner and R.W. Funk, *A Greek Grammar of the New Testament*
BEvT	Beiträge zur evangelischen Theologie
BFCT	Beiträge zur Förderung christlicher Theologie
BJRL	*Bulletin of the John Rylands University Library of Manchester*
BK	*Bibel und Kirche*
BNTC	Black's New Testament Commentaries
BSac	*Bibliotheca Sacra*
BTB	*Biblical Theology Bulletin*
BWANT	Beiträge zur Wissenschaft vom Alten und Neuen Testament
BZ	*Biblische Zeitschrift*
CBQ	*Catholic Biblical Quarterly*
CH	*Church History*
CJT	*Canadian Journal of Theology*
CQ	*Church Quarterly*
CT	*Christianity Today*
CTM	*Concordia Theological Monthly*
DDB	J.D. Davis (ed.), *A Dictionary of the Bible*
EBT	*Encyclopedia of Biblical Theology: The Complete Sacramentum Verbi*
EJ	*Evangelical Journal*
EMQ	*Evangelical Missions Quarterly*
EncChrTh	A. Kuyper (ed.), *Encyclopedia of Christian Theology*
EphCar	*Ephemerides Carmeliticae*
EvQ	*Evangelical Quarterly*
EvT	*Evangelische Theologie*
ExGT	*Expositor's Greek Testament*
ExpTim	*Expository Times*
GTJ	*Grace Theological Journal*
GOTR	*Greek Orthodox Theological Review*

GR	*Gordon Review*
HDCG	J. Hastings (ed.), *Dictionary of Christ and the Gospels*
HeyJ	*Heythrop Journal*
HNTC	Harper's NT Commentaries
HTR	*Harvard Theological Review*
ICC	International Critical Commentary
IDB	G.A. Buttrick (ed.), *Interpreter's Dictionary of the Bible*
Int	*Interpretation*
ISBE	G.W. Bromiley (ed.), *International Standard Bible Encyclopedia*, rev. edn
JBC	Jerome Biblical Commentary
JBL	*Journal of Biblical Literature*
JBR	*Journal of Bible and Religion*
JETS	*Journal of the Evangelical Theological Society*
JewEnc	*The Jewish Encyclopedia*
JPT	*Journal of Pentecostal Theology*
JQR	*Jewish Quarterly Review*
JRH	*Journal of Religious History*
JSJ	*Journal for the Study of Judaism in the Persian, Hellenistic and Roman Period*
JSS	*Journal of Semitic Studies*
JTS	*Journal of Theological Studies*
Kairos	*Kairos: Zeitschrift für Religionwissenschaft*
Lange'sCom	Lange's Commentary on the Bible
MeyerK	H.A.W. Meyer (ed.), Kritisch-exegetischer Kommentar über das Neue Testament
MHist	*Methodist History*
NCB	New Century Bible
NICNT	New International Commentary on the New Testament
NIDCC	J.D. Douglas (ed.), *New International Dictionary of the Christian Church*
NIDNTT	C. Brown (ed.), *The New International Dictionary of New Testament Theology*
NIGTC	The New International Greek Testament Commentary
NovT	*Novum Testamentum*
NovTSup	*Novum Testamentum* Supplements
NTD	Das Neue Testament Deutsch
NTS	*New Testament Studies*
PB	*Presbyterian Banner*
PG	J. Migne (ed.), *Patrologia graeca*
PJ	*Presbyterian Journal*
PL	J. Migne (ed.), *Patrologia latina*
PR	*Presbyterian Review*
RevExp	*Review and Expositor*
RTR	*Reformed Theological Review*
SANT	Studien zum Alten und Neuen Testament
SBET	*Scottish Bulletin of Evangelical Theology*
SBT	Studies in Biblical Theology

ScEs	*Science et esprit*
ScrB	*Scripture Bulletin*
SE	*Studia Evangelica*
SHERK	S. Jackson (ed.), *New Schaff–Herzog Encyclopedia of Religious Knowledge*
SJT	*Scottish Journal of Theology*
SSWW	J.E. Meeter (ed.), *Selected Shorter Works of Benjamin B. Warfield*
ST	*Studia theologica*
StNovT	*Studi Novi Testamenti*
StNovTBul	*Studia Novum Testamentum Bulletin*
Str–B	H. Strack and P. Billerbeck, *Kommentar zum Neuen Testament aus Talmud und Midrasch*
TD	*Theology Digest*
TDNT	G. Kittel and G. Friedrich (eds.), *Theological Dictionary of the New Testament*
TDOT	G.J. Botterweck and H. Ringgren (eds.), *Theological Dictionary of the Old Testament*
TGl	*Theologie und Glaube*
TLZ	*Theologischer Literaturzeitung*
TNTC	Tyndale New Testament Commentaries
TRev	*Theologische Revue*
TrinJ	*Trinity Journal*
TS	*Theological Studies*
TTod	*Theology Today*
TynBul	*Tyndale Bulletin*
TZ	*Theologische Zeitschrift*
UNT	Untersuchungen zum Neuen Testament
USQR	*Union Seminary Quarterly Review*
VE	*Vox Evangelica*
WBBW	E.D. Warfield (ed.), *The Works of Benjamin Warfield*
WTJ	*Westminster Theological Journal*
WW	*Word and World*
ZKT	*Zeitschrift für katholische Theologie*
ZNW	*Zeitschrift für die neutestamentliche Wissenschaft*
ZST	*Zeitschrift für systematische Theologie*

Chapter 1

INTRODUCTION

1. *The Setting of the Problem*

One of the most striking developments in twentieth-century church history has been the growth of Pentecostalism. This movement appeared as a few small sects in the 1910s and 1920s,[1] but by the 1950s it had grown to become the 'third force' in Christianity.[2] Since

1. Some of the best-known accounts of these beginnings include N. Bloch-Hoell, *The Pentecostal Movement: Its Origin, Development, and Distinctive Character* (Oslo: Universitetsforlaget, 1964); P. Damboriena, *Tongues as of Fire: Pentecostalism in Contemporary Christianity* (Washington, DC; Corpus Books, 1969); D.W. Dayton, *Theological Roots of Pentecostalism* (Metuchen, NJ: Scarecrow Press, 1987); S. Durasoff, *Bright Wind of the Spirit* (Englewood Cliffs, NJ: Prentice Hall, 1972); M. Harper, *As at the Beginning: The Twentieth Century Pentecostal Revival* (London: Hodder & Stoughton, 1965); D. Harrell, *All Things Are Possible: The Healing and Charismatic Revivals in Modern America* (Bloomington, IN: Indiana University Press, 1975); K. Kendrick, *A Promise Fulfilled: A History of the Modern Pentecostal Movement* (Springfield, MO: Gospel Publishing House, 1961); W.W. Menzies, *Anointed to Serve: The Story of the Assemblies of God* (Springfield, MO: Gospel Publishing House, 1971); J.T. Nichol, *Pentecostalism* (New York: Harper & Row, 1966), and V. Synan's three works: *The Holiness-Pentecostal Movement in the United States* (Grand Rapids: Eerdmans, 1972); *Aspects of Pentecostal-Charismatic Origins* (Plainfield, NJ: Logos, 1975); and *In the Latter Days: The Outpouring of the Holy Spirit in the Twentieth Century* (Ann Arbor, MI: Servant Books, 1984); E.L. Waldvogel, 'The "Overcoming Life": A Study of the Reformed Evangelical Origins of Pentecostalism' (PhD dissertation, Harvard University, 1977). The most prominent history of worldwide Pentecostalism, however, is W. Hollenweger's condensation and translation of his nine volume dissertation, *The Pentecostals* (London: SCM Press, 1972).

2. A well-known phrase coined by H.P. Van Dusen in his article, 'The Third Force in Christendom', *Life* 44 (June 1958), p. 13. This 'third force' of 20 million included the Churches of Christ, the Church of the Nazarene, Jehovah's Witnesses, Seventh Day Adventists and the Christian and Missionary Alliance. But according to

then this Pentecostal, or charismatic, movement has emerged as the largest branch of Protestantism, with estimates ranging to over 100 million adherents worldwide.[1]

This growth did not occur without opposition. Historically, Pentecostalism has provoked controversy at almost every stage of its development.[2] This has been true not merely because of its tradition-breaking forms of worship and practice, but, significantly for the purposes of this essay, because the emergence of Pentecostalism was a tangible challenge to a theological position maintained in the church for centuries: that the miraculous gifts of the Holy Spirit had ceased. Against this, the salient characteristic of Pentecostalism is its belief in the present-day manifestation of spiritual gifts, such as miraculous healing, prophecy and, most distinctively, glossolalia. Pentecostals affirm that these spiritual gifts (charismata) are granted by the Holy Spirit and are normative in contemporary church life and ministry.[3]

Van Dusen the Pentecostal groups represented the largest segment, numbering 8.5 million at that time.

1. So D. Barrett, *The World Christian Encyclopedia* (London: Oxford University Press, 1982), p. 838. He later upgraded this estimate to 332 million in a heavily documented article, 'The Twentieth-Century Pentecostal/Charismatic Renewal in the Holy Spirit, with its Goal of World Evangelization', *International Bulletin of Missionary Research* 12.3 (July 1988), p. 119. Barrett also projects 619 million by the end of the century (*s.v.* 'Statistics, Global', in S.M. Burgess, G.B. McGee and P.H. Alexander [eds.], *Dictionary of Pentecostal and Charismatic Movements* [Grand Rapids: Zondervan, 1988], p. 813). See also the discussion by W. Hollenweger, 'After Twenty Years' Research on Pentecostalism', *Theology* 87 (November 1984), pp. 403 and 411; Synan, *In the Latter Days*, pp. 9-23; and P. Wagner, 'The Greatest Church Growth is Beyond Our Shores', *CT* 28 (May 1984), pp. 25-31.

2. See Synan (*The Holiness-Pentecostal Movement*, pp. 80, 186), who writes of mob attacks and arson in the 1920s and thereafter; R. Quebedeaux, *The New Charismatics II* (New York: Harper & Row, 1983), pp. 39-44, 56, 193-96, 204-207, 209-10; J.C. Logan, 'Controversial Aspects of the Movement', in M.P. Hamilton (ed.), *The Charismatic Movement* (Grand Rapids: Eerdmans, 1975), pp. 33-46. K. McDonnell, *Presence, Power, Praise: Documents on the Charismatic Renewal* (3 vols.; Collegeville, MN: Liturgical Press, 1980) details some of these conflicts.

3. Commitment to these tenets is Barrett's criterion for identifying adherents to Pentecostalism. See Barrett's *World Christian Encyclopedia*. For a thorough presentation of Pentecostal theology, see F.D. Brunner, *A Theology of the Holy Spirit: The Pentecostal Experience and the New Testament Witness* (Grand Rapids: Eerdmans, 1975), pp. 19-149; Hollenweger, *Pentecostalism*, pp. 291-523, and, more sympa-

This conviction is becoming increasingly widespread in American society. In response to the statement, 'Even today miracles are performed by the power of God' 51% said they 'completely agree', while 29% said they 'mostly agree'. 9% disagreed 'somewhat', but only 6% disagreed 'strongly'.[1]

The cessationist[2] polemic, which was often directed against persons or groups claiming religious authority via any exhibition of divine healings, prophecies or miracles, recurs consistently from within such conflict settings throughout the history of the church and even within rabbinic Judaism. But it emerged in its modern form most prominently in the conflicts between Rome and the Protestant reformers, notably Calvin, then again during the Enlightenment in 'the 'great debate on miracles', and presently in the twentieth-century opposition to the Pentecostal–charismatic movement. In recent years the advancing front of charismatic growth has precipitated showers of polemical books and tracts,[3] virtually all reiterating this cessationist premise.

thetically, the three 'viewpoints' of MacDonald, Williams and Gelpi in R.P. Spittler (ed.), *Perspectives on the New Pentecostalism* (Grand Rapids: Baker, 1976), pp. 57-104.

1. G. Gallup, Jr, and S. Jones, *100 Questions and Answers: Religion in America* (Princeton: Princeton Religion Research Center, 1989), p. 10.

2. The terms 'cessationist' and 'cessationism' shall designate the position which holds that miracles or 'extraordinary' charismata were terminated at or near the end of the apostolic age.

3. The following are representative of the scores of books and articles supporting cessationism: V. Budgen, *Charismatics and the Word of God: A Biblical and Historical Perspective on the Charismatic Movement* (Durham: Evangelical Press, enlarged edn, 1989); W.J. Chantry, *Signs of the Apostles: Observations on Pentecostalism Old and New* (Edinburgh: Banner of Truth Trust, 1976); J. Dillow, *Speaking in Tongues* (Grand Rapids: Zondervan, 1975); T.R. Edgar, *Miraculous Gifts: Are They for Today?* (Neptune, NJ: Loizeaux Brothers, 1983); R.B. Gaffin, Jr, *Perspectives on Pentecost: Studies in New Testament Teaching on the Gifts of the Holy Spirit* (Grand Rapids: Baker, 1979); N.L. Geisler, *Signs and Wonders* (Wheaton, IL: Tyndale Press, 1988); R.G. Gromacki, *The Modern Tongues Movement* (Nutley, NJ: Presbyterian and Reformed Publishing, 1972); E.N. Gross, *Miracles, Demons and Spiritual Warfare: An Urgent Call for Discernment* (Grand Rapids: Baker, 1990); J.G. Howard, Jr, 'The Doctrine of Permanent Spiritual Gifts' (ThD dissertation, Dallas Theological Seminary, 1967); D. Judisch, *An Evaluation of Claims to the Charismatic Gifts* (Grand Rapids: Baker, 1978); J.F. MacArthur, Jr, *Charismatic Chaos* (Grand Rapids: Zondervan, 1992); K. McCaslin, *What the Bible Says about Miracles* (Joplin, MO: College Press, 1988); D. MacLeod, 'Has the

Moreover, an impressive list of scholars,[1] for example Adolph von Harnack, J.N.D. Kelly, Arnold Ehrhardt, Henry Chadwick, Hans von

Charismatic Age Ceased?', *Banner of Truth* 85 (1970), pp. 13-20; L.R. Reid, ' "That Which is Perfect" in 1 Corinthians 13.10' (MDiv thesis, Grace Theological Seminary, 1978); R.L. Reymond, *What About Continuing Revelations and Miracles in the Presbyterian Church Today? A Study of the Doctrine of the Sufficiency of Scripture* (Nutley, NJ: Presbyterian and Reformed Publishing, 1977); R. Ruble, 'A Scriptural Evaluation of Tongues in Contemporary Theology' (ThD dissertation, Dallas Theological Seminary, 1964); H. Sala, 'An Investigation of the Baptism and Filling Work of the Holy Spirit in the New Testament as Related to the Pentecostal Doctrine of Initial Evidence' (PhD dissertation, Bob Jones University, 1966); C.I. Scofield, *The Holy Bible, Scofield Reference Edition* (New York: Oxford University Press, 1909), p. 1224 n. 2; C.I. Scofield (ed.), *The New Scofield Reference Bible* (New York: Oxford University Press, 1968), p. 1245 n. 2; C.R. Swindoll, *Tongues: An Answer to Charismatic Confusion* (Portland, OR: Multnomah Press, 1981); R.L. Thomas, 'The Spiritual Gift of Prophecy in Rev. 22.18', *JETS* 32.2 (June 1989), pp. 201-16; *idem, Understanding Spiritual Gifts: The Christian's Special Gifts in Light of 1 Corinthians 12–14* (Chicago: Moody Press, 1978); S. Toussaint, '1 Corinthians 13 and the Tongues Question', *BS* 120 (October–December 1963), pp. 311-16; M.F. Unger, *The Baptism and Gifts of the Holy Spirit* (Chicago: Moody Press, 1974); J.F. Walvoord, *The Holy Spirit: A Comprehensive Study of the Person and Work of the Holy Spirit* (Grand Rapids: Zondervan, 3rd edn, 1977), ch. XX; C. Whitcomb, *Does God Want Christians to Perform Miracles Today?* (Winona Lake, IN: BMH Books, 1973); G.W. Zeller, *God's Gift of Tongues: The Nature, Purpose and Duration of Tongues as Taught in the Bible* (Neptune, NJ: Loizeaux Brothers, 1978). I am indebted to R.W. Graves, 'Tongues Shall Cease: A Critical Survey of the Supposed Cessation of the Charismata', *Paraclete* 17 (Fall 1983), pp. 26-27, for some of these references. He notes in cessationist writings the bewildering and imprecise variety of points at which the charismata are believed to have ceased, for example, after the writing of 1 Corinthians, the book of Hebrews, or the last New Testament book; at the closing of the canon of Scripture; when the New Testament was 'accepted' or 'circulated'; at the death of the last apostle; the death of the last disciple on whom the apostles conferred a charism; when the apostolic age passed; at the destruction of Jerusalem; when the Church matured in 'love' or in 'doctrine'; until faith was established; 'when the whole knowledge of God designed for the saving health of the world had been incorporated into the living body of the world's thought'.

1.   J.N.D. Kelly, *Early Christian Doctrines* (New York: Harper & Row, 1960), pp. 58-59; A. Ehrhardt, 'Christianity before the Apostles' Creed', *HTR* 55 (1962), p. 107; H. Chadwick, *The Early Church* (Baltimore: Penguin Books, 1967), p. 53; H. von Campenhausen, *The Formation of the Christian Bible* (trans. J.A. Baker: Philadelphia: Fortress Press, 1972), p. 234, and his *Ecclesiastical Authority and Spiritual Power in the Church of the First Three Centuries* (London: A. & C. Black,

Campenhausen and Jaroslav Pelikan, have similarly asserted and explained the disappearance of the 'religion of the Spirit and of power'[1] in the earliest church. These authors are essentially restating the classic Protestant position on this issue: that miraculous spiritual gifts, including prophecy, were in some sense 'foundational' in that they were essential for the initiation and spread of the Christian faith, but, like scaffolding, they were no longer required after the viable structure and doctrines of the church had been established.

This doctrine was not only stated in certain polemics and historical theology but was also virtually the consensus position of older Calvinistic and fundamentalist texts on systematic theology[2] and on the Holy Spirit.[3]

1969), p. 297, where the 'unbalanced ascendancy of office' displaced charismatic expression; J. Pelikan, *The Christian Tradition 1: The Emergence of the Catholic Tradition* (Chicago: University of Chicago Press, 1969), p. 106.

1. A. von Harnack, *The Mission and Expansion of Christianity in the First Three Centuries* (trans. J. Moffatt; London: Williams & Norgate, 1908), pp. 199-213. I am following J.L. Ash, Jr, 'The Decline of Ecstatic Prophecy in the Early Church', *TS* 37 (June 1976), pp. 227-52.

2. E.g. L. Berkhof, *Systematic Theology* (Grand Rapids: Eerdmans, 1953), pp. 177-78; J.O. Buswell, *A Systematic Theology of the Christian Religion* (Grand Rapids: Zondervan, 1963), p. 81: 'God generally ceased to work through "sign" miracles when the New Testament was finished; and [it] is His will that the "miracle of grace", the witness of the Spirit, answered prayer, and supremely, the written Word, shall be the chief sources of knowledge of Himself for His people during this age'; L.S. Chafer, *Systematic Theology*, VI (8 vols.; Dallas: Dallas Seminary Press, 1946), pp. 219-20; C.F.H. Henry, *God Revelation and Authority*, IV (6 vols.; Waco, TX: Word Books, 1979), pp. 284-89; A.A. Hodge, *Outlines of Theology* (New York: Charles Scribner's Sons, 1879), pp. 278-79; C. Hodge, *Systematic Theology*, I (3 vols.; New York: Charles Scribner's Sons, 1871), pp. 635-36. Both of these Hodges (son and father, respectively) gave only implicit approval to the idea of the cessation of miracles. Miracles were regarded by them as divine attestation that Christ and the writers of Old and New Testament documents were the true messengers of God. A.H. Strong, *Systematic Theology* (Philadelphia: Judson Press, 1907), p. 128: 'Miracles are the natural accompaniments and attestations of new communications from God. The great epochs of miracles—represented by Moses, the prophets, the first and second comings of Christ—are coincident with the great epochs of revelation. Miracles serve to draw attention to new truth (as it appears in Scripture), and ceases when this truth has gained currency and foothold.' A similar, though softer, position is sometimes maintained by Catholics. See J.B. Metz, 'Miracle I: Theological', in K. Rahner *et al.* (eds.), *Sacramentum Mundi*, IV (New York: Herder, 1969), p. 44. More recently it appears that most major theologians

2. *The Purpose and Method of this Study*

Many polemical and theological works either express directly or presuppose the position that the miraculous gifts of the Holy Spirit had
ceased. In response, some defenders of present-day charismata establish their case on historical studies which endeavor to show a more or
less continuous line of charismatic activity throughout the centuries.[1]

have shifted from this position; so, J. Rodman Williams, *The Eras of the Spirit*
(Plainfield, NJ: Logos, 1971).

3. Most classical Protestant texts on the Holy Spirit have supported this position,
for example A. Kuyper, *The Work of the Holy Spirit* (Grand Rapids: Eerdmans,
repr., 1979 [1900]), pp. 184-88; W.H. Griffith-Thomas, *The Holy Spirit of God*
(Grand Rapids: Eerdmans, 4th edn, repr., 1963 [1913]), *passim*; J. Owen, *On the
Spirit* (Philadelphia: The Protestant Episcopal Book Society, repr., 1862 [1674]),
Part 2, pp. 474, 475; G. Smeaton, *The Doctrine of the Holy Spirit* (Carlisle, PA:
The Banner of Truth Trust, repr., 1974 [1889]), pp. 55-56, 147; H.B. Swete, *The
Holy Spirit in the New Testament* (Grand Rapids: Baker, repr., 1976 [1910]),
pp. 378, 379. A classic text on the Holy Spirit in fundamentalist circles is
J.F. Walvoord, *The Holy Spirit* (Wheaton, IL: Van Campen Press, 1954), ch. XX:
'Temporary Spiritual Gifts'.

1. S.M. Burgess, *The Spirit and the Church: Antiquity* (Peabody, MA:
Hendrickson, 1984); R.N. Kydd, *Charismatic Gifts in the Early Church: An
Exploration into the Gifts of the Spirit in the First Three Centuries of the Christian
Church* (Peabody, MA: Hendrickson, 1984); J.C. Beker, 'Prophecy and the Spirit in
the Apostolic Fathers' (PhD dissertation, University of Chicago, 1955); G. Williams
and E. Waldvogel, 'A History of Speaking in Tongues and Related Gifts', in
Hamilton (ed.), *The Charismatic Movement*, pp. 61-113; T.A. Campbell,
'Charismata in the Christian Communities of the Second Century', *WTJ* 17 (Fall
1982), pp. 7-25; H.M. Evans, 'Tertullian: Pentecostal of Carthage', *Paraclete* 9
(Fall 1975), pp. 17-21; A.T. Floris, 'Two Fourth-Century Witnesses on the
Charismata', *Paraclete* 4 (Fall 1970), pp. 17-22; *idem*, 'Chrysostom and the
Charismata', *Paraclete* 5 (Winter 1971), pp. 17-22; H. Hunter, 'Tongues-speech: A
Patristic Analysis', *JETS* 23 (June 1980), pp. 125-37; M. Kelsey, *Healing and
Christianity* (New York: Harper & Row, 1973), pp. 135-99; J. LaPorte, 'The Holy
Spirit, Source of Life and Activity according to the Early Church', in E.D. O'Connor
(ed.), *Perspectives on Charismatic Renewal* (South Bend, IN: University of Notre
Dame Press, 1975), pp. 57-99; C.M. Robeck, Jr, 'Visions and Prophecy in the
Writings of Cyprian', *Paraclete* 16 (Summer 1982), pp. 21-25; H. Schlingensiepen,
*Die Wunder des Neuen Testament: Wege und Abwege bis zur Mitte des fünften
Jahrhunderts* (Gütersloh: Bertelsmann, 1933); H.F. Stander, 'Miraculous Charisms
in Eusebius' Time', *Paraclete* 21 (Fall 1982), pp. 11-14; J. Serr, 'Les charisms dans
la vie de l'église; temoinanges patristiques', *Foi et Vie* 72.1 (1973), pp. 33-42; and

Despite the relatively large size of the Pentecostal–charismatic constituency, there has been—with a small, but growing, number of exceptions[1]—very little scholarly effort to trace and evaluate the

E.A. Stephanou, 'The Charismata in the Early Church Fathers', *GOTR* 21 (Summer 1976), pp. 125-46, among others.

1. D.A. Codling, 'The Argument that the Revelatory Gifts of the Holy Spirit Ceased with the Closure of the Canon of Scripture' (ThM thesis, Westminster Theological Seminary, 1974). On a more popular level is the classic older Pentecostal polemic by C. Brumback, *'What Meaneth This?' A Pentecostal Answer to a Pentecostal Question* (Springfield, MO: Gospel Publishing House, 1947). Since this present study was begun, several works have appeared dealing exegetically with the issue of cessationism: W. Grudem, *The Gift of Prophecy in the New Testament and Today* (Westchester, IL: Crossway Books, 1988); M.M.B. Turner, 'Spiritual Gifts Then and Now', *VE* 15 (1985), pp. 7-64; M. Lloyd-Jones, *The Sovereign Spirit: Discerning His Gifts* (Wheaton, IL: Harold Shaw, 1985); D.A. Carson, *Showing the Spirit: A Theological Exposition of 1 Corinthians 12–14* (Grand Rapids: Baker, 1987), pp. 66-76; and G. Houston, *Prophecy: A Gift for Today?* (Downers Grove, IL: Inter-Varsity Press, 1989). A treatment of this issue from a Roman Catholic perspective is in Y.M.-J. Congar, 'Excursus B: The Permanence of the *"Revelatio"* and *"Inspiratio"* in the Church', in *Tradition and Traditions* (trans. M. Naseby and T. Rainborough; New York: Macmillan, 1967), pp. 119-37, and from a charismatic viewpoint, C.M. Robeck, Jr, 'Canon, *Regulae Fidei* and Continuing Revelation in the Early Church', in J.E. Bradley and R.A. Muller (eds.), *Church, Word and Spirit: Historical and Theological Essays in Honor of Geoffrey W. Bromiley* (Grand Rapids: Eerdmans, 1987), pp. 65-91; D. Williams, *Signs, Wonders and the Kingdom of God* (Ann Arbor, MI: Servant Publications, 1989), and J.R. Williams, 'Excursus: On the Cessation of Miracles', in *Renewal Theology: God, The World and Redemption* (Grand Rapids: Zondervan, 1988), pp. 158-68. P.S. Minear provides a thoughtful analysis of the problem in his *To Heal and Reveal: The Prophetic Vocation according to Luke* (New York: Seabury, 1976), ch. 7: 'The Prophetic Vocation Today', pp. 147-66.

A pioneering theological and biblically based polemic for the continuation of 'extraordinary' spiritual gifts appeared in the works of E. Irving (*The Collected Writings of Edward Irving in Five Volumes* [London: Alexander Strahan, 1864]), to whose career but little of his argument B.B. Warfield devotes a chapter in his book *Counterfeit Miracles* (New York: Charles Scribner's Sons, 1918). Much of the rhetoric of the debate among Pentecostal and non-Pentecostal fundamentalists of this century may be traced to an acrimonious attack on Irving by John Darby, the theological father of dispensationalism, which was encapsulated in and disseminated widely by Scofield's *Reference Bible*. See L.E. Dixon, 'Have the "Jewels of the Church" Been Found Again?', *EJ* 5 (Fall 1987), pp. 78-92. A decade or so later, in the 1880s and 90s, a number of healing evangelists such as A.B. Simpson, F.F. Bosworth, A.J. Gordon, R.A. Torrey, John Alexander Dowie and

cessationist position, including its historical and biblical aspects, from a perspective of systematic theology. This study examines a major expression of this cessationist tradition.

The doctrine that miraculous gifts of the Holy Spirit ceased around the apostolic age has evolved over the long expanse of church history, and has found expression in various religious persuasions and philosophical convictions. This study evaluates the historical levels of influence from John Calvin to Warfield and the rationale for this cessationist polemic. It focuses in particular upon B.B. Warfield's thought because this represents the historical culmination of the cessationist tradition and because Warfield was the most prominent modern evangelical advocate for the position. His thought is singled out here because he stands at or near the end of the evolution of cessationism, works within Calvinism, the dominant religious tradition espousing this position, and is steeped in the modern philosophical presuppositions which undergird the recent expressions of cessationism.

Benjamin Breckinridge Warfield (b. 1855) was a professor of didactic and polemic theology at Princeton Seminary from 1887 until his death in 1921. Warfield is perhaps best known as the last of the defenders of Calvinist orthodoxy who remained at Princeton. In a prodigious number of articles, book reviews and monographs[1] Warfield attempted to withstand the rising tide of liberalism which had, he thought, denied the divine inspiration and inerrancy of Scripture. An extension of this concern was the increasing emphasis upon religious experience which, to Warfield, de-emphasized the centrality of propositional revelation which comprised the text of Scripture. This new challenge to Princeton orthodoxy found various expressions in the thought of Albrecht Ritschl and A.C. McGiffert, the subjectivism of the Wesleyan 'higher life' and Keswick movements,

---

R.L. Stanton argued for the recurrence of the church of miraculous healings, but met resistance from most mainline Protestant periodicals. See R.J. Cunningham, 'From Holiness to Healing: The Faith Cure in America 1872–1892', *CH* 43 (December 1974), pp. 506-10, and E. Waldvogel, 'Chapter 4: An Evangelical Theology of Healing', in her 'The Overcoming Life: A Study in the Reformed Evangelical Origins of Pentecostalism' (PhD dissertation, Harvard University, 1977), pp. 122-48.

1. Much of Warfield's published and unpublished writings are collected in his *Opuscula Warfieldii*, located at Speer Library, Princeton Theological Seminary. The definitive bibliography of his works is that compiled by J. Meeter and R. Nicole, *A Bibliography of Benjamin Breckinbridge Warfield, 1851–1921* (Nutley, NJ: Presbyterian and Reformed Publishing, 1974).

and in the charismatic revelations and miracles claimed by many religious groups. Warfield was aware of Pentecostalism as a separate movement, but mentions it only in passing,[1] since during his time it had barely become organized.

To most theological leaders of millions of evangelicals and fundamentalists in North America, the collection of Warfield's work in *The Inspiration and Authority of the Bible*[2] stands as the definitive statement on the nature of biblical revelation. To the considerable degree that this issue stands as a sensitive and divisive problem among evangelicals today, Warfield's work remains a major benchmark for the debate.[3]

1. B.B. Warfield, *Perfectionism*, Part One, in E.D. Warfield (ed.), *The Works of Benjamin B. Warfield*, VII (10 vols.; Grand Rapids: Baker, repr., 1981 [1931]), pp. 326-30; hereafter, *WBBW*.

2. Edited by S.G. Craig with an introduction by C. Van Til (New York: Oxford University Press, 1927).

3. For example, see the articles by evangelical authors: D.P. Fuller, 'Benjamin B. Warfield's View of Faith and History', *JETS* 11 (Spring 1968), pp. 75-83; J.H. Gerstner, 'Warfield's Case for Biblical Inerrancy', in J.W. Montgomery (ed.), *God's Inerrant Word* (Minneapolis: Bethany Fellowship, 1974); D. Jodoch, 'The Impact of Cultural Change: Princeton Theology and Scriptural Authority Today', *Dialogue* 22 (Winter 1983), pp. 21-29; H. Krabbendam, 'B.B. Warfield vs. G.C. Berkhouwer on Scripture', in N. Geisler (ed.), *Inerrancy: The Extent of Biblical Authority* (Grand Rapids: Zondervan, 1980); R. Nicole, 'The Inspiration and Authority of Scripture: J.D.G. Dunn vs. B.B. Warfield', *The Churchman* 97.3 (1983), pp. 198-215; 98.1 (1984), pp. 7-27; *idem*, 'The Inspiration of Scripture: B.B. Warfield and Dr Dewey M. Beegle', *GR* 8 (1965), pp. 93-109; M. Parsons, 'Warfield and Scripture', *The Churchman* 91 (July 1977), pp. 198-220; J.B. Rogers, 'Van Til and Warfield on Scripture in the Westminster Confession', in E.R. Geehan (ed.), *Jerusalem and Athens* (Nutley, NJ: Presbyterian and Reformed Publishers, 1971); E.R. Sandeen, 'The Princeton Theology: One Source of Biblical Literalism in American Protestantism', *CH* 23 (October 1964), pp. 74-87; D. Westblade, 'Benjamin W. Warfield on Inspiration and Inerrancy', *SBT* 10 (1980), pp. 27-43. In H. Lindsell's controversial *Battle for the Bible* (Grand Rapids: Zondervan, 1976), Warfield is cited frequently, e.g. on pp. 70, 106, 113, 150 and 185. Elsewhere he notes, 'Perhaps no theologian of that age is as widely read and has had his books kept in print so long as Warfield'. See also H. Lindsell, 'Warfield, B(enjamin) B(reckinridge)', in J.D. Douglas (ed.), *The New International Dictionary of the Christian Church* (Grand Rapids: Zondervan, 1974), p. 1030. In *Fundamentalism* (Philadelphia: Westminster Press, 1977), p. 262, James Barr states: 'In respect of the doctrine of scripture it was the [old Princeton] tradition, and especially the contribution of Warfield himself, that molded the set of ideas we now

But Warfield's decisive influence was not limited to the evangelical debate on Scripture. He also produced a definitive statement for evangelicals on another issue: the occurrence of modern-day miracles. In the evangelical debates over the continuation of charismatic gifts, Warfield's *Counterfeit Miracles* remains, after seven decades, the major starting point for this discussion as well. Accordingly, this study treats Warfield's *Counterfeit Miracles*[1] as the final, authoritative

know as fundamentalism'. D. Clair Davis also affirms Warfield's significance in 'Princeton and Inerrancy: The Nineteenth-Century Philosophical Background of Contemporary Concerns', in J.D. Hannah (ed.), *Inerrancy and the Church* (Chicago: Moody Press, 1984), pp. 259-60: 'To this day Warfield's *Inspiration and Authority of the Bible* serves throughout Evangelical academia as the starting point'. Similarly, M. Noll, 'Benjamin B. Warfield', in W.A. Elwell (ed.), *Evangelical Dictionary of Theology* (Grand Rapids: Baker, 1984), p. 1156. In his important study *The Uses of Scripture in Recent Theology* (Philadelphia: Fortress Press, 1975), p. 16, D.H. Kelsey describes Warfield as '*the* Princeton theologian far. . . and away the ablest mind defending Calvinist orthodoxy in the United States in the 1880s and 90s' (his italics).

1. New York: Charles Scribner's Sons, 1918. Warfield's impact on modern evangelical thinking on miracles is duly noted by: C.F.H. Henry, *God, Revelation and Authority*, IV (6 vols.; Waco, TX: Word Books, 1979), p. 287; A. Hoekema, *Holy Spirit Baptism* (Grand Rapids: Eerdmans, 1971), p. 59; J. Woodbridge, M. Noll and N. Hatch, *The Gospel in America* (Grand Rapids: Zondervan, 1979), p. 77. Also G. Mallone in *Those Controversial Gifts* (Downers Grove, IL: Inter-Varsity Press, 1983), p. 3, notes, 'B.B. Warfield's teaching on [the] cessation of the gifts has now influenced almost an entire century of the church's life'. Again, a well-known fundamentalist writer, J.S. Baxter, in his somewhat ambiguous defense of modern miracles, *Divine Healing for the Body* (Grand Rapids: Zondervan, 1979), p. 53, repeatedly refers to Warfield and introduces him with 'Other well-known writers. . . might be quoted as supporting this theory' but Warfield, in 'his brilliant treatise', *Counterfeit Miracles*, 'most powerfully represents them all'. In an important new book, *Miracles and the Critical Mind* (Grand Rapids: Eerdmans, 1983), p. 198, C. Brown asserts that Warfield 'was in many ways. . . the doyen of American evangelical polemicists. . . Although he has been dead for over sixty years, his views still carry great weight in evangelical circles on a wide range of issues'. See also L. Monden, *Signs and Wonders: A Study of the Miraculous Element in Religion* (New York: Desclée, 1966), p. 295 n. 92. Buswell, in his *Systematic Theology*, p. 182, affirms that 'the best work in the field (of cessationism) is Benjamin B. Warfield's'. According to Synan (*In the Latter Days*, p. 77), 'The last word on the subject' and 'the ultimate statement of the cessation theory' came from Warfield's *Counterfeit Miracles*. Rodman Williams, 'Excursus: On the Cessation of Miracles', p. 162, interacts mainly with Warfield, introducing him as 'the strongest—in many

and representative expression of cessationism for conservative American evangelicalism.

Warfield's polemic is expressed in the traditional Protestant cessationist propositions about miraculous charismata, for example (1) the essential role of miraculous charismata is to accredit true doctrine or its bearers, (2) while God may providentially act in unusual, even striking ways, true miracles are limited to epochs of special divine revelation, that is, those within the biblical period; and (3) miracles are judged by the doctrines they purport to accredit: if the doctrines are false, or alter orthodox doctrines, their accompanying miracles are necessarily counterfeit.

This study critically examines the central premises underlying Warfield's polemic on miracles, evaluating the validity of his argument primarily on the basis of the internal consistency of his thought. The thesis of this study is that Warfield's polemic—the culmination of a historically evolving argument directed against certain threats to institutional religion—fails because of internal inconsistencies with respect to its concept of miracle, its historical method and its biblical hermeneutics. Insofar as these errors are characteristic of more contemporary forms of cessationism, the latter also fail.

The central failure of Warfield's cessationism is the confusion of the *sufficiency* of revelation, that is, in the unique historical manifestation of Christ and apostolic doctrine as finally revealed in Scripture, with the procedural *means* of communicating, expressing and applying that revelation, that is, via the charismata, including gifts of prophecy and miracles. In other words, the charismata do not accredit the Gospel; they express the Gospel. Just as the act of preaching does not add to the biblical canon, so neither does the gift of prophecy; as a charism of hospitality expresses but does not replace the totality of Christ's gracious sacrifice, so also a gift of healing.

The argument proper of this work occupies its three subsequent chapters. The remainder of this chapter is a brief historical investigation of some key elements in the cessationist polemic which Warfield shares, such as the context of religious conflict precipitating the polemic, and its various justifications, which include its underlying epistemology and view of miracle. Chapter 2 then concentrates systematically upon Warfield's polemic itself, noting the historical

ways the most influential—person to affirm the cessation of miracles' in the early part of this century.

factors precipitating it, and critically examining his rationale for cessationism, including its epistemology and view of miracle. Chapter 2 also evaluates Warfield on the basis of the consistency of his thought and the validity of his scriptural exegesis. Chapter 3 carries this critical analysis further by testing Warfield's rationale for his polemic against the understanding of Scripture which his own hermeneutics implies. This chapter first examines the biblical portrayal of the Holy Spirit and of the kingdom of God and finds them both to be inimical to cessationism. With this biblically-grounded understanding of Spirit and kingdom as a contextual background, Chapter 3 also examines key passages of Scripture relating to cessationism which Warfield and cessationist polemicists generally fail to treat. Chapter 4 offers a summary and conclusions.

3. *Historical Antecedents*

Warfield's cessationism did not, of course, suddenly appear in its highly evolved form at the beginning of the twentieth century. Cessationism developed from a complex stew of post-biblical theologies and philosophies that had long been simmering in their polemical cauldron. Battles over the continuation of certain spiritual gifts drastically distorted the understanding of their very nature and purpose. As certain emphases within doctrines such as Christology, the Holy Spirit, the Kingdom of God and ecclesiology have evolved far from those of the New Testament, the dependent understanding of the charismata and 'miracles' has also become drastically distorted. For example, these days the word 'miracle' conjures up to laypersons apparitions of the Blessed Virgin, canonizing saints, televangelists, narrow escapes or photocopier ads, while 'charisma' describes an attractive personality or a seductive brand of cologne. When we exclaim, 'wonders never cease!' at an unexpected virtue, we are reacting to an implicit cessationism.

Cessationism did not originate within orthodox Christianity but within normative Judaism and in Christian sects during the first three centuries of the Common Era. In Judaism, three major elements of a cessationist position emerged.

First, from the Maccabean era onward, Judaism harbored an ambivalence about prophecy and miracles: lamenting, on the one hand, the loss of prophets and God's miraculous interventions, and on the other, a readiness to accept reports of such activity when it appeared. Hence, a compromise: there was a tendency to view prophecy and miracles on a two-tier level: (1) the classical prophets and miraculous events described in the Scriptures, and (2) the various attenuated forms of prophecy and miracles, such as the *bat qol* and miracle accounts of early rabbis.[1]

Secondly, the feeling nonetheless persisted that the highest level of the Spirit's activity had ended, so that by the end of the first century CE, an unusually pious rabbi might 'merit' the Holy Spirit (that is, the gifts of prophecy and miracles), but not receive it because post-biblical (OT) generations are not worthy.[2]

Thirdly, more importantly, the issue of religious authority between charismatics who, even in legendary accounts, may have wished to use prophecy and miracle to establish their doctrinal credibility, increasingly lost out to those who relied on the interpretive skill and consensus of the academy.[3] Prophecy and miracle working were replaced by

---

1. Literally 'daughter of a voice', an echo, suggesting an inner voice or revelatory impression. On the *bat qol* see the article in *JewEnc*, IV, p. 323. On rabbinic wonderworkers see G. Vermes, *Jesus the Jew* (Philadelphia: Fortress Press, 1973), pp. 77-79. Interestingly, Grudem in *The Gift of Prophecy* utilizes the rabbinic distinction between the OT prophet and later manifestations of less authoritative revelations (for example *bat qol*) in his understanding of NT apostleship and its relation to NT prophecy: the former in both cases express the absolute word of God while the latter is only relatively so.

On the cessation of miracles and prophecy in early Judaism see D.E. Aune, *Prophecy in Early Christianity and the Ancient Mediterranean* (Grand Rapids: Eerdmans, 1983), pp. 103-107; A.I. Baumgarten, 'Miracles and Halakah in Rabbinic Judaism', *JQR* 73 (January 1983), pp. 238-53; B.M. Bokser, 'Wonder-Working and the Rabbinic Tradition: The Case of Hanina ben Dosa', *JSJ* 16 (1986), pp. 42-92; W.D. Davies, *Paul and Rabbinic Judaism* (London: SPCK, 3rd edn, 1970), pp. 208-16; F.E. Greenspahn, 'Why Prophecy Ceased', *JBL* 108.1 (1989), pp. 27-49; Grudem, *The Gift of Prophecy*, pp. 21-33; D. Hill, *New Testament Prophecy* (Atlanta: John Knox, 1979), pp. 33-37; R.A. Horsley, '"Like One of the Prophets of Old": Two Types of Popular Prophets at the Time of Jesus', *CBQ* 47 (July 1985), pp. 435-63; R. Leivestad, 'Das Dogma von der prophetenlosen Zeit', *NTS* 19 (April 1973), pp. 288-99; R. Meyer, 'προφήτης', *TDNT*, VI, pp. 812-28; K. Schubert, 'Wunderberichte und ihr Kerygma in der rabbinischen Tradition', *Kairos* 24.1 (19812), pp. 31-37.

2. E.g. *Ber.* 20a and *Sanh.* 11a.

3. *b. B. Meṣ.* 59b. Opposite results obtained in other cases: *y. Ber.* 3b and *b. Ber.* 52a.

study of the Torah and its scholarly interpretations.[1] In reaction against the radical charismatic messianic pretenders of the revolts against Rome and against the rapidly growing charismatic Christian movement, Judaism became a religion based on the one true God, the written Torah and its scholastic interpretation. Because of that miracles and prophecies, perforce, had ceased.

An early form of cessationism was directed at Jesus. One of the accusations which led to his execution was that he had violated the commands of Deuteronomy 13 and 18, which forbid performing a sign or a wonder to lead the people astray after false gods. The cessationist polemic was directed not only against later charismatic Christians,[2] but intramurally within Judaism by competing rabbis.[3]

The Jewish admission that prophecy and miracles had ceased among them, however, proved an irresistible target for Christian polemics. Apologists such as Justin (c. 100–c. 165), Origen (c. 185–c. 254) and Cyril (315–386), argued that God had withdrawn the Spirit of prophecy and miracles from the Jews and transferred it to the church as proof of its continued divine favor.[4] Thus the church moved

---

1. To the rabbis, the prophets, after all, were merely expositors of the Law: *b. Meg.* 14a; *b. Tem.* 16a; *Exod. R.* 42.8 on 19.3; *Lev. R.* 15.2 on 13.2; *S. 'Ol. R.* 21, 30; *b. B. Bat.* 12a. See the summary of this point in R. Meyer, 'προφήτης, κτλ', *TDNT*, VI, p. 818.

2. *Sanh.* 10.1. The one who will have no part in the life to come is one who 'reads the heretical books, or that utters charms over a wound and says, "I will put none of the diseases upon thee which I put upon the Egyptians; for I am the Lord that healeth thee"'. Abba Saul says, 'Also he that pronounces the Name with its proper letters'. In the *Mishnah* and *Talmud*, from which all anti-Christian polemics were extirpated during the Middle Ages, this passage may have survived. The 'heretical books' could well refer to Christian writings, the healings to Christian practice and the reference to the 'Lord' (Yahweh) could designate Jesus Christ, particularly in the Johannine ἐγώ εἰμί passages.

3. F.E. Greenspahn, 'Why Prophecy Ceased', *JBL* 108.1 (Spring 1989), pp. 37-49, and Vermes, *Jesus the Jew*, pp. 80-82.

4. *Trypho* 87: the charismata came in fullness upon Jesus and 'would find their accomplishment in him, so that there would be no more prophets in your nation after the ancient custom: and this fact you plainly perceive. For after him no prophet has arisen among you'. Further, he notes, when '[Christ] came, after whom, it was requisite that such gifts should cease from you; and having received their rest in him, should again, as had been predicted, become gifts which, from the grace of his Spirit's power, he imparts to those who believe in him'. Earlier Justin had insisted that 'the prophetical gifts remain with us [the church] to the present time. And hence

toward the Jewish aberrant view of miracle: evidentialism, the view that the primary, if not exclusive, function of miracles is to accredit and vindicate a doctrinal system or its bearers.

The second source of cessationism arose within Montanism. Some church fathers reacted against an alleged cessationist statement by a Montanist prophetess. They cite her as claiming, 'After me there will be no more prophecy, but the end (συντέλειαν'),[1] a probable reference to Jesus' use of the word in Mt. 28.20. Against this hint of cessationism some appealed to 1 Cor. 13.10. For example Eusebius records that Miltiades does so against Maximilla and concludes: 'it is necessary that the prophetic charisma be in *all the Church until the final coming*'.[2]

you ought to understand that [the gifts] formerly among your nation have been transferred to us'.

Origen also notes the Jews' own concession about the disappearance of miracles and prophecy within their own community: 'Since the coming of Christ, no prophets have arisen among the Jews, who have *admittedly* been abandoned by the Holy Spirit' (*Contra Celsum* 7.8). Elsewhere Origen insists, 'God's care of the Jews was transferred to those Gentiles who believe in him. Accordingly [they] have not even any vestige of divine power among them. They no longer have any prophets or wonders, though traces of these are to be found to a considerable extent among Christians. Indeed, some works are even greater; and if our word may be trusted, we also have seen them' (*Contra Celsum* 2.8). So also *Commentary on Matthew*. See the discussion in N.R. DeLange, *Origen and the Jews: Studies in Jewish–Christian Relations in the Third Century* (Cambridge: Cambridge University Press, 1976), pp. 81-82, who cites similar points in Origen's *First Principles* I, 3, 7; *Psalms*, Homily XXXVI, III, 10; *Leviticus*, Homily XI, 5. Cyril of Jerusalem makes a similar 'dispensational' argument against the Jews in his *Catechetical Lectures*, 18.23, 26.

This whole line of argument must have been ironically familiar to Jews who had often argued that at one time Gentiles had experienced the Holy Spirit, but because they misused the prophetic gift, as did Balaam for example, or because of epochal religious developments, such as the giving of the Torah or the completion of the tabernacle, the Spirit was totally transferred from any Gentile participation to the Jews alone. See E. Sjöberg, 'πνεῦμα', *TDNT*, VI, p. 383.

1. Epiphanius, *Against Panarion* 48.5.4, cited in P. de Labriolle, *Les Sources de l'Histoire du Montanisme* (Paris: Leroux, 1913), p. 117: μετ' ἐμέ προφῆτις οὐκέτι ἔσται ἀλλά συντέλειαν.

2. δεῖν γάρ εἶναι τό προφητικόν χάρισμα ἐν πάσῃ τῇ ἐκκλησίᾳ μέχρι τῆς τελείας παρουσίας. *Against Alcibiades* in Eusebius, *Church History* 5.17.4. Didymus of Alexandria cites 13.8-10 in full and assigns τό τέλειον to the time after the resurrection and the 'second coming of the Lord (τῆς δευτέρας παρουσίας τοῦ

Despite the theological stand of the fathers against the cessationism of the Jews, Montanists and others, despite the abundant appeals to contemporary prophecies, visions, miracles and especially exorcisms performed to evangelize pagans, and despite the growing interest in miracles as aids to piety, a few leaders of the church nonetheless occasionally turned its opponents' polemic against itself. Most of the expressions of these proto-cessationist explanations follow.

Victorian of Petau (d. c. 304), in a commentary on the Apocalypse, writes: 'The apostles through signs, wonders and mighty deeds overcame the unbelievers. After this the faith of the Church was given the comfort of the interpreted prophetic Scriptures'.[1]

Chrysostom (347–407), in his first homily on Pentecost, complains that he is constantly questioned by his congregation about the absence of tongues-speaking when people are baptized.[2] Almost all of Chrysostom's several dozen references to miracles are associated with

---

Δεσπότου)'; *Concerning Triadus* 3.41 (*PG* 39.984), in Labriolle, *Sources*, pp. 156-57. Earlier, Irenaeus by implication connected the τέλειον with the eschaton: 'we, *while upon the earth*, as Paul also declares, "know in part and prophesy in part" '. (*Against Heresies* 2.28.7 [my italics]). Cf. the same identification with τό τέλειον in *Against Heresies* 4.9.2. Origen (*Contra Celsum* 6.20) makes the same connection: 'And therefore we hope, after the troubles and struggles which we suffer here, to reach the highest heavens ... And as many of us as praise him [there] ... shall be ever engaged in the contemplation of the invisible things of God ... seeing, as it was expressed by the true disciple of Jesus in these words, "then face to face"; and in these, "when that which is perfect is come, then that which is in part will be done away" '. Methodius of Olympus, *The Banquet of the Ten Virgins* 9.2: 'For now we know "in part", and as it were "through a glass", since that which is perfect has not yet come to us, namely, the kingdom of heaven and the resurrection, when "that which is in part will be done away"' '. So also Archelaus, who identified 'the perfect' with the eschaton in *The Disputation with Manes*, 36-37. Cf. J.L. Ash, Jr, 'The Decline of Ecstatic Prophecy in the Early Church'.

1. *Corpus Scriptorum Ecclesiasticorum Latinorum*. This seems to be the only clear connection between the cessation of the charismata and their replacement by Scripture among the church fathers. The charge that Montanist prophecy was creating new Scripture is challenged by D.F. Wright, 'Why Were the Montanists Condemned', *Themelios* 2 (September 1976), pp. 19-20, and C.M. Robeck, 'Canon, *Regulae Fidei*, and Continuing Revelation in the Early Church', in Bradley and Miller (eds.), *Church, Word and Spirit*. Certainly this charge is implicit in the cessationist 'maturity of the church' argument, as in Chrysostom and Augustine, but its exact relation to Scripture echoes the earlier rabbis.

2. *PG*, 50, col. 549.

arguments against seeking them: (1) miracles were once required for weak faith; today, powerful miracles would perniciously allow weak faith among observers; (2) accordingly, when 'true religion took root' in all the world, miracles ceased; (3) to suffer for Christ is much greater than to experience miracles delivering us from that suffering; (4) no one should 'wait for miracles' today because the 'sign greater than all signs' is deliverance from sin; (5) besides, if we choose Christian love as the best spiritual gift, 'we shall have no need of signs'.[1]

Isidore of Pelusium (d. c. 450) follows this latter line somewhat idealistically: 'Perhaps miracles would take place now, too, if the lives of the teachers rivalled the bearing of the apostles'.[2]

Ambrosiaster (d. 384) offers another proto-cessationist theory involving a kind of charismatic entropy beginning with the apostles, who in Jn 14.12 were promised they alone would perform 'greater works'; then Jn 20.22 denotes an impartation of the Spirit conferring ecclesiastical power enabling the successive transfer of the Spirit throughout history via the imposition of hands, and finally, a third level described in Acts 2 in which the Spirit was bestowed on the laity 'whence arises the preaching of the church'.[3]

Augustine (354–430) begins his theological career with cessationist sentiments:

> We have heard that our predecessors, at a stage of faith on the way from temporal things up to eternal things, followed visible miracles. They could

---

1. In (1) *First Corinthians*, Homily VI (on 2.5); *Romans*, Homily XIV (on 8.24); (2) *Acts*, Homily XXXI, *NPF*, 1st ser. XI, p. 196; (3) *Matthew*, Homily IV (on 1.17). This appears as part of a larger point: 'It is usual with God. . . to display his own power' during periods of danger and persecution against God's people, e.g. at the Exodus, at Daniel's time and when the church 'had just come out of error' (apostolic period). (4) and (5), *Matthew*, Homily XLVI, 4 (on Mt. 13.24-30). Chrysostom here wrongly interprets the 'better way' of 1 Cor. 12.31 as a forced choice between love and the charismata, rather than the 'way' in which all the charismata were to be employed.

R.A. Greer has recently insisted that 'Chrysostom's opinion that miracles ceased after the apostolic age is certainly a minority view. . . the miraculous is an important dimension of the church in the fourth and fifth centuries' (*The Fear of Freedom: A Study of Miracles in the Imperial Church* [University Park, PA: The Pennsylvania State University Press, 1989], p. 115).

2. *Epistle* 4.80.

3. *PL* 35, cols. 2289-91.

do nothing else. And they did so in such a way that it should not be necessary for those who came after them. When the Catholic Church had been founded and diffused throughout the whole world, on the one hand miracles were not allowed to continue till our time, lest the mind should always seek visible things, and the human race should grow cold by becoming accustomed to things, which, when they were novelties, kindled its faith. On the other hand we must not doubt that those are to be believed who proclaimed miracles which only a few had actually seen, and yet were able to persuade whole peoples to follow them. At that time the problem was to get people to believe before anyone was fit to reason about divine and invisible things.[1]

Augustine later repudiated this position, and in chapter 22 of his *City of God* provides samples of over seventy miracles he recorded in and around his churches. He complains in *City of God* 22.8 that contemporary miracles are relatively unknown not because they no longer occur, but simply because of bad communication and because people are conditioned (perhaps from statements like his own, above) to disbelieve them.

Gregory the Great (540–604), though a prolific recorder of contemporary miracles, nevertheless wrote (c. 590) what was to become a highly influential metaphor on the cessation of miracles:[2] 'These things [miracles described in Mk 16.17-18] were necessary in the beginning of the Church, for in order that faith might grow, it had to be nourished by miracles; for we, too, when we plant shrubs, pour water on them till we see that they have gotten a strong hold on the ground; and when once they are firmly rooted, we stop the watering. For this reason Paul says: "Tongues are for a sign, not to believers, but to unbelievers"'.[3]

These Christian cessationist tenets followed those of the rabbis: (1) spiritual power is normatively apportioned in descending tiers, at the idealized level of the biblical canon versus the present time. The apostolic level of spiritual power could not, and likely should not, again be approached; (2) only in a return to the (impossibly?) idealized righteousness of the New Testament could the church merit the

1. *Of True Religion* 47.
2. See his *Dialogues*, subtitled *De Miraculis Patrum Italicorum*.
3. *Homily on the Gospels* 29. On the impact of this statement upon Protestant cessationism, see N.L. Brann, 'The Proto-Protestant Assault upon Church Magic: The "*Errores Bohemanorum*" according to the Abbot Trithemius (1462–1516)', *JRH* 12 (June 1982), pp. 9-22, esp. p. 16.

charismata; (3) miracles were once required as scaffolding for the church, which, once established (that is, in Scripture, tradition and institution), no longer required such support. A mild deistic theme seems implicit here: the church required a divine 'jump-start' of power at the beginning, but now more or less runs on its own (cf. Gal. 3.3!) Hence, miracles and prophecy were replaced by piety and the study of Scripture. This last thesis reflected the church's growing apologetic, evidentialist use for miracles which, along with appeals to the exemplary morality and self-sacrifice of early Christians, had acted as a powerful tool for evangelism. Increasingly, in this view, miracles appeared to *prove* the Gospel, not to *express* it.

Still another corollary of cessationism was the common tendency to transmute the 'miraculous' charismata of earlier times into the more 'ordinary' expressions of church ministry; for example, prophecy became preaching or teaching, or the various miracles of healing became metaphors for regeneration, such as the blind seeing the light of the Gospel or the lame walking the paths of righteousness.[1]

In this way cessationism provided the ecclesiastical hierarchy with a ready rationale against complaints of diminished charismatic activity in their churches and an answer to an embarrassing implicit question, 'how can religious authorities as bearers of pure church tradition and praxis be justified if they lack certain charismata which appear to be a normative New Testament expression of Christian experience?' Perhaps the faithful recalled the prediction of 2 Tim. 3.5, of a church 'having a form of religion but denying its [miracle] power ($\delta\acute{\upsilon}\nu\alpha\mu\iota\varsigma$)'. But while a few church leaders may have promoted cessationism out of personal and institutional defensiveness, many simultaneously disseminated contemporary miracle accounts to encourage piety, and even included in their liturgies requests for God's miraculous graces

---

1. On the Christian tradition of spiritualizing of miracles see e.g. Origen, *Contra Celsum* 1.46; 2.48, 42, 94; similarly Augustine, *Sermons on the Selected Lessons of the New Testament* 38.3: 'The blind body does not now open its eyes by a miracle of the Lord, but the blinded heart opens its eyes to the world of the Lord. The physical corpse does not now rise again, but the soul rises again which lies dead in a living body. The deaf ears of the body are not now opened; but how many who have the ears of their hearts closed, let them fly open at the penetrating word of God.' See also the summary on the early practice of spiritualizing miracles by J. Speigl, 'Die Rolle der Wunder in vorconstantinischen Christentum', *ZKT* 92 (1970), pp. 307-10. This metaphorical treatment of miracles led easily to Bultmann's program of demythologization.

as though normative.[1] The role of the devout is no longer to expect miracles, but to pursue virtues prescribed in church Scriptures and doctrines.

Thomas Aquinas (1225–74) ordered the pattern of cessationist tenets which dominated the church until the 20th century.[2] His major new contribution to cessationism was the metaphysics of miracle based on Aristotelian philosophy. A true miracle, Aquinas said, expresses itself beyond any 'means' of nature, absolute and above the power of the created order: it must be purely 'super-natural'.[3] Therefore, starting with the 'facts' of a miracle, an observer can reason to its divine source. While one can never know *how* God performed the miracle, one can certainly know *that* he did. Miracles, then, include

---

1. D.R. Foubister, 'Healing in the Liturgy of the Post-Apostolic Church', *SBT* 9.2 (October 1979), pp. 141-55. Tertullian attempted to integrate the reception of the charismata into Christian initiation liturgies, according to K. McDonnell, 'The Ecclesiology of *Koinonia* and the Baptism in the Holy Spirit: Roman Catholic Perspectives', paper presented to the Society of Pentecostal Studies, CBN University, Virginia Beach, VA, November 13, 1987, p. 15.

2. For the influence of Aquinas on later Christian thought on miracles, see J. Wendland, *Miracles and Christianity* (trans. H.R. Mackintosh; New York: Hodder & Stoughton, 1930), p. 64. For critical appraisals of miracle as an empirical expression of divine sanction in Aquinas, see L.S. O'Breartuin, 'The Theology of Miracles', *EphCar* 20 (1969), pp. 3-4, L. Monden, *Signs and Wonders: A Study of the Miraculous Element in Religion* (New York: Desclée, 1966), pp. 46-47, J.A. Hardon, 'The Concept of Miracle from St Augustine to Modern Apologetics', *TS* 15 (June 1954), p. 243, and B.J. van der Walt, 'Thomas Aquinas' Idea about Wonders: A Critical Appraisal', in K. Rahner *et al.* (eds.), *Dio d l' Economia della Salvezza* (Naples: Edizioni Domenicane Italiane, 1974), pp. 470-80.

3. 'A miracle properly so called is when something is done outside the order of nature. But it is not enough for a miracle if something is done outside the order of any particular nature; for otherwise anyone would perform a miracle by throwing a stone upwards, as such a thing is outside the order of the stone's nature. For a miracle is required that it be against the order of the whole created nature. But God alone can do this, because, whatever an angel or any other creature does by its own power is according to the order of created nature; and thus is not a miracle. Hence, God alone can work miracles' (*Summa Theologica* 1.110.4).

L. Monden is critical of the Thomistic emphasis here: 'The primary note is that God is the author of the miraculous; we, by reasoning, constitute it as a sign. The biblical conception—and the intervention which God himself intends to be significant—is practically abandoned. This debased [rationalistic] conception remained dominant in theology and in apologetics until the end of the last century'— certainly including Warfield's conception (*Signs and Wonders*, pp. 47-48).

such events as instantaneous healings of visibly diseased or broken bodies, the revelation through a prophecy of something impossible for anyone to know, or the bestowal of the gift of the Holy Spirit by the laying on of hands.[1]

According to Aquinas, the central function of miracles was to serve as a *signum sensibile*, a *testimonium*[2] to guarantee the divine source and truth of Christian doctrines, particularly the deity of Christ. To explain the lack of visible miracles in his day, Aquinas asserted that Christ and his disciples had worked miracles sufficient to prove the faith once and for all; this having been done, no further miraculous proof of doctrines could be required.[3] In a number of other places, however, he vitiates this position by maintaining that miracles can recur if they aid in confirmation of preaching and bringing humankind to salvation.[4] But even beyond this, Aquinas suggests that believers of great sanctity may exhibit miraculous gifts of the Spirit, a doctrine that strengthened the veneration of shrines and canonization of saints via miracles.[5] A widespread belief in these last two exceptions, which essentially contradicted cessationism, resulted in the excesses surrounding miracles which precipitated the Reformation.

The Protestant reformers turned the cessationist polemic against not only Roman Catholicism but also the radical reformation, undercutting the claims of both to religious authority they based on miracles and revelations. Because of his special relevance to this study I will

1. *Commentary on 1 Corinthians* 12.2; *Commentary on Galatians* 3.2; *Commentary on Hebrews* 2.1. This latter point may have influenced Warfield's insistence that only the Apostles could confer the Spirit by the laying on of hands; *Counterfeit Miracles*, pp. 22 and 245 n. 48.

2. *Commentary on Hebrews* 2.1; cf. *Summa Theologica* II. II, 178, 2-3; *De Potentia* 6, 5; *Commentary on John* 9, 3: *Commentary on 1 Corinthians* 12.2; *Commentary on Galatians* 3.2. Cf. the comment on 1 Corinthians 12.2: since biblical doctrines are beyond the capacity of people to grasp rationally, miracles are provided to authenticate them, in the sense that any envoy must provide a special sign to establish the royal origin of his message. Cf. *Commentary on 1 Corinthians* 14.1, where any prophet claiming supernatural insight must substantiate his claim with miracles.

3. *Commentary on Matthew* 10.1.

4. *Summa Theologica* II, II, 2, 9 ad 3; 5, 2; 171, 1; 178, 1; 2; III, 7, 7; 27, 5 ad 3; 29, 1 ad 2; 31, 1 ad 2; 43, 1 ad 2.

5. *Summa Theologica* II, II, 178, 1 and 2; III, 43, 1. Cf. his *Commentary on John* 9.3, 1348; on 4.7 and on 2.3.

concentrate on only one of these reformers,[1] John Calvin (1509–64). Calvin popularized the restriction of miracles to the accreditation of the apostles and specifically to their Gospel, though he was less rigid about cessationism than many of his followers in that he held to the tradition that in unevangelized areas, apostles and prophetic gifts could recur to confirm the Gospel.[2]

At least four significant aspects of Calvin's polemic stand out, the first three of which shed light on its underlying strategy and the last of which is an observation on the epistemological basis for Calvin's thesis that the extraordinary (miraculous) gifts of the Spirit did in fact cease with the apostolic age. This rationale was delineated by the following propositions.

1. God's purpose for miracles was to accredit the Word, that is, the Scripture, its doctrines and its first proclaimers.[3] This proposition had the effect of restricting the power of accreditation by miracles to the major Protestant basis of religious authority: Scripture. This limitation to Scripture and the original apostles of accrediting miracles was presented to undercut the religious authority of contemporary miracles thought to accredit the evolving doctrines and the contemporary leadership, derived from 'apostolic succession', of the Roman

1. For Luther's comments on miracles see E.M. Plass (ed.), *What Luther Says: An Anthology*, II (St. Louis, MO: Concordia, 1959), pp. 953-57. He essentially follows the church tradition he received, with the exception of his anti-Romanist miracle polemics.

2. '[Miraculous or revelatory spiritual gifts as a category] either does not exist today or is less commonly seen' (*Institutes* IV, 3, 4 [1057]). Apostles, prophets or evangelists, he says, are not ordinary offices in the church today, but the Lord 'now and again revives as the need of the times demands' (1056).

3. 'Scripture [has] warned us concerning the legitimate purpose and use of miracles. For Mark teaches that those signs which attended the apostles' preaching were set forth to confirm it [Mark 16.20]. In like manner, Like relates that our "Lord. . . bore witness to the work of his graces", when these signs and wonders were done by the apostles' hands [Acts 14.2]. Very much like this is that word of the apostle: that the salvation proclaimed by the Gospel has been confirmed in the fact that "the Lord has attested it by signs and wonders and various mighty works" [Heb. 2.4; cf. 15.18-19]. . . These are the seals of the Gospel' (*Institutes* I. Preface, 3 [16]; I. 8. 4 and 5). The same ideas are expressed in *Tracts and Treatises*, 'Article XI: Of the Miracles of the Saints', pp. 92-93, and *Commentary on the Acts of the Apostles*, II (2 vols.; trans. J.W. Fraser, ed. D.W. and T.F. Torrance; Grand Rapids: Eerdmans, 1966), p. 3 (on 14.3).

Church, as well as the 'Spirit-inspired' (and hence, religiously authoritative) teachings of the radical reformation.

2. Counterfeit miracles are discerned by their association with false doctrines; hence, when miracles were claimed by the Catholics or the radical reformation as accrediting their unscriptural doctrines, such miracles were self-evidently false.[1]

3. While 'visible', 'miraculous', 'extraordinary' or 'temporary' spiritual gifts ceased with the apostles, there is a possibility they may recur if conditions requiring their manifestation warrant. However, these types of spiritual gifts are more likely transmuted into the 'permanent' gifts and offices of contemporary Christian ministry or employed as metaphors for faith in the Gospel.[2]

4. What proof, other than his *a priori* association of miraculous charismata with accreditation of Scripture, does Calvin offer for their cessation? Surprisingly little: he appeals only superficially to Scripture and to the testimony of historical 'experience'.[3] But in the main Calvin assumes the traditions enshrined in Aquinas, rather than attempt systematically to prove his contention.

The Enlightenment era (c. 1650–1790) provided the setting for the next major steps in the development of Warfield's cessationist miracle polemic. Calvin had established a theological rationale for the polemic

1. E.g. *Institutes*, Prefatory Address, 3 (16): 'In demanding miracles of us they act dishonestly. For we are not forging some new gospel, but are retaining that very gospel whose truth all the miracles that Jesus Christ and his disciples ever wrought serve to confirm. But, compared with us, they have strange power: even to this day they can confirm their faith by continual miracles. Instead they allege miracles which can disturb a mind otherwise at rest—they are so foolish and ridiculous, so vain and false!'

2. *Institutes* IV, 3, 4 (1057). Calvin has a two-level view of Christian healing of the sick: the apostolic level of 'manifest powers' versus the affirmation that 'the Lord is no less present with his people in every age; and he heals their weakness as often as necessary no less than of old' (IV, 19, 19 [1467]). He sees the gift of tongues as the ability to preach the Gospel in foreign languages or allegorically in the use of biblical Greek or Hebrew in interpreting Scripture (*The Acts of the Apostles*, I [on 10.46]; cf. *Commentary on 1 Corinthians* [on 14.22]). The gift of discernment involves fairly rational testing of false teaching against Scripture (*Institutes* IV, 9, 12 [1176]).

3. For scriptural 'warnings' about the use of miracles, see *Institutes* Prefatory Address 3 (17, 18); I, 14, 17 (176); I, 18, 2 (232); II, 4, 5 (313); IV, 8, 6 (1153); IV, 9, 4 (1168). On experience as a test for miracles, see *Institutes* IV, 19, 19 (1467); IV, 19, 29 (1477).

based on a few, but important, scriptural proof-texts, but primarily on an evolved and internally inconsistent role of miracles. But during the Enlightenment, the basis of religious authority underwent a profound shift from the Protestant basis of biblical authority to the human authority of perception and reason. The Enlightenment era[1] is generally regarded as the watershed in thought about miracles.[2] But less well known is that during this time in England a 'great debate' raged over the role of miracles in accrediting the truth of religion.[3] In line with a growing quest for certainty in human knowledge and increased confidence in human reason during this period, certain prominent scientists who were also evangelical apologists[4] advanced

1. The so-called Age of the Enlightenment is generally dated between 1648 (the end of the Thirty Years War) and the French Revolution, or in intellectual history from Francis Bacon's *Novum Organum* (1620) to Kant's *Critique of Pure Reason* (1781) (J.C. Livingstone, *Modern Christian Thought from the Enlightenment to Vatican II* [New York: Macmillan, 1971], pp. 1-2).

2. Wendland, *Miracles and Christianity*, p. 210; J.S. Lawton, *Miracles and Revelation* (New York: The Association Press, 1961), pp. 11-14; Brown, *Miracles and the Critical Mind*, p. 23; and P.H. Richards, 'The Nature of Miracle' (PhD dissertation, Union Theological Seminary, 1958), pp. 127-78.

3. D.P. Walker, in a brief but valuable study, suggests that cessationism remained 'such a prominent and tenaciously held doctrine [during the early Enlightenment] partly because of the controversies arising out of Puritan attempts in the 1590s to cast out devils and the savage suppression of these attempts by Anglican prelates' and because of the increased use of contemporary miracle stories by Catholics in their anti-Protestant polemics; 'The Cessation of Miracles,' in I. Mekul and L.G. Debus (eds.), *Hermeticism and the Renaissance: Intellectual History and the Occult in Early Modern Europe* (Washington, DC: Folger Books, 1988), p. 111. See also D.P. Walker, *Unclean Spirits: Possession and Exorcism in France and England in the Late Sixteenth and Early Seventeenth Centuries* (London: Scholar Press, 1981), pp. 66-70, 72-73, and K. Thomas, *Religion and the Decline of Magic* (London: Weidenfeld & Nicolson, 1971), pp. 80, 124, 256, 479 and 485.

4. These men were not, as is usually supposed, a conservative, obscurantist rearguard defending miracles against the enlightened minds of the time, like David Hume, but represented the most prominent scientific pioneers, for example Bishop John Wilkins, founder of the Royal Society for the Advancement of Science, Sir Robert Boyle, 'the father of chemistry and the son of the Earl of Cork', Sir Isaac Newton, and Archbishop Tillotson; R.M. Burns, *The Great Debate on Miracles: From Joseph Glanvill to David Hume* (Lewisburg, PA: Bucknell University Press), pp. 9-18. Conventional wisdom is that David Hume was a trailblazing thinker in the great debate, since he became the *bête noire* for countless orthodox apologists right up to the present day. But Burns has pointed out that David Hume's now famous

the novel thesis that miracles provided a more or less reasonable and empirical proof for Christian doctrine. Against this new apologetic thrust came the response of the Deists,[1] who, in their defense of 'natural' (as opposed to revealed) religion, were concerned, in some cases, not only to deny divine revelation but also the miracles from which it received its accreditation. Here the cessationist polemic was pushed past its ultimate limit, when the Deists challenged not only the possibility of post-biblical miracles but even the possibility of their ever having occurred at all.

Several important developments in the cessationist miracle polemic emerged during the Enlightenment period. First, the increased interest in natural science with the presupposition that God providentially ordered nature subject to fixed laws led to a renewed emphasis on miracles as attesting evidence for Christian religious authority. Apologists now had, they felt, an *empirical* basis for apologetics. Proof of Christianity via miracles was available to any human mind in the same way that all knowledge is accessible, not by revelation, but by 'common sense'. But this new scientific world-view also led to the conviction of a closed cosmology resting on the three pillars of causality, continuity and objectifiability. While for these apologists, miracles, as divine irruptions into the natural order, provided an empirically observable event demonstrating God's presence, later

work, 'On Miracles", at the time of its publication in 1749, 'was very much a tail-end contribution to a flagging debate' (Burns, *The Great Debate*, pp. 9-10). His points had already been repeatedly made, discussed, refuted and even transcended by many other writers. In particular it was greatly overshadowed by a much more substantial book by Conyers Middleton, discussed below. While Warfield's historical method ironically follows Hume on the question of post-biblical miracles, it is Middleton's very similar position that Warfield claims as his own. It is for this reason that Hume's work is properly relegated to this footnote.

1. The expression 'deist' is difficult to define, as those writers usually so described were a very diverse group who held a variety of positions on theoretical issues. Deism is associated with: Lord Herbert, Shaftesbury, Blount, Wollaston, Woolston, Toland, Tindal, Bolingbroke, Morgan, Chubb and Annet. Their central tenet was the all-sufficiency of natural religion. Revealed religion was discriminatory in that it rendered humankind's salvation subject to a historical and geographical accident. They accused the orthodox notion of revelation of being self-contradictory, in that recognition of Jesus as divine implies a pre-existing set of criteria for determining him so. Revelation was merely a 'republication' of innate ideas. Deists also tended to push Calvin's repugnance for 'enthusiasm' to an extreme, applying it to any claim to revelation. See Burns, *The Great Debate*, pp. 13-14.

skeptics either subsumed these events under natural (as against divine) causality or attributed them to enthusiastic imaginations. The strategy of the skeptics was an old one: if miracles were adduced to accredit doctrines and religious authority, the miracles themselves must be discredited. Hence, the cessationist polemic redivivus. Some Enlightenment polemicists went further: they were not merely confining accrediting miracles to the classical era of Christian origins but, certainly in the case of David Hume, were attempting to build an impenetrable wall between the natural and supernatural. Thus the polemic became not cessationist, but abolitionist.

Secondly, these Deistic and other Enlightenment polemicists who so vociferously rejected the credulity of religious dogmatism actually managed to create a dogmatism of their own. Extreme skepticism and rationalism shaped the anti-miracle polemic which arrogantly admitted of no facts beyond one's own experience and preconceptions about nature. The term 'law', as in 'law of nature' became equivocal, somehow being both descriptive and prescriptive. The phrase 'law of nature', then, moved illogically from describing one's consistent but limited understanding of natural phenomena to expressing a dogma prescribing what must always happen to everyone under all circumstances. Hence, if this skeptic does not experience miracles, then no one can experience miracles.

Finally, the area of history as a locus of revelation was thought particularly suspect,[1] first, because of the widespread Protestant suspicion of 'enthusiasm' and its claims to unverifiable revelations, secondly, because of Protestant suspicion of Romanist rule and traditions which had evolved from the dubious testimony of the Church fathers, as over against the idealized period of the New Testament, and thirdly, because of the Deistic desire for a 'natural' religion, rationally and equitably accessible to everyone on the basis of common sense independent of revelation. Following Calvin, the Deistic polemic maintained that *if* miracles had in fact *ever* occurred, all the miracles required for establishing true Christianity had already been performed by Christ and the apostles, no further were needed. A model of history developed during the Renaissance and the Enlightenment consisting of an ideal 'classical' period, for example,

---

1. It is interesting that one of the tasks of modern apologetics is to affirm, against the old Liberal–Deistic notion, that revelation can indeed be found in history. This seems to be a project of for example Rahner, Moltmann and Pannenberg.

the Golden Ages of Greece and Rome or the New Testament era, the 'dark ages' of Roman Catholicism, ignorance and degradation, and the optimistic restoration in the present time of only limited elements of the classical period, but in some ways, for instance, scientifically, transcending it.[1]

Conyers Middleton in his *Free Inquiry into the Miraculous Powers*[2] continued Calvin's attack on Roman Catholics by applying Enlightenment historical-critical methodology to the miracle accounts of the church fathers, accounts which had been adduced as support for Catholic post-apostolic dogmas. As Calvin's theological cessationism profoundly influenced him, Warfield claimed Middleton's skeptical historical methodology as his own.[3]

Conyers Middleton's work in this area greatly outshone that of David Hume, whose now famous essay on miracles contained nothing new in what had by then become a dying issue. Middleton concluded his *Inquiry* with a response to his critics[4] and summarized the major theses of his work for himself. The points put forward here are mirror-image countertheses parodying those put forward by Dr Chapman, an apologist for the early fathers, in a defense of miracles performed by Simeon Stylites.

---

1. Many in Puritan America were more optimistic about the restoration of the biblical age. America could become fully realized as the eschatological 'new Israel' with the attendant outpouring of the Holy Spirit if the covenant with God were faithfully observed. See J. Gilsdorf, *The Puritan Apocalypse: New England Eschatology in the Seventeenth Century* (New York: Garland Publishing, 1989), pp. 102, 110. The 'Latter Rain' movement among Pentecostals followed a similar model of history based on a misconception of Joel 2.23, viz., that the abundant operations of spiritual gifts once confined to the ideal apostolic age were, after the long, dry, dark ages, being restored. The Israeli rainy season is continuous. Joel's reference to the former and latter rains only mean that the season was blessedly long and therefore productive.

2. The full title is *A Free Inquiry into the Miraculous Powers which are supposed to have subsisted in the Christian church from the earliest ages through several successive centuries. By which it is shown that we have no sufficient reason to believe, upon the authority of the primitive fathers, that any such powers were continued to the church after the days of the Apostles* (London: R. Manby and H.S. Cox, 1748).

3. Warfield, *Counterfeit Miracles*, pp. 6 and 28-31.

4. Middleton, *Free Inquiry*, pp. 149-77.

1. That they (miracles) were all of such a nature, and performed in such a manner, as would necessarily inject a suspicion of fraud and delusion.

2. That the cures and beneficial effects of them, were either false, or imaginary, or accidental.

3. That they tend to confirm the idlest of all errors and superstitions.

4. That the integrity of the witnesses is either highly questionable, or their credulity at least so gross, as to render them unworthy of any credit.

5. That they were not only vain and unnecessary, but generally speaking, so trifling also, as to excite nothing but contempt.

And lastly, that the belief and defence of them are the only means in the world that can possibly support, or that does in fact give any sort of countenance, to the modern impostures in the Romish Church.[1]

Middleton's cessationist polemic ostensibly had a practical end: to combat the errors of the Romanists. Most contemporary observers, including John Wesley, however, were convinced there was another motive: 'to overthrow the whole Christian system'.[2] Middleton, he complained, 'aims every blow, though he seems to look the other way, at the fanatics who wrote the New Testament'.[3]

Warfield's philosophical and historiographical approaches to miracles were derived from the Enlightenment era and from Conyers Middleton respectively. The following chapter examines how Warfield applied these views to his cessationist polemic.

1. *Free Inquiry*, pp. 135-37, citing J. Chapman, *Miscellaneous Tracts Relating to Antiquity* (London: S. Birt, 1742), pp. 175-76.

2. J. Wesley, *Journal of John Wesley* (ed. N. Charnock; London: Epworth Press, 1938), III, p. 390 (entry for January 28, 1749).

3. Wesley, *Journal*, V, p. 426 (August 12, 1771). Middleton responds in section V of *Free Inquiry* to Wesley's criticisms which appeared in an extended letter written from January 4 to 24, 1749; *The Letters of Rev. John Wesley, A.M.* (ed. J. Telford; London: Epworth Press, 1931), II, pp. 312-88. For a fascinating account of this conflict between Wesley and Middleton, see T.A. Campbell, 'John Wesley and Conyers Middleton on Divine Intervention in History', *CH* 55 (March 1986), pp. 39-49.

Chapter 2

BENJAMIN WARFIELD'S POLEMIC ON POSTBIBLICAL MIRACLES

Benjamin B. War field's *Counterfeit Miracles* represents the most influential recent expression of the key elements of cessationist doctrine. The thesis of this chapter is that Warfield's polemic fails because of internal contradictions in his concept of miracle and because of weaknesses in his historical method and his biblical hermeneutics. After examining the historical traditions which shaped the argument of *Counterfeit Miracles* and the contemporary conditions which precipitated it, this chapter examines the three essential elements of Warfield's polemic for internal consistency against his own stated presuppositions and interpretive methods.

1. *Theological and Philosophical Traditions in Warfield's Polemic*

Calvinist theology and the Enlightenment epistemology of Scottish common-sense philosophy strongly influenced Warfield's cessationist polemic. Accordingly, I will examine their specific impact on Warfield's thought in the following two sections.

Calvinism
In his own mind, Benjamin Warfield was emphatically a Calvinist. In 1904 he summarized what had long been held at Princeton: 'Calvinism is just religion in its purity. We have only, therefore, to conceive of religion in its purity, and that is Calvinism'.[1] Moreover, Warfield insists that for one to remain truly an evangelical Christian, one must follow Calvin's theology.[2] Even though Calvin and Warfield had faced

1. B.B. Warfield, 'What is Calvinism?', in *SSWW*, I, p. 389.
2. B.B. Warfield, 'Calvinisim', in *SHERK*, II, pp. 359-64. The article is reprinted in B.B. Warfield (ed.), *Calvin and Calvinism* (New York: Oxford University Press, 1931), pp. 353-69. Warfield defines Calvinism as the teachings of

different theological issues, the latter nonetheless saw his work as flowing completely within the stream of Calvin's thought. Where he deviates from it, as in several exegetical points relating to his cessationist polemic, he occasionally does so with apology to, and appreciation for Calvin generally.

When it came to his cessationist polemic specifically, Warfield shared Calvin's struggle to fix the basis of religious authority firmly upon the Scriptures, as against, say, the Roman Catholics, who maintained their claims to theological legitimacy, at least in part, on the authority of post-apostolic tradition, or against the 'enthusiasts' who attempted to found their religious authority upon subjective religious experience. Warfield continued Calvin's polemics against the Romanists using essentially the same arguments and expressions as those of the sixteenth century. But as he saw it, the challenge of the enthusiasts had evolved into an even more menacing threat to Calvinist orthodoxy. The old enthusiastic error of the Anabaptists and Pietists had now become, on the one hand, the sophisticated theology of Schleiermacher, which had come to dominate Protestant theology,[1]

John Calvin, the Doctrinal System of the Reformed Churches, or more broadly, the entire body of theological, philosophical, ethical and political concepts which have become dominant in Protestant nations. 'Calvinism,' he writes, 'is the only system in which the whole order of the world is brought into rational unity with the doctrine of grace.' Elsewhere, he is more emphatic about the identity of Christian orthodoxy and Calvinism: 'There is no true religion in the world. . . which is not Calvinistic—Calvinistic in its essence, Calvinistic in its implication. . . In proportion as we are religious, in that proportion, then, are we Calvinistic; and when religion comes fully to its rights in our thinking, and feeling, and doing then shall we be truly Calvinistic. . . It is not merely the hope of true religion in the world: it *is* true religion in the world—as far as true religion is in the world at all' (Warfield, 'What is Calvinism?', p. 392).

1. For example, Warfield attacked the pronouncements on the subjective principle of authority in the church by A.C. McGiffert in his inaugural address as professor of church history at Union Theological Seminary in New York. The address was contained in his *Primitive and Catholic Christianity* (New York: J.C. Rankin, 1893). On the relation of the early church to scriptural authority, he writes, 'The spirit of primitive Christianity is the spirit of religious individualism, based upon the felt presence of the Holy Ghost' (*Primitive and Catholic Christianity*, p. 19). The early Christians looked to the apostolic writings as a *source* for knowledge of divine truth, but not necessarily the 'sole *standard* of truth' or 'exclusive normative authority. The only authority which was recognized was the Holy Spirit, and he was supposed to

and on the other hand, the subjective perfectionism[1] of the Methodist movement which dominated American religious practice. Moreover, the Calvinistic basis of religious authority, the Scripture, had come under an even more direct attack from a third direction: that of modern, rationalistic biblical criticism. Warfield had labored mightily to counteract the growing impact of these threats to the Princetonian Calvinism of his time.[2]

But our focus in this study must be directed at still another area of polemical concern shared by Calvin and Warfield, that is, the implicit attack on the sufficiency of scriptural authority made by those claiming miracles and extraordinary gifts of the Holy Spirit. We have already seen that, in general, Calvin quite narrowly perceived claims to such powers as *prima facie* attempts to promote extrabiblical, and hence false, doctrines. Such claims, of course, represented a direct challenge to Protestant religious authority in that the latter was specifically based upon a closed canon of Scripture. Warfield is at one with Calvin, then, both theologically and sociologically, in the perceived need to destroy any pretensions to spiritual leadership implied in these claims by exposing their supporting postbiblical miracles as counterfeit. We shall see once again, with Warfield as with Calvin, that the sociological dimension of group conflict provides impetus for

---

speak to Christians of the second century as truly as he had ever spoken through the Apostles' (*Primitive and Catholic Christianity*, pp. 32-33).

In McGiffert's provocative concluding comment we may find some impetus for Warfield's extensive historical polemic in *Counterfeit Miracles* against alleged postbiblical miracles recounted in the first few centuries: 'If we today draw a line between the apostolic and post-apostolic ages, and emphasize the supernatural character of the former as distinguished from the latter, we do it solely on dogmatic, not historical grounds' (*Primitive and Catholic Christianity*, p. 22). Warfield's reaction appeared in his article, 'The Latest Phase of Historical Rationalism', *PQ* 9 (1895), pp. 36-67, 185-210, reprinted in volume IX of his collected works, *Studies in Theology* (New York: Oxford University Press, 1932), pp. 585-645.

1. Perfectionism, of course, was not related directly to the centrality of Scripture, but was concerned rather with questions of soteriology, that is, the sufficiency of God's grace alone for salvation as opposed to 'works righteousness'—the human striving for religious self-sufficiency. Warfield devoted to this topic a substantial percentage of his polemical writings, most of which are now contained in two volumes among his collected works, *Studies in Perfectionism*, I, II (New York: Oxford University Press, 1931).

2. For instance, in the articles collected in his *Revelation and Inspiration* (*WBBW*, I).

his re-application of the cessationist polemic. But for all his insistence that he was a fully orthodox follower of Calvin, Warfield is nonetheless criticized[1] for contaminating his Calvinism with an Enlightenment-era rationalism based on a philosophy which was dominant in American religious thought during the previous century, namely, Scottish common-sense realism.[2]

Scottish Common-Sense Philosophy

The apologetic use of miracles as accreditation for doctrine was, as I have shown, revived by orthodox English empiricists who saw in this approach a way of avoiding either dogmatism and/or fideism by appealing to what was observable in nature for the vindication of Christian faith. This new apologetic was developed as a response to the new intellectual climate that had evolved in the West.

From Descartes throughout the Enlightenment period, thinkers who faced the intellectual dilemma of competing dogmatic claims made by

---

1. For instance, by D. Livingstone, 'The Princeton Apologetic as Exemplified by the Work of Benjamin B. Warfield and J. Gresham Machen: A Study in American Theology, 1880–1930' (PhD dissertation, Yale University, 1948), pp. 342-43 and C.N. Krause, 'The Principle of Authority in the Theology of B.B. Warfield, William Adams Brown and Gerald Birney Smith' (PhD dissertation, Duke University, 1961), pp. 113-34, 222-39 (for exposition) and 227-76 (for critique). Especially see N. Wolterstorff, 'Is Reason Enough?', *RJ* 31 (April 1981), pp. 20-24, A. Plantinga, 'On Reformed Epistemology', *RJ* 32 (January 1982), pp. 13-17, J.J. Makarian, 'The Calvinistic Concept of the Biblical Revelation in the Theology of B.B. Warfield' (PhD dissertation, Drew University, 1963), pp. 107-108 and 226-33, as well as an important study by J.C. Vander Stelt, *Philosophy and Scripture: A Study in Old Princeton and Westminster Theology* (Marlton, NJ: Mack, 1978), pp. 166-84 and 304-13. S. Ahlstrom, in 'The Scottish Philosophy', *CH* 24 (September 1955), p. 269, is sternly critical of the impact of Scottish common-sense philosophy on Reformed theology which replaced the profound insights of Calvin's theocentricity with the premise that 'self consciousness [is] the oracle of religious truth'; that the 'benign and optimistic anthropology. . . veiled the very insights into human nature which were the chief strength of Calvin's theology'. Under the influence of Scottish common-sense philosophy 'a kind of rationalistic *rigor mortis* set in'. I am indebted to Vander Stelt's study for much of what follows in the next section.

2. Vander Stelt, *Philosophy and Scripture*, pp. 15-16, summarizes the various designations given to this movement, including 'natural realism', 'Scottish realism', 'common-sense realism', 'Scottish empiricism', 'common-sense philosophy'. For consistency I have chosen to use the latter term.

clerics searched for a reliable and commonly accepted ground for knowledge. This search led increasingly to a preoccupation with the nature, capacities and limits of the human mind, and further led to the inclination to view the relation of human beings to both nature and God in terms of a knowing subject and a known object. This 'turn toward the subject' in philosophy carried with it the conviction that the ultimate vindication for truth could be established, not in revelation from above, but in the mind of the human knower, the known object, or in some relation of the two. Against a background of religious intolerance and dogmatism, John Locke, for example, had insisted that the human capacity for knowledge was limited to fairly reliable probabilities based on sensory input and experiment. He held that through the correct use of this intellectual capacity, which was common to all, reasonable people could see the truth and settle differences. English philosophers, whether Cambridge Platonists or Lockean Aristotelians, who might have parted company over the innateness of ideas and the empirical nature of knowledge, could agree on viewing revelation rationalistically as a way of securing a common ground for religious peace.

Until the beginning of the eighteenth century, Scotland had been isolated from this intellectual ferment. But with the inception of the United Kingdom in 1707 English rationalism pushed northward, generating conflicts between Presbyterians who either did or did not accommodate themselves to these foreign ideas. The major Scottish universities reacted quickly to these rationalistic notions about religion, revelation and innate human capacities. This response was Scottish common-sense philosophy, which propelled its adherents to the center stage of European thought. Chief among these was Thomas Reid (1710–96) who in 1764 assumed the chair of moral philosophy at Glasgow University. Both Reid and his predecessor, Adam Smith, were friends of David Hume, whose epistemological skepticism precipitated the defensive reaction of Scottish common-sense philosophy. Earlier, while teaching at Aberdeen, Reid had once written to Hume: 'a little philosophical society here is much indebted to you for its entertainment. . . You are brought here oftener than any other man to the bar, accused and defended with great zeal, but without bitterness'.[1] Reid was likely one of the accusers: his *Essays on the*

---

1. S.A. Grave, *The Scottish Philosophy of Common Sense* (Oxford: Clarendon Press, 1960), p. 1 n. 2.

Intellectual Powers of Man (1785) was a direct attack on the views of Hume. It was feared that, as Vander Stelt puts it, 'By reducing matter to sensation, mind to ideas, causality to mere subjective habit, Hume had, in Reid's opinion, robbed philosophy of its source, knowledge of its foundation, belief of its basis, miracles of their trustworthiness, and history of its credibility'.[1] Reid saw his task as rebuilding for theology a solid foundation of epistemological certainty, on which the structure of Christian apologetics could securely rest. The physical, external world could not be reduced to an epistemological fiction, which found its reality either in a spiritual world of ideas, as Berkeley had said, or to a quagmire of doubt about the possibility of any reliable knowledge, as in Hume. What bothered Reid about idealism and skepticism was the damage they did to traditional apologetics, particularly the argument for the existence of God based on evidences of his design in nature.

Reid maintained that God had placed within the intellectual constitution of all normal people certain 'instinctive presuppositions' of self-evident principles or propositions, which serve as a kind of template, or, to use a more modern metaphor, as a central processing unit in a computer, to organize, classify and give meaning to incoming sense data. Human beings are not, however, passive receivers of incoming images, but are active, judging perceivers who immediately and intuitively know external things in themselves.[2] This rational 'common sense',[3] or naive consciousness, both characterizes and validates knowledge. Since knowledge based upon common sense is intuitive, it requires no further proof. Hence, one can not only know *that* something exists, but also can know with certainty *what* it is that exists.[4] Perception, Reid says, involves the elements of the *act* of perceiving, the *object* perceived, and the *conviction* that the object really exists in the external world. This view implies a permanence in subject and

1. Vander Stelt, *Philosophy and Scripture*, p. 23.

2. Vander Stelt, *Philosophy and Scripture*, p. 27. Also, Grave, *Scottish Philosophy*, pp. 110-50 for an extended treatment of Reid's use of the term 'common sense'; particularly in relation to reason.

3. Vander Stelt, *Philosophy and Scripture*, p. 23, notes that '"common sense" is not used here to indicate a power of general knowledge based on ordinary development and opportunities, but to mean a faculty of reason, a source of principles, a light of nature, a capacity for certain original and intuitive judgments which may be used as foundation for deductive reasoning'.

4. Vander Stelt, *Philosophy and Scripture*, p. 24.

object, knower and known, and further implies that truth cannot be established by mere ideas or representations in the mind, but only on the ground of common sense. Truth, then, is static and open to investigation to people irrespective of time or place. Empirically observable facts are as pieces of a mosaic which can be arranged, through the innate human powers of judgment, into coherent and logical wholes. This view led to the expectation that if the evidence for Christianity were properly assembled, the conclusion as to its truth was inescapable.

Reid claimed that the facts of science were not materially different from those of religion in that the faculties of common sense mediated them both. He described the facts and experience of science and faith not as a 'fiction of human imagination', but as a 'touchstone' and the very 'voice of God'.[1]

Ahlstrom, Vander Stelt, Marsden and Noll, among others,[2] have documented the extensive impact of Scottish common-sense philosophy on American thought and culture during the latter part of the eighteenth century and the middle of the nineteenth. Vander Stelt, for example, notes that

> by leaving its imprint upon philosophy and theology as well as upon sociology, psychology, aesthetics, literature, education, economics, and political theory, [Scottish common-sense philosophy] permeated almost every faculty of the academy, institution of society, and activity in culture. Because of its remarkable versatility, it functioned as 'the handmaiden of both Unitarianism and orthodoxy'.[3]

He goes on to point out that although many early American seminaries may have disagreed theologically, they nonetheless concurred on the 'relevance of the *practical* rationalism of SCSP'.[4] The philosophy was

---

1. Vander Stelt, *Philosophy and Scripture*, p. 29, following here O.M. Jones, 'Empiricism and Intuitionism in Reid's Common Sense Philosophy' (PhD dissertation, Columbia University, n.d.), p. 97.

2. Ahlstrom, 'The Scottish Philosophy', pp. 257-58; Vander Stelt, *Philosophy and Scripture*, pp. 57-64; G. Marsden, *Fundamentalism and American Culture: The Shaping of Twentieth-Century Evangelicalism, 1870–1925* (New York: Oxford University Press, 1980), pp. 14-17; M. Noll, *The Princeton Theology, 1812–1921* (Grand Rapids: Baker, 1983), pp. 30-33; and H.F. May, *The Enlightenment in America* (New York: Oxford University Press, 1976), pp. 337-50.

3. Vander Stelt, *Philosophy and Scripture*, pp. 61-62.

4. Noll, *Princeton Theology*, pp. 34-35, points out that at this time Scottish common-sense philosophy was widespread in virtually all American theological

uniquely suited to the anti-elitist democratic American vision of its national mission. Everyone could be expected to share the consensus view of the '*manifest* destiny' expressed in the American political, social and religious agenda because of its clearly 'self-evident' nature.

This common-sense philosophy became particularly entrenched in American Presbyterianism as a function of its strong Scottish roots. The Rev. John Witherspoon, who came from Scotland to Princeton College as its first president in 1768, introduced the dominant common-sense tradition which was faithfully and thoroughly passed down in theological instruction, first in Princeton College, then in the Seminary until the death of Warfield in 1921.[1] Warfield was a disciple of James McCosh, the last prominent defender of Scottish common-sense philosophy, who became president of Princeton College in 1868, the year Warfield entered as an undergraduate.[2]

Princetonians had put this philosophy to work justifying their traditional distinctions between faith and reason as well as the supernatural and the natural. Henry F. May notes they did so at some cost:

> Nowhere were Common Sense principles taught with more enthusiasm than in Presbyterian seminaries, where they were used to reconcile natural religion and revelation in a manner reminiscent of the early eighteenth century, and to play down the moral paradoxes which have always troubled Christians.[3]

circles: 'Early in the century Congregationalist conservatives like Timothy Dwight were. . . diligent. . . in putting the Scottish philosophy to work for the faith. Over the next generation, Congregational moderates like N.W. Taylor or more consistent Calvinists like Edwards A. Park, Unitarians like Andrews Norton, revivalists like Charles Finney, not to speak of the mass of the Presbyterians, whether Old School or New, shared the same philosophical perspective'.

1. See Noll, *Princeton Theology*, pp. 31-33, who traces the transmission of Scottish common-sense philosophy at Princeton through the academic careers of Witherspoon, William Graham (1773), Archibald Alexander (1815–40), Charles Hodge (1841–78), A.A. Hodge (1879-1886) and Warfield (1887–1920).

2. For Warfield's dependence on Scottish common-sense philosophy see: J.H. Gerstner, 'Warfield's Case for Biblical Inerrancy', in J.W. Montgomery (ed.), *God's Inerrant Word* (Minneapolis: Bethany Fellowship, 1974), pp. 102-22; Marsden, *Fundamentalism*, pp. 114-16; Vander Stelt, *Philosophy of Scripture*, pp. 166-84; and J. Wiers, 'Scottish Common Sense Realism in the Theology of B.B. Warfield' (unpublished paper, Trinity Evangelical Divinity School, 1977).

3. May, *The Enlightenment in America*, p. 348. Ahlstrom, in his article, 'The Scottish Philosophy', p. 269, makes a similar observation, i.e., that Scottish common-sense philosophy was essentially an anthropocentric rationalism which

The common-sense philosophy of the Princetonians, then, provided a moral platform on which any observer could stand so as to decide rationally about religious matters, a position which was particularly in evidence in either the empirical, apologetic appeal to, or the polemic denial of, miracles.[1] Warfield also followed this common-sense pattern when he constructed his polemic on miracles, just as he did in his general approach to apologetics and his specific defenses of the authority of Scripture. Warfield's epistemology is nowhere systematically developed, but may be discovered in scattered statements throughout his many writings. The focus here will be, as much as possible, on his work on apologetics and miracles.

In 1908 Warfield wrote an article on apologetics for *The New Schaff-Herzog Encyclopedia of Religious Knowledge*[2] in which he described theology as a science in the same empirical, inductive sense that characterized the so-called 'hard sciences', for example, chemistry, biology, astronomy. As part of its foundation, he reiterated some central premises of Scottish common-sense philosophy:

> If theology be a science at all, there is involved in that fact, as in the case of all other sciences, at least these three things: the reality of its subject matter, the capacity of the human mind to receive into itself and rationally to reflect this subject-matter, the existence of media of communication between the subject-matter and the percipient and understanding mind.[3]

Accordingly, Warfield was extremely optimistic as to the adequacy of the human mind to reason its way to theological truth. As light to a photographic plate, so the rational appeal of the Christian message would almost inevitably imprint itself on the consciousness of a person of common sense.

'rendered the central Christian paradoxes into stark logical contradictions that either had to be disguised or explained away. Reformed theology was thus emptied of its most dynamic element'.

1. In this vein see for example articles by other Princetonian theologians: C. Hodge in 'Miracles', Chapter XII of his *Systematic Theology* (New York: Charles Scribner's Sons, 1871–72), I, pp. 617-36; W.G.T. Shedd, 'Hume, Huxley, and Miracles', *PR* 1 (1880), pp. 22-45, and C.W. Hodge, 'What is a Miracle?', *PTR* 14 (1916), pp. 202-64, esp. pp. 243-48.

2. I, pp. 232-38, reprinted in Warfield, *Studies in Theology* (WBBW, IX), pp. 3-21.

3. Warfield, in *Studies in Theology*, p. 11.

> It is the distinction of Christianity that it has come into the world clothed
> with the mission to *reason* its way to its dominion. Other religions may
> appeal to the sword, or seek some other way to propagate themselves.
> Christianity makes its appeal to right reason, and stands out among all
> religions, therefore, as distinctively 'the Apologetical religion'. It is solely
> by reasoning that it has come thus far on its way to its kingship. And it is
> solely by reasoning that it will put all its enemies under its feet.[1]

Warfield shared the view of his Princeton colleagues that theology
was very like any other natural science, that by following the
Baconian model of observing, arranging and organizing the facts of
Scripture and theology, one could derive all of the essential Christian
truths.[2]

But the cacophony of conflicting theological and philosophical
opinions flooding nineteenth-century America presented a challenge to
Warfield's view of the perceptual homogeneity innate to humankind.
A simple glance at the 'facts' showed that by Warfield's time the
American intellectual consensus, if there ever had been one, had
unraveled. How was it possible for there to be many opposing
theological viewpoints, ranging from Roman Catholicism to
Congregationalism, to revivalistic evangelicalism to Unitarianism to
the 'pure religion' of Calvinism, if the truth could so simply and accurately be ascertained by the person of 'common sense'? Moreover,
how could a man such as Charles Darwin, raised in the evangelical
faith, a man of sober mind and scientific temperament, lose his
Christian faith while scientifically studying nature? This obviously
required explanation. While Warfield remains firm in his optimism
about humanity's coming to faith through reason and evidence, he
must explain why this may occasionally appear not to be the case:

---

1. Cited from Warfield's introductory remarks to F.R. Beattie's *Apologetics: Or,
the Rational Vindication of Christianity* (Richmond, VA: Presbyterian Committee of
Publication, 1903), cited in *SSWW*, II, p. 98.

2. So, for example, C. Hodge, whose *Systematic Theology* (New York: Charles
Scribner's Sons, 1871), obviated, for Warfield, the need to write his own. See
F. Patton, in his 'Memorial Address' for Warfield in *PTR* 19 (1921), p. 387.
Hodge writes: 'If natural science be concerned with the facts and laws of nature,
theology is concerned with the facts and the principles of the Bible. If the object of
the one be to arrange and systematize the facts of the external world, and to ascertain
the laws by which they are determined, the object of the other is to systematize the
facts of the Bible, and ascertain the principles or general truths which those facts
involve' (*Systematic Theology*, I, p. 18).

> It seems to be forgotten that though faith be a moral act and the gift of
> God, it is yet formally conviction passing into confidence; and that all
> forms of conviction must rest on evidence as their ground, and it is not
> faith but reason which investigates the nature and validity of this
> ground. . . We believe in Christ because it is rational to believe in
> Him. . . Of course mere reasoning cannot make a Christian; but that is
> not because faith is not the result of evidence, but because a dead soul
> cannot respond to evidence. The action of the Holy Spirit in giving faith is
> not apart from evidence, but along with evidence.[1]

Wherever rationalism and mysticism have penetrated, says Warfield,
we lose the theoretical basis of religion founded on the knowledge of
fact. With the rationalism of Ritschl religion is historically relativized;
it becomes not a 'knowledge of fact, but a perception of utility'.[2] With
mysticism the convictions of the Christian 'are not the product of
reason addressed to the intellect, but the immediate creation of the
Holy Spirit in the heart'.[3] This latter error was characteristic of the
modern 'enthusiasts', the Methodists, and more specifically, the
Keswick 'Higher Life' movement, against which Warfield had directed
a good deal of polemical attention.[4] So by allowing one's natural
faculties to be diverted, either to false rationalism on the one hand, or
to the formless feelings attributed to the Holy Spirit on the other, one
could wander from the true source of knowledge. Though Warfield
implies in the passage above that religious knowledge flows from a
joint work of the mind and the Spirit, his emphasis consistently favors
the former. And what of Darwin, who became for Warfield the
archetypal erring scientist of his time? Continually exposed as he had
been to the evidence of God's divine plan in nature, why had Darwin's
faith failed? Warfield's answer was that because it had become so
narrowly focused on a single scientific enterprise, Darwin's mind
'atrophied' in other areas, thereby rendering it an untrustworthy
judge of evidence and incapable of following 'the guidance of his

---

1. Warfield, 'Apologetics', *WBBW*, IX, p. 15.
2. Warfield, 'The Latest Phase of Historical Rationalism', *The Presbyterian Quarterly* 9 (1895), pp. 36-67 and pp. 185-210, reprinted in *WBBW*, IX, pp. 585-645.
3. Warfield, 'Apologetics', pp. 14 and 15.
4. These writings are now collected in volumes VII and VIII of *WBBW*.

inextinguishable [religious] conviction'.[1] But Warfield still faced a difficulty: if one accurately observes the tremendous diversity in theological viewpoints, the 'common-sense' model of human mental capacity dies the death of a thousand qualifications and millions of exceptions. Either 'common sense' is 'common' to all, or the term does not carry much meaning. If most people are 'dead souls' who 'cannot respond to evidence', what of Warfield's epistemological premise? Accordingly, once the 'common' of the common sense is surrendered, the epistemological ground of Warfield's apologetics has been washed away.

According to Warfield, nowhere is the suspension of common sense more likely than in dealing with miracles. Hence, one of his major tasks is to come to grips with the confusion surrounding reports of their occurrence and the interpretations of their meaning. Moreover, while Calvinism was for Warfield the ideal theological expression for American Christian belief, he nonetheless found himself beset by a proliferating Babel of competing religious ideas which claimed miraculous sanction for their beliefs. On seeing this situation, Warfield now sharpened his ready-made cessationist polemic from Calvin, honed his common-sense epistemology, and was ready to do battle against those who both misperceived and misapplied true miracles to support their deviant causes.

2. *Benjamin Warfield's Cessationist Polemic*

Warfield's cessationist polemic was founded on his understanding of Calvinism, which in turn was shaped by Scottish common-sense philosophy. I will now turn to the factors that precipitated his cessationism, and the methods, both historical and biblical, by which it was inadequately supported.

Theological Challenges Precipitating Warfield's Cessationism
It is in *Counterfeit Miracles* that several streams of Warfield's life-long polemic concerns converge. In his dealing with the issue of the continuation of the miraculous in its various historical (pseudo-) expressions, Warfield apparently sensed he was in reality confronting

1. Warfield, 'Darwin's Arguments Against Christianity and Against Religion', *SSWW*, II, p. 41. See also *idem*, 'Charles Darwin's Religious Life: A Sketch in Spiritual Autobiography', *WBBW*, IX, pp. 541-84.

a challenge to the uniqueness of scriptural and apostolic authority in the church. This challenge appeared in the form of certain groups who laid claim to the possession of miraculous power,[1] specifically, the Roman Catholics, the Irvingites (indirectly, the Methodists), contemporary faith healers and Christian Scientists. A chapter is devoted to each group and their respective alleged miraculous activities. As we shall shortly see, the very act of a group's claiming miraculous powers was, for Warfield, *prima facie* evidence for its heterodoxy. It is against this common claim to miracles that Warfield is able to direct a general polemic attack collectively on these religious persuasions.

Counterfeit Miracles was written after an upsurge of faith healing activity in American Protestantism which had penetrated broadly across denominational lines in the last three decades of the nineteenth century. As a result, a major controversy over the continuation of healing miracles in the church broke out in a number of ecclesiastical periodicals, the majority of them hostile to the movement.[2] But modern awareness of this early emphasis on healing has been largely obscured as, after the turn of the century, Fundamentalists scrambled to distance themselves from nascent Pentecostalism, in which the objectionable practice of speaking in tongues had increasingly tainted the already suspect practice of faith healing.[3] This late-nineteenth-century interest in healing developed as an outgrowth of the wide-

---

1. *Counterfeit Miracles*, p. 6.

2. R.J. Cunningham, 'From Holiness to Healing: The Faith Cure in America 1872–1892', *CH* 43 (December 1974), pp. 503-506. Cunningham notes that 'the principal periodical controversy of the decade on this subject' was a debate between two prominent Presbyterian clergymen which appeared in the *Presbyterian Review* in 1883–84. Warfield became a co-editor of that periodical in 1890 when it modified its name to *Presbyterian and Reformed Review*.

3. See Cunningham, 'From Holiness to Healing', D. Dayton, 'The Rise of the Evangelical Healing Movement in Nineteenth Century America', *Pneuma* 4 (Spring 1982), pp. 1-18 and Waldvogel, 'The "Overcoming Life"', esp. ch. 4, 'An Evangelical Theology of Healing'. Warfield notes in *Counterfeit Miracles*, p. 159, that already by 1887 'there were more than thirty "Faith Homes" established in America, for the treatment of disease by prayer alone; and in England and on the European Continent there were many more'. He cites a large number of healing conferences and conventions of 'adherents in every church'.

spread 'deeper life', 'holiness', or 'Christian perfection' movement[1]—a phenomenon against which Warfield had devoted two volumes in his capacity as polemicist.[2]

As further impetus for the writing of *Counterfeit Miracles*, new immigration patterns were shifting the blend of the American religious traditions toward Roman Catholicism[3] at a time when it was particularly defensive about its apologetic claims for the miraculous.[4] Beyond this, religious authority was increasingly difficult to ascertain for Christian Americans living in an intellectual atmosphere of subjectivism, where human understanding of truth was ever evolving—expanding and being modified. Unlike his predecessor, Charles Hodge, for whom biblical criticism was a somewhat distant (European) concern, Warfield faced a situation where almost all major American theological seminaries had (to him) capitulated to higher criticism of Scripture, with its resulting loss of theological authority; whole religious denominations no longer preached the Gospel as traditionally understood. Those who opposed such

1. A movement derived from the 'Age of Methodism', as some, for example P. Schaff, described American religious life in the 19th century. This has been more recently argued by C.C. Goen, ' "The Methodist Age" in American Church History', *RL* 34 (1964–65), pp. 562-72 and W. Hudson, 'The Methodist Age in America', *MHist* 12 (April 1974), pp. 3-15.

2. See earlier footnotes. For further background, see T.L. Smith, *Revivalism and Social Reform in Mind-Nineteenth Century America* (Nashville: Abingdon Press, 1957), chs. 7–9; J.L. Peters, *Christian Perfectionism and American Methodism* (Nashville: Abingdon Press, 1956).

3. Between 1830 and 1900, the combined factors of natural increase, immigration and conversion raised the Catholic population to 12 million. A large percentage of the growth figure represented immigrants: some 2.7 million, largely from Ireland, Germany and France, between 1830 and 1880, and another 1.25 million during the 1880s when Eastern and Southern Europeans came in increasing numbers ('The Catholic Church in the U.S.', *1987 Catholic Almanac* [Huntington, IN: Our Sunday Visitor, 1987], p. 388). In the first two decades of the twentieth century, Catholic immigration was at its peak, a trend that may have alarmed Warfield and may have contributed to the urgency and relevance of his treatment of medieval and Roman Catholic miracles in *Counterfeit Miracles*.

On the openness to the miraculous among Catholics of this period see J.P. Dolan, *The American Catholic Experience: A History from the Colonial Times to the Present* (Garden City, NY: Doubleday, 1985), pp. 233-35.

4. See J.A. Hardon, SJ, 'The Concept of Miracle from St Augustine to Modern Apologetics', *TS* 15 (1954), p. 249.

modernism found themselves increasingly shunted aside from what came to be regarded as mainstream American Christianity.[1] This development was crucial to Warfield, since, in his view, sound spiritual life hung on sound theology. The general theological climate of liberalism was particularly odious to Warfield in its treatment of miracles. Liberal theologians typically attempted to explain the presence of miracles in the Bible either by providing naturalistic interpretations (for example, Jesus was walking on a sand bar, not the water; the loaves and fishes were 'multiplied' as the five thousand shared their provisions after being shamed by a small boy's gift of food to the multitude), or by seeking analogies with contemporary psychological or faith healings. For liberals, the sharp distinction between 'natural' and 'supernatural' had blurred, and with it the effectiveness of any Christian apologetic, such as William Paley's classic, based on proof from miracles. This new view of miracle, of course, carried ominous implications for the cessationist polemic. The implications were spelled out for cessationists by an influential American liberal theologian, Horace Bushnell, who, in his book *Nature and the Supernatural as together Constituting the One System of God*,[2] wrote a chapter defending the thesis that 'Miracles and Spiritual Gifts are Not Discontinued'. This conclusion may have represented to liberalism, at least in Warfield's mind, the logical extension of their worldview. It was a position that had to be countered if Princetonian apologetics were to survive, particularly the defense of the authority of scriptural doctrine by proof from miracles. Warfield does not devote a special chapter to liberalism in *Counterfeit Miracles*, but interacts with its ideas frequently throughout the book. His article 'A Question of Miracles',[3] however, is more systematic and directed against those more rationalistic and extreme than Bushnell.

Still another challenge to Warfield's position on the cessation of miracles was that of Christian Science, a religion based on *Science and Health, With a Key to the Scriptures*, by Mary Baker Eddy, which,

1. G. Marsden, *Fundamentalism and American Culture* (New York: Oxford University Press, 1980), pp. 113-16.

2. New York: Charles Scribner's Sons, 2nd edn, 1883. Warfield mentions Bushnell in *Counterfeit Miracles*, p. 247 n. 59. See the important discussion on Bushnell's impact on the question of cessationism in R.B. Mullin, 'Horace Bushnell and the Question of Miracles', *CH* 58 (December 1989), pp. 460-73.

3. Warfield, 'A Question of Miracles', in *SSWW*, II, pp. 167-204.

she claimed, was divinely dictated. The position that these new scriptures supplemented, and in some sense, assumed priority over Christian Scriptures, represented, of course, a significant challenge to Warfield and his view of religious authority. This is particularly true when the religious claims of Christian Science were supported by its apparent emphasis upon miracles of healing.[1] In view of the rapidly expanding influence of Catholicism, Perfectionism, faith healing, liberalism and cults of pantheism, could the spiritual dissolution of true American Christianity (that is, Princetonian Calvinism) be far behind?

Finally, *Counterfeit Miracles* was written shortly after the death of Warfield's invalid wife, who had contracted a severe nervous disorder as a result of being caught in a lightning storm during their honeymoon in Europe many years previously. Outside of his classroom duties, Warfield remained through the years almost constantly beside his wife, reading to her numerous popular novels in which he frequently jotted reviews.[2] We may only speculate on how this tragic long-term illness affected Warfield's perspective on miracles and divine healing.

The dissonant new voices and conditions which challenged Warfield's religious and philosophical world-view required a fully

1. Actually, as J. Daane points out, 'It is a mistake to think of Christian Science as a faith-healing religion. It does not claim to *heal* sickness, for it claims sickness is an illusion' ('Christian Science', *NIDCC*, pp. 221-22).

2. Apparently this was an activity to which he had become attached, according to J.E. Meeter in an interview on 8 November 1983. Meeter's bibliography lists not only 800 entries for articles and books Warfield published, but also almost 800 book reviews as well; J.E. Meeter and R. Nicole, *A Bibliography of Benjamin Breckinridge Warfield*, I (Philadelphia: Presbyterian and Reformed Publishing, 1974). Biographical information on Warfield is scanty: the memorial address cited in *PTR* 19 (1921), pp. 329-30 and 369-91, the brief biographical note in *Biblical and Theological Studies* (Philadelphia: Presbyterian and Reformed Publishing, 1956), in the introduction to *WBBW*, pp. v-ix, and in W.A. Hoffecker, *Piety and the Princeton Theologians* (Grand Rapids: Baker, 1978), pp. 93-160, and surveys of Warfield's theological positions generally, in W.A. Hoffecker's 'Benjamin B. Warfield', in D.F. Wells (ed.), *Reformed Theology in America* (Grand Rapids: Eerdmans, 1985), pp. 60-86. According to Hoffecker, N.B. Stonehouse said that Warfield rarely left his invalid wife's side for more than two hours, and because of her condition did not leave the town of Princeton between 1905 and 1915. Hoffecker is citing Stonehouse's biography, *J. Gresham Machen* (Grand Rapids: Eerdmans, 1954), p. 220.

developed and justified polemic. In the following three sections I will examine Warfield's understanding of miracle, which undergirds the two major arguments for his polemic, those from history and from Scripture.

Warfield's Concept of Miracle

The validity of Benjamin Warfield's cessationism stands or falls completely with the integrity of his Enlightenment era concept of miracle on which it rests. For cessationism to demand the restriction of miracles to approximately the apostolic age, it is crucial first to establish some agreement on how one knows a miracle has appeared or whether Warfield's concept of miracle is an intelligible notion at all. The validity of cessationism depends upon a clearly discernible and internally consistent model of miracle which can be applied transparently and uniformly to all candidate cases as they appear throughout history, both in the biblical accounts and afterward. Any failure in Warfield's miracle model, or in its consistent application to both categories of cases, necessitates a corresponding failure of his cessationist polemic.

Warfield's cessationism further depends upon the normative, that is, biblical, affirmation of an exclusively evidentialist purpose for miracles (his designation of certain gifts of the Holy Spirit). Accordingly, the function of biblical miracles determines their duration: if their sole purpose is to accredit the initial presentation of New Testament doctrine, then they must perforce cease when the doctrine is established. This present section also examines the validity of this centrally important cessationist claim.

Wherever he treats the subject of miracles, we find that Warfield is fighting on two fronts: against those who deny or redefine the traditional understanding of miracle, and against those claiming present-day miracles to attest to the legitimacy of their religious authority. Since our focus is upon Warfield's cessationist polemic, I will treat the first category only insofar as it provides us with Warfield's concept of the miraculous and his criteria for distinguishing true and false miracles. I will consider Warfield's definition and description of miracles as they relate to nature and providential events, the epistemological conflict within his concept of miracle, and finally the function of miracles in his polemic.

Warfield's Definition and Description of Miracle. To ascertain the nature of Warfield's polemic we need first to seek out his understanding of miracle. In his article 'A Question of Miracles'[1] he takes to task those who, for him, vitiate the purely transcendent, divine character of the biblical miracles. Warfield insists at the outset on the need for a 'clearly defined conception' of miracle, and criteria for determining the validity of claims to miracles. 'A miracle,' he writes, 'is specifically an effect in the external world produced by the immediate efficiency of God'.[2] Its two *differentiae* are, first, that a miracle is not merely subjective, but that it is 'objectively real' and not a function only within the mind, and, secondly, that its cause 'is a new supernatural force, intruded into the complex of nature, and not a natural force under whatever wise and powerful manipulation'. I will deal with the first, subjective aspect of miracle in the next section which treats Warfield's epistemology of miracle. Here I will focus more on his ontology of miracle.

Warfield's understanding of miracle in relation to nature is fairly traditional, but he is aware of the cost of tampering too freely with the accepted concept of an orderly nature. Warfield denies that a miracle should be spoken of as 'a violation, suspension, or transgression of the laws of nature'.[3] He seeks to outmaneuver Hume by asserting rather that a miracle is a

> product of a force *outside* [italics mine] of nature, and specifically above nature, intruding into the complex of natural forces and producing, therefore, in that complex, effects which could not be produced by the natural forces themselves. These effects reveal themselves, therefore, as 'new'—but not as neo-natural but rather as extra-natural and specifically as supernatural.

Warfield wants to avoid, on the one hand, the naturalistic dilution of miracle into a natural event, but desires, on the other, to avoid the trap of rendering miracles more objectionable to the critic of the traditional, evidentialist view because of their alien, unnatural,

---

1. Warfield, 'A Question of Miracles', pp. 167-204.
2. 'A Question of Miracles', p. 170. This definition is close to that of his mentor, C. Hodge, in *Systematic Theology*, p. 618: 'an event, in the external world, brought about by the immediate efficiency, or simple volition of God'.
3. 'A Question of Miracles', p. 168.

'lawless' character.[1] The apologist using miracles in this way had long faced the dilemma of requiring both a consistent and inviolable order coexisting with miraculous events interrupting that order, this combination somehow demonstrating their divine origin. Hence, Warfield moves his description of miracle as close as possible to the orderly process of nature, while insisting that the miraculous effect is completely above its powers. For example, the wine produced by the miracle of Cana was real wine, interactive with and effective under the conditions of the relevant natural forces, becoming immediately subject to these forces once it was created. But he stresses that the wine was created miraculously—unambiguously above and beyond the power of nature.

Warfield follows Aquinas and the later traditional Christian concept when he insists that a miracle is not an event which is in any way, however unusual, produced by nature. This is so even if the forces of nature, whether physical, occult or angelic, are 'under the manipulation of the infinite intellect of God'. The forces of nature, he continues, 'under whatever guidance, can produce nothing but natural effects', in which case such events must be classed as 'special providences'. 'Providential' works of God involve the use of 'means', or 'second causes' within nature which God uses to produce effects above their 'natural working'. Miracles cannot be viewed as 'extraordinary events performed through the medium of natural forces, but as the immediate products of the energy of God'.[2] Hence an event may be

---

1. Warfield cites one of his opponents, William Mackintosh, who summarizes the critics' position on the immutability of the natural order: 'Modern thought holds, in the form of a scientific conviction. . . that the universe is governed by immutable laws inherent in the very nature and constitution of things—by laws which are never reversed, never suspended, and never supplemented in the interest of any special object whatever.' To suggest the necessary link between a perceived 'violation' of the laws of nature and divine activity is to ignore a more generally accepted explanation. 'The inference is irresistible. . . to assume that every fact or event, however strange, and apparently exceptional or abnormal, admits of being subsumed under some general law or laws, either already ascertained or yet ascertainable' (*The Natural History of the Christian Religion* [New York: Macmillan], p. 23).

2. Warfield, 'A Question of Miracles', p. 198.

supernatural even to the extent that it is 'startling' or 'remarkable',[1] but it is not necessarily miraculous.

On this basis, then, Warfield makes an important distinction in his polemics against faith healing groups: a person may be physically healed in answer to prayer so that 'the supernaturalness of the act may be so apparent as to demonstrate God's activity in it to all right-thinking minds conversant with the facts'.[2] But he chastises those who claim these healings as 'miracles' because they are guilty of 'obscuring the lines which divide miracles, specifically so called, from the general supernatural'.[3] Warfield felt this clarification to the 'simple reader' was necessary since there were those who attempted to 'reduce the idea of miracles to the level of these Faith Healings, assimilating the miracles of our Lord. . . to them and denying that miracles in the strict sense have ever been wrought, even by our Lord'.[4] Warfield is also reacting here to the liberal theology of divine immanence, the framework within which Modernists attempted to justify Christ's miracles on the basis of historical and contemporary analogies.[5] On one level, to preserve his apologetical tradition of proving the existence of God from the occurrence of empirically-observable miracles, it was crucial that Warfield maintain a strict natural/supernatural dichotomy. Nothing of 'natural means' could be allowed to contaminate a purely divine act. Beyond this, his cessationist polemic demanded a sharp distinction between the 'miraculous' events of the Bible and the 'providential' divine acts, if any, of later history. Any 'analogies', then, between biblical and modern miracles, as the faith healers and the liberal apologists were proposing, were anathema.

---

1. *Counterfeit Miracles*, pp. 185, 191. By 'miraculous' in this case Warfield intends 'to say without means—any means—and apart from means, and above means'.

2. *Counterfeit Miracles*, p. 192.

3. *Counterfeit Miracles*, p. 163.

4. *Counterfeit Miracles*, pp. 161-62.

5. *Counterfeit Miracles*, p. 163. Warfield here cites works by Prebendary Reynolds who refers to a case of hypnotism producing unusual physical effects and concludes, 'This shows how easy it was for our Lord, with His divine knowledge and power, to work every kind of healing'. Warfield disagrees: 'Our Lord's miracles of healing were certainly not faith cures, as it has become fashionable among the "Modernists" to represent' (*Counterfeit Miracles*, p. 302 n. 12).

Warfield emphasizes the *toto coelo*[1] difference between the true miracles of the Bible and events purported to be such from a later time. In his description of biblical miracles Warfield echoes the early Enlightenment quests for religious certainty, absolute truth and the idealization of a past, golden age. The miracles of Christ, for example, 'were but the trailing clouds of glory which He brought from heaven, which is His home'.[2] 'Their number,' Warfield asserts, 'is usually greatly underestimated'.[3] The miracles surrounding Christ's ministry described in the Gospels are 'recorded only as specimens' of a much larger number. The miracles he lists are those of healing, exorcisms, nature-miracles, and raisings of the dead.[4] Warfield's view of the idealized and absolute character of Jesus' miraculous ministry is illustrated when he goes far beyond the scriptural evidence: 'For a time disease and death must have been almost banished from the land. The country was thoroughly aroused... filled with wonder [and] universal excitement'.[5]

The miraculous power resident in Jesus was transmitted to the Apostles, who, 'as a crowning sign of their divine commission', passed

1. *Counterfeit Miracles*, p. 57
2. *Counterfeit Miracles*, p. 3.
3. Warfield, 'Jesus Christ', in *SHERK*, VI, p. 159. 'The number of miracles which He wrought may easily be underrated' (*Counterfeit Miracles*, p. 3).
4. Elsewhere, Warfield states that 'supernatural dreams' in which 'direct divine revelations are communicated' and 'those 'symbolical dreams which receive divine interpretations' share the characteristics of a miracle, as we see below, in that they are 'clustered at two or three critical points in the development of Israel' or in the 'supernatural epochs' ('Dream', in *SSWW*, II, pp. 154-55). He makes the same point in his article, 'Miracle', in *DDB*, pp. 481-82.
    In 'A Question of Miracles', p. 202, Warfield makes a special plea to view exorcism as strictly a clash of spiritual powers, an activity 'which can scarcely be subsumed under the operation of natural forces'. He compares exorcism to the resurrection of Jesus from whom 'both the divine Spirit and the human soul. . . departed into "the other world"', and returned him to life—activity 'over which "natural forces" could have no control' (p. 201). Warfield's view of the miraculous nature of New Testament exorcism here lies in sharp contrast to his reaction to nearly identical reports occurring in later church history.
5. In *Counterfeit Miracles*, p. 3, Warfield offers what he says is a 'pardonable exaggeration' when he writes of Jesus, 'In effect He banished disease and death from Palestine for the three years of His ministry'. The hem of his garment 'could medicine whole countries of their pain. One touch of that pale hand could life restore'.

it on to others in the form of charismata. These Warfield describes as 'extraordinary capacities produced in the early Christian communities by a direct gift of the Holy Spirit'.[1] These spiritual gifts are divided along the classical Protestant lines of 'ordinary' and 'extraordinary', that is, those which were 'distinctively gracious' and those which were 'distinctly miraculous'.[2] Warfield reflects his Reformation attitude toward miracles when he insists that the 'non-miraculous' charismata are 'given preference' in Scripture, and as such are called 'the greater gifts'. To seek after these rather than the miraculous gifts is, according to Warfield, 'represented as the "more excellent way"' (1 Cor. 12.31).[3] Nevertheless, the manifestation of these miraculous gifts were diffused throughout the Apostolic Church on a scale that was 'quite generally underestimated'. And he affirms this widespread operation of the miraculous charismata as a 'beautiful picture' of early Christian worship.[4] He summarizes this ideal portrayal of the church of this period:

1. *Counterfeit Miracles*, p. 3.
2. G. Vos, *The Pauline Eschatology* (Grand Rapids: Eerdmans, 1972), pp. 300-302, a conservative scholar who was a contemporary of Warfield at Princeton Seminary, represents the virtual consensus of mainstream Protestant theology of his time when he down plays this 'ordinary extraordinary' dichotomy as applied to spiritual gifts: 'The central significance in all manifestations of the Spirit, both those that we are accustomed to call ordinary or those called extraordinary, consisted for Paul in the tremendous irresistible power with which the Spirit makes his impact and produces his results in every sphere of operation. This was something inherent in the nature of the Spirit. All the phenomena revealing his presence and working bore witness to this. The fundamental note in his activity was that of divine, unique forthputting of energy.' He urges that the church ought to connect the 'quiet virtues and graces with the constant powerful urge and influence of the Spirit' and not to 'empoverish' Christian eschatological hope by ruling out 'the mighty rushing of the Pentecostal wind'.
3. His predecessor at Princeton, Charles Hodge, and the majority of commentators on this passage would not agree. The gift of prophecy, a 'miraculous' gift of revelation and divine guidance for the community, is highly prized by Paul. Hodge, in *An Exposition of the First Epistle to the Corinthians* (New York: A.C. Armstrong, 1891), p. 294, writes: 'The sense is, "Seek the better gifts, and moreover, I show you a better way to do it"', namely, in the 'way' of love rather than in a competitive spirit in which the possession of spiritual gifts accredits one's spiritual status in the community.
4. Warfield, *Counterfeit Miracles*, pp. 3-4.

[It is] characteristic of the Apostolic churches that such miraculous gifts should be displayed in them. The exception would be, not a church with, but a church without such gifts. Everywhere, the Apostolic Church was marked out as itself a gift from God, by showing forth the possession of the Spirit in appropriate works of the Spirit—miracles of healing and miracles of power, miracles of knowledge, whether in the form of prophecy or of the discerning of spirits, miracles of speech, whether the gifts of tongues or of their interpretation. The Apostolic Church was characteristically a miracle-working church.[1]

By his emphasis on the highly miraculous condition of the Apostolic Church, Warfield appears to be establishing two points: first, he points out the clearly discernible contrast between the miraculous activities of the Apostolic communities and those claimed for the post-Apostolic era. Secondly, Warfield is staking out the boundaries of miracle against 'theologians of the "liberal" school' who 'deny the miraculous character of the charisms', attributing the phenomena to 'known psychological laws' generated from times of excitement or 'great mental exaltation'.[2]

Warfield, then, emphasizes that miracles are unconnected with any process of nature; that they are directly and immediately caused by God; and are to be distinguished from 'providential' works of God in which some natural means is used to produce an unusual effect. But can one know, empirically and rationally, if a given event is a miracle?

The Epistemological Conflict within Warfield's Concept of Miracle. Warfield's approach to how a miracle is perceived is crucial for determining the validity of his concept of miracle, and with it his cessationism. But he attempts to combine two incompatible *a priori* beliefs into one notion of miracle: naturalism and faith. On the one hand, Warfield's common-sense philosophy provided him with the confidence that one could, by sifting the facts, determine if an event was miraculous or merely providential, supernatural or natural. He understands the discernment of miracles in terms of their objectivity and evidence, and from the perspective of naturalistic *a priori* beliefs. On the other hand, Warfield finally must admit that a prior faith commitment determines one's judgment on miracles.

1. *Counterfeit Miracles*, p. 5.
2. *Counterfeit Miracles*, p. 234 n. 6.

A true miracle, Warfield asserts, cannot be dismissed as subjective and personal: it must actually occur 'in the external world. . . objectively real and not merely [as] a mental phenomenon'.[1] He rejects the attempt to transpose 'marvels from the physical to the mental world' as, for example, in the case of the miracle of wine at Cana. Here the wine was not miraculous because of the altered subjective reactions of taste and sight to what was really water, but lay in the fact that water had actually changed to wine. This is a rather simple distinction between the objective and subjective nature of miracle and Warfield mentions it only in passing. But from here the issue of subjectivity becomes more complex. Warfield suggests that miracles may not be judged merely by their 'stupendous' quality, such as a resurrection from the dead versus a modest answer to prayer. More is needed to determine a miracle than a 'spiritual tape line', that is, the subjective impact of an event. Further, if miracles are determined by the perception of God's 'manifest presence and activity', then one's subjective religious experience of a miracle is simply an affirmation that God sustains and directs nature and history. In such a case, 'everything that occurs is a miracle'.[2]

Against these subjective positions, Warfield insists that the identification of a miracle must include a clear, empirically verifiable intrusion of the supernatural into the natural order of events. In 'A Question of Miracles' he then develops his definition of miracle as discussed in the previous section.

Warfield's common-sense philosophy is clearly opposed to a subjective description of miracle and even more so as he interacts with those who, while sharing the conventional definition of miracles as empirical and supernatural events, deny their occurrence. Warfield is mystified at his opponents, for instance, Hume and Huxley, who claim that a miracle is unprovable on *a priori* grounds: 'Why such an event should be incapable of proof. . . is not immediately obvious. If it occurs, it ought to be capable of being shown to have occurred.'[3] He continues, 'The question of miracles, then, is just a question of evidence'. But is it 'just a question of evidence'? As in the case of Darwin's fall from faith, Warfield fails to explain how all human beings can be endowed with 'common sense' to accept the truth as the

1. 'A Question of Miracles', p. 170.
2. 'A Question of Miracles', p. 167.
3. 'A Question of Miracles', p. 175.

evidence dictates and still account for those who reject the evidence for miracles that lies so clearly and objectively before them. All he offers is the critics' presupposition, with no hint of the epistemological grounds by which they arrived there. He observes:

> When the evidence for a miracle presents itself before their minds it scarcely finds a hospitable reception; and when that evidence is exceptionally abundant and cogent, they are compelled to face the question, What kind and amount of evidence would convince them of the real occurrence of such an event, and they thus discover their real position to be that a miraculous event is as such incapable of proof.

In other words, despite the critics' appeals to the lack of provable miracles in history, a miracle is to them 'by definition' impossible from the very outset. To them, an extraordinary event can only fall into one of two categories: a false report, or an event which can be explained, at least ultimately, within a naturalistic world-view. Warfield excoriates those who claim to examine carefully nature and history, declaring, on *a posteriori* grounds, that biblical miracles do not happen when in fact these doubters have already begun their investigation guided by the *a priori* belief that miracles are impossible. Nevertheless, when attacking the occurrence of postbiblical miracles, Warfield is not above an appeal to an identical naturalistic *a priori* belief. For example, though his rigorous demands for veracity seem excessive, Warfield appears to accept the possibility of genuine miracles. In *Counterfeit Miracles* he insists that the 'effects for which miracles are required' would consist of such phenomena as the restoration of an amputated hand, the sudden healing of a broken bone, or replacement of lost teeth.[1] However, some pages earlier, his naturalistic *a priori* belief shows through when he insists that 'bare inexplicability' or 'inscrutability' would prove insufficient grounds for the assertion of a miracle. Even such amazing events as those he described could not qualify as miracles. Warfield, like the skeptics he criticizes, simply subsumes these events, if not under the category 'nature', then certainly under 'not proven to be a miracle'.

Of course, what we have just seen illustrates the contradiction between, on the one hand, Warfield's skeptical *a priori* belief that postbiblical miracles do not occur, and on the other, his assertion that he is reasonable and open to their possibility, and they may be determined only on *a posteriori* grounds to be true miracles when judged

---

1. *Counterfeit Miracles*, p. 191.

as an objective event in the real world, accessible as such to any observer. This type of contradiction is made even more explicit when he points out not only the presuppositions of those who doubt miracles, but those of those who affirm them. In a stunning break from his common-sense epistemology and from the whole empirical basis of his extreme evidentiary miracle apologetic, Warfield makes the following concession:

> The atheist, the materialist, the pantheist are within their rights in denying the *possibility* of miracle. But none other is. As soon as we adopt the postulate of a personal God and a creation, so soon miracles cease to be 'impossible' in any exact sense of the word. We may hold them to be improbable, to the verge of the unprovable: but their possibility is inherent in the very nature of God as personal and the author of the universal frame. . .
>
> The bald assertion that miracles are 'impossible' is, for the theist, obviously mere unreasonable dogmatism.[1]

So Warfield's concept of miracle rests on two mutually incompatible foundations: on the one hand, the belief that a miracle is an event which can be shown as such to any observer, naturalist or theist, simply by viewing the evidence, and on the other, the belief that naturalists and theists necessarily determine the nature of an event from their respective background positions.

These two incompatible viewpoints appeared as a single, unexamined premise underlying the classic Evangelical apologetic on miracles. The miracle apologetic stood on common ground with the Enlightenment-era skeptic in that they could both view nature as a closed system characterized by a chain of cause and effect relationships. They also shared a confidence in human ability to determine by observation an accurate assessment of reality. A startlingly unusual event within a certain religious context, however, would to a theistic apologist indicate the irruption of the 'super-natural', an essentially distinct (divine) cause, into the chain of causality. The naturalist would feel no such constraint and would simply expand his or her view of the phenomena of nature to include such an unusual event. The apologist could charge a betrayal on the part of the naturalist since he or she has refused to perceive the empirically-verifiable evidence of a miracle breaking the natural chain of causality, an

---

1. 'A Question of Miracles', pp. 175-76.

irruption which indicated the hand of God. The naturalist could counter that this interpretation did not play by the mutually accepted rule of natural law, which was, in essence, a program of exclusively natural cause and effect relationships: if one begins with this premise, one ought not arbitrarily change the laws of nature in mid-game.

In the final analysis, the miracle apologetic is a simple question-begging exercise, a sleight of hand maneuver which attempts to reconcile the irreconcilable: theism and naturalism.[1] It purports to stand with the skeptic on a neutral, objective and rationalistic platform, and, from within a naturalistic world-view, to judge whether or not an event is of divine origin. The two positions are not so much contrary from an epistemological standpoint, as they are, at base, opposing commitments of faith.

Warfield has correctly pointed out that the skeptics reject the miraculous on *a priori* grounds. He states, also, that the theist who accepts the possibility of miracles must also begin with some presuppositions. In particular, Warfield, despite his overall appeal to a presuppositionless apprehension of the facts as the ground for the knowledge of miracles, has some *a priori* belief of his own. When he claims that 'the question of miracles. . . is just a question of evidence', the 'evidence' to which he appeals is testimony. In order to establish the reliability of this appeal, he claims that the probability of 'testimony being true rests in part on the known or presumable trustworthiness of the witnesses available in the case, anterior to their testimony to the particular fact now under consideration'.[2] But one such testimony to which Warfield appeals to establish the historicity of miracles is the Gospel of John. Now this is a perfectly acceptable appeal to one sharing an Evangelical faith-position, but much more than what Warfield offers in support of the historical trustworthiness of John is required if he is to satisfy his own requirements for true historical

---

1. Though referring primarily to scriptural inerrancy, the following remarks by Vander Stelt apply to Warfield's view of miracle as well: 'As to the structure of the natural world, Warfield found the basic assumptions of a philosophy of reality and truth that was greatly indebted to SCSP acceptable and helpful in curtailing any threats upon certainty and security. By placing all of this within the larger context of the supernatural, Warfield tried to reinsure the former with the latter. . . a curious fusion of two basically conflicting worlds of thought' (*Philosophy and Scripture*, pp. 182-83).

2. 'A Question of Miracles', p. 180.

testimony. For example, as Brown points out,[1] Warfield offers no corroborating contemporary testimony to John's account of the raising of Lazarus or the healing of the man born blind. Nor can he appeal to the corroborating testimony of similar events occurring in his own experience due to his cessationist theology. So Warfield's selection of John as reliable historical testimony is based on his *a priori* assumptions about the infallibility of Scripture and the evidential function of miracles.

Warfield appeals again to the *a priori* belief in scriptural authority when he offers the following *non sequitur* argument.

> The entrance of sin into the world is . . . the sufficient occasion of the entrance also of miracle. Extraordinary exigencies (we speak as a man) are the sufficient explanation of extraordinary expedients. If, then, we conceive the extraordinary events of the Scriptural record as part and parcel of the redemptive work of God—and this is how they are uniformly represented in the Scriptural record itself—surely the presumption which is held to lie against them is transmitted into a presumption in their favor, as appropriate elements in a great remedial scheme, by means of which the broken scheme of nature is mended and restored.[2]

Again, the proof for miracles is circular: one must stand completely within the Christian tradition, with all its affirmations of divine activity in the physical world, to accept the premises of the argument. Warfield applies a similar type of logic when he extrapolates the likelihood of miracles' occurring from some central supernatural events of the Christian creeds: creation, the incarnation and the resurrection.

> The admission of the truly miraculous character of these three will not only itself suffice to fill the category of 'miracle', taken in its strictest sense, with an undeniable content, and so to vindicate the main proposition that miracles have happened; but will tend to drag into that category others in their train.[3]

1. Brown, *Miracles and the Critical Mind*, p. 201.
2. 'A Question of Miracles', p. 193.
3. 'A Question of Miracles', p. 200. Somewhat later he expands on this principle of miracle-by-association: he wants to 'call attention. . . to the natural tendency that exists to work out from them (major miracles) as a center to the inclusion in the same category of others more or less like them. Just because some are certainly miracles of this order, a presumption is raised that others may be of this order; and this presumption may not unnaturally grown upon us until we are inclined to assign to the same group many which in themselves would never have suggested this classification' (p. 202).

Just how these events would 'drag into that category others in their train' is unclear. In any case, he is begging the question. Miracles, in the evidentialist sense he hoped to employ them, were to indicate the existence of God; but here he is using the existence and power of God to indicate the occurrence of miracles. Ostensibly, the logic is that he is moving from the greater to the lesser: if God could perform the great wonders of creation, the incarnation and the resurrection, how much more easily could he perform lesser miracles in the same general category, for example, the multiplication of the loaves and fishes, the cure of demoniacs and miracles of healing? But even granting the great redemptive wonders, there is no necessity to the claim that God had actually supplemented these works with further, lesser miracles. More to our point, Warfield is again beginning with the same theological *a priori* beliefs: the existence and activity of God as well as the historical reliability of Scripture to attest to miracles. This scriptural starting point underlies Warfield's summary of *a priori* criteria for testing genuine miracles, as we see in his article, 'Miracle' in *DDB*: [1]

> 1) They [true miracles] exhibit the character of God and teach truths concerning God. 2) They are in harmony with the established truths of religion (Deut. 13.1-3). If a wonder is worked which contradicts the doctrines of the Bible, it is a lying wonder (2 Thess. 2.9; Rev. 16.14). 3) There is an adequate occasion for them. God does not work them except for great cause and for a religious purpose. They belong to the history of redemption, and there is no genuine miracle without an adequate occasion for it in God's redemptive revelation of himself. 4) They are established, not by the number of witnesses, but by the character and qualification of the witnesses.

The fourth point here, of course, is a reference to the reliability of the biblical witnesses as against those found in later church history. I will investigate below the specific scriptural arguments Warfield used to support cessationism, but it is necessary here only to point out that his *a priori* belief in scriptural infallibility was foundational to his view of miracles. Elsewhere, a fifth point, related to the first three above, is his insistence that miracles must be disassociated from 'occurrences in which immoralities are implicated' or 'implications of. . . irreligion or of superstition'.[2] Such events may be thoroughly

---

1. *DDB*, p. 299.
2. *Counterfeit Miracles*, p. 121.

marvelous and 'inexplicable', but '*we know from the outset* [italics mine] that God did not work them'. 'It is a *primary principle*,' Warfield writes, 'that no event can really be miraculous which has implications inconsistent with religious truth'. [1]

Moreover, in keeping with his view that the miracles of Scripture were absolute, instantaneous and complete, he points to the numerous failures and to the sometimes partial cures among faith healers and healing shrines,[2] and remarks, 'It must remain astonishing. . . that miracles should frequently be incomplete. We should *a priori* expect miraculous cures to be regularly radical'.[3]

Warfield mentions still another of his criteria for judging reports of miracles: naturalism, that is, the belief that there are no forces, divine or spiritual, which impact upon the physical, material world. This appears inconsistent in light of his attacks on the critics of biblical miracles for employing just such an objection to miracles. But when he treats accounts of postbiblical miracles, Warfield repeatedly describes them as occurring, however inscrutably, only within the natural order. For example, in response to the account of Pierre de Rudder, whose badly broken legs were reportedly instantly healed at the shrine of Lourdes, Warfield repeats not only his usual disbelief of such a report, but adds the observation:

> We are only beginning to learn the marvellous behavior of which living tissue is capable, and it may well be that, after a while, it may seem very natural that Pierre de Rudder's case happened just as it is said to have happened. . . Nature was made by God, not man, and there may be forces working in nature not only which have not yet been dreamed of in our philosophy, but which are beyond human comprehension

1. *Counterfeit Miracles*, p. 122.
2. *Counterfeit Miracles*, pp. 106-109; 196.
3. *Counterfeit Miracles*, p. 109. It is this demand for absolute certainty that characterizes so much modern Evangelical and Fundamentalist thought on spiritual gifts. For example, the inerrant Scripture is frequently contrasted with the reported aberrations surrounding claims for the contemporary gift of prophecy, with the latter faring, in many cases, quite badly by contrast. Recently Grudem, *The Gift of Prophecy*, pp. 17-114, attempted to reconcile this conflict by positing a two-level degree of inspiration and authority for revelation: the first group, the Old Testament prophets and New Testament apostles, that is, those authorized to write Scripture, are contrasted with the second group: New Testament prophets, whose utterances were not regarded as infallible and so lay under the judgment of apostolic tradition and under the discernment of others in the church congregations.

altogether. . . We do not busy ourselves, therefore, with conjecturing
how Pierre de Rudder's cure may have happened. . . We are content to
know that in no case was it a miracle.[1]

Physical healings may happen among such groups as Catholics, faith
healers and Christian Scientists, but Warfield typically attributes such
healings to the power of hysteria, suggestion or 'mind cure'. In these
cases, the power of the sufferer's faith lies in the abilities of the mind
to influence the body, rather than God's response to that faith.
Similarly, he attributes what some believe to be divine revelation or
utterances to the effects of 'deep religious excitement', in turn, a
consequence of 'brutal persecution' and 'widespread oppression'.[2]

When Warfield confronts the question of whether or not biblical
miracles have occurred, he bases his judgment not on an unbiased,
rational examination of the facts, but upon prior assumptions about
the reliability of biblical testimony and its theological corollaries.
When he deals with postbiblical miracles, however, he adopts the
naturalistic background of his rationalist critics. In this Warfield is
ironically and profoundly unbiblical in his outlook. 'The man without
the Spirit', St Paul wrote, 'does not accept the things of the Spirit of
God, for they are foolishness to him, and he cannot understand them,
because they are spiritually discerned' (1 Cor. 2.14), that is, not by
human reason but by revelation of the Holy Spirit.

I will spell out these background beliefs more fully in the section on
Warfield's historical method, but I will now examine briefly still
another of his presuppositions, indeed, the central presupposition of
Warfield's miracle polemic.

The Function of Miracles in Warfield's Cessationist Polemic. Warfield
was confident that if one correctly discerns the 'biblical principle
which governed the distribution of the miraculous gifts' one finds the
'key which unlocks all the historical puzzles connected with them'.[3]
What is this principle that provides him with such confident control of
historical accounts of these miraculous spiritual gifts? These spiritual
gifts were given, Warfield writes, by God, transferred from the
earthly ministry of Christ, to be 'distinctively the authentication of the
Apostles. They were part of the credentials of the Apostles as the

1. *Counterfeit Miracles*, pp. 119-20.
2. *Counterfeit Miracles*, pp. 127, 129.
3. *Counterfeit Miracles*, p. 25.

authoritative agents of God in founding the church'.[1] The ability to bestow the Holy Spirit by the laying on of hands as recorded in Scripture is given 'to teach us the course of the gifts of power, in the Apostles, apart from whom they were not conferred: as also their function, to authenticate the Apostles as the authoritative founders of the church'.[2] Warfield approvingly cites Bishop Kaye who insists that the miracle-working power of the New Testament church

> was not extended beyond the disciples upon whom the Apostles conferred it by the imposition of their hands. As the number of these disciples gradually diminished, the instances of the exercise of miraculous powers became continually less frequent, and ceased entirely at the death of the last individual on whom the hands of the Apostles had been laid.[3]

Under this schema it would be possible, then, to hear of a few miracles still being performed into the second century, though the number of apostolically trained men endowed with the Spirit 'cannot have been very large'.[4] Warfield lists Polycarp, the disciple of John, Ignatius, Papias, Clement, Hermas and possibly Leucius as examples. Hence the miracle reports written by such men as Justin and Irenaeus could be attributed to the activity of these last disciples of the Apostles.

Warfield adds to this rather mechanical view of spiritual entropy a 'deeper principle' of which the above connection of the charismata to the Apostles and their disciples serves only as an illustration. This principle is the 'inseparable connection of miracles with revelation, as its mark and credential'. But even within Scripture miracles do not appear randomly, but rather 'appear only when God is speaking to His people through an accredited messenger declaring His gracious purpose'.[5] Elsewhere, Warfield lists the four periods of revelation accompanied by miraculous confirmation:

> 1. The redemption of God's people from Egypt and their establishment in Canaan under Moses and Joshua. 2. The life-and-death struggle of the true religion with heathenism under Elijah and Elisha. 3. The Exile, when

---

1. *Counterfeit Miracles*, pp. 3 and 6.
2. *Counterfeit Miracles*, p. 23.
3. *Counterfeit Miracles*, pp. 22-23, 245, n. 51, citing *The Ecclesiastical History of the Second and Third Centuries, Illustrated from the Writings of Tertullian* (Cambridge: Cambridge University Press, 1845), pp. 98-103.
4. *Counterfeit Miracles*, p. 25.
5. *Counterfeit Miracles*, p. 26.

Jehovah afforded proof of his power and supremacy over the gods of the heathen, although his people were in captivity (Daniel and his companions). 4. The introduction of Christianity, when miracles attested the person of Christ and his doctrine. Outside these periods miracles are rare indeed (Gen. 5.24). . . . The working of miracles in the apostolic age, although not confined to the apostles (Acts vi.8; viii. 5-7), were the signs of an apostle (2 Cor. xii.12; Heb. ii.4; cp. Acts ii.43; Gal. iii.5).[1]

From the time of creation to the exodus, Warfield tells us, miracles were 'almost totally unknown'. Similarly, 'supernatural' dreams, that is, those communicating direct, divine revelation and those which received divine interpretations, are rare in Scripture and when they occur are 'oddly clustered at two or three critical points in the development of Israel',[2] that is, the birth of Israel as a nation, the period of Daniel and the birth of Christ. The exceptions to these may be classed essentially as 'providential' dreams or reduced to a single case: 1 Kgs 3.5. If the corresponding 'supernaturalistic epochs' of dreams and other miracles demonstrate a less-than-perfect match, Warfield concedes that supernatural manifestations of all types may simply 'be connected with [the]. . . particular periods God's people were brought into particularly close relations with the outside world'.[3] Warfield next takes up the question of why God would not continue to accredit his revelation 'atomistically. . . to each individual, throughout the whole course of history, in the penetralium of his own consciousness'.[4] Indeed, the 'Romish theory' held that miracles continued throughout history, accrediting the truth of Catholic doctrine to the present day. This theory, Warfield writes, is at least more 'consistent and reasonable'[5] than the 'prevailing opinion' of his time which held that miracles continued after the Apostolic age for a few, usually three or four, centuries. Warfield cites Middleton's *Free Inquiry* for reasons maintaining this prevailing opinion.

1. Warfield, 'Miracle', p. 482.
2. Warfield, 'Dream', pp. 154-55.
3. 'Dream', p. 155. This 'cluster theory' of miracles, at least in the Old Testament, seems flatly contradicted by Jer. 32.20, 'You performed miraculous signs and wonders in Egypt and have *continued them to this day*, both in Israel and among all mankind and have gained the renown that is *still yours*'. See Isa. 59.21 for the same sense of continuing prophecy.
4. *Counterfeit Miracles*, p. 26.
5. *Counterfeit Miracles*, p. 35.

The first is that miracles were required to strengthen the church until the civil power of the Roman Empire converted to Christianity and was in a position to protect it. The church, 'being now delivered from all danger, and secure of success, moved under the protection of the greatest power on earth'.[1] Middleton's irony here is perhaps directed at those clerics who felt nothing amiss in referring to the civil government of Rome rather than God as 'the greatest power on earth' protecting the church.

A second reason for the continuation of the charismata for the first few centuries was offered by John Tillotson following an ancient church tradition which compared the infant church to a young plant requiring water until established, after which 'the [miraculous] power ceased, and God left it to be maintained by ordinary ways'.[2]

Some defined these 'ordinary ways' more precisely, echoing Calvin's[3] transmutation of the extraordinary spiritual gifts into the permanent, ongoing gifts of the spirit; for example, 'to gifts of tongues succeeded orderly human teaching; to gifts of healing succeeded healing by educated human skill'.[4] A third general reason maintained that the charismata were granted not as protection for the church, but as 'signs of divine favor' upon it[5] until, as John Wesley had suggested, the Roman Empire had become nominally Christian and 'a general corruption both of faith and morals infected the church—which by that revolution, as St. Jerome says, lost as much of

1. C. Middleton, *Miscellaneous Works* (London: R. Manby, 1755), I, pp. xli, cited in *Counterfeit Miracles*, p. 7.

2. This plant metaphor may be derived from Chrysostom and Gregory the Great. See earlier notes.

3. Calvin, *Institutes* IV, 3, 8 (1061). See above.

4. Bishop M. Creighton, *Persecution and Tolerance* (London: Longmans & Green, 1895), pp. 55-56, cited in *Counterfeit Miracles*, p. 9. Also, the popular work by Godet who makes a similar argument (*Commentary on the First Epistle to the Corinthians* [trans. A. Cusin; Grand Rapids: Kregel, 1977], p. 250): 'Prophecy may be transformed into animated preaching; speaking in tongues may appear in the form of religious poetry and music; knowledge continue to accomplish its task by the catechetical and theological teaching of Christian truth'.

5. Warfield, *Counterfeit Miracles*, p. 8, points out that William Whiston, an Arian, held this position. The charismata accompanied the 'pure religion' of the early church until, to him, the heresy of Athanasianism triumphed in AD 381 when God could no longer continue his miraculous sanction.

its virtue as it had gained of wealth and power'.[1] Implicit of course in Wesley's argument is a challenge to the religious authority and legitimacy of a church without miracles.

Warfield is dissatisfied with these justifications of what he calls the Anglican theory, not only on historical grounds, as he goes on to show throughout most of *Counterfeit Miracles*, but on the ground of inconsistency. If the principle of the above position is that miracles appeared temporarily to plant and sustain the church in unevangelized areas, why then would miracles be limited to the Roman Empire in the first three or four centuries? Why not also the Chinese Empire in the twentieth? For that matter, he continues, the church presently bears no essentially different relation to China than it does to the whole unevangelized, unbelieving world. Still further, could not one take the 'long view' of church history and see the first two millennia of its existence as a 'negligible quantity', which places us even now in the era of 'primitive Christianity', a time still requiring the accreditation of miraculous charismata?

Warfield rejects the 'Anglican theory'[2] not only for its inconsistency, but more importantly, as I have noted, because of the 'inseparable connection' between the miraculous charismata and special revelation, that is, Scripture. To provide an alternative to the Anglican theory, he must show why the charismata cannot continue validly to accredit true, biblical doctrine after the time of the initial revelation. He offers two explanations.

First, echoing Calvin,[3] Warfield implies that since the only function of miracles is to accredit revelation, and since no new revelation is forthcoming after the apostolic age, miracles perforce must cease. As a consequence,

---

1. Warfield, *Counterfeit Miracles*, p. 8; J. Wesley, *Works of Rev. John Wesley* (New York: Carlton & Porter, 1856), V, p. 706.

2. Also called the 'scaffold theory', the miraculous charismata serving as scaffolding for the church while it is being built. After the structure is complete the external and temporary scaffolding is no longer needed. This image implies that the church reached maturity or viability in some institutional or doctrinal sense, and further implies that for the church to regress back to use of the charismata would be a sign of immature faith. See A.H. Strong, *Systematic Theology* (Philadelphia: Judson Press, 1907), pp. 117-36, and W.H. Griffith-Thomas, *The Holy Spirit of God* (Grand Rapids: Eerdmans, 1913, 4th edn, 1963), pp. 44-45.

3. *Counterfeit Miracles*, p. 26-27; J. Calvin, *Institutes*, Prefatory Address, 3 (16).

God the Holy Spirit has made it His subsequent work, not to introduce new and unneeded revelations into the world, but to diffuse this one complete revelation through the world and to bring mankind into saving knowledge of it.[1]

The Holy Spirit's work, then, is divided into two sharply distinct eras: that of revelation and that of proclamation. Warfield admits that when Christ returned to heaven this 'special revelation' did not cease. Instead, the Holy Spirit was poured out in the 'extraordinary working of the powers and gifts'. Only when 'the revelation of God in Christ had taken place, *and had become in Scripture and Church* [italics mine] a constituent part of the cosmos, then another era had begun'.

The ministry of Christ in his exaltation, then, begins with the brief bestowal of spiritual gifts, resulting in the publication of Scripture. At this point, Warfield claims, 'New constituent elements of special revelation can no longer be added. His work has been done'. Since then, God chose not to reveal himself 'atomistically' to each and every soul throughout history 'to meet his separate needs', but rather revelation was granted to humankind as 'an organically complete' package. Just how the Holy Spirit could 'diffuse' this revelation through the world and 'bring' humankind into a 'saving knowledge' of it is unclear if it were not to be revealed 'atomistically' to each individual in some personal, or perhaps subjective, sense.[2] Warfield's view on the one hand protects the finality and authority of normative Christian faith, but on the other, effectively freeze-dries almost all the biblically-described activity of the Spirit and incarnates him into the texts of Scripture.

Warfield also uses cessationism as a shield to protect his Christology: the final and 'complete revelation of God [as] given in Christ':

Because Christ is all in all, and all revelation and redemption alike are summed up in Him, it would be inconceivable that either revelation or its accompanying signs should continue after the completion of that great revelation with its accrediting works, by which Christ has been established in His rightful place as the culmination and climax and all inclusive

---

1. Warfield is quoting H. Bavinck, *Gereformeerde Dogmatiek* (Kampen: J.H. Bos, 2nd edn, 1906), I, pp. 363-64, in *Counterfeit Miracles*, p. 27.

2. See the discussion at the end of Chapter 3 on the 'atomistic' revelation of Christ to individuals as a biblical and normative phenomenon.

summary of the saving revelation of God, the sole and sufficient redeemer of His people.[1]

Here, Warfield confuses 'completion' with 'sufficiency' with respect to the revelation of Christ.[2] Just as it is absurd to say that because the revelation of Christ is 'complete' one cannot speak about it, so it is nonsense to say that God cannot later reveal aspects, emphases or applications of this 'complete' revelation. 'Additional' revelation need not add 'constituent elements of special revelation' to the 'faith once and for all delivered to the saints', any more than the 'illumination' of Scripture adds verses to the Bible.[3] Similarly, miracles, Warfield's corollary to revelation, need not cease if their function is to continue operating within the framework of their functions in the kingdom of God and within the completed and finally established Gospel. Hence it is clear that Warfield confuses *process* (revelation) with *content* (the normative statement of the church's faith).

Warfield sees the mission of Christ, like the function of the Spirit, drastically changing, a view which also contradicts the biblical teaching on Christ's ministry during his exaltation. For that matter, Warfield's understanding of the mission of Christ on earth is profoundly unbiblical. Chapter 4 of this book briefly touches on Warfield's faulty pneumatology and Christology, particularly as they relate to the biblical doctrine of the kingdom of God. These views and Warfield's cessationism are mutually conditioned, and as such require investigation.

A second reason follows from the first and is based on the notion that the final revelation has its locus in Scripture and is, by an

1. *Counterfeit Miracles*, p. 28.

2. Note that in the preceding passage, Warfield moves from talk of 'new' revelation to 'unneeded'. The equivocation begins with his use of the term 'new', which can mean in this context 'repeated' or 'qualitatively different or additional'. 'New' in the first sense need not threaten the content of revealed doctrine any more than preaching about it.

3. See 'Appendix C: The Sufficiency of Scripture' in Grudem, *The Gift of Prophecy*, pp. 299-312. Obviously, the sufficiency of Scripture applies to general theological principles and cannot give guidance for every specific detail of every life, for example, personal, career or many ministry decisions requiring divine revelatory insight. Most of the prophecies in Acts responded to such unique situations, for example, guidance for ministry (11.12; 13.2; 16.6-9), warnings of famine (11.28) or personal danger (20.23; 21.4, 10) which did not add new doctrinal content to the Bible (cf. 1 Cor. 14.24-25).

unspecified process, 'incorporated into the living body of the world's thought', or, has become a 'constituent part of the cosmos'. Warfield cites a similarly nebulous metaphor of Abraham Kuyper, who says that in Scripture God 'has spread a common board for all, and invites all to come and partake of the richness of the great feast'.[1] These rather vague expressions seem only to mask the point that Christian revelation for Warfield is now simply equated with Scripture, and for one to partake of this revelation, apparently, one simply reads the complete, objective, propositional revelation which comprises the text of the Bible. Indeed this seems to be the point Kuyper and Warfield are making in the following passage:

> [God] has given to the world one organically complete revelation, adapted to all, sufficient for all, provided for all, and *from this one completed revelation He requires each to draw his whole spiritual sustenance.* Therefore it is that miraculous working, which is but the sign of God's revealing power, cannot be expected to continue, and in point of fact does not continue, after the revelation of which it is the accompaniment has been completed [italics mine].[2]

For Kuyper and Warfield, miracles have only extrinsic value; they are not in themselves revelation, but merely point to it, deriving their significance only from the fact that they draw attention to the truly important message: that of scriptural revelation.[3] Moreover, one's 'whole spiritual sustenance' has its source in the revelation of Scripture. There is nothing mentioned here of Calvin's *testimonium*[4] of the Spirit bearing witness to the message of the Scripture and to the

---

1. A. Kuyper, *Encyclopedia of Christian Theology* (trans. J.H. DeVries; New York: Charles Scribner's Sons, 1898), pp. 368 and 355-58, cited in *Counterfeit Miracles*, pp. 26-27.

2. Kuyper, *Encyclopedia*, p. 368, cited in *Counterfeit Miracles*, p. 26-27.

3. R.C. Trench, an influential Evangelical writer of the last century, summarizes this extrinsicist position in his *Synonyms of the New Testament* (London: Macmillan, 1865), p. 327: 'The prime object and end of the miracle is to lead us to something out of and beyond itself: that, so to speak, it is a kind of finger-post of God . . . valuable, not so much for what it is, as for that which it indicates of the grace and power of the doer, or of the connection with a higher world in which he stands'.

4. See B. Ramm, *The Witness of the Spirit: An Essay on the Contemporary Relevance of the Internal Witness of the Holy Spirit* (Grand Rapids: Eerdmans, 1959), pp. 11-27. See his comments on Warfield on this subject (pp. 22, 100, 119).

subjective knowledge of salvation in the believer's heart. There is no possibility of any continuing charismata such as divine power or revelation operating in the church for the express purpose of edifying the local congregation. Warfield's view of the miraculous charismata is that function determines duration, and for him, their function is strictly limited to the accreditation of revelation recorded in Scripture and confined to the time during which it was revealed.[1]

In this study I emphatically accept Warfield's premise that the biblically described function of the charismata determines their duration.[2] But, contrary to Warfield, the following chapter argues that the functions of the charismata are not evidential, but salutory and edificatory.

Moreover, many clear commands of Scripture explicitly urge the widespread and continued use of the very charismata Warfield insists have ceased. Warfield's evidentialist view of miracle is not only internally inconsistent but also inconsistent with the biblical view of miracle. If, as Warfield so strongly affirms, Scripture is the basis of theological truth, then it is crucial to determine what Scripture says explicitly and specifically about the function or purpose of the so-

---

1. For a brief but useful sketch of scholarly consensus on the biblical view of miracles which challenges Warfield at key points, see D. Senior, 'The Miracles of Jesus' in R.E. Brown, J.A. Fitzmyer and R.E. Murphy (eds.), *The New Jerome Biblical Commentary* (New York: Prentice Hall, 1990), pp. 1369-73, especially §1, 'Biblical Notion of Miracle', pp. 1369-70. Senior notes that more recent theology is becoming 'discontent' with the traditional view of miracle. He argues that defining miracles as 'beyond the *ordinary* laws of nature' (Augustine), or beyond '*all* laws of nature' (Aquinas) 'divorces miracles from the climate of faith'. Moreover, he continues, viewing nature as a closed system of laws is alien to the Scripture, as is the notion that a miracle is primarily 'something to be wondered at' or marvelous. Above all, NT miracles are 'not only, or even primarily external confirmations of [the Christian] message; rather the miracle was the vehicle of the message. They are "revelation stories". . . Side by side, word and miraculous deed gave expression to the advent of God's redemptive power' being expressions of Christ's war against the kingdom of Satan—the 'primary means of establishing God's reign (kingdom)'. In Acts the miracles 'represent the continuing power of the reign of God inaugurated by Jesus'.

2. This argument has been independently developed also by D.A. Codling in his Westminster ThM thesis, 'The Argument that the Revelatory Gifts of the Holy Spirit Ceased with the Closure of the Canon of Scripture', pp. 81-150; Grudem, *The Gift of Prophecy*, pp. 156-64, implicitly; and Carson, *Showing the Spirit*, p. 156: Warfield's 'argument stands up *only* if such miraculous gifts are theologically tied *exclusively* to a role of attestation; and this is demonstrably not so'.

called 'extraordinary' charismata, using three examples: miracles, prophecy and tongues.

Miracles and the charismata are an essential element in the very nature of the kingdom of God that Jesus presented, of the gospel proclaimed and demonstrated by the disciples, apostles and the church. An examination of Scripture reveals that miracles do not prove the gospel, but are an essential element of it. Miracles represent, in actuality, the displacement of the rule of Satan by the kingdom of God, whether in the realm of the physical, emotional, moral or spiritual; the gospel articulates those events. Hence, to remove the presence of God's charismatic power from the Christian gospel is to destroy its very essence as biblically described. Perhaps it is this fear that prompted the writer of 2 Tim. 3.5 to predict an eschatological struggle against those 'having a form of religion, but denying its power (δύναμις)'. The nature of the gospel is 'miraculous' in the way in which it is presented, and also in the way in which it continues its purpose in the church community.

The New Testament describes the function of prophecy in a variety of cases. The earliest prophets of the New Testament, Zacharias, Elizabeth, Simeon, Anna, John the Baptist and Mary, are all seen as proclaiming or identifying the Messiah, but sometimes in the form of a psalm of worship (Lk. 1.67-79; 1.42-45; 2.25-26; 2.36; 1.76; 1.46-56, respectively). Peter receives a vision concerning the barriers between Jews and Gentiles (Acts 10.11-17) and Paul his apostolic call (Acts 9.3-8). These are not signs 'accrediting' the gospel, but the means by which aspects of the gospel are revealed and presented. But the function of prophetic revelation seems to lose its accrediting function altogether when Joseph is warned for the safety of his family in a revelatory dream (Mt. 2.12, 13, 19, 22), or repeatedly those spreading the gospel are encouraged, warned and directed by the Spirit through various revelations (Acts 5.3; 8.26, 29; 9.10; 10.3, 19; 11.27-30; 16.6-10; 18.9-10; 21.4, 10-12; cf. 27.23). The book of Acts describes prophecy explicitly as having 'exhorted' and 'strengthened' the community (Acts 9.31; 15.32), just as Paul describes its function in 1 Cor. 14.3; cf. 1 Thess. 5.11-22; 1 Pet. 4.10. 'The one who prophesies, speaks to people for their upbuilding (οἰκοδομήν), encouragement (παράκλησιν) and consolation (παραμυθίαν)'. The one who prophesies 'edifies the church' (14.4). From prophecy an outsider or unbeliever will be 'convicted' (ἐλέγχεται), 'called to account' (ἀνακρίνεται), and 'the secrets of his heart will be revealed' (14.25). Conversion and worship will result from this prophetic revelation. This explicit function of prophecy is not tied to an apostle, nor necessarily to Scripture, but to specific, often unknown human needs. As long as the gospel is to be preached and applied, that is, 'to the end of the age' (Mt. 28.20), these functions of worship, prophetic guidance, encouragement, exhortation, edification and conviction will continue to have relevance, and, if function determines duration, sufficient relevance to continue to the parousia of Christ.

The function of the gift of tongues parallels that of prophecy, insofar as it not only indicates the presence of the Spirit (Acts 2.4; 10.44-46; 11.15; 19.6, cf. 8.17-18), but also 'edifies' (1·Cor. 14.4, cf. Jude 20) the speaker, who utters 'mysteries' to God that no one (14.2), including the speaker (14.14) understands. Also, tongues speaking is associated with praise and worship.[1] F.F. Bruce argues that the tongues proclaiming the 'mighty works of God' the foreigners heard at Pentecost were not the preaching of the gospel—it was required that Peter do that later (vv. 14-40)—but probably psalms of praise to God in response to the coming of the Spirit. By using the gift of tongues, Paul says that he can both pray and sing in the Spirit (1 Cor. 14.15), a practice that may have appeared elsewhere among the Christian communities (Eph. 5.19 and Col. 3.16, cf. Jude 20), according to Dunn and L.W. Hurtado.[2] The repeated purposes for both these sample charismata are edification and praise, and represent functions to which every believer in the church is called to perform.

The summary statements about the function of charismata bypass entirely the notion of Warfield's evidentialist accreditation of apostles or doctrine. Instead they are given for 'strengthening' and 'edification' (Acts 15.32; Rom. 1.11; 1 Cor. 14.26), for 'the common good' (Rom. 12.3-8; 1 Cor. 12.7); to know God's purposes (Eph. 1.18-22); so as to be 'pure and blameless' (1 Cor. 1.8; 1.10, cf. Col. 1.10), 'that in everything God may be glorified (1 Pet. 4.11)'. Eph. 4.12 sums up the purpose of the gifts of the Spirit: 'for the equipment of the saints, for the work of the ministry, for the building up of the body of Christ'. It is explicit that these gifts are employed not simply by or for apostles, but ideally by everyone in the Christian community.

1. Bruce, *The Book of Acts*, p. 52.
2. Dunn, *Jesus and the Spirit*, pp. 185-88; 208, 237 and 238; L.W. Hurtado, 'What Are "Spiritual Songs?"' *Paraclete* 5 (Winter 1971), pp. 8-15.

Despite the testimony of Scripture on the function of charismata, Warfield's cessationist polemic requires a narrowly-focused, rationalistic, evidentialist notion of miracle as the only possible base from which to launch his major offensive against post-apostolic miracles: his extensive historical investigation and its underlying historical method.

Warfield's Historical Method

In lieu of a developed theological or exegetical defense of cessationism, Warfield devotes the overwhelming percentage of space in his major polemical work, *Counterfeit Miracles*, to an analysis of specific historical accounts of alleged post-apostolic miraculous events. This present section unpacks Warfield's historical method, demonstrating, that like his concept of miracle, his historical method is flawed. The criteria he applies to sustain the validity and historicity of biblical miracles against their critics are not applied consistently to miracles occurring after the Apostolic age. Similarly, the historical methods for which he condemns the biblical critics, he himself applies to discredit postbiblical miracles.

Against the Anglican thesis, that is, the 'prevailing opinion' that miracles existed for the establishment of the early church (until about the time of Constantine) after which they faded away,[1] Warfield insists that this view 'contradicts the whole drift of the evidence of the facts, and the entire weight of probability as well'.[2] Instead of maintaining, as does the popular opinion, that the charismata gradually diminished after the Apostolic period until they finally dwindled away around the end of the third century, Warfield holds that 'if evidence is worth anything at all' the pattern of charismatic operation in the church is quite the opposite:

> There is little or no evidence at all for miracle-working during the first fifty years of the post-Apostolic church; it grows more abundant during the next century (the third); and it becomes abundant and precise only in the fourth century, to increase still further in the fifth and beyond. Thus . . . there was a steadily growing increase of miracle-working from the beginning on.[3]

1. *Counterfeit Miracles*, pp. 6-9.
2. *Counterfeit Miracles*, p. 9.
3. *Counterfeit Miracles*, p. 10.

Miracles occurring in history after the Apostolic age differ from biblical miracles, according to Warfield, in two ways: most obviously, in the nature of the doctrines in connection with which they claim to have been wrought, and secondly in character.[1] On this second point Warfield approvingly quotes an opponent, John Henry, Cardinal Newman, who suggests several differences.[2] First, biblical miracles confirm divine revelation; ecclesiastical miracles have 'no discoverable or direct object'; secondly, biblical miracles occur for the 'instruction of the multitudes'; ecclesiastical wonders for those who are already Christians' or for 'purposes already effected. . . by the miracles of Scripture'; thirdly, biblical miracles tend to be 'grave, simple, majestic' as opposed to their later counterparts which enter into the 'wildness and inequality' of a romantic character. Fourthly, the miracles of the Bible are 'undeniably beyond nature', whereas those of ecclesiastical tradition are 'often scarcely more than extraordinary accidents or coincidences, or events which seem to betray exaggerations or errors in the statement'. However, it was Newman's task to show that there were important exceptions to these generalizations, and Warfield's to show that there were not.

But the purpose of this section is to examine the criteria Warfield employs for determining whether or not the numerous accounts of miracles in history are valid. Warfield's historical hermeneutic appears to have two foci: the credibility of witnesses and historical probability. These are the classic arguments from the 'great debate' on miracles in early eighteenth-century England,[3] particularly from Conyers Middleton, who so powerfully shaped Warfield's thought on miracles. By the nature of the case, Warfield was forced to investigate a great amount of historical material, which constituted the overwhelming percentage of his book.

The Credibility of Witnesses. Warfield's examination of the witnesses to alleged miracles throughout church history is thoroughly skeptical. He follows Middleton's attempts to discredit them by a critical analysis

---

1. *Counterfeit Miracles*, pp. 53-54.

2. J.H. Newman, 'The Miracles of Ecclesiastical History Compared with those of Scripture as regards their Nature, Credibility and Evidence', in his *Two Essays on Biblical and Ecclesiastical Miracles* (London: Basil M. Pickering, 1873), p. 99, cited in *Counterfeit Miracles*, pp. 53-54, 253 n. 44.

3. See Burns, *The Great Debate on Miracles*, pp. 70-96.

of the world-view of the witnesses, and, as an extension of this, the use of literary forms for conveying theological messages, the vacillating attitude of some prominent witnesses toward miracles, and the mental states of those witnessing or experiencing alleged miracles.

The world-view of those who claim to witness miracles, according to Warfield, is, in each case, suspect, because of the way they apprehended the real world. The early post-apostolic church, he argued, increasingly adopted the intellectual framework of a pagan environment. Warfield notes: 'It is possible that we very commonly underestimate the marvellousness of the world with which the heathen imagination surrounded itself, crippled as it was by its ignorance of natural law, and inflamed by the most incredible superstition'.[1] Citing Theodore Trede, Warfield continues: 'The credulity of even educated people reached an unheard-of measure, as well as the number of those, who, as deceived or deceivers, no longer knew how to distinguish between truth and falsehood'.[2] Even 'Augustine the truthful' in 'a case of marvellous happenings ... shows himself quite unreliable ... a child of his times'.[3] Warfield then goes on to demonstrate Augustine's credulity. Augustine allegedly cites as from first-hand witnesses an apparently old and widely-recounted pagan story of a man resuscitated from the dead, using the same name and circumstances.[4]

Beyond this, Warfield asserts that the identical story was affirmed by Gregory the Great as having happened to an acquaintance of his.[5] This credulity toward the miraculous is, Warfield thinks, typical of all subsequent Roman Catholics:

> The worldview of the Catholic is one all his own, and is very expressly a miraculous one. He reckons with the miraculous in every act; miracle suggests itself to him as a natural explanation of every event; and nothing seems too strange to him to be true. . . [He has a] disposition for miracle-seeking, which [is] altogether unaffected by the modern scientific axiom of the conformity of the course of nature to law.[6]

1. *Counterfeit Miracles*, p. 75.
2. *Counterfeit Miracles*, pp. 75, 249 n. 7.
3. *Counterfeit Miracles*, pp. 76-77.
4. Augustine, however, catalogued some seventy miracles describing a number of them in meticulous, eye-witness detail in chapter 22 of his *City of God*.
5. *Counterfeit Miracles*, p. 78.
6. *Counterfeit Miracles*, pp. 100-101.

Indeed, the very center of Roman Catholic worship, to Warfield, is the altar, which he asserts is a relic chest, a symbol of claims which are utterly at odds with the certainty and authority of the 'modern scientific axiom' of natural law.

World-views are reflected in literary forms. Warfield suggests that in adapting its mode of communication to the surrounding culture, the church came very early to make use of pagan aretalogy (wonder tales) and popular romances, which were usually replete with miracles. Pagan stories (as above) were taken over wholesale by Christian advocates,[1] and with them their very 'conception-world'.[2] With the emergence of monasticism, a new literary form followed: 'a monkish belletristic', as A. Harnack[3] called it. In literature, if not in theology, Warfield feels, 'the saints were the successors to the gods'.[4]

Warfield further challenges the credibility of post-apostolic church witnesses by pointing out the apparently vacillating attitude of some key church fathers on whether or not miracles did in fact occur. Augustine 'bitterly complains' that so little was made of the innumerable Christian miracles when they occurred in his time.[5] The implication here could be that Augustine was only imagining miracles his contemporaries would not or could not confirm. Warfield's view of miracles as compelling proof to as rational and spiritually enlightened an observer as Augustine is here on shaky ground. Warfield further offers quotations from Ambrose, Chrysostom and Gregory the Great, 'who record long lists of miracles contemporary with themselves, yet betray a consciousness that miracles had nevertheless. . . ceased with the Apostolic age'.[6]

The emotional and mental states of witnesses affect their credibility, and Warfield throughout his study notes how reports of miracles may be generated by 'blinding excitement', 'brutal persecution',[7] or by

1. *Counterfeit Miracles*, pp. 19, 20, 62 and 83.

2. *Counterfeit Miracles*, p. 63, citing H. Guenter, *Die christliche Legende des Abendlandes* (Heidelberg: C. Winter, 1910), p. 8.

3. *Counterfeit Miracles*, p. 63, citing Harnack's *Die Moenchthum, seine Ideale und seine Geschichte* (Geissen: J. Ricker, 3rd edn, 1886), p. 27.

4. *Counterfeit Miracles*, p. 93.

5. *Counterfeit Miracles*, pp. 44-45.

6. *Counterfeit Miracles*, p. 46. A page later Warfield cites Chrysostom: '"Of miraculous powers, not even a vestige is left"; and yet he records instances from his day!'

7. *Counterfeit Miracles*, pp. 13 and 129.

being 'inflamed by enthusiasm'[1] (a pejorative Enlightenment phrase of
Warfield's, being applied most frequently to Methodists and
Irvingites), by suggestion or hysteria.[2] The cases of the stigmata indicate 'pathology' or 'morbid neuroses',[3] rather than cases of miraculous participation in the sufferings of Jesus. The fascination with relics
and their miraculous powers, according to Warfield, is an expression,
at base, of 'fetichism'.[4] In contrast to the above witnesses, the writers
in the earliest post-apostolic age 'inculcate the elements of Christian
living in a spirit so simple and sober as to be worthy of their place as
the immediate followers of the Apostles'.[5] It is no accident that saints
of this caliber make 'no clear and certain allusions' to miracles or
charismatic operations contemporaneous with themselves.[6]

Historical Probability From the cases immediately above, we catch a
glimpse of Warfield's historical methodology at work. Though the
literature from the early second century is scanty, 'there is little or no
evidence at all' for asserting the presence of miracles during the first
fifty post-apostolic years.[7] Any mention of miracles in authors during
this time is handled in one or more of four ways. If Warfield encounters a general statement that Christians were endowed with certain
charismata or miraculous powers, he responds that such unspecific
statements afford 'no opportunity of applying those tests by which the
credibility of miracles must be tried'.[8] If the references become
somewhat more specific and compelling, as in the case of Irenaeus'

---

1. *Counterfeit Miracles*, pp. 48, 128-29 and 137.
2. *Counterfeit Miracles*, pp. 111, 199-207, esp. 213; and 153.
3. *Counterfeit Miracles*, pp. 87.
4. *Counterfeit Miracles*, pp. 99-101.
5. *Counterfeit Miracles*, p. 10.
6. *Counterfeit Miracles*, p. 10.
7. Numerous recent studies on this point have demonstrated the presence of such
charismata. See for example J. Reiling, *Hermas and Christian Prophecy: A Study of
the Eleventh Mandate* (Leiden: Brill, 1973); R. Kydd, *Charismatic Gifts in the Early
Church* (Peabody, MA: Hendrickson, 1984); J.E. Davison, 'Spiritual Gifts in the
Roman Church: 1 Clement, Hermas and Justin Martyr' (PhD dissertation, University
of Iowa, 1981), and J.C. Beker, 'Prophecy and the Spirit in the Apostolic Fathers'
(PhD dissertation, University of Chicago, 1955). See earlier note and the
bibliography for further studies.
8. Citing Bishop John Kaye, in *Counterfeit Miracles*, p. 11.

account of one being raised from the dead,[1] Warfield relegates it to the Apostolic age. If such a case appears to be regarded seriously by contemporaries, he dismisses it as 'not esteemed [by them as] a very great thing'.[2] Finally, the frequent references to prophecy during this period seem to be dismissed with hardly a comment.[3] This is despite the fact that Warfield regards the gift of prophecy as falling within the category of miraculous or extraordinary charismata.[4] References to exorcism seem to be either classed as wonder tales, or essentially demythologized.[5] This last point is worthy of more detailed attention.

---

1. 'And so far are they from raising the dead as the Lord raised them, and the Apostles did by means of prayer, and as when frequently in the brotherhood, the whole church in the locality, having made petition with much fasting and prayer, the spirit of the dead one has returned, and the man has been given back to the prayers of the saints' (*Adv. Haer.* 2.31.2). Warfield makes much of the aorist tenses in the latter two verbs, above. This he says indicates that these events took place in the Apostolic age. What more appropriate tense Irenaeus could have used to describe such an event is left unexplained.

2. *Counterfeit Miracles*, p. 16; the implication being, as above, with Augustine, that this contemporary insouciance toward such a report casts doubt on its likelihood. Note that substantial research on near death experiences show this phenomenon to be extremely widespread, but until recently, generally unrecognized and disbelieved.

3. *Counterfeit Miracles*, pp. 11-12. For more recent examinations of prophetic activity during the first three Christian centuries, see Reiling, *Hermas*, Kydd, *Charismatic Gifts*, and Davison, 'Spiritual Gifts'; D. Hill, *New Testament Prophecy* (Atlanta: John Knox, 1979), esp. pp. 186-213; C.M. Roebeck, Jr, 'The Role and Function of Prophetic Gifts for the Church at Carthage, AD 202–258' (PhD dissertation, Fuller Theological Seminary, 1985), also his 'Irenaeus and "Prophetic Gifts"', in P. Elbert (ed.), *Essays on Apostolic Themes* (Peabody, MA: Hendrickson, 1985), pp. 104-14; G.H. Williams and E. Waldvogel, 'A History of Speaking in Tongues and Related Gifts', in M.P. Hamilton (ed.), *The Charismatic Movements* (Grand Rapids: Eerdmans, 1975), pp. 61-113, among others.

4. *Counterfeit Miracles*, p. 5.

5. *Counterfeit Miracles*, p. 20: 'Something new entered Christianity in these wonder-tales; something unknown to the Christianity of the Apostles, unknown to the Apostolic churches, and unknown to their sober successors; and it entered Christianity from without, not through the door, but climbing up some other way. It brought an abundance of miracle-working with it; and unfortunately, it brought it to stay'.

See also *Counterfeit Miracles*, pp. 238-39, citing Harnack: 'The whole world and the circumambient atmosphere were filled with devils; not merely idolatry, but every phase and form of life was ruled by them. . . Christianity won, and expelled

Warfield affirms at one point that the 'cure of demoniacs' as with the resurrection of Jesus 'can scarcely be subsumed under the operation of natural forces'.[1] Yet he is totally committed to Adolph von Harnack's utterly rationalistic understanding of exorcism when he denies the 'miraculous' quality of such events in the early church.[2] In this latter case, demonic powers have become essentially objectifications of superstitious minds! Perhaps more than any other apologetic device, early Christian preachers pointed to the power of Christian exorcism over pagan demonic deities as the most tangible proof for the credibility of the gospel.[3] By 'demythologizing' demonic power in the post-apostolic church, Warfield has attempted to avoid investigating some of the most specific and clearly described cases of what he earlier described as the supernatural power of God in action. Some of these cases, according to Warfield's own criteria of historical credibility, clearly demand, but do not receive, his careful examination.[4] Warfield's rejection of this category of 'miracle' is necessary for his cessationist polemic, but represents a fatal contradiction in his

the demons not only from the tortured individuals whose imagination was held captive by them, but from the life of the people, and from the world'.

1. 'A Question of Miracles', p. 202.

2. Harnack's rationalistic attitude toward miracles in the church at any period resonates closely with Warfield's position on postbiblical miracles: '1) In Jesus' day, a time when there was no sound insight into what is possible and what is not, people felt surrounded by miracles. 2) Miracles were ascribed to famous persons almost immediately after their death. 3) We know that what happens within our world is governed by natural laws. There are, then, no such things as "miracles", if by that is meant interruptions of the order of nature. 4) There are many things that we do not understand, but they should be viewed as marvelous and presently inexplicable, not miraculous' (*What Is Christianity?* [New York: Harper & Brothers, 1957], p. 33).

3. G.W.H. Lampe, 'Miracles and Early Christian Apologetic', in C.F.D. Moule (ed.), *Miracles: Cambridge Studies in their History and Philosophy* (London: Mowbrays, 1965), pp. 215-18.

4. For example Tertullian, *Apology* 22–23; Cyprian, *Epistle* 75, 15; *Whereas Idols Are Not God* 7; Origen, *Contra Celsum* 1, 6, among others. Warfield concedes, with Harnack, that 'from Justin downwards, Christian literature is crowded with allusions to exorcisms, and every large church, at any rate, had exorcists'. 'But this,' Warfield comments, 'is no proof that miracles were wrought, except this great miracle, that [the Church won] its struggle against deeply-rooted and absolutely pervasive superstition' (*Counterfeit Miracles*, p. 239 n. 21).

historical method. Even some of the most vociferous advocates of cessationism today accept the probability of contemporary exorcisms.[1]

Another example of Warfield's historical method comes in his investigation of contemporary faith-healing miracles. In setting out to survey the genuineness of modern faith cures recounted in A.J. Gordon's work *The Ministry of Healing, or, Miracles of Cure in All Ages*, Warfield lays out his procedure:

> The testimony of theologians is. . . a matter of opinion. . . and of the healed themselves is only a record of facts. . . which constitute in their totality the whole evidence before us. What now are these facts? What is their nature? And what are we to think of them? The first thing which strikes the observer. . . is that they stand sadly in need of careful sifting. What we are looking for is such facts as necessitate or at least suggest the assumption, in order to account for them, of the 'immediate action of God, as distinguished from His mediate action through natural laws'.[2]

Warfield then begins his 'sifting' process in four, somewhat vaguely defined and cross-ranked, stages. A healing, to qualify as being a miracle, 'should be immediate, as in cause so in time—without delay as without means—on the exercise of simple faith'. This would eliminate the so-called 'Faith Houses' which seem limited in the range of their cures and in the time required to effect such cures as do occur. A true miracle must exclude all cures which can be paralleled by obviously non-miraculous cures. For example, if a certain type of remarkable cure took place in the context of a non-Christian or anti-Christian religion, and the same type of cure occurred in an orthodox Christian setting, then both cures must be disallowed as being miraculous.[3] Again, for Warfield, a heterodox miracle, or, for that matter, any post-apostolic miracle is a contradiction in terms.

Also excluded from the miraculous are 'all cures which seem to us, indeed, to have come in answer to prayer, but of which there is no

---

1. For example, M. Unger, *Demons in the World Today* (Wheaton, IL: Tyndale House, 1971). For a less popular approach, see the recent work by G. Twelftree, *Christ Triumphant: Exorcism Then and Now* (London: Hodder & Stoughton, 1985).

2. *Counterfeit Miracles*, p. 185, citing A.J. Gordon.

3. *Counterfeit Miracles*, p. 185. This rather bizarre requirement may be in response to Hume's critique that miracles are self-canceling: if rival groups with conflicting doctrines exhibit the same type of miracle, neither is authenticated. See N. Geisler, *Miracles and Modern Thought* (Grand Rapids: Zondervan, 1982), pp. 138-39.

evidence that they have come. . . without all [any possible] means'.[1] A cure may come in a dramatic, sudden, fashion; but solid proof must be offered that no 'natural' means could have entered the case. Finally, since few persons are competent to diagnose correctly the exact nature of a disease, a precise, accurate diagnosis must be guaranteed before a miraculous cure is claimed.[2]

Further on, when examining the cures of Lourdes, Warfield notes that some of the healings were not complete. 'We should *a priori* expect miraculous cures to be regularly radical.' 'Why, after all,' he continues, 'should miracles show limitations?'[3] God would be expected to do a thorough job. This raises an important point in the assessment of all reported charismatic occurrences, and a demand that Warfield, at a number of points, seems to make of his cases, *viz.*, an element of absoluteness, or perfection, something 'unambiguously' true, almost docetic in its transcendence of the mundane.[4] But Warfield ignores the New Testament's own apparent ambiguities in its records of charismatic activity. For example, Paul is told by a prophet 'through the Holy Spirit' not to go to Jerusalem, reported without apology or embarrassment at this anomaly, when it had been made clear that this journey was indeed a divine mission (Acts 21.4, cf. 20.22).[5] Warfield also ignores other New Testament miracle accounts which fail his guidelines, for example, the case of the incomplete healing of Paul's eyes (Acts 23.3-4, where he was unable to identify the high priest; Gal. 4.15; 6.11), his illness (6.14), his failure to heal Trophimus (2 Tim. 4.20), and even Jesus' incomplete, though corrected, healing (Mk 8.24, cf. Mk 6.5).

Moreover, the clear teaching of the New Testament affirms that in appearances of such 'miraculous charismata' as prophecy and divine knowledge, the experiences are described explicitly as 'limited':

---

1. *Counterfeit Miracles*, p. 187.

2. *Counterfeit Miracles*, p. 188.

3. *Counterfeit Miracles*, p. 110.

4. As in his opening paragraphs describing the near total scope of Jesus' healing activities (with a touch of his 'pale hand'), and charismatic operations in the Apostolic church.

5. Grudem has suggested that prophecy in the New Testament often represents 'speaking merely human words to report something God brings to mind'. These 'human words' are frequently full of imperfections and do not bear the ultimate divine authority of say, Old Testament prophets or New Testament apostles (*The Gift of Prophecy*, pp. 89-106).

occurring only 'in part', or as 'in a glass darkly' (1 Cor. 13.7-12). Miracles are regularly rejected or misperceived by onlookers in the New Testament.[1] John records an exceptionally ambiguous miracle that precipitated at least three interpretations (12.28-29). But to Warfield, a miracle is necessarily out of the world of the ordinary and radically transcendent, and as such, no historical event could attain that quality, particularly if perceived by one with a skeptical mindset. It is, of course, reasonable to require accurate records and careful observation in determining the unusual nature of an event, but one senses that that only postpones the problem, and that no amount of 'sifting' will force one out of a determined, non-theistic interpretive frame of reference.

It is ironic that Benjamin Warfield, who to so many was a rock of orthodox stability in a time of dramatic theological change, used many of the same critical techniques on historical miracles that his liberal opponents had used on Scripture. In dealing with miracle accounts through the centuries, Warfield appears to be employing at least rudimentary kinds of literary form criticism; he cites approvingly Adolph von Harnack's rationalization of exorcisms in the early church, and dismisses every claim to miracles as human misperception, be it superstition, mental imbalance or mendacity. The very essence of Warfield's argument against postbiblical miracles seems formed from a template of Harnack's rationalistic liberalism, but also from Hume's *Enquiry*. All have their presuppositions: that miracles cannot happen (for Warfield after the Apostolic age, for Hume, at all); a highly critical evaluation of witnesses to miracles; and a pre-ordained analysis of the improbability of miracle occurrences on a case-by-case basis. While Warfield's attack on the historical reliability of postapostolic miracles represents the greater part of *Counterfeit Miracles*, he insisted that his polemic rested on '*two* legs': a historical

1. For example, Jesus is accused of performing the miracles of Beelzebul (Mk 3.22-23; Mt. 12.24; Lk. 11.15) or a demon (Jn 8.48; 7.20; 10.20). Early Jewish religious authorities may have made these charges on proscriptions against miracle workers who draw people after other gods (Deut. 13.1-11 and 18.15-22), hence, their desire to 'test' Jesus by demanding miracles, thereby further condemning him. Moreover, the signs of Jesus provoke both belief (e.g., Jn 2.11, 23; 4.50, 53; 5.9; 6.14; 21; 9.11, 17, 33, 38; 11.27, 45; 12.11) and unbelief (e.g., Jn 5.18; 6.66; 9.16, 24, 29, 40-41; 11.53). In the ministries of the Apostles, the miracles provoke similarly divided responses (e.g., Acts 4.13-22; 5.17-20, 33-40; 16.19-27) or were misinterpreted (e.g., Acts 14.11; 28.6).

case against post-apostolic miracles, and a biblical justification for cessationism.[1] It is to an analysis of Warfield's biblical arguments for cessationism that we now turn.

Warfield's Biblical Argument

When the limited number of texts Warfield employs in his biblical arguments for cessationism are critically analyzed according to his own presuppositions of the authority and inerrancy of the Bible, and tested against his own scriptural hermeneutic, they fail to sustain his cessationist thesis. Moreover, he fails to treat almost all of the important biblical material relating to his polemic.

Warfield asserts that his polemic stands on two legs: first, that cessationism is supported by the clear teaching of Scripture, and secondly, that it is supported by the facts of history. It appears odd, in view of Warfield's strong commitment to a biblically based theology,[2] that hardly more than a half dozen pages of over three hundred are devoted to this scriptural grounding, and of this, almost nothing in specific exegesis of texts. The remainder of this chapter, after outlining his biblical hermeneutic, tests Warfield's biblical arguments against his own explicit principles of biblical interpretation. The following chapter then reviews important biblical theological arguments

---

1. Warfield is 'sure' of his cessationist position 'on the ground both of principle and of fact; that is to say both under the guidance of the New Testament teaching as to their (i.e., the miraculous charismata's) origin and nature, and on the credit of the testimony of later ages as to their cessation' (*Counterfeit Miracles*, p. 6).

2. Warfield had emphasized in 'The Idea of Systematic Theology' (*WBBW*, IX, p. 63) that natural theology, including historical investigation, would lead to a 'meager and doubtful theology were these data not confirmed, reinforced and supplemented by the surer and fuller revelations of Scripture; and that the Holy Scriptures are the source of theology in not only a degree, but also in a sense in which nothing else is'. Warfield's biblical hermeneutic is somewhat illuminated in this passage dealing with the inspiration of Scripture: 'We follow the inductive method. When we approach the Scriptures to ascertain their doctrine of inspiration, we proceed by collecting the whole body of relevant facts. Every claim they make to inspiration is a relevant fact; every statement they make concerning inspirations is a relevant fact; every allusion they make to the subject is a relevant fact; every fact indicative of the attitude they hold toward Scripture is a relevant fact. . . Direct exegesis, after all has its rights: we may seek aid from every quarter in our efforts to perform its processes with precision and obtain its results with purity; but we cannot allow its results to be "modified" by extraneous considerations [for instance preconceived theology]' (*WBBW*, I, pp. 205-206).

and specific passages regarding cessationism which Warfield failed to treat.

Warfield's Biblical Hermeneutic. As he does with his historical and theological method generally, Warfield shapes his specifically biblical hermeneutic according to the common-sense traditions he received from, *inter alia*, his mentor Charles Hodge.[1] Warfield held that the Bible should first be approached, without any presuppositions, 'as any other book', to discern any peculiarities which 'should modify the applications of the usual, simple rules of interpretation'.[2] Scripture possesses a single such feature, that is, the fact of its divine inspiration. This fact, Warfield continues, both does and does not affect the rules of New Testament interpretation. On the one hand, the Bible's inspiration forces the reader to a greater diligence 'to seek the exact and minute meaning of each passage and word and express only it'. Further, despite variations in their style, focus and peculiarities, the fact of the infallible inspiration of the human writers by the Holy Spirit 'brings the whole book under the authorship of a single Mind; the words of Peter or the words of Paul are alike the words of God'.[3]

1. Hodge, *Systematic Theology*, I, p. 10. See Vander Stelt, *Philosophy and Scripture*, pp. 164-84, and M.A. Noll, 'Common Sense Traditions and American Evangelical Thought', *AQ* 37 (Summer 1985), pp. 216-38, and especially pp. 229-32 where Noll examines the impact of the common-sense philosophy on Evangelical hermeneutics.

2. B.B. Warfield, 'The True Method of Procedure in the Interpretation of the New Testament', p. 6, contained in a folio, *MSS Material on the New Testament*, located at the Alumni Alcove of Speer Library, Princeton Theological Seminary. This article was delivered as an address to the incoming students of Western Seminary at the beginning of the school year 1880–81, and was printed in *PB*, September 22, 1880. Since by Warfield's own account the printed version was inadequate, the manuscript of the address is used here.

3. Warfield, 'True Method', p. 10. The entire New Testament bears 'the stamp of a single mind'; B.B. Warfield, *Biblical Doctrines* (Grand Rapids: Baker, 1929), p. 176. This is not to say that 'when the Christian asserts his faith in the divine origin of his Bible, he does not mean to deny that it was composed and written by men or that it was given by men to the world. He believes that the marks of its human origin are ineradicably stamped on every page of the whole volume. He means to state only that it is not *merely* human in its origin'; *idem, Revelation and Inspiration* (New York: Oxford University Press, 1927), p. 429. Elsewhere, Warfield affirms the human–divine tension in the formation of Scriptures, which 'are conceived by the writers of the New Testament as through and through God's book,

Hence, one must interpret the works of this single author 'in harmony with Himself'.[1]

On the other hand, since the New Testament has come to us in the language of human beings, it is equally subject to the 'rules for the interpretation of human writings'.[2] So on this view, the fact of inspiration does not appreciably affect ordinary interpretive processes. Interpretation lays out for the investigator the facts the author has written. However,

> to *understand* the meaning when arrived at, requires other graces: humility, docility. . . and above all. . . spiritual discernment before we can feel the full sense of the Word, which can be inspired into the heart only by the same Spirit which inspired the words themselves.[3]

But in the paragraph following, Warfield prescinds from the subjective aspect of interpretation, although he describes it as 'the *sine qua non* rather than the *qua*' of interpretation, concentrating instead on the '*objective method*', which is 'indispensable to the accurate attainment of the mind of the Spirit'. Warfield then offers an arrangement of five rules, to be applied sequentially, for interpreting the New Testament. These 'self-evident' rules, listed below, were 'more or less consciously used by every competent exegete from the publication of the New Testament until now'.[4]

The application of these five rules, Warfield claims, represents such a 'safeguard of so careful and scientific an examination [that] we may

in every part expressive of His mind, given through men after a fashion which does no violence to their nature as men, and constitutes the book also as men's book as well as God's, in every part expressive of the mind of its human authors'; *idem, The Inspiration and Authority of the Bible* (Philadelphia: Presbyterian and Reformed Publishing, 1948), pp. 151-52. For a sympathetic review of Warfield's view of the divine–human tension in the formation of Scripture, see A.N.S. Lane, 'B.B. Warfield on the Humanity of Scripture', *VE* 16 (1986), pp. 77-94.

1. Warfield, 'True Method', p. 10.
2. Warfield, 'True Method', p. 16.
3. Warfield, 'True Method', p. 19. Earlier (p. 17) Warfield notes: 'Divine as it is, Scripture has come to us in a human form [of speech], and it is with that form that we [have] primarily to do'. The task of exegesis is to determine the intent of the human author of any New Testament passage by a five-point method, which 'demands that the sense of a passage where once reached through legitimate means be adhered to as the true sense no matter what divinity it implies' ('True Method', p. 18).
4. 'True Method', p. 35.

be able to say with confidence: "this is the mind of the Spirit" '.[1] Warfield recognizes, however, that some passages of Scripture may not yield the full profundity of their meaning to this method, particularly if applied in a 'coldly' intellectual manner. He does concede that the guiding presence of the Holy Spirit is crucial to any meaningful exegesis, much as one may successfully interpret the *Iliad* only if one has 'poetry in his soul'. Nevertheless, Warfield's awareness of the role of the Spirit in illuminating the Scriptures does not fare well against his conception that his principles of interpretation are somehow an inherent characteristic of the human consciousness. For example, Warfield's common-sense philosophy emerges clearly when he insists that his method does not appear as a new discovery, but that his hermeneutic appears throughout history almost as a universal mental archetype, or 'common sense' of humankind:

> It is as old as the Bible itself, and has been unconsciously used by everyone who has tried in a simple-hearted way to understand its words. A man does not need to know logic to reason correctly. When the argument is in him, it will come out; nor has it been necessary for everyone who has interpreted correctly to know he was interpreting after a scientific fashion. All the same, logic and hermeneutics are true sciences; and a knowledge of them will enable many a man to reason and interpret correctly who never could have done so without them.[2]

The first 'self-evident' rule of interpreting Scripture is to base one's exegesis upon an accurate text.[3] Warfield, the text critic,[4] complains that this rule is frequently neglected in the process of interpretation. Even as exegetes know and admit the problem, in practice they 'seldom act upon it!'[5]

The second rule is: 'Obtain the exact sense of every word'.[6] When stating this rather obvious rule, Warfield says he is 'dealing with self-evident propositions', but failure to distinguish, say, between the

1. 'True Method', p. 32.
2. 'True Method', p. 34.
3. 'True Method', pp. 19-22. Warfield apparently found himself limited by the convocation schedule before giving this address to the incoming seminary students because a great deal of interesting material supporting and illustrating each of his rules was crossed out.
4. B.B. Warfield, *An Introduction to the Textual Criticism of the New Testament* (New York: Thomas Whittaker, 7th edn, 1907).
5. 'True Method', p. 20.
6. 'True Method', p. 20.

meaning of a Greek word as it appeared in the Classical period and as it later appeared in Hellenistic usage has caused 'great classical scholars' to flounder sadly in the New Testament.[1] But words in themselves require logical linkages to others to form intelligible language.

Rule three, then, is: 'Construe the words according to the strictest rules of grammar'.[2] Warfield criticizes the 'old school' of interpreters 'who framed a grammar to their own liking for each passage treated'. He illustrates such improper interpretive techniques with several cases relating to the virgin birth and the authority of Scripture, which, he felt, liberal critics of the Bible had ignored. He cites the famous conservative commentator, Lange, who said that the 'publication of Winer's grammar killed [the liberal and rationalistic] Strauss's *Life of Jesus* in Germany'. Warfield wonders whether the similar application of correct biblical grammar would not do the same in America.[3] It is clear that to Warfield, hermeneutics is the handmaiden of polemics.

Rule four is to 'interpret with reference to the historical setting of a passage'. Spelled out, this requires not only that the interpreter approach the task with an understanding of the historical, archaeological and topographical background of a passage, but also that he or she 'be able to enter into the feelings of the contemporary readers'.[4] In this last case, Warfield's emphasis here is upon a knowledge of allusions to the first-century literary and intellectual experience; he does not mention that an understanding of the *religious* experiences of the time might also be useful.

Finally, rule five demands that one 'interpret contextually', keeping in mind the immediate context, which 'must be put in harmony' with the 'broad context' which is 'the object, argument and general contents of the entire book'.[5] Warfield 'cannot too strongly' insist that the sense of a verse cannot be arrived at 'when torn from its context'. Indeed, 'it is very often that the apparent sense is utterly and diametrically altered by the context'.[6] But Warfield is confident that, in one sense, the whole of Scripture is a uniform context.

1. 'True Method', p. 23.
2. 'True Method', p. 26.
3. 'True Method', p. 27.
4. 'True Method', p. 29.
5. 'True Method', p. 30.
6. 'True Method', p. 31.

One may extrapolate from this last rule to another: that one must interpret Scripture *by* Scripture, that is, 'interpreting by the analogy of faith'.[1] This principle follows from the proposition that all Scripture has the stamp of a single infallible author and is therefore a unity. Because Scripture, Warfield continues, 'has but one sense',

> this puts the chief instrument of interpretation in the hands of every Bible reader, by declaring that Scripture is its own interpreter, and that more obscure Scriptures are to be explained by plainer Scriptures.

Human learning may be of some use in the hermeneutical process, but in the last analysis, 'parallel passages alone will give. . . infallible guidance'. Specifically, this suggests that if the meaning of a word or phrase in the Bible, for instance, 'Spirit', or 'Spirit of God', is unclear or ambiguous, one must clarify the obscure reference by consulting all the other relevant biblical contexts where these words appear.

Warfield's Scottish common-sense philosophy, then, has influenced his hermeneutics of Scripture. But our interest in his principles of interpretation for this chapter focuses more specifically on how these principles would, if applied consistently and without cessationist preconceptions, explicate certain patterns of biblical passages relating to the cessation of miracles at the end of the Apostolic period.

One could argue that Warfield's emphasis on common-sense methodology, a hermeneutic which claims by certain fairly mechanical steps to discern 'the mind of the Spirit',[2] betrays a kind of rationalism—a kind of world-view—which is reluctant to taste or

---

1. B.B. Warfield, 'The Westminster Doctrine of Holy Scripture' (*WBBW*, VI, pp. 251-52). He summarizes his section on the Westminster Confession's hermeneutic: 'The rule here set forth is that which is known as "interpreting by the analogy of faith", and its foundation is the assumption of the common authorship of Scripture by God, who is truth itself. If we once allow the Confessional doctrine of the divine authorship of Scripture, it becomes only reasonable that we should not permit ourselves to interpret this divine author into inconsistency with Himself, without compelling reason. This is the Confession's standpoint; and from this standpoint the rule to interpret Scripture by Scripture is more than reasonable—it is necessary'.

2. We are reminded here of T.F. Torrance's critique of Warfield's *Revelation and Inspiration of the Bible* in *SJT* 7 (May 1954), p. 107: 'The basic error that lurks in the scholastic idea of verbal inspiration is that it amounts to an incarnation of the Holy Spirit. . . Dr Warfield's theory of inspiration neglects the Christological basis of the doctrine of scripture, and fails, therefore, to take the measure both of the mystery of revelation and the depth of sin in the human mind'.

even recognize subtle flavors of the miraculous or charismatic in the text it encounters.[1] On the other hand, if this hermeneutic is truly 'scientific' and objective, such reluctance could be transcended by careful compilation and analysis of word meanings derived from their respective contexts, even if one is not willing to enter into the religious experiences as Warfield demands, that is, into the 'feelings' of the writers and their readers. These numinous elements, like any other elements in the text, can be identified and studied, if not personally owned. I will assume this position is viable. Aside from sharing Warfield's certainty that his hermeneutical method can discern the 'mind of the Spirit', we can generally find Warfield's canonical exegetical approach valid and useful. Our agreement with his method is irrelevant, however, since it is from within Warfield's own hermeneutical method that I will evaluate his cessationist polemic.

Since I have described in broad strokes Warfield's biblical hermeneutic, let us now examine his biblical argument for the cessation of the charismata against the background of his own interpretive principles.

Specific Texts Treated in Warfield's Biblical Argument. Warfield is expansive in his descriptions of the miraculous activities of Christ and the Apostolic church, averring that we 'greatly underestimate' the breadth of our Lord's healing ministry, as well as the ubiquitous 'characteristic' occurrence of charismatic phenomena in the early Christian communities.[2] These charismata are classified as 'ordinary'

---

1. This reluctance to perceive in the Bible implications for continuing miracles may not have been solely a consequence of rationalism. There seem to be theological biases against miracles derived from the broad Reformation tradition as well. For example, in his *Preface to the New Testament* of 1522, Martin Luther reveals a view of the canon of Scripture which distinguishes the 'true and noblest books', that is, Romans, Galatians, Ephesians, 1 Peter and the rest of Paul's letters, as well as the First Epistle and Gospel of John from others in the New Testament. His criterion for selecting 'the heart and core of all the books' is that 'these do not describe many works and miracles of Christ, but rather masterfully show how faith in Christ overcomes sin, death, and hell and gives life, righteousness, and blessedness'. The discerning Christian prefers the Gospel of John over the Synoptics only because the latter contain more miracles (*The Works of Martin Luther* [St Louis, MO: Concordia, 1955], XXXV, p. 361). See the discussion in P. Althaus, *The Theology of Martin Luther* (trans. R.C. Schultz; Philadelphia: Fortress Press, 1966), p. 83.

2. *Counterfeit Miracles*, pp. 3-5.

('distinctively gracious'), and 'extraordinary' (miraculous). The former category of gifts is 'preferred' in the classical passage which treats them, 1 Corinthians 12–14, and the quest for these ordinary, post-apostolic gifts is described by Warfield as being 'the more excellent way'.[1] The most favored of the 'miraculous' gifts, prophecy, Warfield describes as a rather ordinary-sounding 'gift of exhortation and teaching',[2] but miraculous in the sense that it was divinely inspired. Further miraculous gifts include: healings, workings of miracles, discernings of spirits, kinds of tongues, the interpretation of tongues and miraculous knowledge.[3]

I have already noted that Warfield believes that the operation of these gifts 'belonged exclusively to the Apostolic age'. Failure to perceive this is a failure of 'an accurate ascertainment of the teaching of the New Testament on the subject'.[4] The question now is, how does

1. *Counterfeit Miracles*, p. 4.
2. Note Calvin's description of prophecy as the application of Scripture to the needs of the church, above.
3. *Counterfeit Miracles*, p. 5.
4. *Counterfeit Miracles*, p. 21. Yet C. Hodge, Warfield's teacher at Princeton, may have set the historical, as opposed to the biblical, thrust for *Counterfeit Miracles* when he wrote: 'There is nothing in the New Testament inconsistent with the occurrence of miracles in the post-apostolic age of the church'. Hodge espouses the Reformed tradition that the 'necessity' of miracles ceased when they achieved their 'great end' as aids to the Apostolic testimony. 'This, however, does not preclude the possibility of their occurrence on suitable occasions, in other ages' (Hodge, *Systematic Theology*, III, p. 452). A more recent Princeton seminary professor, B.M. Metzger (with D.E. Dilworth and J. Rodman Williams), perhaps with an eye to Warfield, served as editor for the Presbyterian position paper on the biblical basis for cessationism: 'We cannot. . . follow the view of some theologians that the purely supernatural gifts ceased with the death of the apostles. There seems no exegetical warrant for this assumption' (*Report of the One Hundred and Eighty Second General Assembly of the United Presbyterian Church, U.S.A. Part I: Journal* [Philadelphia: Office of the General Assembly, Presbyterian Church, USA, 1970], p. 150). A similar statement emerged from the Southern Presbyterian Church a year later; see J.R. Williams cited in K. McDonnell, *Presence, Power and Praise: Documents of the Charismatic Renewal* (Collegeville, MN: Liturgical Press, 1980), III, pp. 287-317. Also, the editor of the conservative Presbyterian periodical, for which Warfield had written, states: 'It can be rather categorically stated that the New Testament simply does not affirm that the Church should expect God to stop working miracles among his people. To take that position is to come perilously close to the approach which is anathema to Reformed hermeneutics, namely, conclusions based on what is said to be the experience of the Church rather than the clear teaching of Scripture. . . We

Warfield make his case from the biblical data? Warfield approaches this task both affirmatively and negatively.

Affirmatively, he builds a case for the authentication of the Apostles as being the messengers of God. While other Christians in the Apostolic age were recipients of the charismata, these gifts 'belonged, in a true sense to the Apostles' as special signs of their office. The charismata are tied in this special sense to the Apostles in that they are not conferred to others with the exception of the two 'great initial instances of the descent of the Spirit' at Pentecost and at the household of Cornelius: 'There is no instance on record of their conference by the laying on of hands by any one else than an Apostle'.[1] Warfield does note Acts 9.17 where a non-Apostle, Ananias, tells Paul, 'the Lord Jesus. . . has sent me that you may regain your sight and be filled with the Holy Spirit', but claims this 'is no exception as is sometimes said; Ananias worked a miracle on Paul but did not confer miracle-working powers'. To preserve his thesis, without any biblical evidence whatsoever, Warfield insists that Paul's miracle-working power was 'original with him as an Apostle, and not conferred by any one'.[2] But if we are to be consistent with Warfield's own examples, the issue here is not conference of miraculous powers, but rather the 'conference' of the Holy Spirit 'by the laying on of hands', the express, divinely given mission of Ananias. This is a fatal exception. Either Warfield must say in this case that Ananias's mission from the Lord Jesus failed, or that the filling of the Holy Spirit in Paul's case was unique among all the other occasions in Acts where there were miraculous accompaniments. Added to this is the fact that nowhere else in the New Testament is Paul portrayed as initially receiving the Spirit. Further, the consensus of current biblical scholarship generally affirms that 'Luke shares with Judaism the view that the Spirit is essentially the Spirit of prophecy'[3] and of other charismata.

have no biblical warrant to restrict the gifts to the early Church, nor to outlaw any specific gift today' (G.T. Aiken, 'Miracles—Yes or No?', *PJ* 33.16 [14 August 1974], p. 9).

1. Warfield, *Counterfeit Miracles*, p. 22.

2. Warfield, *Counterfeit Miracles*, p. 245 n. 48.

3. See E. Schweizer *et al.*, 'πνεῦμα, κτλ', *TDNT*, VI, pp. 408-409. See also the summary of the consensus on this matter by M.M.B. Turner, 'The Significance of Receiving the Spirit in Luke–Acts: A Survey of Recent Scholarship,' *TrinJ* 2 (Fall 1981), pp. 131-58. See below, in Chapter 3, 'The Biblical Portrayal of the Holy Spirit's Characteristic Activity is Inimical to Cessationism'.

Warfield also asserts that the 'cardinal instance' demonstrating his proposition that only Apostles could confer spiritual gifts is the case of the Samaritans and their reception of the Spirit. In this case, after the successful evangelism of Philip in Samaria, the Apostles Peter and John were sent to the Samaritan believers that they might 'receive the Holy Spirit'. Warfield cites Simon the sorcerer: 'Give me also this power, that, on whomsoever I lay my hands, he may receive the Holy Ghost'. From this statement of a sorcerer, whom Luke wished to portray as representing an incorrect understanding of the Spirit's work, Warfield decides that Luke is most 'emphatically' teaching that 'the Holy Ghost was conferred by the laying on of the hands, specifically of the Apostles, and of the Apostles *alone*' (italics mine).

Warfield here is wide of the mark. The explicit reason Luke gives for Simon's failure to 'have any part or share in this ministry' is 'because' (γάρ) Simon's 'heart is not right before God' (v. 21). If Luke wished to teach 'emphatically' the doctrine Warfield imagines he did, here would have been the perfect opportunity to introduce it: Simon was simply not an apostle. Instead, Luke's 'reason' is conditional, implying that on the basis of repentance, he too could receive, and effectively intercede for others to receive, the Holy Spirit (cf. Acts 2.38, 'Repent. . . and you will receive the gift of the Holy Spirit'). Moreover, this passage is of further importance, Warfield contends, because it teaches us 'the source of the gifts of power, in the Apostles, apart from whom they were not conferred: as also their function, to authenticate the Apostles as the authoritative founders of the church'.[1]

Evangelical scholar F.F. Bruce notes: 'Ananias' gesture of fellowship to [Saul] was to much the same effect as the apostles' imposition of hands on the Samaritans: to be thus accepted and to be called "brother" by someone who confessed Jesus as Lord assured Saul of his welcome into the community which he had so recently been endeavoring to extirpate. Ananias had no official status such as Peter and John. He was, for the moment, the risen Lord's messenger and mouthpiece to Saul. Peter and John themselves could discharge no nobler function'. Bruce cites T.W. Manson's 'insistence that [it] is function and not status that is of the essence of the Christian ministry' (F.F. Bruce, 'The Holy Spirit in the Acts of the Apostles', *Int* 27 [April 1973], p. 175). He refers also to H. Küng, *Why Priests? A Proposal for a New Church Ministry* (trans. R.C. Collins; Garden City, NY: Doubleday, 1972), pp. 25-29.

1. Warfield, *Counterfeit Miracles*, p. 23.

This conclusion seems to go well beyond the facts before us. Again, several other plausible interpretations of this passage are more likely,[1] the most usual being that the Apostolic visit from the Jerusalem community was a mission of reconciliation: a confirmation that Jews and the Samaritan outcasts were, at the point of their reception of the Spirit, indeed, one in Christ.[2] The story is not primarily about the conversion of the Samaritans, but the conversion of Peter and the Jewish Christians to an understanding of the scope of God's program of salvation.

In a footnote,[3] Warfield mentions two promising scriptural passages which could imply a firmer foundation for his contention. The first is 2 Cor. 12.12, 'The signs of a true apostle were performed among you in all patience, with signs and wonders and mighty works'. The second is Heb. 2.3b-4, 'It was declared at first by the Lord, and it was attested to us by those who heard him, while God also bore witness by signs

---

1. See for example the summary by F.F. Bruce, *The Book of the Acts of the Apostles* (NICNT; Grand Rapids: Eerdmans, rev. edn, 1988), pp. 168-70. Also, J.D.G. Dunn, *Jesus and the Spirit: A Study of the Religious and Charismatic Experience of Jesus and the First Christians as Reflected in the New Testament* (Philadelphia: Westminster Press, 1975), pp. 176, 182; G.W.H. Lampe, *The Seal of the Spirit: A Study in the Doctrine of Baptism and Confirmation in the New Testament and the Fathers* (London: Longmans & Green, 1951), pp. 70-73; G.T. Montague, *The Holy Spirit: The Growth of a Biblical Tradition* (New York: Paulist Press, 1976), p. 294.

2. See for example F.D. Bruner, in the most comprehensive theological critique of Pentecostalism to date, *A Theology of the Holy Spirit: The Pentecostal Experience and the New Testament Witness* (Grand Rapids: Eerdmans, 1970), pp. 175-76: 'What the Samaritans lacked, as far as we are told, was not the laying on of hands, it was the *Holy Spirit* (vv. 15-16). In no other place in Acts, except at Acts 19.6, are the hands of the apostles recorded in connection with the gift of the Holy Spirit—neither at Pentecost, nor in the post-Pentecost accessions, not even in Paul's conversion itself where Ananias, who was not an apostle, was, according to Luke's account, the agent (or audience) of Pail's initiation. Even in Acts 19.1-7 it was not the apostolic laying on of hands which was either missing or taught' but exclusion into the Christian community through baptism. J. Jervell notes that even if it may be correct to say (if Ananias' bestowal of the Spirit on Paul is excluded) that the 'Spirit is given only when the Twelve are present or a member or a delegate of the Twelve is on the scene', the operative idea is not the role of apostleship in an 'intermediary office' but that they represent the people of God (*The Unknown Paul: Essays on Luke–Acts and Early Christian History* [Minneapolis: Augsburg, 1984], p. 115). See also J.A. Fitzmyer, *Jerome Biblical Commentary*, p.185.

3. Warfield, *Counterfeit Miracles*, p. 245 n. 50.

and wonders and various miracles and by gifts of the Holy Spirit distributed according to His own will'.

In the first instance there is no indication that the signs of a 'true apostle' were limited to the twelve Apostles. As Warfield admits, others performed such signs and wonders who were not apostles, but concedes also, somewhat too restrictively and without biblical proof, that miracles were performed by those upon whom apostolic hands were laid. To the contrary, one could add to the list of non-apostolic miracle-workers, even some who do not follow Jesus (Mk 9.38-41 // Lk. 9.49-50), not to mention those who are not 'known' by God at all (Mt. 7.22-23)!

Moreover, the function of these 'signs of a true apostle' may be better understood by focusing on the function of an apostle, that is, to bear witness to the gospel of the kingdom of Christ (Acts 15.10; 19.8; 20.25; 26.18; Rom. 15.19; 2 Cor. 12:12). The true gospel is normatively expressed in both word and deed; hence these signs did not appear for the purpose of directing the onlookers' attention to the person of Paul, or even to his message, but rather were the characteristic 'signs of the New Age'[1]—normative activities of the Holy Spirit which are part and parcel of the proclamation/demonstration of the gospel. Hence, Paul's argument here is directed against those 'false apostles' or others whose kingdom message consists not in 'power', but in 'talk' or in 'persuasive words of wisdom' (contra 1 Cor. 2.4; 4.19-20; 1 Thess. 1.5) thereby showing that their gospel is not normative—either in its content or presentation. Paul's argument, to be sure, raises disturbing implications for the role of preaching in traditional Protestantism.

The second passage, Heb. 2.4,[2] again, makes no necessary connection between the miraculous operations of the Spirit and the specific

1. V.P. Furnish, *Commentary on II Corinthians* (AB 32A; Garden City, NY: Doubleday, 1984), p. 555.

2. For a cessationist reading of this passage see P.E. Sywulka, 'The Contribution of Hebrews 2.3-4 to the Problem of Apostolic Miracles' (ThM thesis, Dallas Theological Seminary, 1967). On this passage see also T.R. Edgar, *Miraculous Gifts: Are They for Today?* (Neptune, NJ: Loizeaux Brothers, 1983), pp. 103-104, 268-69, 276-77. Edgar's work has ambitiously focused on that which Warfield promised, and failed to achieve, namely, to provide biblical and theological grounding for the cessationist polemic. Edgar's exegesis has been criticized for being less than transparent; see Carson, *Showing the Spirit*, p. 105, and Turner, 'Spiritual Gifts Then and Now', pp. 22-23. Warfield does not argue that because this passage

accreditation of the Apostles. The passage describes three more or less parallel 'witnesses' to the same gospel: the Lord, his hearers, and God via the distributed charismata.[1] In biblical tradition 'two or three witnesses' presenting the same message guarantee its certainty (Deut. 17.7; 19.15; Mt. 18.16; 1 Cor. 14.27; 2 Cor. 13.1). The miracles in this context do not 'accredit' the kingdom of God, but are a manifestation of it; they are not proofs of the gospel: they *are* the gospel. The English expression 'sign' may well suggest an image of a 'sign-post', having little intrinsic significance except as it points to something of vastly greater importance. Certainly this is Warfield's notion of a sign or miracle, but as in the case of the 'signs of a true apostle' above, the very characteristic of the Christian message was that it came expressed

looks back into the past toward God's miraculous presentation of 'so great a salvation' (where the present participle συνεπιμαρτυροῦντος, 'confirmed with', at the end of v. 3 is grammatically contemporaneous with ἐβεβαιώθη, 'was confirmed', at the beginning of v. 4), the author of Hebrews is implicitly affirming these gifts ceased.

But the point of the passage is to parallel and contrast the punishment for rejection of a law that was confirmed by *angels*, against the stronger certainty of judgment for neglecting 'so great a salvation' which was confirmed by *three* witnesses: 'the Lord', 'the ones hearing' him, and by God himself via the charismata bestowed among the churches. Cessationism is an incidental concern here. The mention of miracles and spiritual gifts as past events may only indicate the author's need to strengthen his parallel with the (lesser) angelic initial confirmation of the Law and that of the Christian Gospel. Certainly the charismatic (i.e., prophetic and miraculous) confirmation of the law was not restricted to within a generation of its appearance (Isa. 59.21 and Jer. 32.20), any more than spiritual gifts were restricted to the first generation of Christians. To say that because this passage says God bore witness to the gospel with miracles in the past is not to say he could not continue to do so.

Moreover, the present participle (συνεπιμαρτυροῦντος) may actually indicate an action continuing into the future from the time of the aorist main verb, hence the meaning, '[the salvation] was affirmed to us by those who heard Him, God also continuing to confirm with miracles. . . ' See BDF, §339, p. 174. This passage warrants further study with respect to cessationism, since it can be shown to parallel, *inter alia*, such passages as 1 Cor. 1.4-8 insofar as they deal with testimony of Christ, his hearers, and the continuing 'confirmation' of each member in the church communities via the spiritual gifts until the end of the age.

1. Though see H. Strathmann 'ἐπιμαρτυρέω, κτλ', *TDNT*, IV, p. 510, who seems to vacillate on the meaning of συνεπιμαρτυροῦντος as either an independent witness or as one who simply accepts and confirms what is said or done as true. The context seems to prefer the first interpretation, though the practical difference is nil.

in 'word *and* deed', two aspects of the kingdom of heaven breaking both the mental and physical bondage characterizing the kingdom of this age.[1] The passage further suggests that the gifts of the Spirit were distributed to the Christian community at large, rather than restricted to Apostles (cf. 1 Cor. 12.7 and 11; Rom. 12.6 and 1 Pet. 4.10). In this context, then, these 'signs, wonders, miracles and gifts of the Spirit' do not appear as proofs of apostolic authority but as the normative expression or confirmation of the gospel working in acts of divine power in and through the Christian community.

The prooftexts Warfield positively offers as support for cessationism can be interpreted, in fact, as contradicting it. Now Warfield moves more negatively against his opponents' prooftexts, popularly used to attack cessationism.

Warfield shifts his biblical defense of a cessationist, evidentialist concept of miracle by attacking A.J. Gordon's contention that Scripture 'unambiguously justifies the conclusion that God has continued the gift of specifically miraculous healing permanently in the church'.[2] The verses adduced by Gordon to establish contemporary miraculous healing are: Mt. 8.17; Mk 16.17, 18; Jas 5.14, 15; Jn 14.12, 13; and 1 Cor. 12 in which, he held, no hint was offered there as to the cessation of the charismata. Gordon shared, it appears, much of Warfield's notion of miracle. And it is because he insists, in Warfield's view, on identifying contemporary healings as miracles, even though in some cases they were adduced to accredit Evangelical doctrines, that he becomes part of Warfield's polemical concern.[3] The verses listed above represent the classic prooftexts of the American faith healing movement.[4] The following representation is intended only to be indicative of the respective positions which are considerably more detailed and nuanced than presented here.

---

1. See the discussion below in Chapter 3 on the relation of the kingdom of God to charismatic activity in the church.

2. Warfield, *Counterfeit Miracles*, p. 166.

3. Warfield, *Counterfeit Miracles*, pp. 160-64, is careful to establish just this point: that Gordon is indeed trying to restore modern miracles of healing.

4. See Cunningham, 'From Holiness to Healing', p. 507. In Mt. 8.17, for example, contemporary healings, on the one hand, found a rationale from biblical soteriology, and on the other, provided a miraculous proof against liberals who denied the efficacy of Christ's substitutionary offering for sin.

Mt. 8.17 served faith healers to show that healing was in some way guaranteed in the atonement of Christ, who bore on the cross not only sins but sickness as well.[1] Warfield echoes Luther in countering this with the evidentialist claim that a miracle was strictly an 'object lesson'[2] for a spiritual truth. Mt. 8.17 holds out no promise of 'relief from every human ill' which is to be realized suddenly or completely in this life. Then, possibly reflecting on the tragedy of his wife's extended illness, he declares, 'We live in a complex of forces out of which we cannot escape'. 'Are we,' he continues, 'to demand that the laws of nature be suspended in our case?'[3] Against the roots of perfectionism, or instantaneous 'entire sanctification' of the holiness movement from which much of the faith healing movement evolved, Warfield affirms that while we are no longer under the curse of sin, as Christians, we nonetheless remain sinners. The struggle against 'indwelling sin' is constant, and continues through life.[4] In the same way, we experience a life-long struggle against sickness. Warfield's ultimate argument against this connection of healing and the atonement lay in its 'confusing redemption. . . which is objective, and takes place outside of us, with its subjective effects, which take place in us . . . and that these subjective effects of redemption are wrought in us gradually and in a definite order'. The extent to which these subjective effects of redemption are active in a believer's life could have been fruitfully debated. However, since this debate was framed in the absolute terms of 'miracle', that is, nothing of the provisional, partial or ambiguous, there could be no compromise on healing.[5]

---

1. 'When evening came, many who were demon-possessed were brought to him, and he drove out the spirits with a word and healed all the sick. This was to fulfill what was spoken through the prophet Isaiah: "He took up our infirmities and carried our diseases".'

2. Warfield, *Counterfeit Miracles*, p. 177.

3. *Counterfeit Miracles*, p. 179. Earlier (p. 177) Warfield comments, 'Our Lord never permitted it for a moment to be imagined that the salvation He brought was fundamentally for this life. His was emphatically an other-world religion'.

4. Warfield, *Counterfeit Miracles*, p. 177-78.

5. The analogy, of course, between redemption from sin and redemption from sickness could be argued by pointing out that just as one of the results of the atonement in the believer's present, earthly life is sanctification—a diminution in the expression of sin—so through faith, one may expect a similar diminution in sickness. The deliverance of the body (Rom. 8.22-23) from both sin and sickness is eschatological in nature, but proleptically experienced in this 'time between the

'Realized', or more accurately, 'inaugurated' eschatology was not yet on the horizon of Warfield's practical theology.

Mk 16.17, 18 was set forth by Gordon and others as a mandate for miraculous powers to those who believed. Warfield, the text critic,[1] denied the validity of this assertion on the grounds that this passage was 'spurious', that is, a textual addition to the original autograph of Mark's Gospel. In this he is doubtless correct, though it does represent, likely, a very early view of the relation of charismata and faith. But even if this passage were valid, Warfield continues, 'I should not like to have the genuineness of my faith made dependent upon my ability to speak with new tongues, to drink poison innocuously, and to heal the sick with a touch'.[2] Apparently Warfield either overlooks or does not subscribe to Calvin's distinction between 'saving faith' leading to redemption, justification and sanctification, and 'miraculous faith', described in 1 Cor. 12.9, by which 'miracles are performed in [Christ's] name'.[3] Calvin also notes that 'Judas had faith like that, and even he carried out miracles by it'. Warfield's mentor, Charles Hodge, and Hodge's son Archibald Alexander both make analogous distinctions,[4] so it is odd that Warfield frames his objection to faith for miracles in such a manner.

Jas 5.14, 15 is a command to call for the church elders to pray with faith for the sick, anointing them with oil. This seems a rather

times'. See D.A. Carson, 'Matthew', in F.E. Gaebelein (ed.), *The Expositor's Bible Commentary* (12 vols.; Grand Rapids: Zondervan, 1984), VIII, pp. 204-207. The New Testament clearly does expect a change in sinful behavior after regeneration. In this sense, Christianity is *not* an 'other-world religion'.

1. Warfield, *Counterfeit Miracles*, pp. 167-68, 45 and 59.

2. *Counterfeit Miracles*, p. 168.

3. Calvin, *Commentary on I Corinthians*, p. 262: 'Chrysostom makes a slightly different distinction, calling it the "faith relating to miracles" (*signorum*), and not to Christian teaching (*dogmatorum*)'.

4. C. Hodge develops Calvin's 'saving miraculous' faith distinction in his *Commentary on I Corinthians* (Carlisle, PA: Banner of Truth Trust, 1959), pp. 246-47: 'As faith here is mentioned as a gift peculiar to some Christians, it cannot mean saving faith, which is common to all. It is generally supposed to mean the faith of miracles to which our Lord refers, Mt. 17.19, 20, and also the apostle in the following chapter, "Though I have all faith, so that I could remove mountains", 13.2'. Hodge here assumes that 'the gift meant is a higher measure of the ordinary grace of faith'. See A.A. Hodge, *Outlines of Theology* (New York: Robert Carter, 1861), pp. 358-59.

straightforward prooftext for faith healers, but Warfield dissents by seeing 'no indication' that a peculiar miraculous faith or healing is intended.[1] The anointing oil is not a symbol of the power of the Spirit to be exercised in the healing, as Gordon had interpreted; rather, Warfield would suggest the oil had medicinal value only. This highlights an important element in the nature of miracle for Warfield. If a cure can be shown to have been effected by 'natural means', that is, by any possible intervening agent of cure other than an immediate act of God, then no miracle has occurred. This principle is applied consistently to the whole range of post-apostolic miracles Warfield surveys. Hence Warfield takes some care to establish, in the face of the strong trend within biblical scholarship to the contrary,[2] the medicinal significance, as 'natural means', of the anointing oil. It is more likely, however, that James derived the connection of healing and anointing with oil not from medical practice but from the earliest ṣtrata of Christian charismatic tradition, Mk 6.13, when, after the disciples were given spiritual power (ἐξουσία) over evil spirits in the commission to demonstrate and proclaim the presence of the kingdom of God, they 'drove out many demons and anointed many sick people with oil and healed them'. Here, clearly, is not a description of medical missionaries, but of those who, like Jesus, were empowered for spiritual battle, 'healing all who were under the power of the devil' (cf. Acts 10.38).

1. Warfield, *Counterfeit Miracles*, p. 169.
2. Commentaries available to Warfield usually disagreed on this point; for example J.A. Bengel: 'The only design of that anointing was miraculous healing' (*New Testament Commentary*. II. *Romans to Revelation* [trans. C.T. Lewis and M.R. Vincent; Grand Rapids: Kregel Press, 1981], p. 723, on Jas. 5.14). J.E. Huther would agree with Warfield that anointing with oil was employed for 'refreshing, strengthening and healing of the body', but insists that the healing is a 'miracle' and is precipitated 'not [by] the anointing but [by] prayer' (*General Epistles of James, Peter, John and Jude* [MeyerK, 10; Freiburg: Herder, 1887], p. 157). So also, J.P. Lange, *The General Epistles of James* (trans. J.I. Mombert; New York: Charles Scribner's Sons, 1900), p. 140. Even Calvin seems to disagree with Warfield on the function of the anointing in James (*Tracts and Treatises on the Reformation of the Church* [trans. H. Beveridge; Grand Rapids: Eerdmans, 1956], p. 91). See Warfield's comments in *Counterfeit Miracles*, p. 303 nn. 22-23. For a more modern survey of the interpretive options of this passage, see Shogren, 'Will God Heal Us', pp. 100-107.

From Jn 14.12 comes an interpretation which suggests the promise
to anyone who believes that they will do 'greater works' (greater
miracles) than Christ. Warfield dismisses this view quickly on two
grounds: first, faith healers have yet to produce 'greater works' than
Jesus' raisings from the dead or nature miracles, and, secondly, the
normative interpretation of this passage is that 'spiritual works' refer
to spreading the gospel to the world.[1]

This interpretation reflects the usual post-reformation Calvinistic
spiritualizing tendency when dealing with the miraculous.[2]
Recent scholarship is more nuanced,[3] concluding generally that the

---

1. *Counterfeit Miracles*, pp. 174 and 307 n. 30, where Warfield cites the works
of Luthardt, Godet, Wescott, and Milligan and Moulton. He refers us especially to
the discussion in W. Milligan, *The Ascension and Heavenly High-Priesthood of Our
Lord* (London: Macmillan, 1892), pp. 250-53.

2. See, for example, the conservative Evangelical commentator L. Morris who
changes the usual reference of μείζονα to 'works', to a simple neuter plural,
'things', therefore not referring to miracles, 'but to service of a more general kind'.
'Greater works' 'mean more conversions. There is no greater work possible than the
conversion of a soul' (*The Gospel according to John* [NICNT; Grand Rapids:
Eerdmans, 1971], p. 646). Similarly, Warfield (*Counterfeit Miracles*, p. 4) insists
that Paul urges the Corinthians to seek the 'greatest gifts', which are the 'non-
miraculous' charismata of 'faith, hope and love', though his mentor C. Hodge
disagrees. See note above.

3. See the summary and discussion of the problem of 'greater works' by
R.E. Brown, in *The Gospel according to John* (AB, 29A; Garden City, NY:
Doubleday) pp. 633-34. After a review of promises made by Jesus to his disciples
in the Synoptics and Acts to perform marvelous works, Brown suggests that the
works are 'greater' insofar as they partake of an 'eschatological character', implying
a stage of salvation history more advanced than that of the earthly Jesus.
C.K. Barrett, in *The Gospel according to St. John* (Philadelphia: Westminster
Press, 2nd edn, 1978), p. 384, develops this point further by suggesting that these
same continued works (miracles) are greater not because they themselves are greater
but 'because Jesus' work is now complete'. The disciples are to perform their works
in the new age of the Spirit under the reign of the glorified Christ. 'Greater' then
refers to the time significance of the era in which miracles are performed rather than
to their own intrinsic nature. A similar notion may be behind Jesus' saying that all in
the kingdom of God are greater than John the Baptist. R. Schnackenburg affirms that
'these "greater works" can justifiably be applied to the missionary successes of the
disciples'. But the evangelist intends to characterize these successes as 'the increasing flow of God's power into man's world' (*The Gospel according to St John* [trans.
K. Smyth; 3 vols.; New York: Herder & Herder, 1968], III, p. 72). B. Lindars,
The Gospel of John (NCB; London: Oliphants, 1972), p. 475, takes a continuist

evangelist's intention was that 'greater' miracles were to continue among the disciples in that they were to be performed in a more eschatologically advanced era than during the earthly mission of Christ, namely that of the exalted Lord Jesus.

3. *Summary*

Two major influences which shaped Warfield's cessationist polemic were a narrowed and less ambiguous form of Calvin's miracle polemic against Roman Catholicism, and an Enlightenment era polemic against ecclesiastical miracles, based upon a concept of miracle that was decidedly rationalistic, which in' Warfield's case was governed by his acceptance of Scottish common-sense realism. Warfield's polemic did not appear as an exercise in theological abstraction; it was precipitated by specific groups challenging Princetonian orthodoxy, all of which shared the claim to a religious authority based on performance of miracles. The axe of classical cessationism lay readily at hand to chop out this common root. Warfield insisted that his cessationist polemic stood upon two legs: upon a critical analysis of historical claims of miracles and upon the teaching of Scripture. But these legs, in turn, rested upon a certain understanding

view of miraculous activity and decides that the 'greater works' represent the 'full scope of divine activity in Jesus. . . extended through the world and down the ages'. G.W.H. Lampe is even more emphatic and specific about the nature of these works: 'The divine is at work, in a sense, only proleptically in the pre-Resurrection ministry of Jesus. In his messianic anointing with Holy Spirit and power, and in the operation of that power in his mighty acts, the age of fulfillment is anticipated; but all this was *but a foretaste* [italics mine] of what was to follow when Jesus had been "taken up". The Johannine saying, "He who believes in me, the works which I do shall he do also, and greater things than these shall he do, because I am going to the Father", expresses very clearly Luke's conception of the relation of the works done by Jesus in his ministry to the signs and wonders performed in his name after his ascension. It is as concise a summary of a central Lukan theme as is that other Johannine comment, "[the] Spirit was not yet because Jesus was not yet glorified"' The true beginning of the new age for Luke, according to Lampe, is 'therefore at the Ascension and its counterpart at Pentecost' ('Miracles in the Acts of the Apostles', in C.F.D. Moule [ed.], *Miracles: Cambridge Studies in their Philosophy and History* [London: Mowbrays, 1965], pp. 169-70). W.F. Howard ties the performance of 'greater works' (miracles) to the 'secret of effectual prayer' and that they will appear 'over a wider range than the limited field' of Jesus' earthly ministry (*Christianity According to St John* [Philadelphia: Westminster Press, 1946], p. 162).

of the nature and purpose of miracles. Warfield's concept of miracle, however, is shown to be internally contradictory and is therefore useless as firm ground for his cessationist polemic. To him, a miracle is an event *both* rationally deduced by any observer of 'common sense' *and* determined by a previous commitment of faith. He did not perceive that both could not be true, or that miracles could communicate divine revelation in and of themselves.

When Warfield himself judges the authenticity of biblical miracles, he falls prey to this internal contradiction: he claims to base his evaluation on a detached, rational examination of the facts, but instead he bases his evaluation on prior assumptions about the inerrancy of biblical testimony and theological corollaries to this. Warfield's major theological assumption about miracles is that they have just one purpose, namely to accredit the New Testament apostles and their doctrine. On this basis, for Warfield, any striking or unusual event unconnected with this function could not be considered a miracle. I agree with Warfield's premise that the function of the charismata determine their duration. Scripture explicitly states the function of the charismata: not for accreditation of apostles, but for edification, exhortation, encouragement and equipping of all believers for further service.

Warfield's historical criteria for his evaluation of postbiblical miracles are essentially the same as those for which he condemns the rational critics of New Testament miracles; for instance, continuously directing *ad hominem* arguments against anyone reporting miracle accounts, reductionistically viewing some miracle accounts as mere literary forms devoid of historical credibility, and above all approaching these miracles from a consistently naturalistic background.

In contrast to Warfield's historical argument, the second, biblical, 'leg' on which his polemic stands occupies only a few pages scattered throughout his work. None of the biblical passages Warfield offers as support for his thesis necessarily demand, or can even suggest, a cessationist conclusion. In view of Warfield's commitment to a biblically based theology, it is astonishing that he fails to address almost all of the important Scriptures bearing on his cessationist polemic. The following chapter advances beyond biblical issues that Warfield specifically raised in connection with his polemic to some far more important ones that he omitted.

Chapter 3

A THEOLOGICAL AND BIBLICAL CRITIQUE
OF BENJAMIN WARFIELD'S CESSATIONISM*

This chapter argues that Warfield's claim of basing his cessationist
polemic solidly on Scripture is unjustified, first, because his traditional
Calvinist theology ignores the emphases in at least two biblical doctrines inimical to cessationism, and secondly, because his polemic
contradicts the specific teaching of several passages of Scripture. The
first part of this chapter briefly examines the biblical doctrines of the
Holy Spirit and the kingdom of God as they bear upon cessationism
and as they provide a theological setting for the second part of the
chapter, an exegesis of biblical texts which teach the continuation of
the charismata during this present era of Christ's exaltation.

1. Cessationism and its Conflict with a Biblical Theology
of the Holy Spirit and the Kingdom of God

Warfield's cessationism represented an attempt to protect the idea that
after the final revelation of Christ, there could be 'no new gospel'.[1]
The resulting denial of contemporary charismata is accordingly
reflected in his pneumatology and doctrine of the kingdom of God,
specifically as it relates to the mission of the exalted of Christ. For
example, in *Counterfeit Miracles* he asserts:

> God the Holy Spirit has made it His subsequent work, not to introduce
> new and unneeded revelations into the world, but to diffuse this one

---

*   The substance of the arguments of this chapter was presented in my paper, 'On
the Cessation of the Charismata', read at the Evangelical Theological Society annual
meeting at Santa Barbara, California, December 1970.
    1.   Warfield, *Counterfeit Miracles*, p. 27.

complete revelation through the world and to bring mankind into saving knowledge of it.[1]

Warfield's post-canonical Holy Spirit is strictly limited to activities in the Calvinistic steps of salvation (*ordo salutis*).[2] 'New' revelations are 'unneeded' revelations: Warfield's equivocal use of 'new' here bans from the Holy Spirit any revelatory or miraculous charismata.

Similarly, Warfield seems to shape his doctrine of Christ's exaltation to fit his polemic. The exaltation is a key aspect of the doctrine of the kingdom of God insofar as it impinges upon cessationism:

> When the revelation of God in Christ had taken place, and had become in Scripture and church a constituent part of the cosmos, then another era began . . . Christ has come, His work has been done, and His word is complete.[3]

The exalted Christ seems presently inactive, waiting, it appears, for the preaching of Calvinistic soteriology to accomplish its task in the world.

These representative statements of theological doctrine seem to reflect more of an urgency to protect the authority of Scripture than to describe carefully its teaching. For example, how does the Scripture teach that the Spirit can now 'diffuse' the revelation to 'bring' humankind to a 'knowledge of it' if not by some sort of revelation? In what sense has the exalted Christ's 'work. . . been done'? It is ironic that Warfield, who is best known as the Evangelical defender of the authority of Scripture, and who repeatedly insists that he founds his theology inductively upon it,[4] deviates so drastically from the pattern of biblical data in two doctrines, which by their very nature

---

1. Warfield, *Counterfeit Miracles*, p. 26.
2. Warfield, *Counterfeit Miracles*, p. 27.
3. Warfield, *Counterfeit Miracles*, p. 28.
4. See Chapter 2, above. According to Warfield, systematic theology 'is founded on the final and complete results of exegesis as exhibited in Biblical Theology. . . combining them in their due order *and proportion* [italics mine] as they stand in the various theologies of the Scriptures' (Warfield, 'The Idea of Systematic Theology', *WBBW*, IX, pp. 66-67). However, see K.R. Trembath, *Evangelical Theories of Biblical Inspiration: A Review and Proposal* (Oxford: Oxford University Press, 1987), pp. 20-27 and Kelsey, *The Uses of Scripture in Recent Theology*, pp. 17-30 and 141. Both see a contradiction between Warfield's theoretical and actual dependence on Scripture as his basis for theology.

contradict cessationism: pneumatology and the kingdom of God—the latter particularly as it relates to the exaltation of Christ.

A Biblical Doctrine of the Holy Spirit is Inimical to Cessationism
Warfield's 'biblical' pneumatology, especially his description of the Spirit in today's world, is limited almost exclusively to postbiblical theological questions of ontology and the role of the Spirit in the Calvinistic concepts of regeneration and sanctification.[1] This traditional Calvinist pneumatology and conclusions of traditional biblical exegesis were mutually conditioned, causing generations of scholars to ignore the charismatic implications in the texts before them. Accordingly, Warfield failed to appreciate an emerging consensus in biblical scholarship which pointed out the overwhelmingly charismatic function of the Holy Spirit described in Scripture.[2] Had he

1. Warfield, 'The Spirit of God in the Old Testament', in *WBBW*, II, pp. 101-32, and his 'Introductory Note' to A. Kuyper, *The Work of the Holy Spirit* (trans. H. De Vries; Grand Rapids: Eerdmans, 1979), pp. xxv-xxxix. Also, B.B. Warfield, 'John Calvin the Theologian', in G.S. Craig (ed.), *Calvin and Augustine* (Philadelphia: Presbyterian and Reformed Publishing, 1956), pp. 484, 487, 486; B.B. Warfield, 'John Calvin, the Man and his Work', *WBBW*, V, p. 21. In his 'Introductory Note', p. xxxiii, Warfield insists that the early church provided a limited doctrine of the Spirit, consisting of the person (deity and personality) and 'His one function of inspirer of the prophets and apostles [to write Scripture]'. By contrast, 'the whole doctrine of the work of the Spirit *at large* [italics mine] is a gift to the Church from the Reformation'.

2. For example H. Gunkel, *Die Wirkungen des heiligen Geistes nach der populären Anschauung der apostolischen Zeit und der Geister im nachapostolischen Zeitalter* (Göttingen: Vandenhoeck & Ruprecht, 2nd edn, 1889). The fact that Gunkel's work has been translated into English 90 years after its original publication attests to its revolutionary and continuing impact. See also Leonard Goppelt's high estimate of the work in his *Theology of the New Testament*, II (ed. J. Roloff; trans. J.E. Alsup; 2 vols.; Grand Rapids: Eerdmans, 1982), p. 119. Similar conclusions available to Warfield came from: H. Wendt, *Die Begriff Fleische und Geist* (Gotha: F.A. Perthes, 1878), pp. 139-46; J. Gloel, *Der heilige Geist in des Heilsverkündigung des Paulus* (Halle: Niemeyer, 1888); C. Briggs, 'The Use of רוח in the Old Testament', *JBL* 19.2 (1900), pp. 132-45; W. Shoemaker, 'The Use of רוח in the Old Testament and of πνεῦμα in the New Testament', *JBL* 23.1 (1904), pp. 13-65; H. Bertram, *Das Wesen des Geistes* (NTAbh, 4.4; Münster: Aschendorff, 1913), pp. 28-76. Following Warfield's hermeneutical steps, I classified each Old and New Testament reference to the Holy Spirit ('Spirit', 'Spirit of God', and so on) acording to any contextual description. It came as no surprise that of the 128 apperaances, 76 primarily described prophetic or revelatory activities of the Spirit;

appreciated this, he would have found it almost impossible to speak of the contemporary activity of the Spirit in truly biblical terms without mentioning the continuing appearance of 'extra-ordinary' charismata. The burden of proof for cessationism rests on Warfield and those who would so completely change the characteristic, if not the essential and central, activity of an unchanging God as Spirit.

It is not simply Warfield's failure to grasp the characteristic biblical activity of the Spirit that is so inimical to cessationism, but also the fact that Scripture repeatedly emphasizes the promise of the universal outpouring of this Spirit of prophecy and miracle on 'all people'. This promise is fulfilled not simply to accredited apostles and those 'upon whom apostolic hands were laid', but to all future generations, conditional only upon repentance and faith.[1] The Bible sees the outpouring of the Spirit and his gifts upon the church as characteristic of the age of the messiah and his reign in the kingdom of God.

A Biblical Doctrine of the Kingdom of God is
Inimical to Cessationism
Secondly, Warfield ignores the anti-cessationist implications derived inductively from a biblical portrayal of the kingdom of God.[2] Jesus'

---

18 were charismatic leadership; 14 were divine (miraculous) power; and 18 were the sustenance of life. Only a handful of associations of the Spirit and ethics or ritual purity appeared, and those were somewhat ambiguous. Similar proportions appeared in the more frequent references to the Spirit in the New Testament. Today the consensus of scholarship on the biblical portrayal of the Spirit in terms of charismatic, primarily prophetic, power follows Schweizer *et al.*, 'πνεῦμα, κτλ', pp. 332-455, for example, J. Dunn, 'Spirit in the NT', *NIDNTT*, III, p. 393; D. Hill, *Greek Words and Hebrew Meanings: Studies in the Semantics of Soteriological Terms* (Cambridge: Cambridge University Press, 1967), pp. 108-30; D. Lull, *The Spirit in Galatia: Paul's Interpretation of* πνεῦμα *as Divine Power* (SBLDS, 49; Chico, CA: Scholars Press, 1980), pp. 69-73.

1. See the development of the Old Testament promise of the Spirit into the New Testament in R. Stronstad, *The Charismatic Theology of St. Luke* (Peabody, MA: Hendrickson, 1984), pp. 13-82, Y.M.J. Congar, *I Believe in the Holy Spirit*, I (3 vols.; New York: Seabury; London: Geoffrey Chapman, 1983), pp. 8, 9, 30, 31, and 44. See notes below.

2. Warfield apparently wrote nothing specifically on the biblical theology of the kingdom of God and its essentially charismatic expression in the New Testament. His position is probably the same as that of Charles Hodge, whose three-volume systematics Warfield used in lieu of his own; see Hodge, *Systematic Theology*, II, pp. 596-609. Hodge stresses that Christ as 'King' in his exalted state rules over all

central mission in the New Testament is to inaugurate the kingdom 'in power' and 'in word and deed' (Lk. 4.23-27; 24.19).[1] His signs and wonders are not mere 'signs', in the English sense of extrinsic value, 'pointing' to the truth of the 'gospel' or its bearer.[2] Rather, miracles manifest the essential core activity of his mission: to displace the physical and spiritual ruin of the demonic kingdom by the wholeness of the kingdom of God.[3]

his people 'by his power in their protection and direction. . . by his Word and Spirit', but only 'providentially'. Hodge makes no mention of Christ's bestowal of spiritual gifts or ministries during the exaltation. The church, not charismatic or other divine activity specifically, is the visible expression of the kingdom in this age (p. 604).

1. Since this section was written, a former professor at Fuller Theological Seminary, Don Williams, has published his *Signs, Wonder and the Kingdom of God* (Ann Arbor, MI: Servant Books, 1989) which makes essentially the same points outlined here. So also B.D. Chilton, *God in Strength: Jesus' Announcement of the Kingdom* (Studien zum Neuen Testament und seiner Umwelt, B.1; Linz: SNTU, 1979); J. Kallas, *The Significance of the Synoptic Miracles* (Greenwich, CT: Seabury, 1961), pp. 10-12. See especially J. Jeremias, *New Testament Theology: The Proclamation of Jesus* (trans J. Bowden; New York: Charles Scribners' Sons, 1971), pp. 96-97, §11.i: 'The Βασιλεία as the Central Theme of the Public Proclamation of Jesus'.

2. Warfield, in 'Jesus' Mission According to His Own Testimony', in *WBBW*, II, pp. 255-324, says, ' "Mighty works" were as characteristic a feature of Jesus' ministry as His mighty word itself'. But this is qualified a page later: 'Jesus' mission is to preach a Gospel, the Gospel of the kingdom of God'. The miracles only 'accompany' or 'seal' his mission as messiah; they have no intrinsic value other than proofs validating his preaching and messianic claims.

By contrast, Raymond Brown represents the consensus of modern biblical scholarship when he writes: 'Jesus' miracles were not only or primarily external confirmations of his message; rather the miracle was the vehicle of the message. Side by side, word and miraculous deed gave expression to the entrance of God's kingly power into time. This understanding of the miracles as an intrinsic part of revelation, rather than merely an extrinsic criterion, is intimately associated with a theory of revelation where the emphasis on the God who acts is equal to (or even more stressed than) the emphasis on the God who speaks', *JBC*, p. 787. See also H. vander Loos, *The Miracles of Jesus* (Leiden: Brill, 1965), pp. 280-86; H. Bavinck, *Gereformeerde Dogmatiek* (Kampen: Bos, 3rd edn, 1918), p. 361; Schnackenburg, *God's Rule and Kingdom*, p. 121: 'Miracle might be called the kingdom of God in action'; P.E. Langevin, 'La signification du miracle dans le message du Nouveau Testament', *ScEs* 27 (May–September 1975), pp. 161-86.

3. Warfield insists in *Counterfeit Miracles*, pp. 177-78, that Jesus' healings were an 'object lesson' of his 'substitutionary work', which made 'no promise that this

Such 'miraculous' charismata as prophecies, exorcisms and healings, not only continue through Jesus' earthly ministry, but are bestowed through his followers during his exaltation.[1] Characteristically, the 'word' or preaching is not 'accredited' by miracles, but rather, the preaching articulates the miracles and draws out their implications for

relief [from sickness] is to be realized. . . in this earthly life'. Disease is an expression of natural law and as much may not be 'suspended in our case'.

Recent scholarship shows that Scripture takes the opposite view; see for example Kallas, *Significance of the Synoptic Miracles*, chs. 5 and 6: 'The Demonic-Cosmic Motif in the New Testament' and 'The Miracles Explained by This Motif', pp. 58-102, and A. Richardson, *The Miracle Stories of the Gospels*, ch. 3: 'The Miracles and the Proclamation of the Kingdom of God', pp. 38-58; J. Robinson, *The Problem of History in Mark* (SBT, First Series, 21; London: SCM Press, 1957), pp. 34-39; B. Bron describes the mission of Jesus in terms of its 'Kampfcharakter' against the slavery of anxiety, sickness and death which was encountering 'the inbreaking of the time of salvation and the eschatological new creation' (*Das Wunder: Das theologische Wunderverständnis im Horizont des neuzeitlichen Natur- und Geschichtsbegriffs* [Göttingen: Vandenhoeck & Ruprecht, 2nd edn, 1979], pp. 236-37). See also Fuller, *Interpreting the Miracles*, p. 40: 'Jesus interprets his exorcisms as the beginning of the end of Satan's reign'; W. Kelber, *The Kingdom in Mark* (Philadelphia: Fortress Press, 1974), p. 17: 'Exorcisms and healings are the two principal approaches used to translate the kingdom program into action. In both cases Jesus intrudes upon enemy territory, challenges and subdues the forces of evil which are in the way of the fulfillment of the kingdom of God'; H.C. Kee, 'The Terminology of Mark's Exorcism Stories', *NTS* 14 (January 1968), pp. 232-46; W. Foerster, 'δαιμῶν', *TDNT*, II, p. 19 and W. Schrage, 'Heil und Heilung im Neuen Testament', *EvT* 43.3 (1986), pp. 197-214, who argues that the New Testament vocabulary of salvation and healing should not be subjected to a false dualism: healing is a dimension of the eschatological salvation of the reign of God.

1. Cf. Acts 2.33, 36; 3.6, 16, 21; 4.7-13; Ladd, *Jesus and the Kingdom*, p. 268; Whitely, *The Theology of St Paul*, pp. 124-25; and Lampe, *God as Spirit*, p. 69. See also the important new study by L. O'Reilly, *Word and Sign in the Acts of the Apostles: A Study in Lucan Theology* (Analecta Gregoriana, 243.B.82; Rome: Pontificia Universita Gregoriana, 1987). Also, J. Marcus, 'Entering into the Kingly Power of God', *JBL* 107.4 (December 1988), pp. 663-75, esp. p. 674.

The Gospel of John cannot be excluded from this seamless connection of the Spirit's activity in Jesus' earthly ministry and that of the church. See W.F. Lofthouse, 'The Holy Spirit in the Acts and the Fourth Gospel', *ExpTim* 52 (1940-41), pp. 334-35. A. Richardson, *Introduction to the Theology of the New Testament* (London: SCM Press, 1958), p. 64.

the onlookers.[1] Jesus' charismatic mission (summarized in Acts 2.22; 10.38) continues in the commissions to his disciples (Mt. 10; Lk 9 and 10[2] and Mt. 28.19-20, cf. 24.14) 'until the end of the age'. In the book of Acts the church expresses its commission (1.5-8) to present the kingdom in the power of signs and wonders and the preaching of the word. The summary statements of Paul's mission (Acts 15.12; Rom. 15.18-20; 1 Cor. 2.4; 2 Cor. 12.12; 1 Thess. 1.5) show the continuation of this normative pattern of presenting and living out the gospel in 'word and deed'.[3] The next major section in this chapter examines

1. 'Without miracle the gospel is not gospel but merely word, or rather, words'; J. Jervill, 'The Signs of an Apostle: Paul's Miracles', in his *The Unknown Paul: Essays on Luke–Acts and Early Christian History* (Minneapolis: Augsburg, 1984), p. 95. M.H. Miller describes preaching in Luke–Acts as the way to 'mediate the word of power which effects the miracles which are constitutive of the kingdom' ('The Character of Miracles in Luke–Acts', PhD dissertation, Graduate Theological Union, 1971), p. 193. G. Friedrich, 'εὐαγγελίζομαι', *TDNT*, II, p. 720, has also noted that for Paul, 'εὐαγγελίζεσθαι is not just speaking and preaching; it is proclamation with full authority and power. Signs and wonders accompany the evangelical message. They belong together'. Jervell ('Signs of an Apostle', p. 91) states: 'Miracles assume a quite central role in Paul's preaching, almost to a greater degree than in Acts. . . He. . . states clearly that miracles occur *wherever* he preaches the gospel. This is in itself self-evident, because miraculous deeds were a part of his proclamation of the gospel, and for Paul, proclamation is inconceivable apart from deeds of power'.

2. See W. Kurz. *Following Jesus: A Disciple's Guide to Luke–Acts* (Ann Arbor, MI: Servant Books, 1984), ch. 4, 'Sharing Jesus' Power for Service', pp. 57-67. Kurz implies in the introduction (p. 5) that these early commissions in Luke 9 and 10 were intended by Luke to apply beyond the early disciples mentioned there to Luke's readers generally. So also Williams, *Signs, Wonders and the Kingdom of God*, p. 125; C. Kraft, *Christianity with Power* (Ann Arbor, MI: Servant Books, 1989), p. 136. However, C. Brown, 'The Other Half of the Gospel', *CT* 33 (21 April 1989), p. 27, argues that because this specific commission was brief and limited to the Jews at that time, that commands to heal and exorcise demons can have no application to the later reader. This is clearly not the pattern in the book of Acts, in the summary statements of Paul's mission, nor in the passages investigated below.

3. So C.C. Oke, 'Paul's Method not a Demonstration but an Exhibition of the Spirit', *ExpTim* 67 (November 1956), pp. 35-36. Oke's point is that Paul's miracle-working was not to accredit himself as an apostle, but was performed in humility as an exhibition of the Spirit's normative work among his people. Echoes of these summaries of how Paul 'preached' the gospel appear also in other writers, for example in Acts 26.17-18 and Heb. 2.4, though in this latter case, as in Gal. 3.5 and 1 Cor. 1.5-8, the 'confirmation' of the gospel was God working via a distribution of

representative New Testament passages which show the continuity of kingdom charismata from the apostles to their readers, and beyond them, to the end of the age.

By contrast, Warfield fails to grasp the charismatic significance of several key theological aspects of the kingdom of God. Specifically, Warfield's picture of Jesus' earthly and exalted mission is unbiblical in that it fails to show Christ as the continuing source of the charismata among those who would receive them. Warfield's soteriology, a Calvinistic *ordo salutis* limited to the problem of sin, is also unbiblical in that it fails to grasp the holistic nature of salvation, including healing, revelation and deliverance from demonic power. His eschatology is flawed in that he fails to see the work of the kingdom of God (alternatively, the Spirit of God) as biblically described, that is, that the exalted Christ bestows charismata provisionally in this age as a 'downpayment', the 'firstfruits', or a 'taste of the powers of the age to come'.

The exaltation of Jesus and the resulting outflow of the charismata through his church must be placed in the context of salvation history. The New Testament conception of the flow of history represents a modification of the fairly simple two-part schema shared by the Old Testament and the rabbis, which divided history into two major parts: this present age (from creation to the coming of the messiah), and the age to come (from the coming of the messiah onward). The New Testament saw the two ages as overlapping: the coming of the messiah, Jesus, inaugurated the time of the kingdom and Spirit in the opening victories over the kingdom of Satan. The exaltation of Jesus and the subsequent outpouring of the Spirit continued, and expanded this conflict, through the ministry of his church, a conflict characterized by the restoration of hearts, souls and bodies from the control of the kingdom of darkness, via the preaching of the word and through healings and miracles. The first coming of Jesus represented, in Oscar Cullmann's metaphor, 'D-Day', the decisive battle (properly at the resurrection) which raged on, with its sufferings, victories and

spiritual gifts in members of the various congregations. See F.F. Bruce, 'The Spirit in the Letter to the Galatians', in *Essays on Apostolic Themes* (Peabody, MA: Hendrickson, 1985), pp. 37-38.

The miraculous nature of the term 'deed' in the above expression is confirmed in contemporary rabbinic materials, according to G. Vermes, *Jesus the Jew: A Historian's Reading of the Gospels* (Philadelphia: Fortress Press, 1973), pp. 78-82.

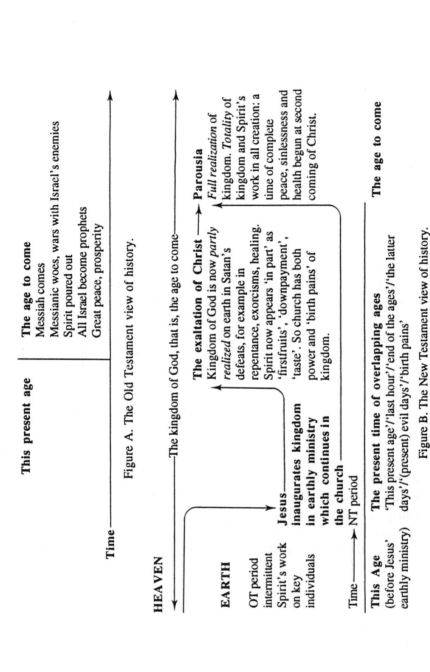

This present age | **The age to come**
Messiah comes
Messianic woes, wars with Israel's enemies
Spirit poured out
All Israel become prophets
Great peace, prosperity

Time

Figure A. The Old Testament view of history.

The kingdom of God, that is, the age to come

The exaltation of Christ → **Parousia**
Kingdom of God is now *partly realized* on earth in Satan's defeats, for example in repentance, exorcisms, healing. Spirit now appears 'in part' as 'firstfruits', 'downpayment', 'taste'. So church has both power and 'birth pains' of kingdom.

Full realization of kingdom. *Totality* of kingdom and Spirit's work in all creation: a time of complete peace, sinlessness and health begun at second coming of Christ.

HEAVEN

EARTH

OT period intermittent Spirit's work on key individuals

Jesus inaugurates kingdom in earthly ministry which continues in the church

Time → NT period

This Age (before Jesus' earthly ministry)

The present time of overlapping ages
'This present age'/'last hour'/'end of the ages'/'the latter days'/'(present) evil days'/'birth pains'

The age to come

Figure B. The New Testament view of history.

defeats, toward its ultimate victory at 'V-Day' (the parousia). Below are diagrams of the Old and New Testament views of history which originated from a Princeton Seminary colleague of Warfield's, Gerhardus Vos.[1]

The original schema of the Old Testament and the rabbis was strictly linear (see Fig. A). The New Testament introduces the over-lapping period of the messianic reign, during which time the church carries out the final commission by the power of the Spirit sent from the exalted Lord Jesus. The first ascending and descending lines represent the incarnation, the inauguration of God's kingdom and the ascension of the messiah Jesus; the third represents his parousia at the end of this present age (see Fig. B).

The New Testament expressly ties the presence of the charismata to the exalted Lordship of Jesus. This theological setting depends on an understanding of the nature of the interim period between the first and second comings of Christ, and its relation to the bestowal of the charismata, which is simply that God, through his exalted Christ in his church, continues his earthly ministry of deliverance through the church (Jn 7.39; 16.7, 17). The 'greater works' of those who believe in him can be performed only *because* Jesus goes to his Father (Jn 14.12, cf. Acts 2.33, 36b, 38-39).

If Warfield's theology had been truly based as inductively and as thoroughly on Scripture as he claimed, his cessationism would have been incongruous with his biblical facts. As additional examples, he fails to perceive that the explicitly stated biblical conditions for the manifestation of the charismata (for instance repentance, faith and prayer) contradict his unconditional, temporary connection of the charismata with the apostles and the introduction of their doctrine.[2]

---

1. G. Vos, *Pauline Eschatology* (Grand Rapids: Eerdmans, 1961), p. 38. See also G.E. Ladd, *Jesus and the Kingdom* (New York: Harper & Row, 1963), p. 268.

2. On *repentance*, see Acts 2.38-39. Repentance, aggressive turning from this present world to enter the kingdom of God and its charismatic blessings, is a strong theme in the teaching of Jesus (for example Mt. 13.44-45).

In the Synoptic Gospels, almost all of the references to *faith* relate it to the power of God for physical needs, primarily healing. Jesus stresses the need for faith for miracles ('your faith has saved you': Mk 5.34 // Mt. 9.22 // Lk. 8.48, cf. 7.50; 'made you whole': Lk. 17.19; Mk 10.52 // Lk. 18.42). The context shows similar connections in Mt. 8.10 // Lk. 7.9, cf. Jn 4.46-54; Mk 2.5 // Mt. 9.2; Lk. 5.20; Mt. 15.28, cf. Jn 11.40. Even for control over the elements Jesus commands faith

He also fails to account for the many explicit biblical commands to seek, desire and employ the very charismata he claims have ceased.[1] How can Warfield ignore these biblically explicit conditions and commands for the continuation of the charismata, if, as he insists, the Bible continues as the normative guide to the church for its faith and praxis?

Our study has outlined both a biblical pneumatology and doctrine of the kingdom of God and their relation to cessationism to provide a

---

(Mk 4.40 // Mt. 8.26 // Lk. 8.25); even to walk on the water (Mt. 14.31), to uproot mountains and trees by faith (Mk 11.20-25; Mt. 17.20-21; 21.20-22; Lk. 17.6, cf. 1 Cor. 13.2). In fact, he says, 'Everything is possible to those who have faith' (Mk 9.23)! Conversely, where there is unbelief Jesus does no miracles (Mk 6.5-6 // Mt. 13.58). This commitment is carried on in the apostolic church. The story of the healing of the lame man teaches explicitly that miracles do not derive from apostolic accreditation, but from the power of faith (in this case, that of the lame man) in the exalted Christ (Acts 3.12, 16; cf. 4.9-12; see the similar teaching in 14.9). Paul commands his readers to 'prophesy according to your faith' (Rom. 12.6; cf. 12.3; Eph. 4.7, 16), and connects the faith of a local congregation, not accreditation of doctrine, with the working of miracles (Gal. 3.5). C.H. Powell, in *The Biblical Concept of Power* (London: Epworth Press, 1963), pp. 185-86, cites a number of similar examples in Paul and concludes: 'Paul has learned that *pistis* [faith] is the way to God's gifts [of power]'.

 Scripture offers many other examples relating *prayer* and the appearance of miracles in the ministry of Jesus and the apostles (for example Acts 4.30; 4.33; 8.15; 9.40; 28.8). See G.W.H. Lampe, 'The Holy Spirit in the Writings of St Luke', in D.E. Nineham (ed.), *Studies in the Gospels* (Oxford: Basil Blackwell, 1952), p. 169. James makes the crucial point that the appearance of miracles is not a function of accrediting prophets, but of righteous, believing and fervent prayer (5.16-17). James points to Elijah as an example for his readers to follow, not a saint to be accredited with miracles. Why cannot this principle be applied to the New Testament figures as well?

 1. The New Testament specifically commands its readers to 'seek', 'desire earnestly', 'rekindle' and 'employ' certain 'miraculous' charismata (1 Cor. 12.31; 14.1, 4, 5 and 39; 2 Tim. 1.6; 1 Pet. 4.10) and implies that their appearance can be suppressed by simple neglect (Rom. 12.6; 1 Cor. 14.39; 1 Thess. 5.19-20; 1 Tim. 4.14; 2 Tim. 1.6). On the latter verse, J.N.D. Kelly affirms that 'the idea that this grace operates automatically is excluded' (*The Pastoral Epistles* [HNTC; New York: Harper & Row, 1963], p. 159). He compares this passage with the 'quenching' of the Spirit of prophecy in 1 Thess. 5.19. Biblical commands, 'let us use', 'strive to excel [in spiritual gifts]', 'desire earnestly', 'do not quench', etc., make little sense if the occurrence of the charismata bears no relation to the obedience of these commands.

theological framework for the final, more fully developed, argument, namely that specific statements of Scripture explicitly teach that the gifts of the Spirit are to continue in the church until the coming of Christ at the end of this present age. Much in the following passages contain echoes of the words of Jesus in the great commission: to duplicate his charismatic work of the kingdom until the end of the age (Mt. 24.14; 28.20). They also reflect the pattern of Peter's earliest sermon: 'In the last days', before the 'day of the Lord', 'You will receive the gift of the Holy Spirit. This promise is for you, your children and for all who are far off—for all whom the Lord our God will call' (Acts 2.17, 20, 39). The background to these verses is the promised eschatological outpouring of the Spirit of prophecy, in all its various manifestations, upon the people of God and upon their descendants forever (Joel 2.28-32;[1] Isa. 47.3; 59.21). Within this theological pattern, then, the next section shows according to Scripture that the kingdom charismata are to function normatively during the final generations of the church.

2. Key Biblical Passages on the Continuation
of the Charismata until the Parousia

Despite his well-formulated rules for developing biblically based doctrine, for example by 'collecting the whole body of relevant facts', and by obtaining 'the exact sense of every word' from its context, Warfield failed to grasp the significance of the pivotal doctrines of Spirit and kingdom as well as almost all of the significant scriptural passages directly bearing on cessationism. By contrast, this section applies Warfield's own hermeneutic to a number of scriptural passages. Three passages, which establish the patterns for subsequent passages, receive more detailed attention: 1 Cor. 1.4-8; 13.8-12 and Eph. 4.7-13. A substantial number of similar passages reiterate the themes of these three, but will be examined only to show that such

---

1. See the important discussion on this passage by W.C. Kaiser, *The Use of the Old Testament in the New* (Chicago: Moody Press, 1985), pp. 89-100. He approvingly cites W.K. Price, *The Prophet Joel and the Day of the Lord* (Chicago: Moody Press, 1976), pp. 65-66: 'Joel's prophecy has *initial* fulfillment at Pentecost, *continuous* fulfillment during the Church Age, and *ultimate* fulfillment at the second coming of Christ'.

reiteration does occur: Eph. 1.13-14, 17-21; 3.14-21; 4.30; 5.15-19; 6.10-20; Phil. 1.9-10; Col. 1.9-12; 1 Thess. 1.5-8; 5.11-23; 2 Thess. 1.11-12; 1 Pet. 1.5; 4.7-12; 1 Jn 2.26-28 and Jude 18-21.

Three Major Passages on Cessationism: 1 Corinthians 1.4-8; 13.8-13; Ephesians 4.7-13

Before dealing directly with the two passages in 1 Corinthians, it is important to point out that the argument of this epistle as a whole considers the nature of this present age before the parousia, whether or not the 'age to come' is thought to be fully realized in our time, and the implications of these two positions. Much of Paul's argument against the variety of problems in the Corinthian church lay in the members' inadequate view of salvation history, their 'overrealized' eschatology.[1] The Corinthian believers apparently felt that the operation of the spiritual gifts evidenced their present eschatological existence, which was manifested in a factious, individualistic spirituality, based on 'knowledge' and utterances (in unintelligible glossolalia) of divine mysteries. They lived 'above and beyond' this present age, so that earthly or material concerns, such as factional conflict, sexual immorality, idolatrous religious associations, and concern for the poor, seemed all vaguely irrelevant to true spirituality.[2] Against these

---

1. For background on the problems precipitating the Corinthian letter, see G. Fee, *The First Epistle to the Corinthians* (NICNT; Grand Rapids: Eerdmans, 1987), pp. 10-15, esp. p. 12, on the Corinthian 'overrealized' eschatology or 'spiritualized eschatology' in which those who see themselves as πνευματικοί, that is, 'people of the Spirit, feel their present existence [is] to be understood in strictly spiritual terms. The Spirit belongs to the Eschaton, and they are already experiencing the Spirit in full measure'. With the gift of tongues they 'have arrived—already they speak the language of heaven'. Fee continues: 'from their point of view it would not so much be the "time" of the future that has become a present reality for them, as the "existence" of the future. They are now experiencing a kind of ultimate spirituality in which they live *above* the merely material existence of the present age'. See also Ellis, 'Christ and the Spirit in 1 Corinthians', pp. 269-77; and his *Prophecy and Hermeneutic in Early Christianity* (Grand Rapids: Eerdmans, 1978), pp. 76-78; F.F. Bruce, *1 and 2 Corinthians* (NCB; London: Marshall, Morgan & Scott, 1971), pp. 49-450; E. Käsemann, *Essays on New Testament Themes* (SBT, 41; trans. W.J. Montague; London: SCM Press, 1964), p. 171.

2. So J.M. Robinson, 'Kerygma and History in the New Testament', in *Trajectories through Early Christianity* (Philadelphia: Fortress Press, 1971), p. 34: 'It would seem to be this heretical interpretation of the kerygma in terms of an already consummated eschaton for the initiated that is behind the various Corinthian excesses

symptoms of a sub-Christian soteriology and eschatology, Paul presented the view of an early Christian tradition, derived directly from the words of Jesus,[1] to the effect that spiritual power was not bestowed for accreditation, but for a revelation of the exalted Christ.

The charismata are *Christocentric*: they are given by God through the exalted Christ Jesus, continuously to confirm the 'testimony of Christ', until the Lord Jesus Christ is revealed, in the 'day of the Lord Jesus Christ'. The charismata are also *ethical* in that they are not granted to exalt the self-centered: they are God's 'grace' and 'graces' (not earned); they are given for relationship—directed to Christ ('while eagerly awaiting. . . and called into fellowship' with God's Son [for example 1.9]); and will continue until the end for the purpose of confirming/strengthening believers to be 'blameless' at the judgment of Christ.

Most relevant for our study is Paul's point that the charismata are *eschatological*. Spiritual gifts express the contemporary presence of the future kingdom of God. But exciting and powerful as these experiences might be, the Corinthians have not yet 'arrived'; there is much more to come.[2] The abundance of the charismata serve usefully to

to which Paul addressed himself in 1 Corinthians'. For a summary of the Corinthian problem in terms of a kind of Jewish gnostic thought, see W. Schmithals, *Gnosticism in Corinth* (trans. J. Steely; Nashville: Abingdon Press, 1971), pp. 117-285; though against this see J.C. Hurd, Jr, *The Origin of 1 Corinthians* (London: SCM Press, 1965), and a mediating position by Bruce, *Commentary on 1 and 2 Corinthians*, p. 21 and R.P. Martin, *New Testament Foundations*, II (Grand Rapids: Eerdmans, 1978), pp. 172-73, 408-409; Conzelmann, *Corinthians*, pp. 15-16.

1. That is, in the words of the great commission (Mt. 28.19-20), where all authority and power is given to Christ who would be with the witnessing disciples 'to the end of the age' and Acts 1.5-8, where the Spirit and power would come upon them for witness 'to the ends of the earth'. This may echo Joel's and Isaiah's prophecies of the bestowal of the Spirit of prophecy 'upon all flesh. . . to your descendants, even to those who are far off' (Joel 2.28-32 in Acts 2.17-27; cf. Isa. 44.3; 65.23; 57.19 in Acts 2.39). As Matthew does implicitly, Acts promises the Pentecostal Spirit of power and prophecy to the full extent of both geographical and temporal limits, contradicting cessationism.

2. Fee, *Corinthians*, p. 12, notes: 'Paul so often views their present existence in light of the future, since neither [Paul nor] they have yet arrived (1.5-8; 3.13-15, 17; 4.5; 5.5; 6.13-24; 7.26-31; 11.26, 32; 15.24, 51-56; 16.22): they are rich, full and reigning, in contrast to the tenuous conditions of Paul's apostolic existence'. See also

promote maturity in believers throughout the present age, but these gifts will be overwhelmed and replaced by the consummation of the age, the 'end', the kingdom in its fullness, that is, the revelation of our Lord Jesus Christ in the 'day' of his glory.[1] Not only do the two passages in 1 Corinthians below respond to these issues, but so do all of the following passages examined in this section. In Corinth, Paul must attack the underlying problem of 'overrealized/overspiritualized' eschatology not by denying the Corinthians' spiritual gifts, but by clearly stating their mission within their limited eschatological framework. Charismata continue the mission of the exalted Lord in confirming and strengthening his church only until it reaches its truly ultimate destiny. Hence, the message to the Corinthians is: spiritual gifts are temporary, that is, for the time of 'eagerly awaiting' the true τέλος: to be blameless at the final revelation of Christ, having been called into fellowship with him and one another. True Christian charismatic experience does not statically accredit the spiritual status of the gifted, but moves the church toward its goal. It necessarily expresses the commission of the exalted Lord, which must continue until the end of the age.

1 Corinthians 1.4-8. 1 Cor. 1.4-8 is part of Paul's bridge-building greeting to the Corinthians, affirming them by thanking God for their development in spiritual gifts. This development is not without problems, as he points out in chs. 12–14. Hence, the passage stresses the 'grace' quality and especially the divine origin of the spiritual gifts—an implicit reminder that these gifts, especially 'knowledge' and 'tongues', do not necessarily confer on the Corinthians high spiritual attainment or status, nor do they mean that the readers are already fully existing in the age to come. The passage also stresses that even those who are spiritually enriched and gifted still must await the ultimate revelation of Christ at his parousia at the 'end'.[2] Indeed, the

D.J. Doughty, 'The Presence and Future of Salvation in Corinth', *ZNTW* 66.1 (1975), pp. 61-90.

1. As W. Grundmann, 'δύναμαι, κτλ', *TDNT*, II, p. 305, points out in connection with charismatic activity in Acts, this eschatological power 'is an expression of the power which works triumphantly in history and leads it to its goal'.

2. The translations will loosely follow the NIV except in cases where special clarity or emphasis is required. Each passage is presented at or near the beginning of each investigation.

very reason that God in Christ provides spiritual gifts is continuously to strengthen and confirm them from now until the end, since they have not yet spiritually 'arrived'.

So in the above context, this long sentence (vv. 4-8) reiterates the themes previously discussed about the Christian experience of the Spirit: the Father bestows the charismatic Spirit 'in' or via the exalted messiah Jesus upon his people, in the form of inspired speech, knowledge and other charismata, by which the church is enriched and strengthened until the parousia at the end of the age. The passage appears without significant textual variants:

> 4 I always thank God for you because of God's grace given you in Christ Jesus, 5 because in every way you have been enriched in him—in every kind of speech and in every kind of knowledge— 6 the same way the testimony of Christ was confirmed in you, 7 with the result that you do not lack any spiritual gift, while awaiting the revelation of our Lord Jesus Christ, 8 who also will confirm you until the end, so that you will be blameless on the day of our Lord Jesus Christ.

How does this passage relate to Warfield's cessationism? I will argue first that this passage is indeed speaking of 'extraordinary' charismata, and secondly, that the teaching of this passage is that these charismata continue to the parousia. First, are we in fact talking about spiritual gifts in this passage? Certainly, in v. 4, the grace of God, τῇ χάριτι, is singular, hence, is no particular gift of the Spirit. But in v. 5 'because' (ὅτι) logically connects this grace with 'every kind of speech[1] and every kind of knowledge', necessarily including charismatic, divinely initiated speech and knowledge.[2] Moreover, v. 7 affirms that the Corinthians do not lack any (μηδενί) spiritual gifts: they experience them all. But the passage does not end abruptly there.

---

1. See BAGD, 'πᾶς', p. 636: πᾶς includes 'everything belonging, in kind, to the class designated by the noun, *every kind of, all sorts of*'.

2. Even Hodge, *First Corinthians*, p. 12, seems to prefer this position, which even in his time was 'the one very generally adopted', though he does offer the suggestion that λόγος and γνῶσις refer to 'doctrinal knowledge' and 'spiritual discernment'. About the charismata mentioned in v. 7: 'The extraordinary gifts. . . seem to be principally intended' (*First Corinthians*, p. 13). Certainly this is the modern consensus. C.K. Barrett, *First Corinthians* (BNTC; London: A. & C. Black, 2nd edn, 1971), p. 37; A. Robertson and A. Plummer, *First Corinthians* (ICC; Edinburgh: T. & T. Clark, 2nd edn), p. 5; Conzelmann, *1 Corinthians*, p. 27.

The next point answers the question, how long is this situation to continue?

Secondly, this passage teaches that all of the spiritual gifts (v. 7) are to continue until 'the revelation of our Lord Jesus Christ', that is, 'the end', 'the day of our Lord Jesus Christ'. This can be shown from the structure of the argument. Paul seems to affirm the importance of the Corinthians' spiritual giftedness while weaning them away from its evidentialist interpretation, that is the idea that they had 'arrived' in a heavenly spiritual existence via the charismata. Paul redirects his readers' focus away from their own spiritual status to the idea that these gifts are graces from God or Christ: they were enriched (divine passive, that is, 'by God', not by their own attainment) with these gifts they had not earned. Moreover, Paul emphasizes that their *present* high level of giftedness ('all speech, all knowledge', v. 5) is 'just as' or 'exactly as' (καθώς, v. 6) their *original* confirming experience with Christ, probably the apostolic witness in the power of signs and wonders and the resulting outpouring of charismata at their conversion or initiation into the Spirit. That is, what they now have in such abundance, they received from others. So far, Paul has tied the Corinthians' present charismatic experience (vv. 4-5) to the past and to its true source outside themselves.

Next (v. 7), from the *past* ('for this reason' [ὥστε]), he ties the *present* ('you do not [now] lack any spiritual gift') to the *future* ('while you are awaiting', or, 'you who are awaiting' [ἀπεκδεχ-ομένους] the ultimate revelation, our Lord Jesus Christ').[1] The Corinthians are not yet in the heavenly places, ruling the universe. They are still 'awaiting' the ultimate revelation, the Lord (exalted) Jesus (earthly, physical, human sufferer) Christ (messiah, divine ruler over the end time). The point for cessationism here is crucial. Paul is arguing that during this present period or condition of 'awaiting', the Corinthians will lack *no* spiritual gift (*all* gifts, including both the so-called 'ordinary' and 'extraordinary' gifts, continue in this period). It is not an accident that Paul describes the Corinthians as 'awaiting' the

---

1. The 'revelation' (ἀποκάλυψις) of Christ here is not a personal revelation of Christ in the present age, but refers to 'the manifestation of Christ when he comes from heaven at the winding up of history, the moment in hope of which the whole creation, including Christians, groans and travails (Rom. 8.22-23). . . [The] coming of Christ in glory' (Barrett, *First Corinthians*, pp. 38-39). Cf. BAGD, p. 92a; A. Oepke, 'καλύπτω, κτλ', *TDNT*, III, p. 583.

revelation of Christ. He is making a key point: this is the time *before* the 'consummation' (συντέλεια, Mt. 28.20) of the age during which Christ or the Spirit will be 'with' them (Jn 14.16-18) in power, to the ends of the earth (Acts 1.5-8). The Corinthians are living in a time of only partially realized eschatology. While it is the time of the Spirit and his gifts, it is also the time of waiting for a fuller revelation, that of Christ and the parenetic implications his life has for their own. This theme is continued and developed in v. 8, where the 'confirmation of [from, by, or about][1] Christ' via the charismata is promised 'until the end (ἕως τέλους)'.[2]

It is important to establish that the spiritual gifts are in fact promised to continue in v. 8, so how can one say, 'via the charismata' here? First, we must consider the immediate context: Paul has just made the point that the charismata exist now, during the 'awaiting' time. The present 'enriching' in and through spiritual gifts is contrasted with the ultimate revelation of Christ: two ages, now and then. Verse 8 shares this pattern. Secondly, the term 'confirm' (ἐβεβαιώθη) is expressed in v. 6 'just as', 'exactly as' (καθώς) the charismata of speech and knowledge in v. 5. To change here in v. 8 the fully charismatic means by which (βεβαιόω) confirms or strengthens to some other means of confirming would amount to equivocation. Fee[3] notes the force of καί, 'Who will *also* confirm you . . .' as a reference back to the first confirmation by God (v. 6) via spiritual gifts. Thirdly, this equivocation would be destructive of Paul's arguments that the gifts are graces from Christ (not personal achievements), and are limited to the 'awaiting' period, in contrast with the ultimate

1. Whether this is an objective genitive ('testimony *about* Christ'), as BDF suggests, or a genitive of origin and relationship ('testimony *from* Christ'), the action is the same: the testimony derives from the charismata, especially those of 'speech and knowledge', which in any case are sent from Christ.

2. So, BAG, 'τέλος', 1, d, ß, p. 819, on this passage and 2 Cor. 1.13 where 'to the end' means 'until the parousia'. So also Fee, *Corinthians*, p. 43, Barrett, *First Corinthians*, p. 39. Though some others, including G. Delling, 'τέλος, κτλ', *TDNT*, VIII, p. 56, take the expression to mean 'fully, wholly and utterly'. This latter meaning diminishes the clarity of spiritual gifts continuing to the end but does not affect the overall eschatological interpretation of the verse. See my arguments against this interpretation, below.

3. Fee, *Corinthians*, p. 43: 'Paul says that in the same way that God first "guaranteed" our testimony to Christ while we were with you, he will *also* "guarantee" or "confirm" you 'to the end"'. See esp. n. 39.

revelation of Christ. Fourthly, the 'who' (ὅς) is the fourth emphasis in this short passage on Christ's involvement in the charismata: the 'grace' was given *in Christ Jesus* (v. 4); the Corinthians were 'enriched *in him* in all speech and all knowledge' (v. 5); the 'testimony of Christ' occurred charismatically, that is, from Christ (v. 6). Paul is also stressing the Christocentric orientation of the charismata in v. 8. Fifthly, the 'confirming' works toward a moral and eschatological end as do the charismata, for example, prophecy, for 'strengthening, encouragement and comfort' (1 Cor. 14.3). Finally, the term βεβαιόω appears significantly in similar contexts about spiritual gifts confirming or witnessing, using the legal metaphor implicit in the word (Mk 16.20; cf. Heb. 2.3; Acts 1.8).[1] Heb. 2.3 uses βεβαιόω in parallel with συνεπιμαρτυρέω by which God, like Christ, 'bears witness with them with signs, wonders, various miracles and gifts'.

Does v. 8 promise that the charismata will continue to the eschaton? One could argue that Paul is saying that Christ will confirm and strengthen the Corinthians 'until personal maturity (ἕως τέλους)', which is not an eschatological time of 'the end'. This interpretation, while conceivable, is doubtful. ἕως with the genitive is almost always used of time, not condition or state. The preposition εἰς would be more appropriate here. This interpretation also contradicts the immediate parallel context of v. 7, which points to a clear eschatological goal: 'awaiting the revelation of our Lord Jesus Christ'. Moreover, the 'maturity' is described as 'blameless' (ἀνεγκλήτους), which, while it is sometimes applied to persons in this present age (1 Tim. 3.10 and Tit. 1.6, cf. Phil. 3.6; though see Col. 1.22 for a closer parallel), is here appositionally connected with 'blameless *in the day of* our Lord Jesus Christ', an expression which could hardly be more eschatological. The rendering could be: 'until (τέλους), that is to say, blameless *in the day* of . . . ' So the teaching, indeed the commitment, of the author in v. 8 is a promise: 'Christ will confirm/strengthen you by means of all the charismata until the end/ parousia'. Given the canonical normativity for the church, one ought not to limit this promise to the Corinthian readers.

So, then, Paul promises that Christ, through his spiritual gifts, will continue the action of progressively 'strengthening/confirming'

---

1. H. Schlier, 'βέβαιος', *TDNT*, I, pp. 600-602.

believers morally, spiritually and physically 'until (ἕως) the end (τέλους)', that is, until the point that the readers are 'blameless in the day of our Lord Jesus Christ'. The gifts continue confirming Christ, progressively strengthening the believers morally and spiritually until the eschaton which is described as 'the end', that is, the point at which the readers are 'blameless', not in this age, but 'in the day of our Lord Jesus Christ'.

1 Corinthians 13.8-13. 1 Cor. 13.8-13 is perhaps the *locus classicus* in the discussion on the continuation of spiritual gifts.[1] To summarize,

1. Since this present study was undertaken, several important studies have appeared on this passage which challenge cessationism generally, and deal with 1 Cor. 13.8-10 in particular. Although there is very little exegetical work relating to cessationism on other equally significant passages, some treat this passage with great thoroughness and overlap with my review here. See for instance D.A. Carson, *Showing the Spirit: A Theological Exposition of 1 Corinthians 12–14* (Grand Rapids: Baker, 1987), pp. 66-72; D.A. Codling, 'The Argument that the Revelatory Gifts of the Holy Spirit Ceased with the Closure of the Canon of Scripture' (ThM thesis, Westminster Theological Seminary, 1974); P. Elbert, 'Face to Face: Then or Now? An Exegesis of First Corinthians 13.8-13', unpublished paper read at the seventh annual meeting of the Society for Pentecostal Studies, Springfield, MO, December 1977; W. Grudem, *The Gift of Prophecy in 1 Corinthians* (Washington, DC: The University Press of America, 1982), pp. 210-19; *idem, The Gift of Prophecy*, pp. 224-52; M.M.B. Turner, 'Spiritual Gifts Then and Now', *VE* 15 (1985), pp. 7-64; Fee, *Corinthians*, pp. 641-52; and on a more popular level, M. Lloyd-Jones, *The Sovereign Spirit: Discerning His Gifts* (Wheaton, IL: Harold Shaw, 1985). Dunn, *Jesus and the Spirit*, p. 424, summarizes this position: 'The classic Calvinist view of 1 Cor. 13.8-13—that glossolalia and prophecy (and knowledge) belonged only to the apostolic, or pre-canonical age, is quite foreign to Paul's thought. . . The charismata are all temporary enough in Paul's view, to be sure, because "the perfect", that is parousia, is imminent; but he does not envisage them ceasing or passing away before the "face to face" knowledge of the parousia'. This study will show, more emphatically and precisely than Dunn's statement, that the teaching of 1 Cor. 13.8-13 is that the cessation of the charismata is *contingent upon* the second coming of Christ.

Some of those interacting with this passage attempt to defend cessationism: T.R. Edgar, *Miraculous Gifts: Are They for Today?* (Neptune, NJ: Loizeaux Brothers, 1983), pp. 333-34; R.G. Gromacki, *The Modern Tongues Movement* (Nutley, NJ: Presbyterian and Reformed Publishing, 1973), pp. 123-24; J.R. McRae, '(to teleion) in 1 Corinthians 13.10', *RQ* 14 (1971), pp. 168-83; L.R. Reid, ' "That Which is Perfect" in 1 Corinthians 13.10' (MDiv Thesis, Grace Theological Seminary, 1978); W. Tamkin, 'That Which Is Perfect: 1 Corinthians

this passage also argues that, in contrast to Christian love, which is manifest both in the present and in heaven, spiritual gifts are temporary, that is, characteristic of the present age, ceasing only at its end, when the full revelation of God will occur. The passage appears, with no significant textual variants, as follows:

> 8 Love never ends. If there are prophecies, they will be ended; if tongues, they will cease; if knowledge, it will be ended. 9 For we know incompletely and prophesy incompletely; 10 but when the complete has come, at that point, the incomplete will be ended. 11 When I was an infant, I talked as an infant, I thought as an infant, I reasoned as an infant. When I became a man, I ended infantile things. 12 In the present time we see through a mirror indistinctly or indirectly, but then, face to face; in the present I know incompletely, but then I shall fully know to the extent I was fully known. 13 Now faith, hope and love, all three, are present; but the greater of these is love.

After placing this passage in the overall context of Paul's argument, this brief study attempts to validate the summary above by answering a few key questions relevant to my thesis: first, are the charismata in fact the focus of this passage? Secondly, to what does the ἐκ μέρους refer in v. 9? Thirdly, is there significance for cessationism in the change of verbs, καταργηθήσονται to παύσονται, in v. 8? Fourthly, to what does τὸ τέλειον refer in v. 10? Fifthly, what is the contribution of the grammar of v. 10 to the necessary conclusion that Paul predicted the continuation of the charismata until the end of the age? And finally, what is the contribution of vv. 11-13 to the central idea of v. 10?

The context of this passage reflects what I have already discussed in my analysis of the previous passage, that is, the argument Paul was making about the relation of spiritual gifts to the eschatological goal of the Christian life. Spiritual experiences did not prove that the Corinthians had 'arrived' in the fullness of wisdom and power characteristic of the age to come. Spiritual gifts, Paul implied, were a *means to an end*, in terms of testimony to Christ and the fulfillment of his

13.10' (BD thesis, Grace Theological Seminary, 1949); R.L. Thomas, 'Tongues. . . Will Cease', *JETS* 17 (Spring 1974), pp. 81-89; S.D. Toussaint, 'First Corinthians Thirteen and the Tongues Question', *BS* 120 (October–December 1963), pp. 311-16. These are only a few of many such references to this passage in cessationist writers.

commission to disciple all nations until the end of the age. This last event they had not yet truly experienced; it was still in the future.

In the immediate context of 13.8-13, we see Paul continuing and developing his overall argument. Chapters 12–14 deal again with spiritual gifts. Again Paul stresses a Christocentric focus for the charismata (12.3, cf. 11.23-33) which implies service (12.5), not status. And again, Paul emphasizes the divine origin of the gifts (12.4-11): they are not human creations or possessions. Above all, Paul attacks the factionalism which had developed, at least partly, from the view of certain charismata as accrediting the status of the one gifted. He does this, as I have said, by stressing that these miracles are *charis*mata ('graces'), that their source is divine, and that God's one Spirit works through many people and gifts for the common good (12.4-31). Hence, the experience of the Spirit must be unifying, not divisive; it must be broad-based and diverse, not focused, as the cessationist polemic would have it, on a few individuals with 'the best' gifts. Just as one body is necessarily constituted of many parts working harmoniously for the good of the whole, no one in the body of Christ can deny the importance of any member's gift or function, be it another's or one's own. Conversely, no one can demand that all members possess an identical gift or function: the body cannot exist without unity in diversity. The gifts are given for humble service, which takes pride only in another's honor (12.12-31). Ultimately, Paul's view of the Corinthians is not that they are 'too charismatic', but that they are not charismatic enough. He not only encourages a display of a broader diversity of gifts, but urges them to seek the 'greater gifts', particularly the 'extraordinary' gift of prophecy (12.31; 14.1, 5, 39). But the way in which to manifest these gifts is in love.[1]

1. The choice of the 'greater gift' in 12.31 is not between the charismata or love; as C. Hodge notes, 'The idea is not that he intends to show them a way that is better than seeking gifts, but a way *par excellence* to obtain those gifts. The other view is indeed adopted by Calvin and others, but it supposes the preceding imperative (*covet ye*) to be merely concessive, and is contrary to 14.1, where the command to seek the more useful gifts is repeated. The sense is, "Seek the better gifts, and moreover, I show you a better way to do it"' (*First Corinthians*, p. 24).

Chapter 13 appears in the context of a discussion of spiritual gifts as an integral part of Paul's argument.[1] The point of the first three verses is that the motive for expressing spiritual gifts is not self-aggrandizement or accreditation, but edification of others in love. The first verses of this chapter show that the most spectacular evidence of divine power is pointless without a loving motive. After a brief discussion of the characteristics of love in vv. 4-7, Paul presents his final argument about love and the charismata: love is eternal, the charismata are temporary. The present time is characterized by the charismata of prophecy, tongues and knowledge, as well as faith, hope and love. But love is greater because it appears both in the present *and* in eternity.[2] The question is, however, just how temporary are the charismata? How long do they continue?

The teaching of vv. 8-13 is that the charismata will continue until the 'end (τὸ τέλειον)', a reference to the end of the age, as described in 1 Cor. 1.4-8, above. Let us unpack the passage by responding to the questions raised above.

Are the charismata being discussed in this passage? Godet,[3] following the early Protestant tendency to see miracles as metaphors,

---

1. Although there is controversy about how this chapter on love appeared in this context—by editorial blunder or by design. As we shall see this chapter is crucial to Paul's message to the Corinthians. See the discussion in J.T. Sanders, 'First Corinthians 13: Its Interpretation Since the First World War', *Int* 20 (April 1966), pp. 159-87.

2. For support of this interpretation see Conzelmann, *First Corinthians*, p. 225: 'Now . . . love and the charismata are set in antithesis to each other, and we have the eschatological argument that the latter will cease. They are accordingly, unlike love, not the appearance of the eternal in time, but the manifesting of the Spirit in a provisional way. Thus these very gifts hold us fast in the "not yet". . . .'.

3. See above, Chapter 2, on Calvin's idea of 'the transmutation of spiritual gifts'. Calvin's hermeneutical device seems to have influenced F. Godet, *Commentary on the First Epistle to the Corinthians* (trans. A. Cusin; London: T. & T. Clark, 1886), p. 250; also W.F. Howard, 'First and Second Corinthians', in *ABC*, p. 1188: 'Prophecy (or Scripture) and knowledge (or Theology), as G.G. Findlay happily suggested, serve our needs now, but of necessity leave much unexplained. These gifts belong to the present order, but will have had their day when immediate communion brings us into the presence of Him who knows perfectly'; cf. Toussaint, 'First Corinthians Thirteen and the Tongues Question', p. 314, who argues that prophecy here is the 'content' of prophecy and knowledge, i.e. 'doctrine'. Against the notion that preaching is prophecy, see R.B.Y. Scott, 'Is Preaching Prophecy?', *CJT* 1 (April 1955), p. 16 and G. Friedrich, 'προφήτης, κτλ', *TDNT*, VI, pp. 854-

concedes that while 'the total abolition of the gifts cannot take place before the end of the present economy, there may come about a modification in their phenomenal manifestation'. For example, prophecy transmutes into preaching, tongues into oratory or music, and revealed knowledge into 'catechetical and theological teaching of Christian truth'. This view does not bear scrutiny. In the first place, such a proposal does violence to Paul's argument in this passage: he is placing spiritual gifts into their proper eschatological context. If, before the eschaton, they are to change into purely human abilities, his argument is made pointless by such an equivocation. Further, the NT is aware of these distinctions, for example between examples of preaching or teaching and prophetic utterance (Acts 13.1; 1 Cor. 12.28-29; Eph. 4.11; Rev. 2.20; cf. *Did.* 11.10-11): preaching involves a conscious arrangement, application and presentation of the Christian tradition. Prophecy is primarily revelation and utterance. The tongues mentioned in 1 Corinthians 14 are quite the opposite of oratory: they are unintelligible even to the speaker (14.14, 15). As with tongues, the distinction between human and divinely revealed knowledge was made abundantly clear in the first three chapters of this epistle. Such an attempt to change meanings of terms so distinguished by the first-century reader is anachronistic. Prophecy, tongues and knowledge are gifts of utterance and revelation, doubtless included in the category of 'all kinds of speech and all kinds of knowledge' cited in 1 Cor. 1.5, above.[1]

55. So also, Hodge, *1 Corinthians*, p. 271, against Toussaint: 'It is not knowledge in the comprehensive sense of the term that is to cease, but knowledge as a gift; as one of the list of extraordinary endowments mentioned above'. Knowledge surely will not pass away in heaven, where we will 'know even as we have been known', but the gift of revealed knowledge (1 Cor. 12.8) is to cease.

1. So, Barrett, *First Corinthians*, p. 300; Fee, *Corinthians*, p. 643; Robertson and Plummer, *First Corinthians*, p. 296-97; 'Three prominent χαρίσματα are taken in illustration of the transitory character of the gifts: to have gone through all would have been tedious'. The attempt is specious to separate the gift of tongues from prophecy and knowledge on the grounds that vv. 9 and 12 list only the latter two and do not mention tongues. See Toussaint, 'First Corinthians Thirteen and the Tongues Question', p. 315 and Edgar, *Miraculous Gifts*, pp. 336-37. Against this, Fee, *Corinthians*, p. 644 n. 21; Conzelmann, *1 Corinthians*, p. 226: 'In the omission of speaking in tongues we are not to find any special intention.' Also, Carson, *Showing the Spirit*, p. 67, argues that the omission is stylistic, as does Grudem, *Prophecy in 1 Corinthians*, p. 21. Cf. Barrett, *First Corinthians*, p. 305.

The term ἐκ μέρους in v. 10 echoes the same phrase in the preceding verse. It refers to the limited character of the representative gifts of knowledge and prophecy, except that in v. 10 it moves from an adverbial function to a more substantive one, acquiring an article, τὸ ἐκ μέριον, hence the meaning, 'the partial *thing*'. The ἐκ μέρους of v. 10, then, also refers to the charismata; if not to the whole body of gifts, which is most likely, then at least to prophecy, tongues and revealed knowledge.[1]

The doctrine of continuing spiritual gifts has been challenged because Paul uses different verb voices in v. 8. The change is from the passive verbs καταργηθήσονται and καταργηθήσεται, which refer, according to this interpretation, to the passing away of ('the content of') prophecy and knowledge (= scripture or doctrine), to the middle voice verb employed for the 'supernatural' gift of tongues (παύσονται, 'will cease'). The argument is that the middle voice implies the translation, 'tongues will cease of themselves', that is, they are not 'caused' to cease (at the parousia), which might have been implied if Paul had used the active voice (παύσουσιν). Hence, grammatically, the gift of tongues may cease at any time before, and independently of, the eschaton.[2] The passive voice applied to the continuation of ('the content of') prophecy and knowledge implies they were 'caused' to cease by the coming of Christ. In other words,

---

1. Barrett, *First Corinthians*, pp. 305-306; Fee, *Corinthians*, p. 645; cf. Hodge, *1 Corinthians*, p. 271; Conzelmann, *1 Corinthians*, p. 226; J. Schneider notes in his article, 'μέρος', *TDNT*, IV, p. 596: 'The adverbial ἐκ μέρους, along with the verbs γινώσκειν and προφητεύειν, serves in 1 Cor. 13.9, 12 to denote the situation of Christians in this age. There is now no perfect knowledge, no full exercise of the prophetic gift. Though controlled by the Spirit, the earthly existence of Christians stands under the sign of the partial. Only in the future aeon will what is partial (τὸ ἐκ μέρους, 1 Cor. 13.10) be replaced by what is perfect (τὸ τέλειον)'. But Schneider goes on to show that μέρος has a broader eschatological dimension: 'salvation history, insofar as it applies to Israel is also put by Paul in the category of μέρος'. Israel's partial (ἀπὸ μέρους) hardening refers to the present condition, which will continue until the predestined full number of Gentiles will come in, and 'thusly all Israel will be saved' (Rom. 11.25-26). See also Grudem's extended comment on the meaning of μέρος here in *Prophecy in 1 Corinthians*, pp. 148-49 n. 59.

2. Thomas, 'Tongues Will Cease', p. 81; Toussaint, 'First Corinthians Thirteen and the Tongues Question', pp. 314-15; Gromacki, *The Modern Tongues Movement*, pp. 128-29. D.A. Carson cites these scholars' treatment of παύσονται in this context as an example of an 'exegetical fallacy' (*Exegetical Fallacies* [Grand Rapids: Baker, 1984], pp. 77-79).

enscripturated prophecy and knowledge may continue until the parousia, but tongues will not.

We have already dealt with the transmutation of spiritual gifts into metaphors, but five additional problems emerge with this interpretation of παύσονται. (1) It is one thing to say that tongues ceased 'of themselves', or simply 'ceased', and quite another to insist, on this apparent grammatical basis, that this cessation necessarily has no external causation, that is, the coming of Christ. As a matter of fact, the action of the same aorist middle of παύω necessarily involves causation in Lk. 8.24, where the wind and waves 'ceased' (ἐπαύσαντο), not 'of themselves', but *at Jesus' command*. An uproar of the crowd in Ephesus 'ceased' (παύσασθαι) only after the rioters were threatened and dismissed by a town official, a clear case of causation (Acts 19.40; 20.1). (2) The appeal to the middle voice of παύω to show cessation of tongues independent of the eschaton is a conclusion based on a faulty understanding of the so-called middle voice in certain semantic contexts, where, as in this case, it acts simply as an active, deponent, intransitive verb.[1] (3) The context is ignored: even if a reflexive (middle) usage of παύομαι were the case, the charism of tongues is still part of the ἐκ μέρους charismata that stand in contrast to the τέλειον and are abolished by it. (4) Since tongues is listed in 1 Cor. 12.10, 28 and 29 as a gift initiated and maintained by the Spirit of God, it is absurd to imply they cease 'of themselves' apart from any action of the Spirit. (5) This interpretation ignores the obvious parallel of the verbs, καταργηθήσονται // παύσονται // καταργηθήσεται used of prophecies, tongues and knowledge, respectively.

---

1. W. Veitch, *Greek Verbs Irregular and Defective: Their Forms, Meaning and Quantity* (Hildesheim: Olms, 1967), pp. 515-16. In researching this very question, Elbert ('Face to Face', pp. 26-27) in an act of academic overkill, from his collection of some 2000 cases, examined over 400 examples of παύω/παύομαι in their various forms. He corroborated the observation of Veitch, and added a further corollary, that without exception, in order to express a thing simply ceasing, 'when no object is involved (as in 1 Cor. 13.8), the middle form is universally preferred'; that in Koine Greek, 'παύομαι is a deponent verb in the sense that the use of middle endings does not necessarily indicate the middle *or* passive idea since the middle form conveys a simple active meaning'. See also Carson, *Exegetical Fallacies*, pp. 78-79.

The meaning of the term τὸ τέλειον in this passage has been the subject of some discussion.[1] The consensus of commentators rightly takes this phrase both as a contrast to the 'in part' of the present age

1. Some understand τὸ τέλειον in this context to indicate:

a. Mature love which obviates the childish desires for the most spectacular gifts: G.G. Findlay, *St Paul's First Epistle to the Corinthians* in *ExGT*, II, p. 90; N. Johansson, 'I Corinthians 13 and 1 Corinthians 14', *NTS* 10 (April 1964), pp. 389-90; E. Miguens, '1 Cor. 13.8-13 Reconsidered', *CBQ* 37 (January 1975), pp. 87-97. Others in this category suggest that a 'mature church' is intended: Criswell, *The Baptism, Filling, and Gifts of the Spirit*, p. 134 and Swete, *The Holy Spirit in the New Testament*, pp. 378-79; others suggest the maturity of believers: H.C. Shank, *More of Christ: Preliminary Thoughts Concerning a Reformed Antidote to the Current Charismatic Movement*, p. 23. In what sense the church was 'mature' as it moved toward its dark ages remains unclear.

b. The canon of Scripture, which, when completed, will need no revelatory gifts, which necessarily add to its material. See J. Walvoord, *The Holy Spirit* (Wheaton, IL: Van Kampen Press, 1954), pp. 178-79; W.E. Vine, *An Expository Dictionary of New Testament Words* (Old Tappan, NJ: Fleming H. Revill, 1966), p. 221; W.G. Bellshaw, 'The Confusion of Tongues', *BSac* 120 (April–June 1963), pp. 151-52; Toussaint, 'First Corinthians Thirteen and the Tongues Question', p. 314; and G.B. Weaver, 'Tongues Shall Cease', *GTJ* 14 (Winter 1973), p. 22. Thomas, in 'Tongues Will Cease' and in his later book, *Understanding Spiritual Gifts* (Chicago: Moody Press, 1978), p. 13, identifies τὸ τέλειον tentatively with both positions (canon and maturity of the church): 'Which of these would happen first the writer did not know'. Edgar, *Miraculous Gifts*, pp. 333-44, opts for a personal, rather than corporate, eschatology ('the individual's presence with the Lord') as identifying τὸ τέλειον, hence, the passage makes no statement as to the historical cessation of the gifts.

c. The millennium is the 'perfect', during which the charismata will be reactivated after their hiatus during the church age, according to C.R. Smith in his *Tongues in Biblical Perspective* (Winona Lake, IN: BMH Books, rev. edn, 1973). For a survey of other interpretations, see Graves, 'Tongues Shall Cease', pp. 22-28.

Against these positions see the arguments of Fee, *Corinthians*, pp. 644-45, Turner, 'Spiritual Gifts Then and Now', p. 37; Carson, *Showing the Spirit*, pp. 66-76; Grudem, *Prophecy in 1 Corinthians*, p. 210-19; K.S. Hemphill, 'The Pauline Concept of Charisma: A Situational and Developmental Approach' (PhD dissertation, Cambridge University, 1976), pp. 113-20, and F.F. Bruce, *Tradition Old and New* (London: Paternoster Press, 1970), pp. 14-15. Bruce shares the widespread Evangelical conviction that the chance that 'the concept of the completed New Testament canon was present in Paul's mind is extremely improbable'.

and a reference to its termination at the parousia.[1] This interpretation is justified for several reasons.

1. Among conservative Protestant commentators, F.F. Bruce, *The Letters of Paul: An Expanded Paraphrase* (Grand Rapids: Eerdmans, 1965), p. 107; *idem, 1 and 2 Corinthians* (London: Oliphants, 1971), p. 128; A. Clarke, *Clarke's Commentary*, IV (Abingdon: Cokesbury Press, n.d.), pp. 268-69; C.R. Erdman, *The First Epistle of Paul to the Corinthians* (Philadelphia: Westminster Press, 1948), pp. 122-23. Erdman, a Princeton Seminary contemporary of Warfield, has a difficult time with the implications of his own exegesis: '"They shall be done away". Let it be granted here that the spiritual gifts which had been bestowed on the Corinthian church were confined to the Apostolic Age. Though Paul does not here so affirm it, this limitation probably was a fact; it is rather certain that these exact gifts no longer exist. But the contrast here was not between the Apostolic Age and the present time, but between the present age as a whole and the future age which is to be ushered in by the return of Christ.' See also Hodge, *First Corinthians*, p. 272; Godet, *First Corinthians*, p. 250; F.W. Grosheide, *Commentary on First Corinthians* (NICNT; Grand Rapids: Eerdmans, 1953), pp. 309-10; E. Harrison, *Wycliffe Bible Commentary* (Chicago: Moody Press, 1962), p. 1252; C.F. Kling, *A Commentary on the First Epistle of Paul to the Corinthians* (Lange'sCom; New York: Charles Scribner's Sons, 5th edn, 1868), pp. 271-72; L. Morris, *The First Epistle of Paul to the Corinthians* (TNTC; Grand Rapids: Eerdmans, 1958), p. 187; Toussaint, 'First Corinthians Thirteen and the Tongues Question', p. 313; among others, commentaries by P.E.B. Allo, *Saint Paul Premièr Epître aux Corinthiens* (Paris: Le Coffre, 2nd edn, 1956), pp. 347-48; Barrett, *First Corinthians*, p. 306; F. Baudraz, *Les Epîtrès aux Corinthiens* (Geneva: Labor & Fides, 1965), p. 106; J. Hering, *La Première Epître de Saint Paul Aux Corinthiens* (Paris: Delachaux & Niestlé, 1949), p. 120; D.H. Lietzmann, *An Die Korinther, I, II* (Tübingen: Mohr, 1949), p. 66; H.A.W. Meyer, *First Corinthians* (MeyerK; New York: Funk & Wagnalls, 6th edn, 1884), p. 305: 'With the advent of the *parousia* the other charismata too (12.8ff.) surely cease altogether'. See also J. Moffat, *The First Epistle of Paul to the Corinthians* (New York: Harper, 1938), p. 201; Robertson and Plummer, *First Corinthians*, p. 297; H.-D. Wendland, *Die Briefe an die Korinther* (NTD, 7; Göttingen: Vandenhoeck & Ruprecht, 1961), p. 106.

In some related works: G. Bornkamm, *Das Ende des Gesetzes* (Munich: Chr. Kaiser Verlag, 1961), pp. 103-105; N. Hugedé, *La métaphor du miroir dans les Epîtres de Saint Paul aux Corinthiens* (Paris: Delachaux & Niestlé, 1927), p. 17; the Evangelical theologian, C.F.H. Henry, *Personal Christian Ethics* (Grand Rapids: Eerdmans, 1957), pp. 484-85; K. Maly, *Mundige Gemeinde* (Stuttgart: Katholische Bibelwerk, 1967), p. 195 and G. Delling, 'τέλος, κτλ', *TDNT*, VIII, pp. 75-76 and J. Schneider, 'μέρος', *TDNT*, IV, 4, p. 596.

See also the more developed arguments by Carson, *Showing the Spirit*, pp. 67-76, Fee, *Corinthians*, pp. 644-45 nn. 22 and 23; Grudem, *Prophecy in 1 Corinthians*, pp. 210-19 and *The Gift of Prophecy*, pp. 228-52; Hemphill, 'The

1. It is the unanimous testimony on the meaning of τὸ τέλειον in this context by some early church fathers who were embroiled in a cessationist controversy over Montanists who, like the Corinthians, claimed spiritual perfection attested by the gift of prophecy. These fathers also reacted against an alleged cessationist statement by a Montanist prophetess. They cite her as claiming: 'After me there will be no more prophecy, but the end (συντέλειαν)',[1] a probable reference to Jesus' use of the word in Mt. 28.20. A number of early fathers argue against cessationism by appealing to 1 Cor. 13.10 for rebuttal of that logion or to the Montanist claims to spiritual perfection. Eusebius records that Miltiades cites 1 Cor. 13.10 against Maximilla and concludes: 'it is necessary that the prophetic charisma be in all the Church until the final coming'.[2] Against the presently realized 'perfect' existence claimed by the Montanists, the fathers employed 1 Cor. 13.8-12, especially v. 10, to show that the 'perfection' (τὸ τέλειον) was yet future at the coming of Christ.[3]

2. The τὸ τέλειον of 13.10 is closely aligned with a similar eschatological context in 1.8 (τέλους), as discussed above. The point is made in both passages that spiritual gifts remain until the 'end'.

3. The τὸ τέλειον in the protasis of v. 10 stands in contrast to the ἐκ μέρους in the apodosis.[4] The 'complete' is contrasted with the 'incomplete' acquisition of knowledge via prophecy and revealed

Pauline Concept of Charisma', pp. 113-20, and Turner, 'Spiritual Gifts Then and Now', p. 39. Calvin, *First Corinthians*, p. 281, identifies the perfect with the 'last judgement' and remarks, 'it is stupid of people to make the whole of this discussion apply to the intervening time'.

1. Epiphanius, *Against Panarion* 48.5.4 (*PG* 41.855), cited in de Labriolle, *Sources*, p. 117: Μετ' ἐμέ προφήτις οὐκέτι ἔσται, ἀλλά συντέλειαν.

2. δεῖν γάρ εἶναι τό προφητικόν χάρισμα ἐν πασῇ τῇ ἐκκλησίᾳ μέχρι τῆς τελείας παρουσίας (*Against Alcibiades* in Eusebius, *Church History* 5.17.4).

3. Pseudo-Athanasus, in his *Dialogue of an Orthodox with a Montanist*, argues forcefully and in some detail from the whole passage against the Montanist position on spiritual perfection, and concludes by identifying the analogies in 13.11-12 (of childhood, seeing in a mirror and face to face, knowing partially and being fully known) with the τέλειον. Jerome, *Epistle* 41.5.35-36, also quotes 13.10 and 12 in the same context, making the same point, as does Augustine, in *Against Faustus*, 33.17.30 (*PL*, 42, 506 in Labriolle, pp. 185-86), in *On Heresies* 26.5, and again in *Praedestinatus* 1.26.5.

4. BAG, 'τέλειον', p. 816; esp. G. Delling, 'τέλειον', *TDNT*, VIII, p. 75: 'In the Pauline corpus the meaning "whole" is suggested at 1 C. 13.10 by the antithesis to ἐκ μέρους'.

knowledge in v. 9. Grudem notes that since the knowledge of the τὸ τέλειον is so great that it will render the present method of gaining knowledge useless (τὸ ἐκ μέρους καταργηθήσεται), only the consummation could qualify for such a contrast.[1]

4. Paul several times uses the term καταργέω in 1 Corinthians in ways parallel to the eschatological context here, in that the present expressions of 'this age' will be 'nullified' by the coming of the end: the 'things that are' (1.28); the rulers, authorities and powers of this age (2.6; 15.24); the stomach and food (6.13); and death (15.26).[2]

5. As we shall see below, the parallel analogies of vv. 11, 12 and 13 further confirm the view that τὸ τέλειον refers to the eschaton. The eschatological meaning of τὸ τέλειον, then, is essential to the passage it occupies. It is to an examination of that crucial verse that we now turn.

The grammar of inspired prediction of St Paul in v. 10 has great significance for the cessationist polemic: ὅταν δέ ἔλθῃ τὸ τέλειον, τὸ ἐκ μέρους καταργηθήσεται, 'but when the complete has come, at that point, the incomplete will be ended'. This contingent connection has been questioned by D.A. Carson, who, while agreeing that τὸ τέλειον refers to the second coming of Christ, nonetheless suggest that the gifts of prophecy and tongues in this context could disappear at any time preceding the parousia.[3] However, the grammar of this verse simply precludes that interpretation. ὅταν appears here with the aorist subjunctive (ἔλθῃ) in the subordinate clause, followed by the future passive καταργηθήσεται. Grammarian J.H. Moulton notes the significance of this pattern:

> One result of the aorist action has important exegetical consequences, which have been insufficiently observed. It affects relative, temporal or conditional clauses introduced by a pronoun or conjunction with ἄν.. . The verbs are all futuristic, and the ἄν ties them up to particular occurrences. . . The aorist, being future by virtue of its mood (subjunctive), punctiliar by its tense, and consequently describing complete action, gets a future-perfect sense in this class of sentence; and it will be found most important to note this before we admit a less rigid translation.[4]

1. Grudem, *Prophecy in 1 Corinthians*, p. 213.
2. *Prophecy in 1 Corinthians*, p. 214.
3. 'The Holy Spirit', *WTJ* 43 (Fall 1980), pp. 58-78.
4. J.H. Moulton, *Grammar of New Testament Greek* (Edinburgh: T. & T. Clark, 3rd edn, 1961), I, p. 186; III, p. 112. So also A.T. Robertson, *A Grammar of the Greek New Testament* (New York: G. Doran, 1914), pp. 972-73; BAG, p. 592a;

The implication for our translation, then, is that the partial (charismata) pass away, not simply 'when', 'whenever', or 'at the point of', but more precisely, 'immediately after' the appearance of the perfect, that is, the event which virtually *causes* the ἐκ μέρους to be ended. I am not arguing that these charismata will continue beyond the parousia for any significant length of time, but only that the grammar does not allow any cessation of the ἐκ μέρους, until the action referred to by ἔλθῃ τὸ τέλειον is complete. Again, the subjunctive ἔλθῃ in these contexts assumes a future perfect tense. Perhaps an even more precise paraphrase of the verse could be: 'When the perfect will have completely arrived, only at that point, and not a moment before, will the partial be ended'.[1]

Finally, the point of v. 10 is illustrated by the analogies of vv. 11, 12, and possibly 13; they repeatedly contrast the present age with the eschatological perfection to come.[2] In v. 11 Paul uses a personal example contrasting his imperfect level of speech and knowledge at infancy to that of adulthood. Some cessationists have insisted that this analogy applies best to the maturity of the church or individual believer, or the 'completion' of the church by the inclusion of the

---

BDF, §382; J.H. Thayer, *A Greek–English Lexicon of the New Testament* (Wheaton, IL: Evangel, 1974), p. 458b; J.H. Moulton and G. Milligan, *The Vocabulary of the Greek Testament* (London: Hodder & Stoughton, 1930), p. 462.

Carson, *Showing the Spirit*, p. 70, claims that this passage teaches that 'a charismatic gift or gifts could. . . have been withdrawn earlier than the parousia', for example, the gift of apostleship (1 Cor. 12.28). But on the basis of the grammar of this verse, and on the basis of the flow of Paul's argument throughout the epistle, it would appear that the *principle* Paul is attempting to establish is the contrast of the uniform (prescriptive) condition of this present age with its gifts, and their abrogation only at the appearance of the age to come. On the continuation of the gift of apostleship see the discussion on 1 Corinthians 12 and Ephesians 4, Appendix II, below.

1. Passages with similar grammatical structure are: Mt. 9.15; 10.19; 19.28; 25.31; Mk 2.20; 12.23, 25; Lk. 5.35; 9.26; 13.28; Jn 4.25; 7.31; 8.28; 15.26; 16.13; 21.18; Acts 23.25; 24.22; Rom. 11.27; 1 Cor. 15.28, 54; 16.3, 5; Col. 3.4; 2 Thess. 1.9-10; Rev. 11.7; 20.7.

It is interesting that some textual witnesses on this passage show a scribal tendency to enhance the 'then, and not until then' meaning of this verse by adding a τότε before ἐκ μέρους (K, L, Syr., Chrysostom, and others). See Robertson and Plummer, *First Corinthians*, p. 297 and N–A[26].

2. Again, this position is the consensus among the commentators.

Gentiles.[1] But as Carson and others have pointed out, such a leap from infancy to 'maturity' (if maturity is understood either in terms of theological awareness or praxis) on the basis of the completion of the canon of Scripture, the spiritual or ethical maturity of the church, or the inclusion of the Gentiles, 'is irrelevant to the context of 1 Cor. 13' and 'trivializes the language of verse 12'.[2] It is also historical nonsense, certainly if Warfield's dim view of the later post-apostolic church is our guide. Compared to the writings of the New Testament, Warfield would affirm that the writings of the second-century church show a significant *loss* of sophistication in terms of the depth of understanding and articulation of the Christian faith. This view also assumes the 'maturity' of the post-canonical church to be greater than Paul the Apostle himself, who admits that now he sees indistinctly and knows incompletely (1 Cor. 13.12). Moreover, was he saying that because the canon was completed, or because Gentiles entered the church, he would suddenly see 'face to face' and know even as God knows him? Was the 'maturity' of the church manifested in the fact that 'all Asia' abandoned Paul at the end of his ministry (2 Tim. 1.15; 4.16)? Or in the fact that throughout the Pastoral Epistles, written near the end of Paul's life, the apostle describes all kinds of strife, heresies and immoralities in the church? Is it because the church possessed a completed Bible or a body of established doctrine that it is called 'mature'? The Bible and orthodox doctrine were in the possession of the worst medieval popes, the driest of dead Protestant orthodoxy or liberalism, and indeed, of Satan himself!

Taken at face value, however, these cessationists, including Warfield, are saying that the 'maturity' or 'completion' of the church need not have anything to do at all with the individual believer, except that he or she has moved into a new historical epoch,[3] and in some undefined sense thereby 'participates' in the church's 'maturity'.

1. For example, J.R. McRay, 'Τό Τέλειον in 1 Corinthians 13.10', *RQ* 14 (1971), p. 183, who maintains that Paul is 'using τέλειος to mean the inclusion of the Gentiles' into the church, so that of Jew and Gentile 'God had created of the two one new man', though he also says that 'the generation upon whom he laid his hands and imparted χαρίσματα experienced τὸ τέλειον'. For others who interpret τὸ τέλειον as 'maturity' or as the completion of the canon see above.

2. Carson, *Showing the Spirit*, p. 71, and Turner, 'Spiritual Gifts Then and Now', p. 39.

3. The connection between the 'mature church' view of cessationism and Warfield's is apparent in the following quotations: 'Prophecy and miracle, word and

The maturity is the *event* of the canon's completion, or the inclusion of the Gentiles into the church. To say that when the ink dried on the last apostolic writing even a few in the church suddenly shifted into a new era of doctrinal awareness or sense of theological completion is historically naive. Not only were these writings not thoroughly disseminated, there was considerable debate for decades, if not centuries, as to what should be included in the canon. How could the writing of the last book of what was to become the canon have affected, at that point, the masses within the church?

This same view applies to the reception of the Spirit at Pentecost, where the 'church' receives the gift of prophecy promised in Joel 2 in a single historical incident, which seems to have the effect of leaving later members of the church to participate in this type of experience of the Spirit only vicariously or by imputation.[1] Similarly,

deed, inspiration and regeneration go hand in hand in the completion of special revelation. But when the revelation of God in Christ had taken place, and had become in Scripture and church a constituent part of the cosmos, then another era began. . . . It has not been God's way to communicate to each and every man a separate store of divine knowledge of his own, to meet his separate needs. . . . He has given to the world one organically complete revelation, adapted to all, sufficient for all, provided for all, and from this one completed revelation He requires each to draw his whole spiritual sustenance. Therefore it is that miraculous working which is but the sign of God's revealing power, cannot be expected to continue, and in point of fact does not continue, after the revelation of which it is the accompaniment has been completed' (Warfield, *Counterfeit Miracles*, pp. 26, 27).

1. For example, R.B. Gaffin, Jr, 'The Holy Spirit', *WTJ* 43 (Fall 1980), p. 74. On the basis of 1 Cor. 12.13 Gaffin says: 'All believers, without exception, share in the gift of the Spirit by virtue of their union with Christ, and correlatively, their incorporation into his body, the church, which he (permanently) baptized with the Spirit at Pentecost. The gift of the Spirit is present in the church on the principle of "universal donations"'. This universal 'gift' of the Spirit must be distinguished from his 'gifts', which are given on the 'principle of differential distribution. . . by divine design. . . and not because of lack of faith or the failure to seek a particular gift'. Gaffin's conception of the church as an abstraction somehow distinct from the sum of its members is puzzling: even with one's 'union with Christ' in what sense is the church 'permanently baptized'? How does every believer experience the singular historical event of Pentecost by 'universal donation'? By reading about it in the Bible? Gaffin's abstraction is a way of denying to future generations of Christians the personal participation in the characteristic and normative activities of the Spirit as they occurred at Pentecost. All this is simply another way of saying, 'the way the Spirit operates today is different than he operated at Pentecost: the Spirit today is limited to his role in the Calvinistic *ordo salutis* as well as to some other gifts which

the subsequent charismatic outpourings of the Spirit in the book of Acts are to be understood as having primarily 'epochal', and therefore by implication unrepeatable, significance for individuals, serving mainly as signs of the key, historically distinct stages of the church's expansion.[1]

We have seen that some have interpreted 1 Cor. 13.11 as referring to the immaturity of the Corinthian church which will move into adulthood at the completion of the canon of Scripture, or growth in love, or the inclusion of the Gentiles. But these interpretations suffer from either an anachronistic reading of dogmatics into this passage, or from forcing onto Paul's analogy a view of 'maturity' which is alien to the context and flow of his eschatological argument. Instead, v. 11 is an analogy contrasting infancy with adulthood in an *eschatological* framework, a point of view which supports, illustrates and mutually conditions the surrounding statements.

Upon what does this 'maturity' of the Corinthians depend? Not upon their own spiritual growth or upon reception of a canon of Scripture, but upon the second coming of Christ. Earlier (1 Cor. 2.6), Paul affirms that he speaks 'a message of wisdom among the mature (ἐν τοῖς τέλοις)'. But it is not a wisdom characteristic of those of this present age—of 'those being ended/abolished (τῶν καταρ-γουμένων)'. This secret wisdom has been hidden by God, but 'destined for our glory [an eschatological term] before time began' (1 Cor. 2.7). No human has seen, heard or even conceived of this wisdom which God has prepared (1 Cor. 2.9). Ignorance, then, is the condition of the present age, but yet, amazingly, the future has, in some sense, come: 'but God has revealed it to us by his Spirit' (v. 10)! Paul goes on to describe the astonishing scope of this present revelation in vv. 10-15, and summarizes the tension between the normal human condition and those 'mature' in the Spirit: '"For who

appear sovereignly "without regard to human faith, desire or denial"'. Gaffin's notion of contemporary believers' participation in the Holy Spirit seems closely related to Warfield's postulate (*Counterfeit Miracles*, p. 26) that the final revelation in Scripture precludes the 'mystic's dream': 'new and unneeded revelations into the world', that is, spiritual gifts. Cf. I.H. Marshall, 'The Significance of Pentecost', *SJT* 30.4 (1977), pp. 347-69.

1. For example, Warfield, *Counterfeit Miracles*, p. 23. In response to this position, see Carson, *Showing the Spirit*, pp. 137-58. For a review of Carson's position see Appendix II.

has known the mind of the Lord that he may instruct him?" But we have the mind of Christ'. But is this wisdom—this 'mind of Christ', which is revealed by the Spirit—complete in this age?

No. The tension is far from resolved, not only among the Corinthians, but also among the apostles. Regarding the Corinthians, while 'God's Spirit lives in' them (1 Cor. 3.16), they are not 'spiritual, but worldly [of this present age]—mere infants in Christ [unable to digest solid food, that is, the revealed wisdom of the age to come] . . . still worldly' (3.1, 2). Their wisdom, even revealed wisdom, and ability to judge are circumscribed by the present human limitations.

Hence, in the context of the Corinthians' attempting to use their revealed wisdom to judge others, Paul spells out necessary rules reflecting this limited condition. (1) The first rule recognizes that the present incompleteness will be ameliorated only by the coming of Christ: 'Therefore, judge nothing before the appointed time; wait till the Lord comes. He will bring to light what is hidden in darkness'. (2) The second rule showing the incompleteness of revealed wisdom is its dependence upon the established body of Christian doctrine: 'Do not go beyond what is written'—likely a reference to Old Testament Scripture (4.6) and, perhaps, the established tradition of the early church (4.7).[1] (3) Present revelation is incomplete and cannot, therefore, be grounds for boasting, since everything the Corinthians (or any other believer) have was given them from God or from others, who obviously have more than the ones receiving (4.7, cf. the discussion on 1.4 and 5, above).

Even Paul and Apollos share this present human condition of limited revelation (4.6, 3): 'God will judge, I do not even judge myself'; cf. 13.12, 'I know in part, I prophesy in part'. Paul has applied to himself (and, by implication, to other apostles) a principle of deference both to the eschatological judgment of Christ and to the limitations of Scripture and tradition (4.6)—all this because in the present age, revealed wisdom, the mind of Christ, is incomplete.[2]

---

1. Fee, *Corinthians*, pp. 167-69 and Barrett, *First Corinthians*, pp. 106-107.

2. Many of the same themes emerge in Rom. 11.34–12.12; that is, the quotation from Isa. 40.13 on the superiority of divine wisdom, the 'renewal of the mind' as opposed to conformity to the world, humility, to 'prophesy according to the measure of faith' (cf. above, to use 'wisdom' within limits of Scripture and tradition), and serving others during the eschatological 'affliction', 'in hope' (of the eschaton), not seeking judgment on others, but allowing the Lord to repay evil (v. 19).

This excursus on the nature of maturity in 1 Cor. 13.11 returns us to the original intent of Paul in this verse: that the comparison of infancy to adulthood is analogous to the contrast between this present age, with its limited speech and knowledge, and the age to come. A chart of the parallels in vv. 9-12 might be instructive. The four segments from left to right are vv. 9-12 which are to be read as divided into two temporal stages, the present and the age to come. Evidence that these verses are indeed parallel, repeating the same argument, lies in the fact that there are three elements in each verse: the imperfect/ immature perception in the present age, the transition event and the consequence. Each sentence is characterized by a 'now' and 'then' aspect, contrasting the quality of perception in the two ages.

Verses	9-10	11	12	
	(Now our) knowledge is imperfect prophecy is imperfect	I used to speak as a child think as a child reason as a child	Now I see dimly, indirectly	Now I know in part
	when the perfect comes the imperfect will be ended	when I became man I gave up infantile things	then I shall see face to face	then I shall know as fully as I am known

Thus Paul is continuing his argument about the value of spiritual gifts: the charismata are valuable and desirable in this present period, but when Christ returns, their usefulness is at an end. As Barth has written, 'because the sun is rising, all lights go out'.[1]

Verse 12 continues the parallel most clearly. The 'now' (ἄρτι) is twice contrasted with the 'but then' (τότε δέ). The ideas of revelation and knowledge are clearly present in the 'seeing indirectly or in a riddle' (ἐν αἰνίγματι), in a mirror,[2] and knowing and being known.

1. K. Barth, *The Resurrection of the Dead* (trans. H.J. Stenning; New York: Arno Press, 1977) p. 81.
2. The metaphor of the mirror here involves much more than a reflection in a simple looking glass (or polished metal). Mirror gazing (captromancy) had a connotation, without the modern negative aspects, of crystal-ball gazing, and, like the casting of lots (cf. Acts 1.26), was a fairly accepted form of prophecy or discerning mysteries among the rabbis and Greeks of the time. See R. Kittel, 'αἴνιγμα (ἔσοπτρον)', *TDNT*, I, pp. 178-80. But the point of the comparison seems simply to be the contrast of the (present) indirect vision, as opposed to the 'face to face'

As in vv. 9-11, these expressions of revelation and/or knowledge are seen as incomplete in contrast to the 'but then', where Paul (using himself as an example)[1] will 'see face to face' and 'know even as [he is] fully known'. Let us briefly examine two key elements in these contrasts.

The first illustration in v. 12 appears to be based, at least partly, on Num. 12.8, where 'we', like the prophets and unlike Moses, receive revelation δι' ἐσόπτρου ἐν αἰνίγματι rather than 'mouth to mouth' or 'face to face', as in the language of theophany.[2] We are not to construe the present vision, the gifts of the Spirit, as distorted or false, but merely indirect, and therefore, as in the other illustrations in this context, incomplete when compared to the presence of God in the age to come.[3]

The second illustration in v. 12 repeats this point: 'in the present I know in part [ἐκ μέρους, paralleling the use of ἐκ μέρους in vv. 9 and 10], but then, I shall know to the extent that (καθώς)[4] I was fully known'. Again, the ἐκ μέρους appears in the same context, and is contrasted with the time when Paul will know 'exactly as' or 'to the extent that' God knew him on earth. The passive here (ἐπεγνώσθην) is most likely a divine passive.[5] The aorist suggests a point of view in

vision (of God) in the age to come. So Hugedé, *La métaphor du miroir*, pp. 145-50 and the consensus of commentators.

1. For the apostle Paul to use himself as example here has important implications for cessationists who feel τὸ τέλειον is the canon of Scripture or the maturity of the church. Even an apostle like Paul, upon whom canonical revelation and doctrine is based, finds himself in the same position with respect to divine revelation as his Corinthian readers: in a time of incomplete revelation, both await the same full revelation of God's knowledge. In light of the church's checkered history, will such cessationists argue that the revelation in the canon, or the maturity of the church, has surpassed that of the apostles? Paul himself acknowledges that in this life he is not yet 'mature' (Phil. 3.12).

2. See Grudem, *Prophecy in 1 Corinthians*, p. 147, who notes that in the Septuagint, πρόσωπον πρὸς (or κατὰ) πρόσωπον 'is clearly used of seeing God personally, as in a theophany'; see Gen. 32.30; Deut. 5.4; 34.10; Judg. 6.22; Ezek. 20.35; cf. Exod. 33.11.

3. So Grudem, *Prophecy in 1 Corinthians*, pp. 145-50; Carson, *Showing the Spirit*, pp. 71-72; Fee, *Corinthians*, pp. 647-49; Meyer, *First Corinthians*, pp. 306-307.

4. Fee, *Corinthians*, p. 649, notes that Paul uses this word 25 times, in every case with the connotation, 'exactly as', or, 'it makes an exact comparison'.

5. Meyer, *First Corinthians*, p. 307.

the eschaton, set by the future tense of ἐπιγνώσομαι, hence almost a pluperfect sense: 'I will know to the extent I *had been* known'. Verse 13 seems to carry on the argument of vv. 9-12, though less clearly.

Verse 13 represents another possible parallel to the foregoing. The beginning of this section, vv. 8-13, begins with 'Love never ends'—implying that other things will. As the argument develops, the charismata are shown to contrast with love: while the charismata are operative in this age, love is superior in that it is the same taste of heaven in the 'now', but unlike the charismata, will continue in heaven. There is little disagreement among the commentators on this point.

But is there a further parallel to those of vv. 9-12 in v. 13? Barrett, Carson and others[1] have argued that Paul is not making the same analogy which contrasts the permanence of love with the temporary nature of faith and hope, thereby paralleling faith and hope with the charismata. But Calvin and the majority of commentators in the older Christian tradition, according to Meyer, argue otherwise.[2] Other Pauline texts show that faith which becomes sight is no longer faith, nor is hope which is realized (Rom. 8.24-25; 2 Cor. 5.6-10; 4.17-18). Moreover, faith is listed as a charism in 1 Cor. 12.9, and, more importantly, as miracle-working faith in the present context (13.2). Further, the overall argument, contrasting love with the temporary characteristics of the present Christian life, would also support the contrast of love with the 'temporary' faith and hope. If, however, the use of μένει for faith and hope suggests that they will 'remain' past the coming of Christ, then, 'the eschatological intention [of Paul] is by no means lost'.[3]

Paul then spells out how this love is applied to the actual situation in Corinth. He wishes that they 'all spoke with tongues', as he did (1 Cor. 14.5, 18). But because of its superior power to edify both the church and visitors, unless the tongues are interpreted, prophecy is far more desirable in the congregational setting. Nevertheless, Paul does

---

1. Barrett, *First Corinthians*, pp. 308-11; Carson, *Showing the Spirit*, pp. 72-76; Bultmann, 'ἐλπίς, κτλ', *TDNT*, II, pp. 530-33; and 'πίστις, κτλ', *TDNT*, VI, p. 221; Conzelmann, *First Corinthians*, pp. 230-31; Meyer, *First Corinthians*, pp. 308-10.

2. Meyer, *First Corinthians*, p. 308; Baudraz, *Corinthians*, p. 107; Hering, *Corinthians*, p. 212-13; Calvin, *First Corinthians*, pp. 282-85; Fee, *Corinthians*, p. 651.

3. Conzelmann, *First Corinthians*, p. 231.

not throw out the charismatic baby with the bath-water of conflict: 'be eager to prophesy, and do not forbid speaking with tongues. But everything should be done in a fitting and orderly way' (1 Cor. 14.39, NIV). These themes dealing with the proper use of the charismata that Paul has established in the passages reviewed above recur not only throughout 1 Corinthians, but also throughout the Pauline and other New Testament writings. In them we hear echoes of Paul's thanksgiving for God's graces given through the exalted Christ to the readers, who are enriched and edified in every form of wisdom and knowledge via the revelations they received, continuing until they are found blameless at the end of the age. In all the surveys of these familiar passages, it is important to remember that the terms 'grace',[1]

---

1. Conzelmann, 'χάρις, κτλ', *TDNT*, IX, pp. 372-415, notes that in the New Testament, '*Charis* shows affinity to the ordinary use of πνεῦμα. χάρις, like πνεῦμα, is given both for the moment and lastingly' (p. 392). 'Specifically Pauline is the use of the word to expound the structure of the salvation event. The linguistic starting-point is the sense of "making glad by gifts"' (p. 394). John Nolland ('Grace as Power', *NovT* 28 [October 1986]) follows the thesis of G.P. Wetter, *Χάρις: Ein Beitrag zur Geschichte des altesten Christentums* (Leipzig: Hinrichs, 1913), cited by W. Grundmann, 'δύναμαι/δύναμις', *TDNT*, II, p. 311 n. 90, and takes Conzelmann to task for taking an overly-traditionalist view of the action of grace, that is, as supernatural power (p. 376), but power focused on 'overcoming sin' (p. 395). While this is certainly a major objective of God's grace, Nolland demonstrates the more specific *activity* of χάρις, which appears in the LXX and in the New Testament as 'a tangible [charismatic] power in the believer' ('Grace as Power', p. 31). Nolland makes an even stronger case for the writings of Luke in 'Luke's Use of Χάρις', *NTS* 32 (October 1986), p. 615, where he argues that 'Luke's major use of χάρις is in reference to a tangible divine power dramatically present with Jesus and the church of Acts'. Dunn makes the same point in *Jesus and the Spirit*, pp. 202-205: 'For Paul grace means *power*, an otherly power at work in and through the believer's life, the *experience* of God's Spirit. . . Paul's most earnest and constant wish for his converts is that they may experience grace, may know ever afresh the gracious power of God existentially moving in and upon their lives'. Certainly, as we view the uses of χάρις in the context of church ministries and spiritual gifts, this usage also seems most reasonable in Paul. Warfield (*Counterfeit Miracles*, pp. 3-4) wished to distinguish between the 'ordinary' and 'extraordinary' gifts of the Spirit, 'that is [those] which were distinctively *gracious*, and those which were distinctively *miraculous*' (italics mine). Again on p. 23 Warfield insists that the whole Samaritan episode in Acts 8 'was of great importance in the primitive church, to enable men to distinguish between the gifts and grace and the gifts of power. Without it there would have been danger that only those would be accredited as Christians who possessed extraordinary gifts'.

'wisdom/knowledge', 'body' (as a metaphor of the church), 'power', and above all, 'Spirit', must be defined according to Warfield's principle of 'scripture interpreting scripture', that is, 'gaining the exact sense of the words' by comparing them with other, more descriptive, contexts, particularly the ones just reviewed. But we need not expend much effort on showing the charismatic characteristics of these terms, since Warfield has not only conceded, but warmly affirmed, that during the time these letters were written, spiritual gifts were widespread in the church. Those who took part in 'ordinary church worship. . . might often have a miraculous gift to exercise, "a revelation, a tongue, an interpretation", as well as "a psalm or a teaching"'. Warfield also lists miracles of healing, of power, of knowledge, of prophecy and the discernment of spirits.[1] Despite this concession, the following investigation must continue to point out the charismatic elements in the passages where there may be doubt over actual reference to them in the text. Once this is established the study then concentrates upon the issue of their continuation.

Ephesians 4.7-13. Eph. 4.7-13 reiterates the themes of 1 Corinthians[2] to affirm that the gifts of the exalted Christ, which are required for the upbuilding of the church, continue until certain ideal eschatological goals are achieved by everyone in the Christian community.[3] Briefly, this survey examines the context of the passage

1. Warfield, *Counterfeit Miracles*, pp. 4-5.

2. Dunn, *Jesus and the Spirit*, p. 347, notes the 'obvious parallels between Eph. 4.3. and 1 Cor. 12.13, between Eph. 4.7 and Rom. 12.3; 1 Cor. 12.11 ('to each'), and between Eph. 4.12-16, Rom. 12.4-7, and 1 Cor. 12.14-27. It is eminently arguable that these parallels are not merely formal, but reflect the actual parallel between the situations envisaged in Eph. 4 and that of Rom. 12, 1 Cor. 12 (see also Eph. 4.25; 5.30); in which case the "gifts" of 4.11 are less likely to be offices, and we would probably be better advised to understand them more as regular ministries, like the prophets and teachers of 1 Cor. 12.28 and the "overseers and deacons" of Phil. 1.1'.

3. Barth, *Ephesians* 4–6, p. 437; 'In 4.11 it is assumed that the church at all times needs the witness of "apostles" and "prophets". . . Ephesians 4 does not contain the faintest hint that the charismatic character of all church ministries was restricted to a certain period in church history and was later to die out'. He notes Calvin's position on the transmutation of the functions of apostles, prophets and evangelists into the preaching of the gospel by pastors and teachers, and concludes, 'thus he sought to refute the Roman Catholic doctrine regarding the transition of

and certain key elements within the passage itself, specifically focusing on the nature of the gifts and their time of termination.

> 7 To each one of us was given grace according to the measure of the gift of Christ. 8 Because it says, 'Having ascended on high, he led captivity captive; he gave gifts to mankind'. 9 (How can it mean, 'he ascended' unless he also 'descended' into the lower, earthly part? 10 The 'one descending' is one and the same as the 'one ascending' far above all the heavens, in order that he might fill everything). 11 He gave some apostles, some prophets, some evangelists, some pastor-teachers 12 for the training of the saints, for the work of service, for the building of the body of Christ, 13 until we all arrive at the unity of the faith and of the full knowledge of the Son of God, toward a complete adult, toward the measure of the stature of the fullness of Christ.

The context of Eph. 4.7-13 is an appeal for love and 'the unity of the Spirit' within the congregation. Paul echoes his unity theme from 1 Cor. 12.4-6, 13 in Eph. 4.3 and 5 ('one body and one Spirit', and 'one Lord, one faith, one baptism, one God and Father of us all'). Another theme is unity in diversity in the use of spiritual gifts distributed by the sovereign Lord. Paul employs virtually the same words as in 1 Corinthians ('To each was/is given. . . '), and certainly the same general concepts. As in 1 Corinthians and Romans 12, he employs the 'body' metaphor to describe the operation of spiritual gifts (4.4, 12, 16). And finally, the goal of the spiritual gifts is not accreditation, but upbuilding of those in Christ, ('according to the empowering distributed to each single part, [Christ] makes for the growth of the body upbuilding itself in love').

The nature of the gifts requires review. First, as in all the previously discussed passages, the parenetic emphasis concerning the gifts points out their grace-quality and their source in the exalted Christ (v. 7). The controversial[1] quotation from Ps. 68.18 referring to Christ also suggests to every Christian reader a paradigm of earthly ministry, and perhaps battle and suffering, before entering into an exalted state of ultimate rule.[2] Secondly, the extent of the giftedness

---

apostolic authority to the bishops and the pope'. In apparent response, Barth affirms, 'The author of this epistle did not anticipate that the inspired and enthusiastic ministry was to be absorbed by, and "disappear" into offices and officers'. See Appendix II: 'Does the Spiritual Gift of Apostleship also Continue?'

1. See Barth's survey, *Ephensians 4–6*, pp. 472-77.

2. Dunn, *Jesus and the Spirit*, §55, 'Sharing in Christ's Sufferings', pp. 326-38: 'To experience the exalted Christ therefore is to experience not merely new life but

bestowed on believers is qualified by 'the measure of the gift of Christ (κατὰ τὸ μέτρον τῆς δωρεᾶς τοῦ Χριστοῦ)'. There may be two equally legitimate interpretations here. First, we might say that κατὰ τὸ μέτρον means 'within the limits of the distribution pattern with which Christ measures out' the gifts, implying that the recipients should neither belittle anyone's gifts, including their own, nor over-exalt certain gifts, but should preserve the productive diversity of charismata which together upbuild the whole body. Secondly, κατὰ τὸ μέτρον might mean 'equal to', or 'to the extent of' the quality and/or abundance of Christ's giftedness. Interpreting κατὰ τὸ μέτρον in v. 7 in the first sense may reflect a similar reference in 4.16 (cf. 1 Cor. 12.7, 27). But even in 4.16 the ideal of each part (gift) operating ἐν μέτρῳ seems to refer, not only to 'operating within the limitations of', but also to the 'extent' or 'full potential' of each part of the body which contributes toward mutual upbuilding. This is certainly a strong theme in Rom. 12.3-8;[1] 1 Cor. 12-14; and 1 Pet. 4.10, where

new life which is life through death, life out of death, and which always retains that character. As soon as the exalted Christ is separated from the crucified Jesus, charismatic experience loses its distinctive Christian yardstick. . . and character'.

1. Rom. 12.3 uses μέτρον in this context: '[You believers are not to] think of yourself more highly than you ought, but soberly to evaluate yourself in accordance with the measure of faith God has distributed to each (ἑκάστῳ ὡς ὁ θεὸς ἐμέρισεν μέτρον πίστεως)'. Superficially, one's status in the community appears to depend on the level of faith imparted: if one is allotted great faith, one will be great in the church and vice versa, as C.E.B. Cranfield suggests in his, '"Μέτρον πίστεως" in Romans 12.3', *NTS* 8 (1961–62), pp. 345-51. Against this notion, one could argue that competition and status-seeking represent a striving to compensate for powerlessness, that is, fear, which is a condition of faithlessness. Hence, when God distributes faith, the recipient's position on earth is secure in God who will vindicate all slights: he or she is empowered enough to be 'weak'; confident enough to be a humble servant. The implication then, is not that God distributes various amounts of faith to different people, which should result in different levels of status, but that the great measure of faith distributed by God to all should be reflected in a great measure of humility and service.

Clearly, while all this is true, and even relevant to the passage, its central meaning is lost, since the above interpretation does not explain a parallel pattern in v. 6: 'if one's gift is prophesying, let him use it in proportion to his faith (κατὰ τὴν ἀναλογίαν τῆς πίστεως). Here the meaning seems to be, as in v. 3, 'Know your spiritual limitations: if you do not have the revelation of faith for a certain gift or job, do not attempt it in "the flesh"'. See Dunn, *Jesus and the Spirit*, pp. 211-12, who cites F.J. Leenhardt, *The Epistle to the Romans* (London: Lutterworth, 1961): 'The

the believers, toward the goal of upbuilding in love, are encouraged to use their gifts diligently to their full extent. We should further note that the object of the measure in Eph. 4.7 is not Christ, but the gift of Christ, implying not only that Christ was distributing the gifts, as is clear from other verses, but also that the gifts are given, ideally at least, to the extent Christ was gifted (cf. Jn 14.12).[1] μέτρον is also used in the sense of 'extent' in v. 13, when it refers to the goal of ultimate maturity: 'toward the measure of (εἰς μέτρον) the stature of the fullness of Christ'.

κατὰ τὸ μέτρον can be interpreted as 'to the extent or quality of' Christ's gift, if we consider the following. Paul in Ephesians is emphasizing and encouraging the present experience of life in the Spirit-power of the age to come. In contrast to his teaching against the 'over-realized eschatology' of the Corinthians, his claim that the charismata are restricted in both quality and duration, Paul in Ephesians emphasizes the exalted position of the believer (for example

expression [of prophecy] should neither fall short of, nor exceed the controlling inspiration' (310). In 1 Pet. 4.10, the use of καθώς (*to the degree that* one has received a gift) implies support for this interpretation. Because of Rom. 12.3, most commentators now reject the older suggestion that the 'analogy of faith' means 'according to a standard of doctrine'. See W. Sandy and A.C. Hedlam, *The Epistle to the Romans* (ICC; Edinburgh: T. & T. Clark, 5th edn, 1971), pp. 356-57 and Warfield, 'The Westminster Doctrine of the Holy Spirit'.

However, among earlier prominent Protestant commentators, see first the ambiguous position of W.G.T. Shedd, *A Critical and Doctrinal Commentary upon the Epistle of Paul to the Romans* (New York: Charles Scribner's Sons, 1879), pp. 363-64: 'subjective faith is meant. . . communicating only what God has revealed to him', though later he adds the more traditional caveat, insisting also on 'the objective rule of faith'. A prophecy must harmonize with that body of doctrine which has come down from the beginning. No alleged Christian tenet can be correct which conflicts with other Christian tenets. C. Hodge, *A Commentary on the Epistle to the Romans* (New York: Armstrong, rev. edn, 1878), p. 615, is more traditional. After exploring more subjective interpretations of faith in this passage, he decides that the 'analogy of the faith' is conformity to 'instructions of men whose inspiration was beyond doubt', that is, the apostles and their Scriptures (p. 621). He recognizes, however, that this understanding is denied by many of the strict philological interpreters'. R. Haldane, an even earlier influential Protestant commentator, opts for the canon of Scripture as the analogy of faith (*Exposition of the Epistle to the Romans* [New York: Robert Carter, 5th edn, 1847], p. 547).

1. This seems to be the point of Acts 1.8-9 when Luke alludes to the account of the Spirit's transfer from Elijah to Elisha in 2 Kgs 2.1-18.

2.6, 'seated us with [God] in heavenly realms') and uses much more expansive and enthusiastic language about the apparently limitless nature of the grace gifts in this age (for example 1.7-8, 18-19, 22; 2.7; 3.16, 19-20). So when Paul describes the grace given to 'each of us', 'according to the gift of Christ', he perhaps has in mind the tradition that Jesus received the Spirit 'without measure or restriction'[1] and that to this 'extent' the abundance of spiritual gifts is supplied here to the believers. It may well have been, however, that this Ephesian emphasis on being 'seated in heavenly realms' and the somewhat more blurred distinction between the extent of God's Spirit in the present and future represented an early emphasis in Paul's gospel. It may have been this presentation, filled with spiritual excitement and a sense of the 'presence of the future', that caused the Corinthians to err into their 'over-realized' eschatology.[2] Consequently, in contrast to Eph. 3.7, Paul was forced to clarify to the Corinthians the extent and limitation of the charismata in this present age, even though in the age to come the Spirit may be in some sense bestowed 'without measure', or perhaps to the ultimate 'measure of Christ's gift'. Whatever the precise meaning of κατὰ τὸ μέτρον, referring to either 'distribution' or 'abundance' of spiritual gifts or a blend of the two, the actual listing of the gifts in this passage remain the same.

The specific gifts from the exalted Christ mentioned in v. 11 are 'apostles, prophets, evangelists, and pastor-teachers'. The gift of apostles, of course, appeared also in the lists of charismata in 1 Cor. 12.28 and 29. Both lists contain a problem which is central to the issue of cessationism, namely, the appearance of 'apostles'.[3]

It may be significant that each of these 'gifts' in Eph. 4.11 is a category of person; the idea of 'office' here seems alien, at least in the more modern ecclesiastical sense. In keeping with the metaphor of Psalm 68, these people could be considered slaves with certain abilities who were captured from the slavery of this world and given to the church by the exalted Lord. This is not only the case for Paul, who sees himself as a 'slave' in service to the church (2 Cor. 4.5) and to God (Rom. 1.1; Gal. 1.10; Eph. 6.6), but indeed, all members of the

---

1. K. Deissner, 'μέτρον, κτλ', *TDNT*, IV, p. 634.

2. So Hurd, *Origin of 1 Corinthians*, p. 285, where he lists the characteristics of the Corinthian community indicating their belief they were 'living proleptically in the Kingdom'.

3. See Appendix II below.

church have been 'redeemed' (Gal. 4.5; Tit. 2.14), or 'purchased' (1 Cor. 6.20; 7.23; 1 Pet. 2.1) from a condition of slavery. So perhaps, in the above sense, they are given as gifts to each other. Certainly this parallels the metaphor in 1 Corinthians 12 of bodily members or charismatic functions given as gifts to the church.

The implication of the Ephesian metaphor for cessationism hangs on the use of 'he gave' (ἔδωκεν, aorist)[1] in v. 11. Was this a singular, punctiliar act as some would say the aorist tense implies? If so, this would argue for the uniqueness and cessation of the apostles and prophets.[2] But it would also require the cessation of the other categories of ministry, evangelists and pastor-teachers, since they are placed in parallel construction and are characterized by the accusative plural endings. If the giving of these gifted people to the church is an ongoing process, then similarly, there is no exegetical warrant for artificially dividing these ministries into categories of 'extraordinary' and 'ordinary', suggesting that one group is no longer given by the victorious Lord but that the other continues. Exegetically, the gifts continue or cease as a single group. But is the giving of apostles, prophets and others an ongoing process?

The time of termination for the gifts in v. 11 is explicit from the relationship of the main verb, ἔδωκεν, and the preposition, μεχρί ('until'). The purpose of (πρός) the gifts of some apostles, prophets, evangelists and pastor-teachers is the training of the saints, specifically, 'for' or 'directed toward' (εἰς) the work of ministry, for (εἰς) the upbuilding of the body of Christ. All this is to continue 'until' (μέχρι) a certain goal is achieved. What is that goal?

1. The use of the aorist here may possibly reflect the writer's lack of awareness of any problem relating to the continuation of these gifts. Because of his eschatological expectations, he may have failed to envision a further generation of ministries emerging in the church before the coming of Christ. More likely, he is simply preserving the tense of the quotation from Psalm 68. In any case, the commitment of the author is that the subsequent ideal goals for these gifts represent a clear, fully eschatological end for their duration.

2. As Stagg and Carson have shown, the aorist tense cannot be limited simply to punctiliar action in the sense of 'once and for all in the past', but, depending on the context, can denote repetitive and even future continuous action; F. Stagg, 'The Abused Aorist', *JBL* 91 (June 1972), pp. 222-32 and Carson, *Exegetical Fallacies*, pp. 69-75. Hence, the gifts of the exalted Christ could be given continuously to the church.

Where πρὸς/εἰς/εἰς describes the function of these gifts (training for ministry and upbuilding), μέχρι defines their duration in terms of a specific standard of spiritual development: '*until* we all arrive at the unity of the faith and of the full knowledge of the Son of God, at a complete adult, at the measure of the stature of the fullness of Christ'. Several observations are in order. First, note that the standard to be reached is essentially perfection: *all* of the church (no possibility for laggards or the immature) are to attain the following: first, 'the unity of the faith'. Whether this refers to unity of doctrine[1] or of their power of faith, or to unity generally, can anyone argue that this goal was achieved fully at any time in either the New Testament or in subsequent church history? Does it occur now? Certainly not over cessationism! If not, the goal remains unreached. The second goal is 'the full knowledge of the Son of God'. Do any spiritual gifts, religious experiences, the completed canon of Scripture, the creeds, or even the millions of words expounding them lead the church to a 'full knowledge' of Christ? Do any of these means even have the capacity to lead 'all' the church into such knowledge? The third goal is the state of being 'a complete man' or 'adult'. This could speak of a certain level of maturity attainable in this age (1 Cor. 2.6; 14.20; Phil. 3.15; Heb. 5.14), but more likely follows the image of 1 Cor. 13.11 ('when I became a man'),[2] and as such represents a purely eschatological state. The fourth goal is 'the measure of the stature of the fullness of Christ'. To claim that all in the church have reached the same level of maturity as Christ is, to say the least, grandiose.

Even Paul the apostle has not reached this goal. This is true for the following reasons. First, the 'we' ending of καταντήσωμεν includes the writer[3] who expects to be among those who remain in the present

---

1. On this passage see especially J. Calvin, *Sermons on Ephesians* (Carlisle, PA: Banner of Truth Press, 1973), p. 381, on 'the unity of the faith', which emerges 'in the age of perfection'. Earlier he argues that this condition is fulfilled only eschatologically, when 'we shall see Him face to face [1 Jn 3.3]'. At the present life, 'we see in part, and we know in part [1 Cor. 13.9], for as yet we walk but in faith'.

2. So A. Oepke, 'ἀνήρ', *TDNT*, I, p. 363. Also Calvin, *Sermons on Ephesians*, p. 381: 'St Paul says that we shall never be at the full measure of our stature until we are rid of this body. So then, the spiritual age of Christians is attained when they are gone out of this world'.

3. Eph. 1.1 and 3.1 so identify the writer, hence, for Warfield, against a great deal of contemporary controversy about a later authorship of this epistle, the case is closed.

'until'. Secondly, the verb καταντήσωμεν appears in the subjunctive mood, representing both Paul and the church in a counterfactual or at least a contingent situation. Thirdly, in Phil. 3.11-16 Paul shows that for him this goal or a very similar one remains unreached: 'Not that I have already attained this or already have become perfected... I do not consider myself to have taken hold of it'. He insists that he is still striving toward the goal of knowing Christ 'in the power of his resurrection and the sharing of his sufferings' and continues in this present time to pursue the 'goal of the high calling of God in Christ Jesus'. He further urges that 'those of us who are "mature" (τέλειοι)' should recognize this tension between a partly realized, but still future, eschatological maturity, 'and if you think otherwise, God will reveal that to you also'. Fourthly, even if one should deny the apostle's own insistence that he, in Eph. 4.13, had not personally reached that goal, the criterion for the cessation of the gifts mentioned remains impossibly inclusive and exhaustive: everyone ('we all') in the whole of the Christian community is to equal the 'stature of the fullness of Christ' at or near the end of the apostolic age. Fifthly, v. 14 further develops the contrast between the present infantile state of both the readers and the writer (ἵνα μηκέτι ὦμεν νήπιοι) and the fullness of Christ to come (cf. v. 15). It is conceivable that the maturity Paul describes in v. 13 is not fully eschatological at all, since it is lived out in vv. 14-16 in contemporary expression. The ἵνα, 'so that' (v. 14), connects a present world situation to be overcome (the 'winds' [or spirits or prophecies] of false doctrines), with the maturity of v. 13, while vv. 15-16 is a exhortation to practice lovingly various spiritual gifts to upbuild the Ephesian church.

But even here the goals are expressed as above: 'so that (ἵνα) we may no longer be infants' (expressed in a counterfactual or contingent subjunctive, ὦμεν, affirming that they are now infants, not mature). Further, the goal for the reader (and the writer), 'that we might grow up into [Christ the Head] in every respect', is expressed in another counterfactual subjunctive, αὐξήσωμεν ('we might grow') requiring the understanding that they, and even Paul, have not yet attained that goal.

Eph. 4.7-13, then, serves as a parallel to 1 Cor. 1.4-9 and 13.8-13 in that the operations of spiritual gifts are to continue until 'the end', 'the parousia', or 'the coming of our Lord Jesus Christ'. The Ephesians passage, however, describes 'the end' in terms of the ultimate spiritual growth of the believer into the absolute 'full measure of perfection found in Christ' (NIV). Like 1 Cor. 13.11, Eph. 4.13 uses the metaphor of the mature person to portray the heavenly state of believers.

The themes of the three passages investigated above recur in those below which are treated more briefly; that is, the idea that in this present time the kingdom of God is advanced through the characteristically charismatic Spirit for strengthening, confirming and edifying the church via the whole range of spiritual gifts until the end of this present age at the second coming of Christ and the church's entrance into heavenly glory.

Shorter Studies on Key Passages relating to Cessationism
Besides Eph. 4.7-11, above, several other Ephesian passages illustrate the themes of each member mutually upbuilding the body in love via the operations of the Spirit toward the eschatological goal of identity with Christ. These are echoed by similar passages from several other New Testament epistles.

Ephesians 1 initiates a major theme of charismatic activity in that it has some important references to the work of revelatory charismata and works of divine power in the church. Paul begins the epistle by affirming that God already 'has blessed us with every kind of spiritual blessing ($\pi\acute{\alpha}\sigma\eta$ $\varepsilon\acute{\upsilon}\lambda o\gamma\acute{\iota}\alpha$ $\pi\nu\varepsilon\upsilon\mu\alpha\tau\iota\kappa\widehat{\eta}$, v. 3)[1] in Christ'. To exclude the full range of charismata from this would be perilous, for in the following verses (1.8, 9, 17-20, cf. 1 Cor. 1.4-8), he describes these riches more fully as being specifically the 'abounding grace' of 'all wisdom and understanding', 'a Spirit of wisdom and revelation', and a power that is the same as that which raised Christ from the dead, that is, the so-called 'extraordinary' charismata.

Ephesians 1.13-14. The eschatological terminal point of the charismata emerges in the following verses (1.13-14):

1. Barth, *Ephesians 1–3*, pp. 101-102, suggests that the term, 'spiritual blessings' refers to something 'belonging to the heavenly world', or to 'special (charismatic) gifts of God. . . whose meaning can be understood and explained through spiritual interpretation, by inspired men only'; 'above all, those things or events are called "spiritual" that are a result and evidence of the presence of the Spirit'. Evidence of this spiritual blessing is: 'Now they cry "Abba, Father". . . now manifold "spiritual gifts" (charismata) are manifest among them. Obviously they offer tangible evidence of God's blessing'.

13 In (Christ), when you believed, you were marked with a seal, the
promised Holy Spirit, 14 who is a down-payment guaranteeing
(ἀρραβών) our inheritance until (εἰς) the redemption of the possession—
to the praise of his glory.

Here Paul describes the Spirit acting as a 'seal', that is, a stamp of
ownership, which warns all who see it that the believer is under God's
protection.[1] Another metaphor, that of the ἀρραβών, also comes into
play. Both figures, referring to the Spirit (seal and downpayment),[2]
carry eschatological significance as to how long the charismatic Spirit
operates among the readers. Specifically, he continues his charismatic
work in the believers *until* (εἰς) they receive the full redemption of
the possession, in other words, when believers receive the fullness of
the Spirit at the consummation of the kingdom.

Ephesians 1.17-21. In 1.17-21, yet again, this same pattern of spiritual
gifts at work throughout the time before the eschaton is repeated. As
in 1 Cor. 1.4-8, Paul gives thanks for them, and keeps asking that

17 the God of our Lord Jesus Christ, the glorious Father, may give you
the Spirit of wisdom and revelation in the full knowledge of him. 18 I
pray also that the eyes of your heart may be enlightened in order that you
may know the hope to which he has called you, the riches of his glorious
inheritance in the saints, 19 and his incomparably great power for us who
believe, according to the working of his mighty strength, 20 which he
exerted when he raised him from the dead and seated him at his right hand
in the heavenly realms, 21 far above all rule and authority, power and
dominion, and every title that can be given, not only in the present age,
but also in the age to come.

---

1. According to G. Fitzer, 'σφραγίς, κτλ', *TDNT*, VII, p. 949, the Holy Spirit
'is now the seal with which the believer is marked, appointed and kept for the
redemption. It shows that he is God's possession *until* [italics mine] the day of
redemption'. The visible expression of the seal of the Spirit, according to Barth in his
Ephesians 1–3, is, at base the gift of prophecy (p. 142), but it is wider than that: it is
'an exhibition of God's love and power' (p. 141).

2. See the discussion on ἀρραβών as a downpayment of the Spirit above, and
J. Behm, 'ἀρραβών', *TDNT*, I, p. 475: 'The Spirit who God has given them is for
Christians the guarantee of their full possession of salvation'. The ἀρραβών is the
essence of the full payment, just as two similar concepts, 'firstfruits' (ἀπαρχή) and
'taste' (γεύομαι), also apply to the reality of the powers of the Spirit which exist in
the present age and the age to come (2 Cor. 5.5; Eph. 1.14; Rom. 8.23; Heb. 6.4, 5)
during the 'time between the times'.

This passage is full of implications for cessationism. First, the Spirit is characterized by 'wisdom and revelation', again, two of the charismata, and by extension, further characterized as an 'incomparably great power' (v. 19). Secondly, Paul is praying that his readers may know (in the biblical sense of 'experience'), 'his incomparably great power (δύναμις) for us who believe[1] [present participle, πιστεύοντας, or, believers in general]'. This power is described as 'like' (κατά with the accusative)[2] the power of the resurrection of Christ. Paul strenuously emphasizes the 'excelling (ὑπερβάλλον) greatness' of this power, which is like, he insists, the 'operation ["energizing"] of the might of his strength' (κατὰ τήν ἐνέργειαν τοῦ κράτους τῆς ἰσχύος αὐτοῦ)'. A description of 'miraculous' power—like that of the ultimate miracle, the resurrection—normatively at work in the Christian church could hardly be more explicit.[3] Thirdly, as in so many other passages in the New Testament, Paul ties the distribution of the charismata, in this case miracle power, to the exaltation of Christ, not to his apostleship, as Warfield would insist. The fourth, and for our study most significant, point is that this power is to be experienced 'not only in the present age, but also in the one to come'. One might object that this last quotation only applies to the exaltation of Christ and not to the power in the church.

But Paul's prayer is that God 'may give' (δώη, aorist subjunctive) gifts of wisdom and knowledge, both, as we have seen, known to be contemporary, in this present age. Connected with this main verb, 'may give', is the perfect participle πεφωτισμένους, indicating action completed before the action of the main verb, that is, 'hearts having been enlightened' in order that the readers may 'know the *hope* to which they were called'. Could 'hope' be a characteristic of the age to come if the object of the hope is realized? Moreover, the final words of this long sentence, comprised of vv. 15-23, further qualify the

1. That this power (δύναμις) is for this present age is apparent in 3.16 and 20, cf. 1 Cor. 12.10 and 29, and Acts 1.8.

2. BAG, p. 408: 'κατά with the accusative serves in general to indicate the nature, kind, peculiarity or characteristics of a thing'.

3. Dunn points out in *Jesus and the Spirit*, p. 209, that 'the ἐνέργειν word group is normally used for the operations of the divine (or demonic)'. Paul chooses this verb deliberately in 1 Cor. 12.3-10 and in Eph. 1.19 (see *Jesus and the Spirit*, n. 53) 'to underline his conviction that all charismata are effected by divine power'. The gifts of the Spirit are only so 'in so far as they are the action (ἐνεργήματα) of God's Spirit in and through the individual'.

activity of the exalted Christ toward his church during the 'present age': 'God has placed all things under his feet [including the demonic powers]'[1] and placed him as head over all things which are 'for' [that is 'given to'] the church, his body, the fullness of him who fills everything in every way'.[2] This last phrase certainly seems broad enough to include the distribution of the charismata. Further, the placement of δόξα and its cognates indicate a strong eschatological overtone to the contexts.[3]

.1. This placing of the demonic rulers under Christ's feet, and the church's participation in his power, recalls the commissions to the disciples: 'I have seen Satan fall like lightning from heaven. I have given you authority to trample on snakes and scorpions, and to overcome all the power of the enemy' (Lk. 10.19). In Mt. 28.18, Jesus affirms, as does Paul, above, that God gave Jesus 'all authority in heaven and in earth', which in Jesus' continual presence with the disciples, would be theirs 'until the end (συντέλεια) of the age'. In Rom. 15.20 Paul refers to the same eschatological hope of the Christian: 'the God of peace will soon crush Satan under your feet'. On the significance of the messianic conquest of evil spirits see especially R. Leivestad, *Christ the Conqueror: Ideas of Conflict and Victory in the New Testament* (London: SPCK, 1954), pp. 40-49; 92-114; Barrett, *Holy Spirit and the Gospel Tradition*, pp. 46-68, and L. Sabourin, *The Divine Miracles Discussed and Defended* (Rome: Catholic Book Agency, 1977), pp. 81-102.

2. Barth, *Ephesians 1–3*, pp. 200-10, after reviewing an astonishing number of interpreters, concludes that the concept of fullness represents 'the revelation of God's glory to the world in Jesus Christ; the power exerted by God in Christ *and in the Church* [italics mine] for the subjection of the powers and the salvation of all mankind. . . in brief, the presence of the living God and his Messiah among his chosen people for the benefit of all creation. . . and that the saints will attain or will be filled with, all of God's and the Messiah's fullness' (p. 209). Certainly, as we see in the note above, this fullness includes charismatic operations of the Spirit. As Barth said earlier with respect to the 'filling' of the body by the head (Christ): ' "Filling" means both the presence felt by the exertion of power *and* the exertion of power by immediate presence' (p. 190).

3. The manifestations of God's δόξα exhibit a similar present–future tension to that of love, power, and the charismata; that is, they appear to some degree in the present age, but are fulfilled in the age to come. On this (and esp. Eph. 3.16, below) see R. Kittel, 'δόξα, κτλ', *TDNT*, II, pp. 250-51: 'For the believer the πνεῦμα is the ἀπαρχή and the ἀρραβών of the new thing which brings with it δόξα. Hence, proleptically, prayer may be made that "according to the riches of His glory God may grant you His Spirit. . . " (Eph. 3.16). In both cases [i.e. in Eph. 3.16 and 1 Pet. 4.14] there is to be διὰ τοῦ πνεύματος [through the Spirit] a full working of eschatological δόξα in the present life of the believer'.

So the point here is to establish that the operations of the charismata are fixed at the very least 'in the present age' with the strong suggestion that the power of God, which the church now experiences, will also, like love in 1 Cor. 13.13 and the exaltation of Christ, continue in the 'age to come'.[1] The themes of the above passages in Ephesians are further developed in Ephesians 3.

Ephesians 3.14-21. This passage offers strong intimations of Paul's repeated schema of the charismata continuing until the end:

> 14 For this reason I kneel before the Father. . . 16 I pray that by means of his glorious riches he may, by power (δύναμει), grant that you become mighty through his Spirit in the inner person, 17 that Christ reside in your hearts through faith, having been rooted and established in love 18 in order that you might be empowered to grasp the dimensions [of Christ's love], 19 and to know that Christ's love is greater than knowledge—all this that you may be filled with the fullness of God. 20 Now to the One ultimately powerful to do immeasurably more than all we ask or imagine, 21 to the extent of the power working in us, to Him be glory in the Church and in Christ Jesus throughout all generations, for ever and ever! Amen.

We must notice the parallels with 1 Cor. 1.4-8 and 13.8-14. Here again, Paul prays that God the Father would grant the Spirit to the readers to reveal to them knowledge of Christ and to be 'filled with the fullness of God', which is an ideal state partially realized in the present, and fully realized in the eschaton.[2] The 'fullness of God', among other things, may reflect the condition of being 'filled with the Spirit' which is clearly a repeated phenomenon producing charismatic activity (Eph. 5.19; cf. Acts 2.4; 4.8, 31; 9.17; 13.9, 52).

The doxology (vv. 20-21) repeats the above theme. Paul begins by praising God and further describing him in terms of his provision of δύναμις available to his people if any believer ('we') ask (as in asking for fillings of the Spirit, as Paul has done).[3] God is glorified by the miracle power presently working in the church. The range of things

---

1. The Matthean picture of the return of Christ certainly includes the idea of power continuing in the fully realized kingdom since Christ comes 'with power and great glory' (μετὰ δυνάμεως καὶ δόξης πολλῆς, Mt. 24.30).

2. See again Kittel, 'δόξα', pp. 250-51.

3. Cf. the echo of Jesus in Lk. 11.10-13, 'If you [fathers], then, though you are evil, know how to give good gifts to your children, how much more will your Father in heaven give the Holy Spirit to those who ask him!'

for which believers are commanded to 'ask' certainly includes the charismatic Spirit. God's being 'glorified' by miracles is a common theme in the Synoptic and Johannine Gospels.[1] If the essential nature of the Spirit is charismatic, then mere mention of the Spirit in this context of his operation in the church would indicate that the charismata are involved here. But this is confirmed and made explicit by the repeated references to 'knowledge' and 'power' as the descriptors of the Spirit's or God's working in this passage.

But the crucial point here is that an eschatological context governs the operation of the charismata. The doxology addresses God, 'The Powerful Enabler' (τῷ δυναμένῳ, cf. Mk. 14.62), whose unlimited and unimaginable activity works 'according to the power (δύναμις) energizing us [the Church]'. This appears to refer to the ideal and most complete range of the charismata.

What is the connection of the first part of the doxology (v. 20) to the second (v. 21)? The first describes God as the incomprehensible 'Enabler displayed in the Church', which seems to parallel and identify the 'glory in the Church', in the second.[2] The parallel implies that the powerful activity of God in the church is also the 'glory' of God and Christ. If this is true, then the charismatic power uninterruptedly continues toward a twice-mentioned eschatological end: 'throughout all generations' and 'for ever and ever'. These last two phrases echo the promise of the perpetually granted Spirit of prophecy in Isa. 59.21

---

1. For example, Mt. 9.8; 15.31; Mk 2.12; Lk. 5.26; 7.16; 18.43; Jn 11.4; 12.28; Acts 11.18. 'The vision of his glory is promised in the entire ministry of Jesus, and in so far as particular miracles are part of this, they are to be regarded as evidence of the fellowship between Jesus and the Father. . . The Johannine conception of the δόξα of Jesus corresponds to the present possession by Jesus of the powers of the age to come' (Howard, *Christianity according to St John*, p. 163). 'The divine presence and power were apprehensible by those who had the faculty of faith. It is in this sense that in and through the σημεῖα He manifested His glory' (C.G.H. Dodd, *The Interpretation of the Fourth Gospel* [Cambridge: Cambridge University Press, 1954], p. 207, cf. 211). On the eschatological significance of δόξα, see the discussion above.

2. On the similarities of 'power' and 'glory' in the New Testament see S. Aalen, 'Glory', *NIDNTT*, II, p. 48; Richardson, *Introduction to the Theology of the New Testament*, pp. 62-67; G. Molin, 'Glory', *EBT*, p. 297.

(cf. Isa. 47.3).[1] Paul continues to recycle his themes once again in the next passage.

Ephesians 4.30. 'And do not grieve the Holy Spirit of God, with whom you were sealed for the day of redemption.'

Eph. 4.30 also suggests an eschatological end point for the operation of prophecy in the church. Superficially, it would appear that God the Spirit is 'grieved' by certain sinful verbal behavior, which is true. But the expression, 'grieve the Holy Spirit' is likely a reference to rejection of prophetic guidance or inspired words from God as in Isa. 63.10 (cf. 1 Thess. 5.19-20). The previous verse (Eph. 4.29) also suggests that prophecy is the subject here when it limits speech to the purpose of 'upbuilding' (οἰκοδομήν), that it might give 'grace' (χάριν). This instruction seems to describe the work of the Spirit as prophecy, which, as a 'seal' (a protecting identification mark), will upbuild and protect continuously 'until/toward/unto (εἰς) the day of redemption', a decidedly eschatological context. This theme continues in the following passage.

Ephesians 5.15-19. This is an exhortation to apply spiritual gifts to the present 'evil days', probably an allusion to the time of the messianic suffering leading up to the parousia.

> 15 Be very careful, then, how you live—not as unwise but as wise,
> 16 making the most of every opportunity, because the days are evil.
> 17 Therefore do not be foolish, but understand what the will of the Lord
> is. 18 Do not get drunk on wine, which leads to debauchery. Instead, be
> filled with the Spirit. 19 Speak to one another with psalms, hymns and
> spiritual songs.

Twice previously in the immediate context, Paul contrasts the present with the future. The present is a time to imitate God (5.1) by abandoning immorality. The future is a time of the 'inheritance in the Kingdom of God' and the time of God's wrath (vv. 5, 6). Again in vv. 8-14 the works done in this present 'darkness' will be exposed in the light of Christ after the resurrection. The pattern is repeated in vv. 15-19 with the exhortation to use wisely every opportunity during

---

1. ' "And this will be my covenant with them," says the Lord. "My Spirit, who is on you, and my words that I have put in your mouth will not depart from your mouth, of from the mouths of your children, or from the mouths of their descendants from this time on and forever," says the Lord.'

the present evil days. Specifically this is spelled out in a series of contrasts: 'Be careful how you live, not as unwise but as wise'. Wisdom throughout Ephesians usually derives from revelation (1.9, 17; 3.10, cf. 1 Cor. 2.6, 13; 3.19; 12.8; Col. 1.28). The same observation applies to the following parallel contrast: 'Do not be foolish [spiritually unaware, imperceptive], but understand what the will of the Lord is'. And again in the next verse the point becomes even clearer: 'Do not get drunk with wine, which leads to debauchery, but be filled with the Spirit'. The analogy of being filled with wine and with the Spirit is an old one in biblical literature (for example Jer. 3.9; Amos 2.12), derived perhaps from the similarity of responses of intense emotion, speech or even song (Isa. 24.9; 28.7; Zech. 10.7). At Pentecost those who were filled with the Spirit and speaking in tongues were accused of being 'filled with new wine' (Acts 2.13, 15). Similarly, according to the custom of the Nazirites, the prophet John the Baptist was forbidden to imbibe wine or other fermented drink; instead he was to be 'filled with the Holy Spirit' (Lk. 1.15). The charge that Jesus, unlike John, was a drunkard (Mt. 11.19-20 // Lk. 7.33-34) may have been an attempt to discredit his status as a prophet or the source of his inspiration.[1]

In any case, the immediate consequence of being 'filled with the Spirit' is the responsibility to 'speak to one another' and 'make music in your heart to the Lord' through the medium of music, via Old Testament psalms and hymns as well as 'spiritual songs (ᾠδαῖς πνευματικαῖς)'. The term 'spiritual songs' probably has some connection with Paul's charism of 'singing' with his (and God's) Spirit (1 Cor. 14.13-17)—a practice he parallels with the gift of 'speaking' in tongues.[2] Is Eph. 5.18-19 a passage about the usage of the charismata during this present age? It appears that the use of the term 'spiritual songs' and the other charismatic content of this passage have significance for the continuation of the charismata in the present era.

---

1. Lk. 7.33-34. See I.H. Marshall, *The Gospel of Luke* (NIGTC; Grand Rapids: Eerdmans, 1978), p. 302; A. Plummer, *St. Luke* (ICC; New York: Charles Scribner's Sons, rev. edn, 1898), p. 208.

2. Dunn, *Jesus and the Spirit*, p. 208: 'Eph. 5.19 and Col. 3.16 speak of "spiritual songs", that is, of songs prompted by the Spirit and manifesting his inspiration'. See esp. pp. 187, 238-39 and L.W. Hurtado, 'What Were Spiritual Songs?', *Paraclete* 5 (Winter 1971), pp. 8-17.

A passage parallel to Eph. 5.18-19 is Col. 3.16, which carries a clearer charismatic overtone, particularly, a sense of divine given-ness:[1] 'Let the word of Christ dwell in you richly, in all wisdom, teaching and admonishing each other via psalms, hymns and spiritual songs in grace, singing in your hearts to God; and everything you do in word or deed, do all things in the name of the Lord Jesus'. As in other passages, for instance 1 Cor. 1.4-8 and the Ephesian passages examined above, which speak of the charismatic community in action, certain key words and phrases recur in Col. 3.16-17: 'word of Christ', 'dwell in you', 'richly', 'in all wisdom' (cf. 1 Cor. 1.5; Eph. 1.9, 17; 3.10; Col. 1.9, 28; 2.3), 'word and deed' (cf. Rom. 15.19)—all of which in their contexts refer to charismatic worship and ministry. It would seem that Col. 3.16 demonstrates the charismatic nature of Eph. 5.18-19, and as such strengthens the case for these activities to continue during these present evil days and as a 'seal' 'until the day of redemption'.

Thus the three Ephesian passages (4.14-16, 30 and 5.15-19) reiterate Paul's pattern of encouraging the development of edifying spiritual gifts in his congregations in the days before the parousia. However, there remains one further passage in Ephesians meriting investigation.

Ephesians 6.10-20. Here Paul explicitly commands the use of the charismatic power of the Spirit in contexts associated with two familiar eschatological themes.[2]

> 10 Finally, be empowered (ἐνδυναμοῦσθε) in the Lord and in the might of his strength. 11 Put on (ἐνδύσασθε) the full armor of God so that you can take your stand against the devil's schemes. 12 For our struggle is not

---

1. Dunn, *Jesus and the Spirit*, p. 238.
2. On this passage and the role of power in the eschatological Christian community generally, see Grundmann, 'δύναμαι/δύναμις', pp. 313-14: 'The community is rescued from the power of Satan and finds itself in a new mode of existence. In this existence, however, it is beset by perils and conflicts, and it waits for the final deliverance and the destruction of its enemies. The power of Christ granted to the community is thus by nature a power to protect and preserve', and by which 'all hostile forces can be overcome'. Grundmann identifies the eschatological outworking of charismatic power in the Ephesians 6 passage with 1 Pet. 1.5: 'Through faith you are shielded by God's power until the coming of the salvation that is ready to be revealed in the last time'. Again, the activity of the 'miraculous' δύναμις (as Grundmann describes it on p. 315) in the church is, according to Peter, to continue until the full revelation of its salvation 'in the last time'.

against flesh and blood, but against the rulers, against the authorities, against the powers of this dark world and against the spiritual forces of evil in heavenly realms. 13 Therefore put on the full armor of God, so that when the day of evil comes, you may be able to stand your ground and after you have done everything, to stand. . . 17 Take the helmet of salvation and the sword of the Spirit, which is the word of God. 18And pray in the Spirit on all occasions with all kinds of prayers and requests. . . 19 Pray also for me, that whenever I open my mouth, words may be given me so that I will fearlessly make known the mystery of the gospel, 20 for which I am an ambassador in chains. Pray that I may declare it fearlessly, as I should.

The first theme is the empowering with the eschatological Spirit. In vv. 10 and 11 the command to be 'empowered' (ἐνδυναμοῦσθε) is associated with the being 'clothed' (ἐνδύσασθε) with the full armor of God. This association of words parallels the command of Jesus in Lk. 24.49 ('I send the promise of my Father upon you. . . [to be] clothed (ἐνδύσησθε) with power (δύναμιν)'. The second aspect of Paul's command, to combat the demonic powers, is also a major theme in Jesus' own ministry, both earthly and exalted, and is, therefore, an integral feature of the disciples' commission as well.[1] Paul had promised his Roman readers that, in the eschatological battle with the demonic powers, 'the God of peace will soon crush Satan under your feet' (Rom. 15.20). This promise is an outgrowth of the *proto-evangelium* tradition in Gen. 3.15, developed in Lk. 10.18-19 (cf. Mk. 16.17-18), in which Jesus affirmed to his disciples that they had been given 'authority (ἐξουσίαν) to tread on serpents and scorpions and over all the power (δύναμιν) of the enemy'.[2] A further parallel of

---

1. See the first part of this chapter, above, and Sabourin, *Divine Miracles*, p. 76.

2. Too much has been made of the demonic ruling forces behind political powers, rather than the more personal demonic spirits as described in the Gospels and Acts, for example by G.B. Caird, *Principalities and Powers: A Study in Pauline Theology* (Oxford: Clarendon Press, 1956), pp. 1-30; Ling, *The Significance of Satan*, pp. 56-61. C.H. MacGregor is typical of this position in his 'Principalities and Powers', *NTS* 1 (1954), p. 19: 'Paul has in view demonic intelligences of a much higher order than the "devils" who possessed the poor disordered souls that meet us in the Gospel pages'. Twelftree and Dunn, 'Demon Possession and Exorcism in the New Testament', pp. 221-22, have urged that we not 'attempt to drive a wedge between Jesus' exorcistic ministry and the wider ministry of healing both of Jesus himself and of the first Christians. The manifestations of Satan's authority, of the grip and ill-effects of evil, were not confined to demon-possession, and Paul (and the other New Testament writers) were very conscious of the malignant power of evil

Eph. 6.12 to the great commission is the reminder that Jesus has 'all authority in heaven and on the earth' (Mt. 28.18), just as Paul commissions his readers to confront the 'world-rulers' (κοσμοκράτορας) and the spiritual forces of evil 'in the heavenlies (ἐν τοῖς ἐπουρανίοις)'.

One specific way in which these demonic forces are to be combated is through the 'sword of the Spirit, which is the word of God'. To say that the sword of the Spirit or the word of God in this context is simply Scripture would be anachronistic.[1] Rather, the reference is to the prophetic inspiration of Christ which slays the demonic forces arrayed against God (Rev. 1.16; 19.13, 15, 21), even resistance in the human heart (Heb. 4.12, cf. 1 Cor. 14.24-25). But the reference does not seem to be to inspired preaching or proclamation; rather, the 'sword' is to be 'taken' 'by means of (διά) all prayer and petition, praying all the time in the Spirit' (v. 18). Apparently it is in prayer and intercession that the 'wrestling' against the demonic powers takes place. It is only later that the readers are asked to pray also for Paul that when he opened his mouth, 'words might be given him' (by God/Christ/the Spirit; note the divine passive voice) so that he could 'fearlessly make known' and 'fearlessly declare' the gospel. This seems a clear paraphrase of Jesus' words to his disciples in Lk. 21.12-19, where they are warned against fear (vv. 9, 11 and 14) and warned of persecution; they are warned against preparing their own defenses but promised that Christ would give 'words [literally "a mouth"] and wisdom' that no one could refute. Both Matthew's and Mark's versions are more explicitly charismatic: 'At that time you will be given what to say, for it will be the Spirit of your Father speaking through you' (Mt. 10.19b-20); 'say whatever is given you at the time, for it is not you speaking, but the Holy Spirit' (Mk 13.11).

It is striking that especially in Mark and Luke, these instructions come in an apocalyptic context, and are introduced in Mark by the

---

that darkened men's minds, enslaved their passions, and corrupted their bodies'. I would further suggest, in view of Paul's action in Acts 16.11-20, his promise in Rom. 15.19, his mention of 'discernment of Spirits' in 1 Cor. 12.9-10 and the summary of Jesus' ministry in Acts 10.38, that with respect to the character of the demonic a clear continuity exists from the theology of the Synoptic Gospels to Paul.

1. So, Dunn, *Jesus and the Spirit*, p. 227; Barth, *Ephesians 4–6*, pp. 799-800: 'It is clear that the mere quotation of Bible texts does not in itself exhaust the use of the "word of God"'.

remark that 'the gospel must first be preached to all nations'. In view of the gospel parallels with Eph. 6.10-20, it would seem that Paul's preaching may have had a strong eschatological overtone. Certainly this is the contention of Johannes Munck in his groundbreaking work, *Paul and the Salvation of Mankind,*[1] in which he argues that Paul's mission to the gentiles ('to all nations') was an attempt to fulfill the commission of Christ ('to all nations/to every creature') and precipitate the eschaton.

The point, then, is that in Paul's mind, the use of the Spirit's gifts and power in an eschatological struggle against the demonic forces, both in prayer and in fearless proclamation, represented the church's task of the end time, of the last days. It was a commission that was to continue until the mission was completed at 'the end of this age' (Mt. 28.20).

The following passages further demonstrate the themes already established in 1 Corinthians and Ephesians: Paul's prayer for God or the exalted Christ to bestow on his communities confirmations of the gospel and knowledge of God's will, via the powerful graces (charismata) of all wisdom, knowledge, discernment, and miracle power (δύναμις), to be continually built up in love and righteousness until the end of this present age at the parousia or 'day of Christ'.

Philippians 1.9-10. This passage briefly reiterates the themes discussed above. In the immediate context, Paul, as he did with his congregations in Corinth and in Ephesus, is praying for the Philippians, partly because they 'share in God's grace (χάρις)' with Paul. This powerful grace is described in its immediate context as 'defending and confirming (cf. βεβαιώσει, v. 7) the gospel'. We have seen that the 'grace' to 'confirm' the gospel involves the operation of the revelatory, if not miraculous, charismata (1 Cor. 1.6, 8; cf. Mk 16.20; Heb. 2.3). The passage itself emphasizes this point:

> 9 And this is my prayer: that your love may abound more and more in knowledge and all perception, 10 toward the goal that (εἰς) you may be able to discern what is best, in order that you (ἵνα) may be pure and blameless until (εἰς) the day of Christ.

---

1. Richmond, VA: John Knox, 1959, pp. 333-34. So also A.J. Hultgren, *Paul's Gospel and Mission* (Philadelphia: Fortress Press, 1985), pp. 143-45.

Here the sharing of Paul's grace appears in a familiar pattern: to 'abound in love' increasingly, 'in knowledge', 'all perception' and in discernment. Based on previous patterns, above, this knowledge, perception and discernment include charismata of revelation, where once again, Paul is confident that the Holy Spirit, from the exalted Christ (v. 11) will preserve his community in the truth as the members mutually minister and upbuild via their spiritual gifts. But how long does this process continue? These charismata operate in the church so that it might remain continually 'pure and blameless *until* (εἰς) the day of Christ'. This revelatory charismatic activity, again, works among the members of the church toward a clearly and fully eschatological goal, which is realized only at the parousia.

Colossians 1.9-12. Col. 1.9-12 shares language and themes with 1 Corinthians and Philippians, but especially with Ephesians 1.15-23.

> 9 For this reason, since the day we heard about [your faith in Christ, v. 4, and love in the Spirit, v. 8], we have not stopped praying for you and asking God that you be filled (πληρωθῆτε) with the knowledge of his will through all spiritual wisdom and understanding (ἐν πάσῃ σοφίᾳ καὶ συνέσει πνευματικῇ). 10 And we pray this in order that you may live a life worthy of the Lord and may please him in every way: bearing fruit in every good work, growing in the knowledge of God, 11 being strengthened with all power (ἐν πάσῃ δυνάμει δυναμούμενοι) according to his glorious might so that you may have great endurance and patience, and joyfully 12 giving thanks to the Father, who has qualified you to share in the inheritance of the saints in the kingdom of light.

Once again, Paul is praying that the congregation 'be filled'—an expression associated with the Holy Spirit and his gifts—with 'knowledge' ('full knowledge', ἐπίγνωσις), 'in all wisdom and spiritual understanding'. This last phrase emphasizes the divine, charismatic nature of this perception: '*all* wisdom' certainly includes, if it is not limited to, the 'gift of wisdom' (1 Cor. 12.8), while the 'understanding' is explicitly qualified by 'spiritual' (πνευματικῇ). Grammatically, both the 'all' (πάσῃ) and the 'spiritual' are connected with the substantives 'wisdom' and 'understanding'. 'Spiritual wisdom and understanding' does not here mean 'being humanly clever about religious matters', but denotes 'wisdom and understanding produced by the Holy Spirit'.[1] The Colossians, like the Ephesians, are promised to be empowered 'in all power (ἐν πάσῃ δυνάμει)' to the extent of 'the might of [God's] glory' (v. 11). This inclusive and expansive description of God's power, a word frequently used in the New Testament of miracles, certainly includes God's power for healing and other 'mighty works'.

Further, this process is ongoing toward an eschatological end. Paul's prayer is for the Colossians 'to walk worthily of the Lord, pleasing Him in every way (εἰς πᾶσαν ἀρεσκίαν), in every good work'[2] continually 'bearing fruit' and 'growing in the full knowledge of God'. All this is to continue despite the eschatological woes requiring 'great endurance and patience'.[3] The movement of this

---

1. T.K. Abbott, *Ephesians and Colossians* (ICC; Edinburgh: T. & T. Clark, n.d.), pp. 202-203: 'πνευματικῇ, given by the Spirit. Compare 1 Cor. xii. 8, ᾧ μὲν γὰρ διὰ τοῦ πνεύματος δίδοται λόγος σοφίας. The word is emphatic in this position, marking the contrast with the false teaching, which had λόγος σοφίας, a pretence of wisdom (ii.23) which really proceeded from ὁ νοῦς τῆς σαρκός, the mind of the flesh (ii.18)'.

2. 'Every good work' here must include charismatic ministries. See John's use of ἔργον in Jn 10.25; 14.11, 12.

3. As in Col. 1.11, above. See H. Schlier, 'θλίβω', *TDNT*, III, pp. 143-48; D.E.H. Whiteley, *The Theology of St Paul* (Philadelphia: Fortress Press, 1972), p. 126. The use of 'patience' (ὑπομονή) here recalls the characteristic presentation and living out of the gospel in 2 Cor. 12.12. The peculiar association—one might say, paradox—of suffering and power (i.e., the charismata) in the Christian life is a strong one, the avoidance of which may have been a central temptation of the primitive Christian community (Mt. 4.1-10; Lk. 4.1-12, cf. 2 Cor. 11; 12.1-13).

Suffering, like the charismata, is essential to the Christian experience because it is a characteristic of the eschatological overlap and the conflict of the two ages: the present evil age and the age to come. Christian sufferings are the eschatological 'messianic woes', the 'birth pains' of the new age (Mt. 24.8; Rom. 8.22, cf. Str–B, I, p. 950), which are to continue until the full 'revelation of the sons of God' (Rom. 8.18-19).

Suffering, then, implies the continuation of the charismata, in that they both characterize this present age and will not cease until the present conflict is resolved at the coming of Christ. See G. Bertram, 'ὠδίν', *TDNT*, X, pp. 667-74. Also, just as Christians are commanded to continue the charismatic mission of Christ only until the 'end of the age', so also their suffering, which Christ's mission necessarily precipitates as it confronts the 'god', or demonic rulers 'of this age', will only last until the end of the age. Christ holds out suffering in this present time 'as a sure prospect for all disciples'—a condition which will be resolved at his return. So, W. Michaelis, 'πάσχω', *TDNT*, V, pp. 932-35, and B. Gärtner, 'Suffer', *NIDNTT*, III, p. 725.

passage is toward the eschatological sharing 'in the inheritance of the saints in the kingdom of light' (v. 12). The following verse (v. 13) also has a strong eschatological overtone, associated with the word 'kingdom'. Here, as throughout the Synoptic Gospels and elsewhere, the final conflict between the 'power of darkness' and the kingdom of the Son is portrayed. God has 'delivered (ἐρρύσατο)' and 'transferred (μετέστησεν) us' into 'redemption' as part of that struggle. Having been thus redeemed,[1] the continuing role of the church is that 'we [including Paul and the community] proclaim him, counseling and teaching everyone in all wisdom, so that we may present everyone perfect (τέλειον) in Christ' (v. 28). Paul affirms that he continues to labor to this end (implying that his readers ought to imitate him; cf. 1 Cor. 4.16; 11.1; Gal. 2.18–3.5; Phil. 3.17; 1 Thess. 1.6; 2 Thess. 3.7, 9; cf. Heb. 13.7), and repeats the characteristic way in which he presents the gospel, in 'word and deed': 'according to the operation of [Christ] working in me in power (ἐν δυνάμει, v. 29)'. It is apparently this characteristic kind of messianic, eschatological, kingdom of God empowerment in which the Colossians were to continue their various ministries (Col. 1.11). This point is amplified in a further passage.

1 Thessalonians 1.5-8. Certainly in 1 Thess. 1.5-8 Paul, who shares Moses' wish that all Israel would receive the Spirit of prophecy, commends the Thessalonians for becoming 'imitators of us and of the Lord'.

> 5 Our gospel came to you not simply with words but also with power, with the Holy Spirit and with deep conviction. . . 6 you became imitators of us and of the Lord; in spite of severe suffering, you welcomed the message with the joy given by the Holy Spirit. 7 And so you became a model to all the believers in Macedonia and Achaia. 8 The Lord's message rang out from you not only in Macedonia and Achaia— your faith in God has become known everywhere.

What did the new believers imitate? Paul has just recounted how 'our gospel came to you not in words only, but also in power (ἐν δυνάμει) and in the Holy Spirit'. As Jesus transmitted his mission and authority to his disciples, so here Paul is passing on both his mandate and the method of presenting the gospel, which was spread (as was the norm

---

1. The redemption here implies, with Eph. 4.7, 11, that the charismatic members of the body of Christ, the church, are given to the church as booty, as slave gifts looted from the 'power of darkness' (cf. Mk 3.27; Mt. 12.29).

in other churches: Acts 6.7-8; 8.4-13; 11.21; 1 Cor. 1.4-9; Gal. 3.2, 5; Phil. 1.7) by the charismatic community at Thessalonica. Paul affirms that they 'became a *model* to *all* believers', to those whom the Thessalonians themselves had reached with the gospel, when they 'sounded out the word of the Lord' throughout the Greek peninsula (v. 8).[1] A crucially important point emerges here. Warfield had conceded that miracles continued, but only, and somewhat mechanically, among those 'upon whom apostolic hands were laid'.[2] Here the 'modeling' of the Thessalonians for those they encountered demands that the mission to present the gospel in word and power was not limited to the first generation of believers, who were physically touched by the apostles, but was available to subsequent generations as well. In any case, the imposition of hands is not hinted at in this passage. Indeed, as in most of the previous passages examined, *prayer* correlates with transmitting the Spirit or the mission to proclaim and demonstrate the gospel. This passage shows that the apostolic laying on of hands was clearly not a requirement for fulfilling the great commission in word and miracle. How long was this process to continue? Paul's frame of reference is again the eschaton: the report of the Thessalonians' performance included not only their good reception of the gospel and their rejection of idolatry, but that they now 'wait for [God's] Son from heaven' (v. 10). As in all these other passages, either implicitly or explicitly, the present messianic age of charismatic activity continues until the coming of the Lord Jesus Christ.

1 Thessalonians 5.11-23. This passage continues the themes of eschatological, charismatic empowering:

> 11 Therefore, encourage one another and build each other up, just as in fact you are doing. . . 16 Be joyful always; 17 Pray continually; 18 give thanks in all circumstances, for this is God's will for you in Christ Jesus.

---

1. What the Thessalonians 'modeled' to the new believers in Macedonia and Achaia, of course, was not only their presentation of the gospel in word and power, as they imitated Paul, but the way in which they received the gospel, that is, with joy amid severe suffering.

2. Warfield, *Counterfeit Miracles*, p. 23: 'My conclusion then is, that the power of working miracles was not extended beyond the disciples upon whom the Apostles conferred it by the imposition of their hands'. Earlier (p. 22) Warfield says: 'The Holy Ghost was conferred by the laying on of hands, specifically of the Apostles, and of the Apostles alone'.

19 Do not quench the Spirit; 20 do not treat prophecies with contempt.
21 Test everything. Hold onto the good. 22 Avoid every kind of evil.
23 May God Himself, the God of peace, sanctify you through and
through. May your whole spirit, soul and body be kept blameless at the
coming of our Lord Jesus Christ. 24 The one who calls you is faithful and
he will do it.

In this passage the clear, stated continuation of the charism of
prophecy until the 'coming (παρουσία) of our Lord Jesus Christ' is
not explicit. But against the intense apocalyptic background of
1 Thessalonians (4.13–5.11), Paul's urgings not to quench the Spirit
or despise prophecy assume a definite eschatological cast. The immediate context provides three further reasons to associate the immedi-
acy of the eschaton with the activity of prophecy. First, the contextual
framework of the exhortations to prophesy parallels that of
·1 Corinthians 12, 13 and 14: the exhortation to recognize and respect
the various ministries in the church (1 Thess. 5.11 // 1 Cor. 12); to do
so lovingly (1 Thess. 5.13-15 // 1 Cor. 13); and to encourage prophecy, but to regulate it (1 Thess. 5.19-21 // 1 Cor. 14). The framework
might even be extended to include the resurrection chapter (1 Cor.
15), where, in vv. 23-24, the whole person including the body is to be
preserved 'blameless at the coming of our Lord Jesus Christ'.
Secondly, the last phrase is a distinct parallel of 1 Cor. 1.8 and Phil.
1.10, where the revelatory charismata are given to strengthen the
community until the 'end' (1 Cor. 1) so it will appear 'blameless in
[or, 'until', Phil. 1] the day of our Lord Jesus Christ'. The parallel is
enhanced by observing the similarity of 1 Thess. 5.24 with 1 Cor. 1.9,
that is, that the 'faithful God' will complete this sanctifying work (cf.
the similar idea in Phil. 1.11). But Paul's use of a particular word in
reference to the Spirit may have significance for our thesis.

Thirdly, Paul's selection of the metaphor of quenching the Spirit
may have importance for cessationism. Here, 'quench', as Jeremias has
suggested, seems an allusion to the 'dominant view of orthodox
Judaism', that the sins of Israel caused the cessation of prophecy[1] at
the death of the last writing prophets of the Old Testament: Haggai,

---

1. Jeremias, *New Testament Theology*, pp. 80-82. Cf. also E. Sjöberg,
'πνεῦμα, κτλ', *TDNT*, VI, pp. 383-87 and Meyer, 'προφήτης, κτλ', pp. 813-28.
Cf. Chapter 1 above on the cessation of prophecy in rabbinic Judaism.

Zechariah and Malachi.[1] Jeremias further points out that the New Testament presupposes such a view among its Jewish contemporaries.[2] It was precisely the Christian claim that in the exalted Jesus the age of the messianic outpouring of the Spirit of prophecy had arrived (Acts 2.17; 7.51-60) that was so startling and infuriating to many Jewish hearers.[3]

1. Jeremias cites *t. Soṭ.* 13.2. Cf. Str–B, I, p. 127 §b. W.C. van Unnik has argued in '"Den Geist löschet nicht aus" (1 Thessalonicher v. 19)', *NovT* 4 (1968), pp. 255-69, that while one could imagine killing prophets and repressing charismatics, it is hard to conceive of stifling the Holy Spirit. Hence, he says, πνεῦμα in 1 Thess. 5.19 refers properly to Spirit-inspired utterances.

2. As in the case where the remark of the disciples of John at Ephesus did not mean that they had never heard of the Holy Spirit, but that they had not heard he was present again. 'The sharp antithesis in Mark 3.28-29 is only comprehensible in the light of the idea that the Spirit has been quenched' (Jeremias, *New Testament Theology*, p. 82).

3. Jeremias, *New Testament Theology*, p. 82, summarizes the possible significance of 1 Thess. 5.19-20 against the background of first-century Judaism: 'The idea of the quenching of the Spirit is an expression of the consciousness that the present time is alienated from God. Time without the Spirit is time under judgment. God is silent. Only in the last days will the disastrous epoch of the absence of the Spirit come to an end and the Spirit return again'.

The Jewish cessationist position regarding the Spirit of prophecy and power very soon became a target of Christian writers, not only those of the New Testament, but also later Christian apologists who opposed the Jewish cessationist polemic, as in the case of Justin Martyr, *Dialogue with Trypho the Jew* 87: 'The prophetical gifts remain with us [right] to the present time. And hence you ought to understand that [the gifts] formerly among your nation have been transferred to us. . . This fact you plainly perceive [that] after [Christ] no prophet has arisen among you. . . It was requisite that such gifts should cease from you; [but] should again, as had been predicted, become gifts which, from the grace of the Spirit's power, He imparts to those who believe in him, according as He deems each man worthy thereof'. See also Origen (c.185–c.154), *Contra Celsum*: 'God's care of the Jews was transferred to those Gentiles who believe in him. Accordingly it may be observed that after Jesus' advent the Jews have been entirely forsaken and possess nothing of those things which from antiquity they have regarded as sacred, and have not even any vestige of divine power among them. They no longer have any prophets or wonders, though traces of these are to be found to a considerable extent among Christians. Indeed, some works are even greater; and if our word may be trusted, we also have seen them'. Cyril of Jerusalem (AD 318–386), *Catechetical Lectures* 18.26, employs a similar dispensational argument: 'The first [Old Testament] church was cast off [but] in the second, which is the universal church, God hath set, as Paul says, first

Hence, it may well be that when Paul urges the community not to 'quench the Spirit' nor to 'despise prophesying', he is not simply affirming the value of prophecy. Rather, he may implicitly be saying, 'do not regress back into the contemporary Jewish belief that the Spirit of prophecy has ceased; this essentially denies your participation in the kingdom of God or, more specifically, in the era of the messiah, Jesus, who bestows the Spirit on you, that is, in the kingdom of God'. It is likely not accidental that this command is bracketed by references to 'Christ Jesus' and the 'coming of our Lord Jesus Christ', the one who, in Paul's mind and in the view of the earliest communities, is associated so primally with the inauguration of the age of the Spirit and the outpouring of his gifts. In vv. 19 and 20, then, to deny the Spirit (of prophecy) is, by implication, to deny Christ's exaltation and charismatic work in his body, the church (Mt. 12.28-32), as Warfield has done.[1] The motivation to quench prophecies in the Christian community of Thessalonica may well have had its source in the confusion reflected in the second letter: 'Do not become shaken or disturbed because of some prophecy [literally, πνεύματος] or message [λόγου] or letter supposed to be from us, to the effect that the day of the Lord has already come' (2 Thess. 2.2). Indeed, this second Thessalonian letter focuses on the problem and consequences of discerning true and false revelations. The revelations to those at Thessalonica have not appeared only as prophetic utterances or 'words', but as 'power (δυνάμει)' and 'with the Holy Spirit' (1 Thess. 1.5). As an extension of the present bewildering variety of 'spirits', both divine and demonic, the miracles of the exalted Christ working through his apostles and subsequent generations of their true 'imitators' will have their opposites in the counterfeit and deceptive miracles worked by the power of the 'lawless one' (2 Thess. 2.9). Those who persecute the Thessalonian believers and refuse to 'obey the gospel of our Lord Jesus' are to be 'shut out from the presence of the Lord and from the glory of his strength on the day he comes to be

apostles, secondly prophets, thirdly teachers, then miracles, then gifts of healings, helps, governments, divers kinds of tongues and every kind of power'.

1. Dunn, *Jesus and the Spirit*, p. 263. See the possible further connection with Jesus' words on despising prophecy and other works of power in J. Jeremias, *The Unknown Sayings of Jesus* (trans. R. H. Fuller; London: SPCK, 1964), pp. 100-101.

glorified in his holy people and to be marveled at among all those who have believed' (1.9-10).

2 Thessalonians 1.11-12. Here, Paul's prayer for his community is for their glorification in the Lord Jesus:

> 11 Toward which (εἰς ὅ) [glorification], we constantly pray for you, that our God may count you worthy of his calling, and that he may fulfill every good purpose and work of faith in power (ἔργον πίστεως ἐν δυνάμει). 12 We pray this so that the name of our Lord Jesus may be glorified in you, and you in him, according to the grace of our Lord Jesus Christ.

This glorification is spelled out in two stages. The first is eschatological and is described in three passages: (1) the previous context of the future revelation of the Lord Jesus from 'heaven in blazing fire with his powerful angels', in which the Thessalonians will be glorified; (2) 'toward which' (time) Paul prays that they be worthy of God's calling (v. 11),[1] and (3) the repeated glorification of the Thessalonians in Christ and they in him (v. 12). The second stage, the present time before the parousia, actually overlaps with the third. Paul prays that the community may be 'counted worthy' (ἀξιώσῃ) even now, just as the same aorist subjunctive verb form 'may fulfill' (πληρώσῃ) applies to the present working of God among them.[2] That 'present working' invites investigation.

Paul prays that God may 'fulfill' two (perhaps appositional and overlapping) objectives: 'every purpose of goodness' (πᾶσαν εὐδοκίαν ἀγαθωσύνης)', and 'every[3] work of faith in power' (ἔργον πίστεως ἐν δυνάμει). The last phrase is of particular significance for our thesis.

---

1. This seems to be equivalent to the fully eschatological 'blameless' or 'mature' state toward which the charismata worked in this present age (1 Cor. 1.8; 13.10; Eph. 4.13; 1 Thess. 1.23).

2. The familiar eschatological overlapping of the present and the age to come is associated particularly in the terms δόξα/δοξαζω ('glory/glorify'). The Johannine association of δόξα with miracle is close to the usage in this passage (for instance Jn 2.11; 12.28), as is the word 'work'. See Dodd, *Interpretation of the Fourth Gospel*, pp. 207-12.

3. The single 'every' (πᾶσαν) likely modifies both phrases, 'purpose of goodness' and 'work of faith in power'. So, E. Best, *The First and Second Epistles to the Thessalonians* (HNTC; New York: Harper & Row, 1977), pp. 269-70.

The juxtaposition of the words 'work', 'faith' and 'power' strongly implies miraculous charismatic activity in the Thessalonian Christian community, as they also appear in Gal. 3.5 and 1 Cor. 12.9-10 where the three root words are similarly connected in clear references to miracles.[1] Moreover, while it is God who effects this activity, the connection with faith here also requires present human involvement in the miraculous charismatic expression. Finally, it is God's and Christ's 'grace' (χάρις) that provides both the means and the extent of this miracle-working power, a concept repeated in many similar charismatic contexts, particularly in the recorded teaching of Jesus.

But the important point is that the grammar of this passage requires miraculous activity to continue into the eschaton. This is evident from the use of the εἰς ὅ, which begins v. 11, and which requires the subsequent activity for which Paul prays (including the 'work of faith in miracle-power') to continue 'into' the parousia. It is also evident from the use of 'So as/in order that' (ὅπως) at the beginning of v. 12. Here, the *purpose* of every 'work of faith in power' is the eschatological mutual glorification of the saints and the name of the Lord 'in' each other. But again the mutual glorification here may reflect the present/ future tension of God's eschatological glory breaking into this present age, as was so often the case in Johannine thought. The same pattern recurs in Petrine thought as well.

1 Peter 1.5. '[You] who are shielded by God's power until the coming of the salvation that is ready to be revealed in the last time.' 1 Pet. 1.5 maintains the eschatological framework for the continuing power of God. This power seems likely to be associated or identified with 'the grace that was to come to you' in 1 Pet. 1.10. Beyond the miraculous implication of δύναμις here, one can only speculate that the kind of power and grace operative in their midst may be further described in 1 Pet. 4.11, which apparently includes, among other gifts, that of prophecy.[2] In any case, the key point here is that this charismatic

---

1. The intimate and necessary connection of miracles and faith in the teaching of Jesus and the apostolic church is discussed in Chapter 3, above, in further detail.

2. Ellis, *Prophecy and Hermeneutic in Early Christianity*, p. 24. The λόγια θεοῦ in 1 Pet. 4.11 are 'the words spoken by the charismatic'. See R. Kittel, 'λόγιον', *TDNT*, IV, p. 139. J.N.D. Kelly (*A Commentary on the Epistles of Peter and Jude* [BNTC; London: A. & C. Black], p. 180) denies the λόγια are ecstatic phenomena, for example glossolalia, but rather are 'routine functions like teaching and

power of God is seen to be operative among the readers 'until' (NIV, Greek εἰς) the salvation 'revealed in the last time'. A similar pattern seems to emerge near the end of this epistle.

1 Peter 4.7-12. 1 Pet. 4.7-12 is strikingly Pauline in its tone, diction and content,[1] particularly as this passage reiterates Paul's pattern of exhortations on spiritual gifts. As in Romans 12, 1 Corinthians 1, 12 and 13, throughout Ephesians and in the other Pauline passages discussed above, the writer of 1 Peter emphasizes the motive of love against a background of the impending 'end of all things' when he encourages charismatic ministry in the Christian community:

> 7 The end of all things is near. Therefore be clear-minded and self-controlled so that you can pray. 8 Above all, exhibit an intense love, because love covers a multitude of sins. 9 Provide hospitality to one another without grumbling. 10 As each one has received a spiritual gift, so serve each other as good stewards of the varied grace of God. 11 If anyone speaks, do so as the oracles of God; if anyone serves, do so by the strength supplied by God, in order that in everything God may be glorified through Jesus Christ, to whom is the glory and the might into eternity.

The charismata are mentioned in general terms: 'speaking' and 'serving', but they are specified as charismata in a number of ways. First, they are the 'varied grace' of God, a term describing a broad range of charismata.[2] As does Paul, so Peter here implies an exhorta-

---

preaching'. He qualifies this apparent 'ordinary extraordinary' distinction by affirming that 'these, too, though lacking the outward tokens of Spirit-possession, should be regarded (he implies) as the true sense charismatic, for what the Christian spokesman enunciates, if he is faithful, is God's word; he does not simply repeat the divine message, *but God speaks through him*' (italics mine). The λόγια, Kelly recognizes, are 'used in classical Greek and the LXX for divine utterances'. Kelly seems to reverse his position in mid-paragraph, finally affirming that the 'routine' teaching and preaching are commanded here to become essentially prophetic utterances. He appears to distinguish between 'ecstatic' and less flamboyant forms of revelation, not between divinely or humanly inspired speech, that is, 'extraordinary' and 'ordinary' charismata.

1. Kelly, *Peter and Jude*, p. 177.

2. 'Peter has in mind (cf. v. 11) the charismata of primitive Christianity to which Paul especially refers, cf. Rom. 12.6-8; 1 Cor. 12.4-11' (H. Seesemann, 'ποικίλος, κτλ', *TDNT*, VI, p. 485). The word is used to describe the 'various', or 'many kinds' of miracles (δυνάμεις) in Heb. 2.4.

tion to preserve church unity via charismatic diversity, that is, not to despise either the so-called 'miraculous' or 'non-miraculous' gifts, but to retain and develop them all. Secondly, those who speak or serve should do so 'charismatically', not through mere human ability. The ones speaking to the community should do so to the extent God speaks through them, as exercising a χάρισμα (v. 10). This appears at least to be an exhortation to exercise the gift of prophecy, paralleling the exhortations of Rom. 12.6; 1 Cor. 14.1, 3, 5, 13, 26, 39; and 1 Thess. 5.19, 20. The readers are not to try to do by human means what God has ordained to do through them by his Spirit (cf. Gal. 3.3, 'Having begun via the Spirit, are you now being completed via the flesh?'). Thirdly, the function of the activities also indicates their charismatic character, as we have seen in so many of the passages examined above: they are 'received to serve others' (NIV),[1] that is, for the mutual edification of the body of Christ.

The eschatological terminal point for the exercise of these charismata is indicated in three ways. First, Peter's exhortations about spiritual gifts appear only as they are exhorted toward their eschatological goal ('the end of all things is near. Therefore. . . Above all. . . '). Secondly, the conclusion of the passage represents the eschatological goal of all Christian activity: the glory of God; and concludes with a doxology which refers to God's ultimate and eternal power.[2] Thirdly, the context leads immediately into Christian suffering or the messianic woes, into which all true disciples, however gifted ('on whom the Spirit of glory and of God rests', v. 14), must enter. These sufferings, like the charismata, will end when believers 'share in the glory that is to be revealed' (5.1) or, 'receive the crown of glory that will never fade away' (5.4). A similar pattern emerges in the Johannine writings.

1. That is, in the spirit of a logion of Jesus placed in the context of ministering spiritual gifts to others: 'Heal the sick, raise the dead, cleanse the lepers, drive out demons. Freely you have received, freely give' (Mt. 10.8).

2. See 1 Pet. 5.8-11 for a similar paradigm: all believers are to resist the devil (a central activity of the kingdom of God) and to suffer. But the God of *all grace* (inclusive of the charismata) will eschatologically restore his faithful ones, steadfast, into 'eternal glory'. The doxology, with its reference to eschatological glory and power, is repeated from 1 Pet. 4.11.

1 John 2.26-28. 1 Jn 2.26-28 is an exhortation, in an eschatological context, to rely on the revelatory work of the Spirit, whether directly to individuals or through gifts of prophecy, in order to combat false teachers:

> 26 I am writing these things to you about those who are trying to lead you astray. 27 As for you, the anointing you received from him remains in you, and you do not need anyone to teach you. But as his anointing teaches you about all things, and as that anointing is real, not counterfeit—just as it has taught you, remain in him. 28 And now, dear children, continue in him, so that when he appears we may be confident and unashamed before him at his coming.

The writer's seemingly extreme appeal here to direct revelation to preserve orthodoxy is startling, since so much conflict and false teaching seems to have derived from 'spirits' and false prophets among them (1 Jn 4.1).[1] There are, of course, other guidelines for identifying those who are in the truth,[2] but the community finds it possible to thwart those who are of the Antichrist 'only in the anointing power of the Spirit', the χρῖσμα. The χρῖσμα reveals to the community 'all things' (1 Jn 2.20, οἴδατε πάντα), and is closely related to other Johannine teaching from Christ about the

---

1. W. Grundmann, 'χρίω, κτλ', *TDNT*, IX, p. 572: 'A notable feature in the ecclesiastical situation in which the Johannine Epistles were written is that the author does not refer the community to an authoritative teaching office but reminds it of its reception of the χρῖσμα which is itself the teacher and which makes the community independent of a teaching office [at least in the modern ecclesiastical sense]. This shows how strongly in John the understanding of the Messiah is determined by the anointing of the Spirit and how the relation between the Son and sons, which is based on reception of the Spirit, finds an echo in the connection between the anointed One (χριστός) and the anointed [the Christians].' Dunn, *Jesus and the Spirit*, pp. 353, 352, points out, however, that as in Paul, the Johannine literature expects the dynamic interaction of present revelation and apostolic κήρυγμα: 'Present inspiration is known and expected; but a right understanding of Jesus is always normative'.

2. For example, those who: exhibit selfless love (1 Jn 2.9-11; 3.10c-18; 4.7-12, 16, 20-21); do not break fellowship with the community (2.19; 4.6); are not antinomian (1.5-10; 2.4-6, 29; 5.18); can and do ask God for cleansing from sin willingly and immediately (1.8-9; 2.1-2, 12; 3.19-22; 4.18; 5.14-15); remain within the framework of the original Christian tradition (1.1-3; 2.7, 13, 14, 24, 26-27); especially emphasize the centrality of Jesus Christ (1.1, 3, 7b; 2.22-24; 4.1-3, 15; 5.1, 5-12); and those to whom the Spirit bears witness to the truth (2.27; 3.24b; 4.13; 5.7).

παράκλητος (Jn 14.26; 15.26; 16.13-14), the prophetic Revealer, Teacher and Witness to the Son (1 Jn 5.6) who was to be with the Christian community during the exaltation of Christ.[1] So in what temporal context does the writer of 1 John see the operation of this revelatory χρῖσμα?

The χρῖσμα appears in a clear-cut eschatological context and represents an ongoing bestowal of the revelatory Spirit in continuing response to the coming Antichrist and to his prototypes who have already appeared. Their appearance in the community is evidence of 'the last hour' (ἐσχάτη ὥρα, v. 18). John has just affirmed that this present κόσμος 'is passing away, but the one who does God's will remains into the age to come' (ὁ δὲ ποιῶν τὸ θέλημα τοῦ θεοῦ μένει εἰς τὸν αἰῶνα). The association of the Antichrist and the 'last hour' is a central theme of New Testament theology, in which demonic forces are unleashed against the kingdom of God in a final spasm of evil, deception and destruction. John's 'hour', or even more significantly, '*last* hour', emphasizes the decisive moment of conflict before the end,[2] which nevertheless characterizes and includes 'the whole Christian era'.[3] It is difficult to imagine an 'hour' later than the

1. So Grundmann, 'χρίω, κτλ', p. 572 and D. Müller, 'Anoint', *NIDNTT*, I, p. 123. However, Grudem, *The Gift of Prophecy*, p. 28, seems to want to limit the similar language in the Gospel of John strictly to apply to the twelve disciples who were thereby empowered to write Scripture. But the parallel here of Jn 16.13-16 and 1 Jn 2.27 (also Mt. 23.9) seems to answer the hermeneutical question of how matters originally addressed to the first disciples apply to the church at large. This strongly implies that the whole church ideally and normatively participates in and continues the mission of the original disciples, even as they did the mission of the Lord Jesus. Again, are not Luke's numbers, 12, 70 (72), or 120, while historical, also archetypal of the elect, both Jew and Gentile?

2. See Richardson, *Introduction to the Theology of the New Testament*, pp. 203-10. R. Schnackenburg, 'Hour', *EBT*, pp. 379-82 summarizes the parenetic intent of this word in Johannine literature: it 'serves as an admonition to his disciples to recognize the eschatological hour which has come with him and is still to be completed and, at the same time, to take cognizance of their salvation and the task which awaits them [in] suffering and persecution. . . joy and confidence. . . peace and the assurance of victory'.

3. See J.G. Gibbs, 'Hour', *ISBE* (rev. edn, 1979), IV, p. 769, referring to 1 Jn 2.18, 'a time known by the "many antichrists" that come during its duration'; D. Guthrie, *New Testament Theology* (Downers Grove, IL: IVP, 1981), p. 855. He notes 'John's acute awareness that the "hour" permeates the whole of the present era'.

'last hour' during which certain spiritual gifts are to cease.[1] The whole time of the messianic woes, during which the people of God are charismatically empowered against the forces of the Antichrist, continue until the final intervention of the messiah at his coming.

The crucial connection of the prophetic anointing with the eschaton is that it 'remains in you' (μένει ἐν ὑμῖν, a plural meaning 'the whole church'), and continues to teach the readers to 'remain in Him' (Christ). How long is this situation to continue? Verse 28 exhorts the readers to 'remain in Him, so that when He is manifested we may have confidence and not be ashamed in His coming (παρουσία)'. This terminal point of the 'remaining' condition reminds us of virtually all of the passages examined, beginning with 1 Cor. 1.8. The flow of this passage, then, certainly suggests that the 'anointing' on the readers, which is to combat the eschatological forces of the Antichrist and his surrogates, is to continue as long as this anointing is required. John

---

1. This same argument applies to the special creation of a sub-divided sixth 'dispensation' of the 'Church Age' in theological dispensationalism so widespread in fundamentalism. Each dispensation represents a 'period of time during which man is tested in respect of obedience to some *specific* [italics mine] revelation of the will of God' (Scofield, *The Scofield Reference Bible*, p. 5 n. 4). Griffith-Thomas popularized a belief among dispensationalists today that, because 'Jews seek signs, and Greeks seek wisdom' (1 Cor. 1.22), miracles appeared primarily to confirm the word to Jews, while Greeks responded more readily to reasoned preaching. The gifts of the Spirit were 'transitional': the records of them in Acts 'were demonstrations of power to vindicate the Messiahship of Jesus of Nazareth, but not intended for permanent exercise in the normal conditions of the Christian Church when Christ had been rejected by Israel' (Acts 3.19-21). Consequently, miracles rapidly diminished after Acts 9, or 15, and the 'normal graces' of the Spirit predominated in the Gentile Christian Churches 'as associated with the Apostle Paul' (Griffith-Thomas, *The Holy Spirit of God*, pp. 45-49). A similar position is assumed by Anderson, *The Silence of God*, p. 162: 'As scripture plainly indicates [miracles] continued so long as the testimony was addressed to the Jew, but ceased when, the Jew being set aside, the Gospel went out to the Gentile world'. A review of the summary statements in the New Testament of Paul's ministry to the Gentiles, however, shows both that the content of his gospel did not change from Jew to Gentile, and that the conclusions of Griffith-Thomas and Anderson do not bear biblical scrutiny (Acts 15.12; Rom. 15.18-19; 2 Cor. 12.12; 1 Cor. 2.4; 1 Thess. 1.5; cf. Acts 19.11; 28.7-9; especially note the universal promise of the Spirit of prophecy in Acts 2.39). Interestingly, Griffith-Thomas presented this theory of a sub-divided 'Church Age' dispensation as part of a series of lectures to Princeton Seminary in 1913, during Warfield's tenure and before *Counterfeit Miracles* was written.

does not appeal only to a body of teaching, to apostolic authority, or to Scripture in this passage, but to the prophetic anointing remaining in the community. Certainly, John elsewhere provides several other objective checks on false teaching and revelation (as noted above), but these do not preclude the witness of immediate revelation to the community, until the coming of Christ. Our final passage continues the themes developed in this present section.

Jude 18-21. Jude 18-21 reflects, like the previous passage, conflict between false teachers and the faithful community:

> 18 'In the last times there will be scoffers who will follow their own ungodly desires.' 19 These are the men who divide you, 'natural' (ψυχικοί) men who do not have the Spirit. 20 But you, beloved, build up yourselves in the most holy faith, praying in the Holy Spirit. 21 Keep yourselves in God's love as you wait for the mercy of our Lord Jesus Christ to bring you to eternal life.

The 'charismatic' element appears in the exhortation that the readers, in contrast to those who 'follow mere natural instincts and do not have the Spirit' (NIV),[1] should instead be 'building themselves up in the most holy faith' by 'praying in the Holy Spirit'. The idea of 'edification' in connection with prayer in the Holy Spirit is familiar from 1 Cor. 14.4 ('the one who prays in a tongue [prays in the Spirit, 14.14, 15] edifies himself'). But whether Jude is exhorting the readers to pray specifically in tongues is problematic, though if prayer is associated with the Holy Spirit in biblical texts, then that prayer necessarily has at least some charismatic dimension.[2]

The eschatological element here is familiar; it includes the struggle of the faithful community against false prophets (vv. 11, 19) and demonically tinged (vv. 4, 6, 13) evil. This is part of the messianic war of the kingdom of God. Dunn has suggested that Jude may be facing a situation here which is much like that of Corinth (1 Cor. 2.13-15),[3] and we might add, of 1 John, in which divisive intruders of a proto-gnostic, antinomian bent have penetrated the community. As

---

1. The NIV translation implies these men were not prophetically gifted by the Holy Spirit.
2. 'A reference to charismatic prayer, including glossolalic prayer, may therefore be presumed for Jude 20'; Dunn, *Jesus and the Spirit*, p. 246, cites Green, *II Peter and Jude*, pp. 183-84.
3. Dunn, *Jesus and the Spirit*, p. 246.

John, Jude understands the appearance of these scoffing, boasting and unspiritual intruders as a characteristic of 'the last times' (v. 18). Certainly the situation has already been foretold (v. 17, cf. Mk 13.22/Mt. 24.24, cf. 1 Tim. 4.1). The command to combat these men by steering into truth the doubters and those influenced by this invasion (vv. 22, 23), then, assumes the eschatological struggle against evil—a struggle which both obediently mirrors the mercy of Christ, and continues onward until the readers themselves are 'brought to eternal life'.

An important issue which Warfield raises in *Counterfeit Miracles* emerges from several of these passages: the revelation of Christ given 'atomistically' to believers, a situation he describes as the 'mystic's dream'.[1] Warfield argues that the Holy Spirit no longer introduces 'new and unneeded revelations into the world', and in the same breath, that the present task of the Spirit is to 'diffuse this one complete revelation through the world and to bring mankind to a saving knowledge of it'. Chapter 2 touched on Warfield's confusion of the *means* of revelation and its *content*, that is, that one necessarily affected the other. A whole range of divine revelations and miracles can, and in fact do, occur which in no way diminish the authority of 'final revelation' in Christ and Scripture; for example, cases in which the gospel requires application: guidance, discernment, correction, healing, exorcism and so on, none of which adds a single word to the Bible or creeds. But does the New Testament in fact predict 'atomistic' revelation of Christ's purposes and will to meet each person's 'separate needs'?

Many of the passages just surveyed provide evidence that the 'testimony of Christ is [repeatedly] confirmed' 'until the end' to church members through revelatory charismata, including miracles (1 Cor. 1.4-8). The list continues in the following: Eph. 1.8-10 ('making known the mystery of his will', cf. v. 18); 3.18 ('empowered to grasp the dimensions. . . '); 4.13 (spiritual gifts 'until we all arrive at the unity of the faith and of the full knowledge of the Son of God'); Phil. 1.9-10 (knowledge and perception to 'discern what is best. . . until the day of Christ', cf. Col. 1.9-12); 1 Pet. 1.5 ('shielded by God's power until. . . the last time'); and finally, 1 Jn 2.27 ('his anointing *remains in you* . . . and teaches you about all

---

1. Warfield, *Counterfeit Miracles*, p. 26.

things. . . that anointing is real and not counterfeit'). 'Extraordinary' spiritual gifts, for example prophecy and other revelatory works, are to function normatively in the church 'confirming' (Heb. 2.3-4) the apostolic testimony of Christ. This testimony is confirmed not by the mere occurrence of 'wonders', but by the fact that these events themselves repeat and apply the gospel in all its expressions until the end of this age, reminding of the exaltation and rule of Christ over every situation: comfort, warning and edification; healing and deliverances; the presentation/proclamation of the kingdom of God in the power of the Holy Spirit.

3. *Summary*

The evidentialist function ascribed by Warfield to miracles, the foundation for cessationism, is reductionistic and superficial in view of their dominating roles in the biblically formulated doctrines of pneumatology and the kingdom of God. An application of Warfield's biblical hermeneutic to the scriptural data on the Holy Spirit reveals a portrayal of the Spirit's activity as characteristically, if not exclusively, charismatic. To speak of the Spirit's 'subsequent work' as functioning only within the Calvinistic *ordo salutis*, and not in the wider range of charismata, is anachronistic. As he operates within the traditional stages of 'salvation', as Calvinism conceived it, the work of the Spirit is thoroughly revelatory and lies on a continuum of revelatory activity which would include the charismata of 1 Corinthians 12. Warfield's limitation on contemporary work of the Spirit is not only to confuse the object of revelation with its mode of presentation and application, but is also to alienate theology from its clear and authoritative biblical grounding.

Similarly, Warfield's understanding of the present work of Christ in his exaltation falls far short of the biblical teaching. The Bible teaches that Jesus' earthly mission was to inaugurate the kingdom of God in charismatic power, and that he is to continue that mission through Christian believers, beginning with his disciples and their converts until the end of the age. The central expression of the kingdom of God is its divine power displacing the rule and ruin of the demonic. Hence the New Testament miracles did not appear in order to accredit preaching, but rather the preaching articulated the miracle, placing it in its christological setting and demanding a believing and repentant response. In the present, the exalted Christ continues to pour out his charismata upon his church to continue his kingdom mission. Christ's work is emphatically not 'done', as Warfield would suggest, but remains active in his church through his presence and distribution of the whole variety of spiritual gifts.

In this chapter I have examined passages which exhibit a single point: the Scriptures explicitly teach that spiritual gifts equip the church for its mission *specifically* until the end of the age. The broad range of God's graces, on a seamless continuum from what the classical Protestant tradition would call 'illumination' to prophecy and the working of miracles, is 'set in the church' for its edification, guidance, correction, comfort and worship of God. The foregoing passages presuppose, explicitly or implicitly, that these charismata are bestowed on the church as the central function of the lordship of the exalted Jesus, and teach directly that they necessarily continue all during this present age until he returns. Further, the charismata serve as Christ's equipment for the intervening time of the 'messianic war', waged not against humanity but against the demonic powers tyrannizing it. Such eschatological warfare necessarily involves casualties; but suffering as a function of charismatic service in Christ only further indicates the duration of the battle and its victorious conclusion at the parousia. Against Warfield's position that the Holy Spirit no longer reveals divine truth 'atomistically', to each believer, several passages have shown that the charismata are normatively expected to reveal divine truth to each and every believer; that, indeed, the very structure of the church body is established to that end. Revelation and miracles, however, are to remain within the theological and moral framework of 'final' revelation in Christ as revealed once and for all in Scripture.

The following chapter attempts to draw the foregoing themes into a fuller coherence and significance.

Chapter 4

SUMMARY AND CONCLUSIONS

Many Evangelicals today would affirm Bishop Butler's stern rebuke to John Wesley: 'Sir, the pretending to extraordinary revelations and gifts of the Holy Ghost is a horrid thing, a very horrid thing'.[1] What is the reason for such a revulsion to contemporary charismatic experience? Simply because, in the long evolution of Christian theology, miracles have come to signify the additional revelation of qualitatively new Christian doctrine, principally, in Scripture. To claim a revelation or a miracle represents an attempt, essentially, to add new content to the Bible.

The modern conflict over the cessation of miraculous gifts has antecedents as old as the fairly sophisticated arguments of early rabbinic Judaism. But the cessationist doctrine found its classic expression in post-Reformation era Calvinism: (1) the essential role of miraculous charismata was to accredit normative Christian doctrine and its bearers; (2) while God may providentially act in unusual, even striking, ways, true miracles are limited to epochs of special divine revelation, that is, those within the biblical period; (3) miracles are judged by the doctrines they purport to accredit: if the doctrines are false, or alter orthodox doctrines, their accompanying miracles are necessarily counterfeit.

Since it is widely believed that Scripture alone is the basis for Protestant doctrine, it is no wonder, then, that the traditional post-Reformation arguments against contemporary miracles (cessationism) have been widely disseminated. But the case for the continuation of the whole range of God's gifts and graces has only recently been articulated in terms beyond the usual appeals to personal experience, based more on serious historical and biblical study. Even within the

1. Cited by R.A. Knox, *Enthusiasm* (Oxford: Oxford University Press, 1950), p. 450.

latter area, the case for continuing spiritual gifts generally rests on a very few biblical texts, usually centering on 1 Cor 13.8-10. Theologically, the case is advanced on the simple assertion that because miracles are not limited to evidential functions in the Bible, and because prophecy is given mainly for 'edification, exhortation and encouragement' and not construed as an addition to a sufficient Scripture, the basic cessationist premise (that miraculous charismata necessarily accredit new doctrine) is bypassed. If the function of the charismata determines their duration, then their edificatory, rather than simply evidential, functions determine their continuation.

The doctrine of cessationism, however, deserves a more thorough examination of its foundational premises, and a broader investigation of the relevant biblical witness, than it has heretofore received. It is to this need that this project is addressed. The purpose of this study is ultimately irenic, undertaken with the hope that a biblical understanding of charismatic function in its eschatological setting may defuse the conflict over cessationism.

The doctrine that revelatory and miraculous spiritual gifts passed away with the apostolic age may best be approached by examining the central premises of the most prominent and representative modern expression of cessationism, Benjamin B. Warfield's *Counterfeit Miracles*. The thesis of this study is that Warfield's polemic—the culmination of a historically evolving argument—fails because of internal inconsistencies with respect to its concept of miracle and its biblical hermeneutics. I would argue that contemporary cessationism stands upon certain post-Reformation and Enlightenment era conceptions of miracle as evidence, upon highly evolved, postbiblical emphases about the Holy Spirit, the kingdom of God and their normative expressions in the world. The central fault of Warfield's cessationism is that it is far more dogmatically than scripturally based. His cessationism represents a failure to grasp the biblical portrayal of the eschatological outpouring of the Spirit of prophecy, expressed characteristically in the charismata, which are bestowed until the end of this age by the exalted Christ as manifestations of the advancing kingdom of God.

In this work I have reviewed the historical evolution of Warfield's cessationism and the concept of miracle on which it depends; I have then examined Warfield's cessationist polemic itself and tested it for internal consistency with respect to its concept of miracle, its historical method and its biblical hermeneutics. Finally I have examined representative passages of Scripture which summarize the recurring theme in the NT that Spiritual gifts are granted for the advance of God's kingdom and the maturity of the church until the end of this present age. This present chapter recapitulates on this and concludes with a review of some biblical principles applicable to cessationism.

1. *The Historical Evolution of Cessationism and its View of Miracle*

Benjamin Warfield's 'Protestant polemic' against continuing miracles is 'Protestant' in that it seeks to protect the core principle of religious authority on which his tradition was based: the final, normative revelation of Christ in Scripture. From before the turn of the century until Warfield responded with his work *Counterfeit Miracles* in 1918, Protestant religious authority had come under increasing attack, in Warfield's view, from a variety of competing religious movements. Warfield perceived that these religious bodies—for example Roman Catholics, proto-Pentecostals like the Irvingites, faith healers, Christian Scientists and the theological liberals—were to some degree heterodox, because they all shared an ominous flaw in faith or practice: openness to contemporary miraculous gifts.

Cessationism did not originate within orthodox Christianity, but within normative Judaism in the first three centuries of the Common Era. An early form of cessationism was directed at Jesus. One of the accusations which led to Jesus' execution was that he had violated the commands of Deuteronomy 13 and 18, which forbid performing a sign or a wonder to lead the people astray after false gods. The Mishnah and Talmud developed a sophisticated cessationist polemic, used not only against early charismatic Christians, but intramurally within Judaism by competing rabbis.[1]

Christian theologians at first attacked Jews with their own cessationism, but not until the fourth century did they employ the polemic against other Christians. These apologists, for example Justin and Origen, argued that God had withdrawn the Spirit of prophecy and miracles from the Jews and transferred it to the church as proof of its continued divine favor. Thus they came to share with Jews an aberrant view of miracle: evidentialism. This is the view that the primary, if

---

1. See Greenspahn, 'Why Prophecy Ceased', pp. 37-49.

not exclusive, function of miracles is to accredit and vindicate the bearer of a doctrinal system.

Against some Christian sects who claimed unique access to the Spirit, or claimed that the charismata would cease with them, the orthodox repeatedly cited 1 Cor. 13.10 as proof for the continuation of spiritual gifts in all the church until the parousia. By the time of Chrysostom (d. 407), however, cessationism provided the ecclesiastical hierarchy with a ready rationale against complaints of diminished charismatic activity in mainline churches. Their cessationist arguments ran in two contradictory directions: miracles either appeared unconditionally (that is, they had been required as scaffolding for the church, which once established no longer required such support), or conditionally (that is, if the church became more righteous, the charismata would reappear).

John Calvin turned the cessationist polemic against Roman Catholicism and the radical reformation, undercutting their claims to religious authority based on miracles and revelations. Calvin popularized the restriction of miracles to the accreditation of the apostles and specifically to their gospel, though he was less rigid about cessationism than most of his followers. Nevertheless, from Aquinas through the Enlightenment, the concept of miracle assumed an increasingly rationalistic cast, until it became a cornerstone of the Enlightenment apologetic of Locke, Newton, Glanville and Boyle, but a millstone in Hume.

Hume's skepticism about the possibility of miracles, the ultimate cessationist polemic (which exemplified Warfield's historical-critical method in his examination of postbiblical miracle claims), precipitated the response of Scottish common-sense philosophy, a somewhat rationalistic apologetic made widely popular by William Paley's *Christian Evidences*. Paley argued from the divine design of nature, predictive (messianic) prophecy and from (biblical) miracles. Scottish common-sense philosophy epistemology was short-lived in Europe but came to dominate American thought so thoroughly that for about a century the Romantic reaction, so widespread in Europe, scarcely gained a foothold.

Nowhere had the Enlightenment era Scottish philosophy been more warmly nurtured than at Princeton Seminary, where Warfield was its last major proponent. Warfield seems unconscious of the impact of Scottish common-sense philosophy on his thought, but his *Counterfeit*

Miracles rests solidly on its epistemology, as does his concept of miracle.

Warfield's concept of miracle requires an essentially deistic view of nature invaded by a supernatural force so utterly transcendent that, to an impartial observer acquainted with the facts, no possible natural 'means' could produce such an effect. An event must be instantaneous, absolute and total to qualify as a miracle. A startling, dramatic healing may occur today so that 'the supernaturalness of the act may be apparent as to demonstrate God's activity in it to all right-thinking minds conversant with the facts'. But to call such an event a miracle is to obscure the division between miracles and the 'general supernatural'.[1] Similarly, Warfield divides NT spiritual gifts into those which are 'distinctively gracious' ('ordinary' gifts) and those which are 'distinctly miraculous' ('extraordinary') gifts.

On the one hand, Warfield insists that making such distinctions is 'simply a question of evidence',[2] and on the other a matter of one's background assumptions. It is no surprise, then, that when Warfield spends the greater part of *Counterfeit Miracles* 'sifting' the evidence on postbiblical miracles throughout church history, he arrives at 'an incomparable inventory of objections to the supernatural'.[3] Warfield has decided their fate at the outset when he insists that miracles may only occur as 'the credentials of the Apostles' and 'necessarily passed away' with them.[4] Warfield's cessationism involves a double standard: in *Counterfeit Miracles* he applies to postbiblical miracles the rationalistic critical methods used by Hume and Harnack, the same methods that he attacks in liberal critics who apply them to the biblical accounts.

Biblically, discernment of a miracle is neither 'simply a question of evidence', nor is it simply based on one's *a priori* position. A miracle is an event perceived, in varying degrees of accuracy (see for example Jn 12.29), by divine revelation. 'The natural man cannot accept the matters [gifts] of the Spirit' for they are 'discerned by the Spirit' (1 Cor. 2.14).

Not only is Warfield's understanding of miracle discernment unbiblical, but so is his understanding of their function. By demanding a

1. Warfield, *Counterfeit Miracles*, p. 163.
2. *SSWW*, p. 175.
3. Brown, *Miracles and the Critical Mind*, p. 199.
4. *Counterfeit Miracles*, p. 6.

strict evidentialist function for miracles, Warfield confuses the sufficiency of revelation, that is, in the unique historical manifestation of
Christ and essential Christian doctrine, with the ongoing means of
communicating, applying and actualizing that revelation via such
charismata as prophecy and miracles. We see below that the charismata do not so much accredit the gospel as express and concretize the
gospel. Just as sound and inspired preaching applies, but does not
change, the all-sufficient Scripture, so true gifts of prophecy, knowledge or wisdom reveal human needs, directing them to God's truth
within the eternally-sealed limits of the biblical canon. Just as gifts of
administration or hospitality tangibly express the gospel and advance
the kingdom of God, but do not alter its doctrinal content, so likewise
gifts of healing and miracles.

For Warfield, the inerrant authority of Scripture was the bedrock
of his theology. So it is ironic that in only a few scattered pages of
Counterfeit Miracles does he seek scriptural support for his cessationist polemic.

2. A Biblical/Theological Response to Cessationism

Warfield's polemic failed to comprehend the broad sweep of biblical
theology when it addressed the crucial eschatological dimension of the
charismata in pneumatology and in the presentation of the kingdom of
God. These doctrines, as they appear in classical Protestant systematic
theologies, have been grotesquely misshapen by a long evolution of
tangential dogmatic conflicts. Even after competent biblical studies
have been published on these areas, not only Warfield but most other
systematicians have been reluctant to utilize the results. Warfield's
evidentialist function for miracles, the foundation for cessationism, is
reductionistic and superficial in view of the dominating role for
miracles in the biblically formulated, eschatologically conditioned
doctrines of pneumatology and the kingdom of God.

A Biblical Doctrine of the Holy Spirit is Inimical to Cessationism

Warfield's desire to limit the Spirit's contemporary miraculous and
revelatory work is not only to confuse the finality of revelation with
its mode of presentation and application, but also to change the essential character of the Holy Spirit as biblically defined and to alienate his
pneumatology from its clear and authoritative biblical grounding. If

we apply Warfield's own biblical hermeneutic to every scriptural context on the Holy Spirit, it reveals a profile of the Spirit's activity that is characteristically, if not exclusively, miraculously charismatic—virtually the consensus of serious biblical scholarship. In a broad sense, the Spirit of the Bible is the Spirit of prophecy. To speak of the Spirit's 'subsequent [post-apostolic] work' as functioning only within the Calvinistic *ordo salutis* demonstrates that the Holy Spirit of post-Reformation cessationism is far removed from the portrayal of the Spirit in the canonical Scriptures. Most significantly, Warfield's pneumatology fails to account for the great Old Testament promises of the specifically prophetic Spirit *to be poured out upon all eschatological generations who believe*, beginning with those in the New Testament era (Isa. 47.3; 59.21; Joel 2.28-32; cf. Acts 2.4, 38).

A Biblical Doctrine of the Kingdom of God is Inimical to Cessationism

Warfield also failed to address the important implications of the doctrine of the kingdom of God. Its nature is essentially that of warfare against the kingdom of Satan and its ruinous effects (Mt. 4.23; 9.35; 10.6, 7; 12.28 // Lk. 11.20; Lk. 9.2, 60; 10.1-2, 9, 11; Acts 10.38). The NT teaches that Jesus' earthly mission was to inaugurate the kingdom of God in charismatic power, and that he is to continue that mission through Christian believers, beginning with his disciples and their converts and continuing until the end of the age. As a rabbi's good disciples, his followers are to duplicate and continue exactly his work ('teaching them to obey *all* that I commanded you,' Mt. 28.20), in this case, to demonstrate and articulate the inbreaking Kingdom. This is shown by: (1) an analysis of the commissioning accounts of Matthew 10, Mark 6; Luke 9 and 10; Mt. 28.19-20 (cf 24.14); Lk. 24.49 and Acts 1.4, 5, 8; (2) the characteristic way in which the kingdom is demonstrated and articulated in Acts; and (3) the summary statements of Paul's ministry among the Gentiles throughout his epistles (Rom. 15.18-20; 1 Cor. 2.4; 2 Cor. 12.12; 1 Thess. 1.5, cf. Acts 15.12). Thus, the 'signs of a true apostle,' or of any Christian, do not accredit anyone as a bearer of orthodoxy, but rather characterize the way in which the commissions of Jesus to proclaim and demonstrate ('in word and deed') the eschatological kingdom of God are normatively expressed by any believer. Whether in the context of an unevangelized crowd of pagans, or within the church community itself, wherever the Spirit displaces the kingdom of darkness in its various manifestations of evil, whether sin, sickness or demonic possession, the kingdom of God has provisionally arrived. Such victories of repentance, healing or other restoration from the demonic world represent a continuing, though partial, experience of the fully realized and uncontested reign of God to come.

An essential element of the kingdom of God is divine power—directed toward reconciliation of humanity to God, of righteousness, peace and joy—displacing the rule and ruin of the demonic ('The kingdom of God does not consist in talk, but in δύναμις', 1 Cor. 4.20). Of the 98 contexts of divine δύναμις in the NT, 65 refer to what the Protestant tradition would designate as 'extraordinary' or 'miraculous' charismata. 33 of the cases refer to the power of God without clear indication in the immediate context as to the exact way in which God's power is working. The NT miracles do not appear simply to accredit preaching (or, 'the word'); rather the preaching in most cases articulates the miracle, placing it in its christological setting and demanding a believing and repentant response. The exalted Christ continues to pour out his charismata upon his church to empower his kingdom mission until the end of the age (see below). It is simply unbiblical to say, as Warfield does, that after an initial outpouring of spiritual gifts in the apostolic age to reveal and establish church doctrine, the exalted Christ's 'work has been done'.

The Specifically Eschatological Dimension of the Doctrines of Pneumatology and the Kingdom of God is Inimical to Cessationism
Warfield's failure to grasp the eschatological implications of cessationism is perhaps the most crucial. He nowhere notices that the OT promises of the Spirit of prophecy and miracles apply to the entire time between the two comings of the messiah; that Jesus' 'authority/ power' granted in his commissions to his church is extended to all nations and is to continue until the end of the age—a frequently repeated theme in the NT epistles. The Spirit of revelation and power is bestowed throughout this age as his own 'down-payment,' 'first-fruits' or 'taste' of 'the powers of the age to come', until the time of the fullness of the Spirit in the consummated kingdom of God.[1] Warfield never really argued against this view of the place of

1. See the diagrams of NT salvation history with respect to the outpouring of the charismata in this present age in Chapter 3.

charismata in biblical theology, which was common in the scholarship of his day.

Finally, Warfield the exegete, beyond his failure to engage with the theological issues above, failed even to acquaint himself with the brief but significant passages of Scripture which teach the continuation of the charismata. It is because Warfield is first and foremost the biblicist, and because he claims to have structured his whole polemic on 'two legs', an investigation into history and *Scripture*, that this omission is so glaring and so disappointing.

New Testament Passages Reiterating the Pattern of Continuing Charismata during the Time of Christ's Present Exaltation until the End of the Age

The following citations paraphrase the results of the brief exegetical surveys in the previous chapter and restate the role of the charismata in the eschatological framework outlined above: the charismata continue during this age to minister toward the (as yet unrealized) goal of complete maturity of the church. Again, expressed biblically, the divine 'Spirit' is presented in Scripture as associated primarily with and essentially performing charismatic operations. The paraphrases below are not to be construed as exegeses, but as summarizing the meaning of the passages exegetically treated above in Chapter 3.

1 Corinthians 1.4-8. I always thank God for you because of God's grace (including the whole range of charismata) because in *every way* you have been enriched in him—in every kind of speech (including prophecy) and in every kind of knowledge (including the gift of revealed knowledge). You are doing this now *exactly as* (καθώς) the testimony of Christ *was* confirmed in you (that is, charismatically, by the apostles and evangelists who first demonstrated and articulated the gospel to you)—with the result that you do not *now* lack *any* spiritual gift during the time you are awaiting the revelation of our Lord Jesus Christ. (The Lord) will *also* (not merely when the gospel first came to you, or even only now) *continue to confirm/strengthen* you (in the same way as you are now experiencing the charismata in the time you are 'awaiting' the end) *until the end*, so that (via the strengthening and purifying charismata which generate growth and progressive maturity) you will be blameless on the day of our Lord Jesus Christ.

1 Corinthians 13.8-13. Love never ends: it continues on into the age to come. But wherever the charismatic operations of prophecies, tongues speaking or revealed knowledge occur, they will be ended. Like childhood, they all represent an incomplete, yet necessary, stage of God's eternal plan.

But when will these three (representative) gifts, that is, the charismata generally, cease? The eschatological principle is this: when the complete (end) arrives, at that precise point, the incomplete will be ended. Specifically, when Christ returns at the end of this present age, then, and not a moment before, the charismata—gifts of prophecy, tongues and revealed knowledge here offered as examples—which are incomplete compared to the ultimate heavenly realities they only now indicate, will all come to an end, having served their temporary purpose.

Let us note three or four illustrations of this point. First, as babies (the state of infancy here representing the present age) we babble, think and reason like babies (this representing the charismata, present in this age, of speech and knowledge). But at adulthood (our existence in the age to come) we attain vastly greater powers of communication, thinking and reasoning.

Secondly, in the present age, the charismata only serve as indirect or indistinct perceptions of God or his will, like looking into a mirror or a photograph. But in heaven, the mirror or photograph (the charismata) are unnecessary if we can see God 'face to face'. At that point these items, which had helped preserve the somewhat distant relationship, will have served their purpose and will be discarded, since we will have the real person before us.

Thirdly, in this present age I can know God, but the charismata reveal him to me only in glimpses and hints. But then, in heaven, I will know God (καθώς) exactly as and to the same degree that God knows me now. Of what use will be those tentative and imprecise gifts of revealed knowledge under those conditions?

Fourthly, faith, hope and love all have a role in this present age, but, like the other charismata, faith (a charism of revelation that can produce miracles or any other aspect of God's salvation), and hope (another gift of God which is superseded if it results in the presence and reality of its object), will be unnecessary in the age to come because of their anticipatory character; in heaven, the waiting will be over. By contrast, love is greater, because, unlike faith, hope and the other charismata, love never ends.

Ephesians 4.11-13. (The ascended Christ) gave some apostles, prophets, evangelists, and pastor-teachers (not to accredit the gospel or its bearers, but) for the perfecting of the saints toward the work of ministry, toward the building up of the body of Christ. (But for how long?) These gifts are distributed, in principle (v. 7), 'to each' *until* (μέχρι)—an ongoing process of distribution—we *all arrive* at the unity of the faith, at the *full* knowledge of the Son of God, at full, mature adulthood, that is, at the level of stature (maturity) of the fullness of Christ. Even Paul has not 'attained' this state (Phil. 3.12).

Ephesians 1.13-23. In the context of believers' receiving 'all wisdom and understanding' (1.8) and Paul's continued prayer for the same (1.17) and to experience ('know') '[Christ's] incomparably great power', like that of the resurrection, Paul describes the time-frame: 'In him, when you believed, you were marked with a seal, the promised Holy Spirit, who is a deposit [or first installment—the first payment of the same to follow] guaranteeing our inheritance [described as incomparably great, like resurrection power, in 1.19], *until* (εἰς) the redemption of those who are God's possession—to the praise of his glory'. This state of affairs is active in believers and is paralleled to the exaltation of Christ which occurs 'not only in the present age, but also in the one to come' (1.21-23, cf. 2.6).

Ephesians 3.14-21. Paul's prayer is that the readers may 'have power through the Spirit' that in love they '*may have power together with all the saints* [an explicit universal application]. . . to the goal that you may be filled to the measure of all the fullness of God. Now to him who is able to do immeasurably more than all we ask or imagine, *according to the power that is at work within us*, to Him be glory, *in the church* and in Christ Jesus, *throughout all generations* for ever and ever. Amen'. Cf. Isa. 59.21.

Ephesians 4.30. With Eph. 1.13-23 above, the time-frame of the Spirit's prophetic presence in the believer is restated: 'Do not grieve the Holy Spirit of God [an allusion to ignoring prophetic warning, for example Isa 63.10? Cf. Eph. 4.29] with whom you were sealed [an ongoing mark of ownership and protection] *until* (εἰς) the day of redemption'.

Ephesians 5.15-19. In the present evil days (characteristic of the time of the messianic woes [Mt. 24.9-12; 1 Tim. 3] preceding the parousia, don't be drunk on wine, but continue to 'be filled with the Spirit [cf. Jer. 23.9; Amos 2.12; Acts 2.13, 15; Lk. 1.15]). Speak to one another with psalms, hymns and spiritual songs' (glossolalic singing? 1 Cor. 14.13-17)—perhaps representative of the whole range of charismatic/ prophetic operations to continue during these 'present evil days'.

Ephesians 6.10-20. Be empowered (closely associated with 'miracle/ mighty work' in the NT) in the Lord and in his mighty power. . . struggling against demonic forces. . . with sword of Spirit, the word of God (prophecy) and constant prayer. Since we are in the time of the messianic woes that Jesus predicted standing before magistrates and the like, we should pray that words will be given to us (divine passive). Cf. Mt. 10.19b-20 // Mk 13.11: 'it is not you speaking but the Holy Spirit'.

Philippians 1.5-10. 'Christ who has begun a good work in you will carry it on to completion until the day of Christ Jesus. What work? Sharing in God's grace (and imitating Paul, 3.17; 4.9—necessarily including the charismata [cf. Mt. 28.20, 'teaching them *all* that I have commanded you'] in defending and confirming—a word in this context speaking of charismata, signs and wonders. And this is my prayer: that your love may abound more and more in knowledge and perception (charismata of revelation), so that you may be able to discern what is best and may be pure and blameless *until* (εἰς) the day of Christ.

Colossians 1.9-12. We have not stopped praying for you and asking God to fill you with the knowledge of his will through *all* Spiritual wisdom and understanding (revelatory gifts). . . being strengthened with *all power*. . . to build spiritual maturity, looking toward (though already provisionally experiencing) the inheritance of the saints in the kingdom of light. Indeed we have already been brought into that kingdom.

1 Thessalonians 1.5-8. In view of the rabbi–disciple model in the Philippians passage cited above, the normative transmission of the gospel in 'word and deed' appears in this passage. 'Our gospel came to you not simply with words, but also with power (ἐν δυνάμει), with the Holy Spirit and with deep conviction. . . You became imitators of us and of the Lord. . . And so (it follows) *you yourselves became models* to all the believers in Macedonia and Achaia.' The pattern of the gospel's normative pattern of transmission in the miraculous power of the Spirit was carried over into a *third* generation, two away from Paul; those upon whom apostolic hands would not be laid! All this has the the goal of building Christian maturity until the end of this age.

1 Thessalonians 5.11-23. In a strong eschatological context of the parousia Paul encourages believers to continue edifying each other in love: 'Do not put out the Spirit's fire; [that is] do not treat prophecies with contempt. Test them and heed the good ones, in view of the goal of being blameless at the coming of our Lord Jesus Christ. The One who calls you will be faithful to preserve you [using these charismata, cf. 1 Cor. 1.4-8].'

2 Thessalonians 1.11-12. For which—in an ongoing process toward the goal (that you will be counted worthy at the coming of Christ) we constantly pray for you that our God will count you worthy and may fulfill your every good purpose *and every work of faith in power* (ἐν δυνάμει), so that the name of our Lord Jesus might be glorified in you and you in him.

1 Peter 1.5. Through faith you are being shielded by God's power (ἐν δυνάμει), *until* (εἰς) a salvation ready to be revealed at the last time.

1 Peter 4.7-12. The end of all things (the goal and context of this warning) is near. . . Each one should use whatever spiritual gift he or she has received to serve others, faithfully administering God's grace in its various forms. If anyone speaks, it should be as the oracles of God. Most commentators see this as a reference to NT prophecy. The parenesis is given against the approaching end, with the understanding that prophecy is to be operative up until that point.

1 John 2.26-28. As an antidote to false prophets, John encourages the gift of prophecy: 'Dear children, *this is the last hour*. . . But *all of you have an anointing* from the Holy One, and all of you know the truth. . . As for you, the anointing you received from him remains in you, and you do not need anyone to teach you. But as his anointing teaches you about all things and as that anointing is real, not counterfeit—just as it has taught you, remain in him. . . continue in him, so that when he appears we may be confident and unashamed before him at his coming'. This passage is strikingly parallel to the promise of the Paraclete to the apostles (Jn 14.26; 15.26; 16.13-14). Here the promise is to the general readers.

Jude 18-21. (As Jesus prophesied) '*In the last times*. . . there will be those who follow their own human desires, and who do not have the Spirit. By contrast, you, beloved, during these same "last times", *edify yourselves in your most holy faith by praying in the Spirit*'. 'Praying in the Spirit' means praying in response to the direct leading of the Spirit—a revelatory process, or, as in 1 Cor. 14.4, 14, 15, in glossolalic prayer ('one who "*prays in the Spirit*" *edifies* himself').

Each of these passages, then, continues the pattern of Jesus' commissions to his disciples to demonstrate and articulate the kingdom in the power of the Spirit—to the twelve, the 70 (72), the 120—as archetypes of 'all of the Lord's people' (including the readers of these verses) whom Moses wished would all be filled with the Spirit of prophecy (Num. 11.29; cf. Isa. 59.21; Joel 2.28-30; 1 Cor. 14.1, 5, 39).

The Clear Statements of Scripture regarding the Charismata are Inimical to Cessationism
Warfield also fails to perceive that the explicitly stated commands to fulfill the biblical conditions for the manifestation of the charismata (for example repentance, faith and prayer) contradict his unconditional, temporary connection of the charismata with the apostles and the introduction of their doctrine. He also fails to account for the many explicit biblical commands directly to seek, desire and employ the very charismata he claims have ceased. How can Warfield ignore these biblically explicit conditions and commands for the continuation

of the charismata, if, as he insists, the Bible continues as the normative guide to the church for its faith and praxis?

The NT repeatedly stresses to its readers that the appearance of God's charismatic power correlates with human response, specifically, in faith and actions. But it is clear that all people, quickened by the Spirit, are commanded, either by precept or example, to respond in faith and prayer to God's graces.[1]

Closely related to the argument above that the function of the charismata determines their duration is the argument from Scripture that the appearance of the charismata depends, not on accrediting functions, but on human responses to explicit biblical commands; we should seek, request and employ the charismata, on the basis of prior repentance and obedience toward God, via faith and prayer. To deny that these commands of Scripture, woven so thoroughly throughout the fabric of the NT, have relevance today, is to call into question the very relevance of the scriptural canon for the church of any age. These are not commands simply to the apostles, but often by apostles to the 'laity'. In any case, all these biblical commands can be construed as parenetic to the church at large. Biblical commands, 'seek', 'rekindle', 'employ', 'let us use', 'strive to excel [in spiritual gifts]', 'desire earnestly', 'do not quench', and so on, make little sense canonically if the occurrence of the charismata bears no relation to the obedience of these commands.

Moreover, cessationism is inimical to at least five further important NT principles regarding the charismata.

1. Paul implicitly challenges the belief that the miraculous gifts of the Spirit were granted only for the establishment of doctrine for the church, which would then carry on more or less under its own interpretive intellect with a greatly restricted activity of the Spirit. Paul exclaims to the Galatians who were tempted by a resurgent Judaism to exchange their calling as prophets for that of the scribes and a religion of Torah-study and works-righteousness: 'Having begun in the Spirit [the context indicates a miracle-producing Spirit], will you now be completed, or reach maturity (ἐπιτελεῖσθε) in the flesh?' Paul does not force a choice between the charismata of prophecy and miracle versus biblical precepts; he insists upon both. Scripture itself affirms the ongoing process of spiritual perfecting (maturing) in this age as

---

1. See Chapter 3.

being normatively developed by the whole range of the charismata, which, within the framework of Scripture, reveal Christ even as they illuminate, apply, express and actualize his gospel. Against cessationism, the NT insists that the church is both initiated *and matured* by the whole range of the Spirit's gifts.

2. Rom. 11.29 states a principle that could hardly be more clearly anti-cessationist: that from God's side, his radical and unconditional grace offers to sustain the above process throughout the present age: 'God's gifts (χαρίσματα) and his call are irrevocable—not repented of, or withdrawn'. The context shows that the human failure to receive God's call, or charismata, does not at all require that they are sovereignly withdrawn in church history, but rather that they cannot become manifested in those who reject them. Accordingly, it may be this very unhappy state of the church that Paul foresaw: an intellectualized quasi-deism among those having 'a form of religion, while denying its power (δύναμις)' (2 Tim. 3.5).

3. Still another Pauline principle is that no one member, or charismatic function, of the body of Christ can say to another, 'I have no need of you' (1 Cor. 12.21). Cessationism says precisely that. Similarly, no one who is gifted in a specific way may demand that all the body take on that particular attribute. The point of 1 Corinthians 12 is that for a body to be a body at all it must have *all* its functions working reciprocally for the good of the whole, each recognizing not only its own value but also the crucial importance of the others. By its very nature, cessationism violates this key biblical principle.

4. The cessationist schema that miracles cluster around great revelatory events to establish the truth of that revelation does not bear scrutiny. Jeremiah lays down an explicit principle about the distribution of divine signs and wonders in Jer. 32.20: 'You performed signs and wonders in Egypt *and have continued them to this day, both in Israel and among all mankind*'. Moreover, while new, enscripturated revelation abounded during and just after the exodus, there was relatively little new doctrinal content added during the miracle-working time of Elijah and Elisha, and certainly no more new revelation in Daniel than, say, Isaiah, Jeremiah, Ezekiel or the other prophets.

Moreover, the greatest new revelation of all was announced by John the Baptist, who 'did no miracle' (Jn 10.41). The contention that miracles faded and ceased as one moves toward the end of Acts is misleading. Much of the last part of Acts relates to an imprisoned

Paul, who, when released for normal ministry at the end of the book, practically empties the island of Malta of its sick (Acts 28.9)! Further, to argue that because 'Jews seek signs and Greeks seek wisdom' (1 Cor. 1.22), Christian evangelism moved from being characterized by miracles to being characterized by reasoned discourse (and remained as such for the rest of church history) flies in the face of Paul's own characterization of his highly charismatic gospel among the Gentiles (Acts 15.12; Rom. 15.19; 2 Cor. 12.12; 1 Thess. 1.5). More importantly, following the tradition of Jesus who refused signs to those who demanded them for evidential proof (Mk 8.11-12; Mt. 12.38-39; Lk. 11.16, 29), Paul insists that his reaction to the unbelieving demand for a sign (or wisdom) is not willingly to provide them, as this argument would have it, but to preach the 'wisdom and power of God', Christ crucified, only to those who could receive it.

5. Finally, the essence of cessationism—the limitation of miracles to new revelation and its bearers—contradicts another biblical principle, namely, the biblical desire to see the Spirit of prophecy and miracle to be as broadly spread as possible. The classic case is Num. 11.26-29 where Joshua is threatened by the loss of Moses' 'accreditation' by the prophetic Spirit. Moses replies: 'Are you jealous for my sake? I wish all the Lord's people were prophets and that the Lord would put His Spirit on them!' The subsequent OT prophets foresaw an ideal time when the Spirit would be bestowed broadly upon all categories of humanity (Joel 2.28-29, cf. Acts 2.17-18, 21, 39). Similarly, Jesus refused to stop those who cast out demons in his name, though not directly associated with him (Mk 9.38-40 // Lk. 9.49-50). No doubt this logion was recorded for the church in response to exorcists, or perhaps those exercising spiritual gifts generally, who were not only not apostles, but were not even church members! At that point the 'accrediting' function of miracles becomes a little thin. Paul prays for 'all the saints [Jew and Gentile]' that they might experience gifts of revelation, knowledge and power (δύναμις) at the level of resurrection power that Jesus experienced (so also 1 Cor. 12.6; 14.1, 5, 24, 39; Gal. 3.5, 14; Eph. 5.18; Col. 1.9-14). Against cessationism, then, this brief sketch shows the biblical (and divine) impulse to offer the power of the Spirit to all who would respond to it, rather than limit it to a few founders of the Christian community whose status must be enhanced.

3. *Implications and Conclusions*

The frequent failure to respond to God's commands to manifest the kingdom of God in power is fully shared by most believers, 'charismatics' and non-charismatics alike. Both groups shape their theology and consequent practice on the basis of their own experience—or lack of it—rather than on a fresh and radical (in its original sense) view of Scripture. The presence or absence of certain charismata in one's experience proves nothing at all about one's spiritual status or destiny (Mt. 7.21-22). Neither group (charismatics or non-charismatics) is more or less 'saved' than the other; both are at once sinful, but justified by grace alone. Nevertheless, the NT offers patterns as to how the gospel is to be presented, received and lived out. We must not attempt to reframe our failures into virtues, that is, by allowing what the NT describes as 'unbelief' in and for the gifts of God, to be construed as having chosen 'the better way' of a 'stronger faith' without them. The rabbis' intellectualized biblical knowledge which led to their cessationism prompted Jesus to affirm that they knew 'neither the Scriptures nor the power of God' (Mt. 22.29 // Mk 12.24).

Much divisiveness over the gifts of the Spirit today derives from a premise common to both sides of the debate: evidentialism. If spiritual gifts are adduced as proofs of spiritual status or attainment, rather than used as tools for humble service for others, then conflict naturally follows. The core temptation to the first and Last Adam (Christ), and by extension to all of us, was to use spiritual knowledge and power to accredit one's independent and exalted religious status, instead of through them rendering glory, obedience and service to God. Spiritual gifts are powerful weapons against the kingdom of darkness; but misapplied in evidentialist polemics they can wound and destroy the people of God.

The charismata, then, reflect the very nature of God, who does not share his glory with another. Similarly, God is a Spirit of power, 'who changeth not'. If the church has 'begun in the Spirit', let us not attempt to change God's methods to complete our course in the weakness of human flesh. Since it is the Father's pleasure to 'give good gifts to them who ask Him', it must be our pleasure to receive them humbly.

Appendix I

'EVIDENCE' OF THE SPIRIT IN ACTS?

D.A. Carson (*Showing the Spirit*, pp. 137-58) presents a fairly sophisticated attempt to help some passages in Acts conform to a traditional Evangelical experience of the Holy Spirit and to divorce them from an overly Pentecostal interpretation. Carson lays out an exposition of the various outpourings of the Spirit in Acts, showing that the experience of speaking in tongues came corporately upon certain representative groups (the first believers, Acts 2; the Samaritans, Acts 8; the Gentiles, Acts 10-11, and the disciples of John in Ephesus, Acts 19). Carson maintains that Luke uses the visible charismatic presence of the Spirit coming on each of these groups to show their incorporation into the church directly by the work of the Spirit.

Carson's survey of contemporary 'charismatic' issues is generally a model of irenic charity, scholarship, balance and biblical insight. But his treatment of the practical application of the above passages demands scrutiny. First, Carson contends that all spiritual gifts (except apostleship in its 'tightly defined sense') continue throughout this age; that '*all* who live under this new covenant enjoy the gift of this prophetic [in a broad sense] Spirit' (p. 153); while 'some gifts, notably tongues, function in Acts in ways particularly related to the *inception* of the messianic age' (that is, as evidence for the inclusion of groups into the church), 'there is no exegetical warrant' for cessationism, 'once the crucial points of redemptive history have passed'. This is true because these gifts, notably tongues, also 'are tied *to the Spirit, to the new age*' (p. 155). Carson insists that 'non-charismatics have often been content to delineate the function of tongues where they appear in Acts, without adequate reflection on the fact that for Luke the Spirit does not simply inaugurate the new age and then disappear; rather, he *characterizes* the new age' (p. 151).

On the other hand, having said all this, Carson wants to deny the Pentecostal doctrine that these texts in Acts can be adduced to 'tell us that a *particular* manifestation of the Spirit attests the Spirit's presence or filling of baptism in every believer this side of Pentecost' (p. 155). 'Charismatics have erred in trying to read an individualizing paradigm into material not concerned to provide one' (p. 151, cf. p. 140: 'Luke's emphasis in Acts 2 is not on paradigms for personal experience but on the fulfillment of prophecy'). According to Carson, one can normatively expect the Spirit's presence at conversion in a fairly traditional Protestant profile: 'The Christian *knows* the Lord by the Spirit; the believer senses him, enjoys his presence, communes with him'. The Spirit seems to arrive in two stages: 'The Spirit in a

Christocentric fashion manifests himself in and to the believer; the believer in turn shows the Spirit' in a range of charismata much broader 'than the few over which so much fuss has erupted today' (p. 155). Though these latter gifts are not spelled out, they doubtless focus on tongues. He is right, of course, but like Protestant pneumatology generally, Carson's profile of Spirit-filling is less palpably charismatic than Luke's, and probably the rest of Scripture.

Carson implicitly recognizes that his contemporary model of Spirit-filling is not that of the four cases above, but dismisses the disparity on the grounds that in these cases the Spirit with gifts of utterance was granted as 'attestation' of *new groups* entering the church, and that where Luke records cases of Spirit-filling to *individuals* (hence our model for contemporary experience) no gift of tongues was given (for example Acts 4.8, 31; 6.3, 5; 7.55; 9.17; 11.24; 13.9, 52 [his examples, p. 150]). Several observations are in order.

First, Carson fails to distinguish between the *use* to which Luke puts these cases of Spirit-filling ('*attestation*', if this word is not too contaminated by rationalistic notions) and the nature of the experience itself. A heartbeat may be used to prove someone is alive, but to act in this way as 'proof' is not the essential function of the heartbeat. The heart may continue to beat irrespective of whether it is ever used as 'proof' of life. Similarly, because gifts of utterance may be used as proof of the presence of the Spirit, such proof does not change the essential and characteristic expression of the Spirit's coming. Carson's implication is that God added the gifts of utterance in the Spirit-filling experiences in these cases strictly for their polemical or didactic value, and that the ideal, essential, or 'normal and expected' Spirit-fillings cannot now be associated with gifts of utterance. To see otherwise is a 'hermeneutically uncontrolled' exercise of applying personally what Luke intended as only historically informative.

Accordingly, if we apply Carson's theology practically, a first-century Samaritan reading the Acts 8 account would be expected to respond: 'I can take comfort that Samaritans as a group were once accepted into the church by receiving the Spirit characterized by gifts of utterance, but since I am an individual and a few years too late, I cannot expect to receive the Spirit in the same way'. Or even more remarkably, following Carson's construction on p. 150, 'Because I am not "a baptized follower of the Baptist, an enthusiastic supporter of the Baptist's witness to Jesus", a "believer in Jesus' death and resurrection", and am "ignorant of Pentecost", I therefore cannot expect normatively to receive the Spirit accompanied by gifts of utterance!' Why do these cases sound so odd, forced, mechanical and implausible? Simply because they represent logical non-sequiturs—the same logical fallacy that Carson identified above: 'accrediting' gifts do not cease (or, fail to continue in the same pattern) simply because they were once used for that function.

Secondly, Carson's argument violates the very notion of 'epochal' in this context and Luke's theological intention as well. These kinds of epochal events, almost by definition, are epochal because they not only initiate an era, but serve as the prototype for subsequent events of the same kind. For example, Lindberg's Atlantic flight was 'epochal' precisely *because* all other ocean crossings of the same kind, that is, by humans in aircraft, have followed. Hence, when Luke identifies representative groups as being incorporated into the church by means of receiving the Spirit, all 'attested' by gifts of utterance, they are 'epochal' or 'prototypical' in that they set the pattern for and share the essential characteristics of individuals in similar groups to follow. In other words, to the reader they would say: 'If your group received the Spirit [Acts 2 probably includes *all* groups, incidentally], then you can too!' A heavy burden of proof rests on those who would then change the essential characteristics of the experience for a later reader of Acts.

Moreover, by the very choice of a particular charismatic experience showing the incorporation of these groups into the church, Luke has necessarily appealed to an *ideal case*, a normative event, or at least a touchstone characteristic of receiving the Spirit (Acts 2.4 and 11.17). The highly charismatic mode of receiving the Spirit described in the four cases above cannot be portrayed as some 'special case', historically unique, to show that he has come, if, as Carson insists, by this specific means Luke intends to show the *universality* of the Spirit's reception, with its implication for including diverse groups into the church. It follows that a central characteristic of this charismatic experience is universal applicability. Indeed this is the point of Acts 2.17, as well as Paul's summaries of his mission: in each new area, he is not attempting to introduce some new epoch, but the gospel in its normative, and universally bestowed power (Acts 15.12; 26.18; Rom. 15.18-19; 2 Cor. 12.12; cf. Heb. 2.4).

The crucial question, though, turns on what are 'essential characteristics' of the Spirit in Luke's four stories? Carson seems to argue that because Luke used the four stories to *demonstrate the scope of the gospel*, we can derive no further normative implications from them.

Carson's thesis fails to comprehend the significance of Luke's device of using gifts of utterance to demonstrate the inclusions. Carson insists, broadly, that the coming of the Spirit with gifts of utterance attests to new epochs—'introducing a new group, until as the gospel expands throughout the empire there are no new groups left' (p. 145). This may be true, but he omits a crucial prior step, common to each case, from Luke's logic: in each case Luke appeals to the presence of the gifts of utterance to indicate the presence of the Spirit. Luke does not only answer in each case, 'Who is included in the church, and how do you know it?' (answer: four groups who received the Spirit), but also, 'How does one know it is the Spirit?' The consistent answer Luke gives is, 'gifts of utterance'. They are the only phenomenon in Acts common to all cases in which the process of Spirit-filling is actually described. This latter point answers Carson's objection that when the Spirit came upon individuals as opposed to the groups, above, no 'tongues' were mentioned. This is correct, but neither does Luke describe a Protestant, generic, highly subjective filling of the Spirit. When Luke describes the process of being filled with the Spirit, charismatic utterance of some type is the norm.

How do we know that Luke sees the characteristic expression of the Spirit to be gifts of utterance? An analysis of Acts 2 shows that the extended crowd response to the Pentecostal phenomena is leading to Peter's 'this is that': the Spirit has come—through the exalted, vindicated Jesus. The goal of the message is that this *same* gift of the Spirit, following repentance, baptism and forgiveness, is available to *all*—not limited to generations, as Carson would have it, or geography (Acts 2.39 with echoes of Isa. 44.3; 59.21). The Protestant reflex is to identify the Spirit here (2.39) in non-charismatic terms. But linguistically, unless it is further qualified, the description of another event by the same name, in the same context, especially as it is still occurring (2.33, 'that which see and hear' in the present tense), retains the same characteristics. Luke is at pains earlier to describe his characteristic appearance by adding to Joel's prophecy about the promised Spirit, 'and they shall *prophesy*' (Acts 2.18). Luke goes on to include 'tongues' under the rubric of prophecy. Acts 8.18 indicates at least *visible* phenomena accompanying the Spirit-filling (cf. 2.33), probably gifts of utterance of some sort. In Acts 11.15, 16 Peter *twice* appeals to their own experience verifying the coming of the Spirit to the Gentiles. In Acts 19.6 the process of the Spirit's 'coming' is described in terms of utterances: tongues and prophecy.

Carson's distinction between the 'epochal' four cases of the Spirit's coming and those to individuals takes a different turn if we widen the characteristic signs of the coming of the Spirit from tongues to gifts of utterance. Using Carson's examples, individual correlations of the filling of the Spirit and gifts of utterance are much closer than he implies in his contemporary descriptions of Spirit-filling. Acts 4.8, 30-31, associate Spirit-filling with revealed utterances, based likely on a fulfillment of Lk. 12.11-12 // Mk 13.11; Mt. 10.20. Acts 6.3 and 5 are not descriptions of the process of Spirit-fillings; the verification of Stephen's being filled with the Spirit follows immediately in his prophetic message. Acts 7.55, again, is the direct connection of the filling of the Spirit and an utterance of a prophetic vision. Acts 9.17 reports a healing, but does not specify that Saul received the Spirit at that precise time as he does in the four 'epochal' cases. At any rate, Luke may have intended Paul's 'seeing', at least secondarily, as revelation. 11.24, again, does not describe the actual filling experience, and in any case the filling did not seem to require special verification. In 13.9, Paul's cursing Elymas is the clearest possible case of prophetic utterance. 13.52 is a summary statement bracketed by the highly effective spread of the 'word'—prophetic utterance—amidst persecution (again Lk. 12.11-12). Moreover, the verb 'were filled' is imperfect, implying, like the powerful utterances of the 'word', an ongoing process.

Carson argues that prophecy and/or tongues as an expected contemporary accompaniment of Spirit-filling is invalid because of the 'distinctive abnormality' of the Ephesian disciples of John, namely, that they 'believed' (were converted) but had not yet received the Spirit. Two issues require disentangling here. It is one thing for Carson to argue against a doctrine of 'subsequence' (that is, that Spirit-filling necessarily comes after conversion—a doctrine likely derived more from the Protestant *ordo salutis* doctrine and the experience of early Pentecostals), and another to argue against the essentially charismatic characteristics of the Spirit, which he seems also to do. On the first point, it is perhaps presumptuous to believe that the NT even addresses the question of 'sequence' of Spirit-filling in relation to 'conversion'. Luke even notes that there are those outside the Christian community, and even not converted at all, who exercise spiritual gifts (Lk. 9.49-50; 11.19; 9.1 included Judas! Cf. esp. Mt. 7.21-23). The NT lacks interest in the precise order of soteriological stages, in contrast to later Protestant scholastics. Rather, the NT's concern is purely pragmatic: the important point is not *when* the Spirit fills an individual, but *that* he or she is filled. Classical Pentecostals may well pragmatically stress the 'when' in order to insure 'that' people experience the power of the Spirit.

This raises a problem with the over-schematization of the Spirit experiences in Acts, that is, the implicit evidentialism associated with these 'epochal' advances in the church's growth. Hermeneutically, one must distinguish between the rhetorical devices used by an author to make a single point (for example Luke's group-inclusion schema) and the ontology and theology of the events and ones similar to those he describes. For example, because of Luke's usage, should we then say that Paul's account of the gospel reception and its spiritual gifts by the Thessalonians is necessarily 'epochal' (1 Thess. 1.5, 'We know. . . that [God] has chosen you, because our gospel came to you not simply with words, but also with power, with the Holy Spirit. . . you became imitators of us'), as would the Galatians, who received the Holy Spirit and performed miracles (Gal. 3.2, 5)? Must all the charismatic expressions of Paul's preaching be repetitively 'epochal' and 'unique' signifying their death as a normative expression of the gospel with the apostle's death (Rom. 15.19; 2 Cor. 12.12; 1 Cor. 2.4; cf. Heb. 2.3, 4)? Recall that 'signs of an apostle', 2 Cor. 12.12, only indicate not that Paul is among the exclusive band of 'true' apostles, but that, because these signs are normative to Christian mission, he is not a 'false' apostle. Hence, the question of cessationism is irrelevant here.

The conclusion to the above discussion points up a small but practically important distinction between Carson's expectation of the Spirit's activity and my own, namely, that while Carson believes the Spirit is 'prophetic' by nature, encompassing a broad range of gifts and graces, his practical portrayal of that Spirit-filling in contemporary experience seems muted, internalized and virtually identified with what we today would call 'conversion'. Certainly, there is a meaningful sense in which we 'receive' the Spirit at conversion. But by contrast, I believe that the overwhelming biblical evidence, particularly in Acts, is that a 'filling of the Spirit' is much more visibly and demonstrably 'prophetic', based on the fairly consistent models in Acts and elsewhere—in the cases of both groups and individuals.

One must also agree with Carson that there are many 'fillings' of the Spirit. But one must not confuse the past tense, 'filled', with the passive voice, 'filled': that because someone *once* had been 'filled' with the Spirit, he or she is *now* necessarily 'Spirit-filled'. One might hold that there are various levels or intensities of the work of the Spirit in individuals, but being 'filled with the Spirit' represents, in most cases, a palpable, powerful, and relatively brief experience of the Spirit, like Old Testament descriptions of prophetic experiences, for some charismatic service. True, an individual does receive the Spirit at conversion, but this is only one of many experiences of the Spirit, often below the level of awareness, both before *and* after a decision to receive Christ (Rom. 1.18, 28; 11.29).[1] The minimum 'level', if you

---

1. An apparent exception, however, may be the clear difference drawn in Jn 14.17 between those whom the Spirit is 'with' and 'in'. This distinction is likely based, however, in large part, on the coming new age of the Spirit (cf. Jn 7.39).

will, with respect to the Spirit and the Christian is that true children of God hear and heed the Spirit's revelation—the ideal of the 'Law written on the heart' (the seat of spiritual consciousness and will, for example Jn 10.3, 27; Rom. 8.14; Jer. 31.33; 2 Cor. 3.3).[1] However, the emphasis of the NT with respect to the Holy Spirit is to be 'filled', repeatedly and constantly, a condition which strongly implies, not one's ecclesiastical status, but the continual involvement in powerful, charismatic spiritual ministry in advancing the kingdom of God.

---

1. This may be the thought behind the idea of 'blasphemy of the Holy Spirit': that revelation can be perceived is a given, attribution of that revelation to Satan represents a *deliberate* denial of that which one *knows*, via the Spirit, to be true. In this state, quite understandably, no one could receive grace and forgiveness.

Appendix II

DOES THE SPIRITUAL GIFT OF APOSTLESHIP ALSO CONTINUE?

The appearance in 1 Cor. 12.28 and Eph. 4.11 of 'apostles' as a gift of the Spirit raises the question as to the continuation of this gift, and its implications for others, until the parousia. This question is a controversial one because of the Reformation concern to shift ecclesiastical authority from the Pope (the 'last apostle') to the NT apostles. If the later are seen to command this ultimate authority, then a claim for the continuation of the gift of apostleship implies the possibility of additional, *ex cathedra* Christian doctrine. I would argue, however, that the NT view of apostleship does not carry this implication of ultimate authority, and so arguments for the continuation of the gift of apostleship need not provoke the traditional negative responses. This is a complex problem and the following discussion will be brief. With certain qualifications, I would refer the reader to Grudem, *The Gift of Prophecy*, pp. 25-66 and 269-76, as well as Carson, *Showing the Spirit*, pp. 88-91, 96-97, 156 and 164. Carson suggests that 'the only χάρισμα bound up with obsolescence is apostleship in the tightly defined sense'. However, Carson may be too restrictive when he spells out 'the reason for the obsolescence of this χάρισμα [which] lies not in its connection with the Spirit but in its connection with the resurrected and exalted Christ, who now no more appears to human beings as the personal, resurrected Lord. Until his return, he manifests himself to us only by his Spirit; and therefore the peculiar commission and authority of the first apostles, which turned on personal contact with the resurrected Jesus, cannot be duplicated today'.

One could argue, however, that if Paul's 'contact with the resurrected Jesus' were a visionary experience, 'in the Spirit', as it seems to be, then little if anything in the apostolic commissions and authority transcend what could, in principle, be granted today. Indeed, in defending his apostleship, while Paul insists that he has 'seen the Lord', he seems to undercut the significance of mere physical association with Jesus as determinative for apostleship by the principle that 'we no longer know [experience/interact with] [Jesus] according to the flesh, but according to the Spirit' (2 Cor. 5.16)—again, an appeal to the Numbers 11 principle of universalizing, rather than restricting, experiences of the Spirit. The standard 'requirement' that an apostle must be chosen from those 'who have been with us' from John's baptism to the ascension (Acts 1.21-22) is problem-plagued. Matthias is never heard from again. Paul certainly failed to qualify. Judas' twelfth place is filled, but what of Paul and others who are called apostles? Hermeneutically, we face a problem some associate with Pentecostals: to what extent does Lucan historical reporting of a stage of spiritual development intend to sanction it as repeatable and normative? Specifically, did the eleven apostles have an immature understanding of the 'twelve' as representing the people of God? Or did the Spirit fill the missing place and introduce the new Israel of God (the 120 and the thousands that followed) at Pentecost?[1]

The crucial exception which has emerged in traditional teaching about apostles, however, is the authority to write Scripture (2 Pet. 2.15-16). Despite this, even assuming conservative positions on authorship, over half of the NT was written by *non*-apostles, a fact which questions the essential relationship of apostles to the finality of doctrine.

The *apostolic commissions* to present the gospel (whether in word and deed, or in word only), as well as the more general ethical and religious injunctions to the apostles/disciples as recorded in the Gospels and Acts, are universally accepted, in principle at least, as canonically normative and binding for the church *of all ages*, particularly Mt. 28.19-20, which, read in concert with the other commissioning accounts, commands the hearers to present the gospel to the world charismatically. This speaks against the apostles' having exclusive authority.

Moreover, one basis of apostolic authority is not at all exclusive; it seems to lie in its faithfulness to the earliest Christian traditions (1 Cor. 4.6; 15.1-3; Gal. 1.8). Specifically, the 'signs of an apostle' (2 Cor. 12.12) are essential characteristics of the gospel as normatively promulgated. By contrast, false apostles preach a kingdom that consists in talk, rather than power (δύναμις, 1 Cor. 4.20). Even revelation of the gospel is not unique to the apostles. The 'revelation' of Paul's gospel, which did not come from other apostles or from humanity (which seems to involve the inclusion of the Gentiles, Gal. 1.11-12; 2.2; Eph. 3.2-3), is characteristically 'revealed' by Christ to the community as well, either through confirming prophecies or by direct revelation (for example 1 Cor. 1.8; Eph. 1.7-10, 17-23. Cf. the similar pattern in Jn 14.25-26; 16.13-14 and 1 Jn 2.27, where essentially the same promise is made to both the apostles and the local community.[2] Apostolic authority seems to be based more on the status of a person as church planter (or 'father') to his congregation than on simple recognition of his status as an apostle.

Significantly, apostleship is no guarantee of infallibility. The apostle Peter capitulates before 'men from James' (Gal. 2.12) over Judaizing teachings. These same men have approved Paul's Gentile mission (Gal. 2.6), although Paul seems cool toward them and had not consulted with them at the beginning of his ministry (Gal. 1.17, 19). It seems possible that they are the 'super-apostles', who boast of their status as servants of Christ but are Judaizers in 2 Cor. 11.22-23a (cf. Gal. 2.12). Only given the real prospect of error among the apostles would it be sensible to warn that the words of an apostle should be weighed against the normative Christian tradition (2 Cor. 4.1-6; Gal. 1.8).

---

1. Note that while the apostles prayed for divine indication of who should be chosen to fill Judas's position, there is no indication, as opposed to other prayers in Acts, that the Spirit responded.

2. See Dunn, *Jesus and the Spirit*, pp. 346-47 and 351-52.

The circle of apostles does not seem particularly exclusive. A very early tradition (for example 1 Cor. 15.5-8) seems to place in sequence, and thereby contrast, the resurrection appearances of Jesus to 'the twelve' and then to 'all the apostles', implying others. Throughout the NT several people are incidentally (one cannot prove that the presence or absence of the title is deliberate or random) called 'apostles': Barnabas (Acts 14.14; 1 Cor. 9.6), James (1 Cor. 9.6; Gal. 1.19), the brothers of the Lord (1 Cor. 9.6), Andronicus and Junia (a woman? Rom. 16.7), Silas (1 Thess. 2.6), unnamed 'apostles of churches' (2 Cor. 8.23), Judas and Silas (Acts 15.22), Apollos (1 Cor. 4.1, 6, 9). The mention of these break the number of the 'twelve' who probably symbolize, via a kind of corporate solidarity, or as prototypes, the complete people of God in Christ. Certainly this seems to be the usage of the twelve (and multiples) in the Book of Revelation and the 120, 'all' filled with the Spirit in the Book of Acts. Paul's conflict with judaizing 'apostles' (Gal. 1–2; 2 Cor. 11–12) reflects no sense of a closed circle of apostles, unless some of them are the original twelve ('super-apostles', Gal. 1.17-19; 2.2, 12, that is, 'men from James', before whom even Peter and Barnabas recanted; 2 Cor. 3.1). Certainly, early Christian literature seems to reflect a tradition of many apostles besides the twelve.[1]

Apostleship is on the list of spiritual gifts (1 Cor. 12 and Eph. 4) which explicitly continue until the parousia, as I have outlined above. Moreover, since the gift of apostleship is listed 'first' in 1 Cor. 12.28 and Eph. 4.11, on what grounds can we deny its continuance if it is not one of the 'higher ($\mu\epsilon\acute{\iota}\zeta$ova) gifts' commanded immediately afterward in the context to be eagerly sought (1 Cor. 12.31)? Why would an offer be made to the readers which could not be fulfilled? On what grounds is this gift to be exempted from these lists?

P.R. Jones interprets Paul's claim to see the resurrected Jesus 'last of all' as a claim to be the last apostle.[2] But such a connection is simply not made explicitly in the passage. Paul is not attempting here to establish himself as the *last* in the circle of apostles, but only saying that he was the last (and therefore, perhaps, least) of a certain group who saw the resurrected Lord Jesus. Who was this group? Peter, the twelve, over 500 brethren, James (Jesus' brother?), then *all* the apostles (excluding Paul, or including many other apostles, for example the 70 [72]?)—certainly many others, as well as perhaps two (different?) groups of apostles. Many in subsequent church history have claimed to see the resurrected Jesus, including the writer of

---

1. *Herm. Sim.* 9.15, 16, cf. *Herm. Vis.* 3.5; *Herm. Sim.* 9.25 knows of 40, while several others (Irenaeus, *Adv. Her.* 2.21.1; Tertullian, *Against Marcion* 4.24) mention 70 or 72 and Eusebius says (*Church History* 1.12.4), 'many others who were called apostles in imitation of the Twelve, as was Paul himself'. *Did.* 11.4-6 gives pre-eminence to the twelve, but describe itinerant missionaries also as 'apostles' led by the Spirit. See the ground-breaking discussion in J.B. Lightfoot, *St Paul's Epistle to the Galatians* (Grand Rapids: Eerdmans, 10th edn, 1957), pp. 92-100; in W. Schmithals, *The Office of Apostle in the Early Church* (New York: Abingdon Press, 1969), pp. 239-40 and L. Goppelt, *Apostolic and Post-Apostolic Times* (London: A. & C. Black, 1970), pp. 178-82. More generally, see F.H. Agnew, 'The Origin of the NT Apostle-Concept: A Review of Research', *JBL* 105 (March 1986), pp. 75-96.

2. See the extensive argument of P.R. Jones, 'I Corinthians 15.8—Paul the Last Apostle', *TynBul* 36 (Winter 1985), pp. 3-34.

Revelation (ch. 4). The 'last' sighting of Jesus need not imply that the viewer is the 'last' apostle!

What is the point of this passage? To prove Paul was the last apostle? No, but at most, to show that he was unusually graced by God, despite its inappropriateness and suddenness, to become a witness of the resurrected Lord. The point is not that Paul is the 'last apostle', but that his preaching is valid despite his lowly status among the witnesses. The passage is not attempting to establish the limits of the apostolate. Rather it is attempting to confirm the truth of the Christian tradition Paul and others are proclaiming. At very least, one might then assert that the gift of apostleship, in the sense of a pioneer missionary, called, commissioned and empowered by Christ, could normatively function in the world today.[1] It is debatable whether the term 'apostle' is ever used in the NT in a sense much stronger than this.

The argument by analogy based on the metaphor of apostles (and prophets) as *foundational* to the church (Eph. 2.20 and 3.5) does not support the cessation of apostleship. Some cessationists have approached Eph. 2.20 as *the* authoritative flow chart of the universal church. The apostles and prophets serve as a 'foundation' in the sense that they collectively represent a kind of oral 'interim NT', their gifts and functions being extinguished when normative doctrine is set down in writing within the first generation or two of the church.[2] Generally, this argument is framed against the mindset of Reformation-era polemics and Enlightenment rationalism, with unexamined premises about Popes, apostolic succession and authority, miracles, 'ordinary and extraordinary' spiritual gifts, and even the essential nature of the gospel itself. There are at least four premises in this argument.

1. The metaphor of 'foundation', to support cessationism, requires that the *definitive* function or apostles and prophets is to establish the parameters of church doctrine, particularly as it appears in the NT. Hence, when their collective function is complete, the gifts of apostleship and prophecy necessarily pass from the scene.

---

1. See for instance K. Giles, 'Apostles Before and After Paul', *Churchman* 96 (1985), pp. 241-56; J.H. Schütz, *Paul and the Anatomy of Apostolic Authority* (SNTSMS, 26; Cambridge: Cambridge University Press, 1975). On a more popular level: M.C. Griffiths, 'Today's Missionary, Yesterday's Apostle', *EMQ* 21 (April 1985), pp. 154-65; J.A. Hewett, 'Apostle', in S. Burgess, G. McGee and P. Alexander (eds.), *Dictionary of Pentecostal and Charismatic Movements* (Grand Rapids: Zondervan, 1988), p. 15; E.F. Murphy, *Spiritual Gifts and the Great Commission* (South Pasadena, CA: Mandate Press, 1975), pp. 193-221. At the very least, the NT concept of apostleship is perhaps too fluid to establish clear criteria for its cessation. See R. Schnackenburg, 'Apostles Before and During Paul's Time', in W. Gasque and R.P. Martin (eds.), *Apostolic History and the Gospel* (Grand Rapids: Eerdmans, 1970), pp. 287-303.

2. For example by R.B. Gaffin, Jr, *Perspectives on Pentecost: Studies in New Testament Teaching on the Gifts of the Holy Spirit* (Phillipsburg, PA: Presbyterian and Reformed Publishers, 1979), pp. 93-116; R.L. Thomas, 'Prophecy Rediscovered? A Review of The Gift of Prophecy in the New Testament and Today', *BS* 149 (January–March 1922), pp. 83-96; K.L. Gentry, *The Charismatic Gift of Prophecy: A Reformed Response to Wayne Grudem* (Memphis: Footstool, 1989); R.F. White, 'Gaffin and Grudem on Eph. 2:20: In Defense of Gaffin's Cessationist Exegesis', *WJT* 54 (1992), pp. 303-20; and F.D. Farnell, 'The Gift of Prophecy in the Old and New Testaments', *BS* 149/596 (October–December 1992), pp. 407-10.

Recent advocates of cessationism are sensitive to charges that this argument is anachronistic, that it is unlikely that the 'foundational' apostles and prophets involved were at all aware of their role as an interim NT. Nevertheless, the argument remains essentially unaltered: these 'foundational' gifts are strictly limited to this brief, transitional function.

The problem with this view is that not only does the NT nowhere explicitly state that this is the *only* role for apostles and prophets, it does not even state that this is *one* of their roles! In Ephesians, the explicit roles given for apostles and prophets are that they are to work in concert with evangelists, pastors and teachers in equipping the saints until ultimate unity and Christian maturity is achieved in all. If the duration of the gifts is necessarily connected with their function, as these cessationists argue, then clearly the task of apostles and prophets is not complete until every single member of the church reaches the same level of Christian maturity as Christ himself (Eph. 4.13). Most cessationists would agree with St Paul (Phil. 3.12) who does not have the temerity to make the claim that he has attained that level, particularly as we still have not reached 'unity of the faith' even on the issue of cessationism. To claim that the *only* function of apostles and prophets in the NT is to formulate doctrine for inclusion in the Bible is in itself unbiblical. But if there are other roles for them, then the 'foundational' argument fails.

2. The 'foundation' argument requires a view of apostles and prophets as the only Protestant Popes, that is, as the unique receivers and articulators of Christian revelation, a role that no one may subsequently share. The counter-argument could be that the NT sees these gifts as first and definitive, but certainly not unrepeatable. Rather, they are actually prototypes, role models for others to follow. The original experience of Christ's revelation is 'epochal' in the sense discussed above: pioneering and offered as a model for others to follow. For the church, then, the apostolic and prophetic gift is 'foundational' not only in the sense that the apostles and prophets first announced the gospel in some areas, but that all further revelation about Christ is delineated, articulated, qualified, and offered for reduplication by its original receivers. Hence, this passage shows not that the gifts of apostleship and prophecy ceased, but rather that since these people's experience is 'foundational' and archetypal, their experience and functions therefore continue. Most importantly we must remember that the apostles and prophets only communicated their revelations; they did not create them, *ex cathedra*. They were not, after all, God. Hence their lives, experiences with Christ and ministries are, to the extent that they followed Christ, necessarily exemplary and repeatable, inviting rabbinic pedagogical imitation as do Jesus and Paul.[1] At least three points support this. First, Paul lays stress on the 'connection' of Jews and Gentiles via access to the Father, not simply through a funnel of apostolic authority, but 'through [Christ]. . . *by one Spirit*' (the Revealer) in Eph. 2.18. Secondly, just as Paul received by revelation his gospel of reconciliation between God, Jews and Gentiles (3.3), so now the church, by reading (3.3-4) and by revelation by the power of the Spirit (3.16-18) is similarly to grasp the scope

1. C.N. Beard, 'Gospel Proclamation in Word and Miracle' (MA thesis, Regent University Divinity School, 1992).

of God's love (*inter alia*, the inclusion of the Gentiles). Thirdly, Christ gave[1] these apostles and prophets *until* (μέχρι) ultimate, eschatological goals of Christian upbuilding and maturity are achieved (4.13). That is, apostles and prophets (however theologians may have later labeled them) are envisioned to be continuously at work until the eschaton.

A profound irony on this point appears: despite the insistence on the integrity of the immutable doctrinal 'foundation', conservative Protestants willingly accept the drastic reshaping of doctrines away from their biblical emphases via discredited Greek philosophical premises and the evolution of systematic theology over two millennia. For proof, contrast the biblical emphases on the doctrines of the Holy Spirit and the kingdom of God against systematic theology of Protestant orthodoxy. Since we have been raised with these grotesque distortions of emphasis, we remain comfortable with them.

3. To preserve the 'foundation' argument, Christ as 'cornerstone' must lie at the same chronological level as the apostles and prophets, that is, as part of the first-generation 'foundation'.[2]

The cessationist argument by analogy collapses if Christ is not limited to the 'foundation' in Eph. 2.20. The foundation metaphor probably echoes the tradition of Jesus about Peter's revelation/confession: 'You are Peter (Πέτρος) and upon this rock (πέτρᾳ, revelation about Christ) I will build my church' (Mt. 16.18). This 'rock' seems to consist of a revelatory process and its content—a revelation of Christ and his significance. Hence in Eph. 2.20 apostles and prophets represent the 'foundation' of the church, of which Christ Jesus is the 'cornerstone', 'key-stone' or 'head of the corner', who, via the Spirit, continually and individually reveals himself, holds the structure together, both from above and from below (1 Cor. 3.11).[3] Since Christ seems to be portrayed not only as a *foundation* stone but also as a *final* stone in the temple of God, Eph. 2.20 argues against the cessationist chronological schema of successive generations of believers (courses of stones) being built on the deposit of doctrine represented by the apostles and prophets.

The death of Christ does not spell the end of his work in the church via the Spirit (and his gifts). If he continues to be 'fitted into' each person in the temple who exists 'in him' or 'in the Lord', then the implications for this continuing activity for the other parts of the 'foundation' are interesting indeed. Do we not have here the same idea as in Eph. 1.21-22, where Christ permeates the church 'not only in the present age, but also in the one to come'? The pattern here suggests that the activity and presence of Christ is not limited to an initiatory period in this age, followed by inactivity,

---

1. 'Gave' (ἔδωκεν, aorist tense) need not mean that Christ gave these gifts once and for all never to repeat them in any other generation. Otherwise, today we would have no claim to the gifts given to evangelists, pastors and teachers, which are here listed seamlessly with apostles and prophets. It is reasonable to ascribe to this tense the eternal view of Christ in the same sense that he 'chose us before the foundation of the world' (Eph. 1.3). In this same context 'he lavished [his grace] on us with *all* wisdom and understanding' (1.8). See the discussion on Eph. 4.7-13 above.

2. For example by Farnell, 'Is the Gift of Prophecy for Today?', p. 409.

3. I cannot improve on the argument for this by Barth, *Ephesians 1–3*, pp. 317-19.

followed by more of his presence in the age to come, as cessationism would suggest. Like Christ, the presence and activity of apostles and prophets are continuous in this present age.

4. The most unsettling premise of the 'foundational' argument is the notion employed of what ultimately *is* the 'foundation'—the most important element or core value—of the church. Some cessationists appear to be insisting that the 'foundation' is the established doctrine of the NT documents.

As one committed to the infallibility and inerrancy of Scripture, I would never seek to minimize the central significance of the Bible for faith. Nevertheless, the Bible in general, and Ephesians in particular, does not identify itself as the foundational core of the church. Rather, this core is the ongoing series of revelatory encounters with Christ, which open our hearts to the Scriptures. The disclosure experience of Christ, although within its biblical framework, is truly the foundation of the church. St Paul was concerned that Christians' faith rested *not* on *words*, but on 'a demonstration of the Spirit's power' (1 Cor. 2.14).

Christian Fundamentalism lies close to the rabbinic tradition of 'it is not in heaven', meaning that the Torah was given once and for all, and that ultimate religious authority now rests with the interpretive abilities of the scribes, as against any further miraculous or revelatory experience. Cessationists tend to model their *heilsgeschichte* after the (dubious) rabbinic doctrine that following the last book in the Bible (OT) there were no more prophets.[1] Cessationists may counter that they still uphold the doctrine of illumination, the view that the Spirit continues its 'revelatory' work in the clarification and application of Scripture. This is a sound and biblical position, but one that is often in practice ignored.[2] In any case, the doctrine of illumination is no substitute for, although it is on a continuum with, either the life-changing spiritual encounter with Christ or his continuing revelatory gifts of the Spirit.

A central aspect of the messiah's coming was to inaugurate the age of the (prophetic) Spirit, to fulfill the Law; to move the locus of perceiving God's mind and will into the heart (the spiritual center of perception), away from the external coercion of the Law. The scribal suppression of the Spirit's revelatory presence prompted Jesus to say, 'You know [in the sense of "divinely understand"] neither the scriptures nor the power of God!' The loss of one necessarily indicated the loss of both. It was against this Judaizing tendency among the Galatians that an exasperated Paul asked, 'Having begun in the [revelatory, miracle-working] Spirit, will you now be completed in the [Godless human abilities] of the flesh?'

The explosive nature of the contemporary debate on apostleship, of course, parallels the contention over modern miracles. The Reformation wished to cut the root of ultimate religious authority from the popes by denying apostolic succession. As it did with miracles, the polemics of the day failed to discern the relation between 'authority' and apostleship. From the conceptions of miracles and apostleship flows, not the coercive political or ecclesiastical power characteristic of this evil age, but a

---

1. See Greenspahn, 'Why Prophecy Ceased', pp. 37-39.
2. C. Pinnock, 'The Work of the Holy Spirit in Hermeneutics', *JPT* 2 (1993), pp. 3-23.

spiritually-discerned authority and influence, apprehended only by those with spiritual perception (1 Cor. 2.11-14). However, since the notion of apostleship is so historically bound up with the idea of ultimate religious authority, anyone now claiming apostleship might justifiably be regarded with suspicion. Nevertheless it is possible that no real biblical impediment exists to someone today functioning as, or even being gifted as, an apostle, at least in the way that the apostle Paul defined himself.

BIBLIOGRAPHY

Achtemeier, P.J., 'Gospel Miracle Tradition and the Divine Man', *Int* 26 (April 1972), pp. 174-97.

—'The Origin and Function of the Pre-Marcan Miracle Catenae', *JBL* 91 (June 1972), pp. 198-221.

—'The Lucan Perspective on the Miracles of Jesus: A Preliminary Sketch', *JBL* 94 (1975), pp. 547-62.

Adler, N., *Das erste christliche Pfingstfest: Sinn und Bedeutung des Pfingstberichtes Apg. 2.1-13* (Neutestamentliche Abhandlungen, 18.1; Münster: Aschendorff, 1938).

—*Taufe und Handauflegung: Eine exegetische-theologische Untersuchen, von Apg. 8.14-17* (Neutestamentliche Abhandlungen, 19.3; Münster: Aschendorff, 1951).

Agnew, F.H. 'The Origin of the NT Apostle-Concept: A Review of Research', *JBL* 105 (March 1986), pp. 75-96.

Agrimson, J.E. (ed.), *Gifts of the Spirit and the Body of Christ* (Minneapolis: Augsburg, 1974).

Ahlstrom, S.E., 'Scottish Philosophy and American Theology', *CH* 24 (September 1955), pp. 257-72.

—*A Religious History of the American People* (New Haven: Yale University Press, 1972).

Allis, O.T., 'Personal Impressions of Dr Warfield', *Banner of Truth* 89 (February 1971), pp. 10-14.

Amsler, S., 'La fonction prophétique de l'église et dans l'église: remarques à partir de l'Ancien Testament', in J. Panagopoulos (ed.), *Prophetic Vocation in the New Testament and Today* (Leiden: Brill, 1977).

Anderson, A.A., 'The Use of "*RUACH*" in IQS, IQH, and IQM', *JSS* 7 (Autumn 1962), pp. 293-303.

Anderson, R., *The Silence of God* (London: Hodder & Stoughton, 5th edn, 1899).

Armstrong, W.P., *Calvin and the Reformation* (New York: Fleming H. Revell, 1909).

Arndt, W.F., 'Does the Bible Teach that Only Christians of the Apostolic Age Would Possess Miraculous Powers?', *Concordia Theological Monthly* 10 (December 1930), pp. 730-35.

Arnold, C.E., *Ephesians: Power and Magic—The Concept of Power in Light of its Historical Setting* (Cambridge: Cambridge University Press, 1989).

Arrington, F.L., 'Paul's Aeon Theology in I Corinthians' (PhD dissertation, St Louis University, 1975).

Ash, J.L., Jr, 'The Decline of Ecstatic Prophecy in the Early Church', *TS* 37 (June 1976), pp. 227-52.

Aune, D.E., *Magic in Early Christianity* (New York: de Gruyter, 1980).

—*Prophecy in Early Christianity and the Ancient Mediterranean* (Grand Rapids: Eerdmans, 1983).

—*Prophecy in the New Testament and the Ancient Mediterranean World* (Grand Rapids: Eerdmans, 1983).

Baer, H. von, *Der Heilige Geist in den Lukasschriften* (BWANT; Stüttgart: Kohlhammer, 1926).

Bailey, J., *The Idea of Revelation in Recent Thought* (New York: Columbia University Press, 1956).

Baillie, L.A., 'An Exegesis of Significant New Testament Passages Concerning Temporary Spiritual Gifts' (ThM thesis, Dallas Theological Seminary, 1970).

Baker, D., 'The Interpretation of 1 Cor. 12–14', *EvQ* 46 (October–December 1974), pp. 224-34.

Balmer, R.H., 'The Princetonians and Scripture', *WTJ* 44 (Fall 1982), pp. 352-65.

Baltensweiler, H., 'Wunder und Glaube im Neuen Testament', *TZ* 23 (July–August 1967), pp. 241-56.

Bamberg, S.W., 'Our Image of Warfield Must Go', *JETS* 34 (June 1991), pp. 229-41.

Bammel, E., ' "John Did No Miracle": John 10.41', in C.F.D. Moule (ed.), *Miracles: Cambridge Studies in their Philosophy and History* (London: Mowbrays, 1965).

Banks, W.L., *Questions You Have Wanted to Ask About Tongues But. . .* (Chattanooga: AMG Publishers, 1978), pp. 34-37.

Barnes, R.S., 'The Miraculous Gifts of the Holy Spirit: Have they Ceased?', *Journal of Pastoral Practice* 7 (Winter 1984), pp. 18-35.

Barnett, D.L., and J.P. McGregor, *Speaking in Tongues: A Scholarly Defense* (Seattle, WA: Community Chapel Publications, 1986).

Barnett, M., *The Living Flame: Being a Study of the Gift of the Spirit in the New Testament, with Special Reference to Prophecy, Glossolalia, Montanism and Perfection* (London: Epworth Press, 1953).

Barr, J., 'The Miracles', in D.G. Miller and D.Y. Hadidian (eds.), *Jesus and Man's Hope*, II (Pittsburgh: Pittsburgh Theological Seminary, 1970).

—'Miracles and the Supernatural', in *Fundamentalism* (Philadelphia: Westminster Press, 1977), pp. 235-59.

Barrett, C.K., 'The Holy Spirit in the Fourth Gospel', *JTS* 1.1 NS (1950), pp. 1-15.

—'Christianity at Corinth', *BJRL* 46 (March 1964), pp. 269-97.

—*The Holy Spirit and the Gospel Tradition* (London: SPCK, 1966).

—*Jesus and the Gospel Tradition* (London: SPCK, 1967).

—*The Signs of an Apostle* (London: Epworth Press, 1970).

Barrett, D.B., 'The Twentieth-Century Pentecostal/Charismatic Renewal in the Holy Spirit, with its Goal of World Evangelization', *International Bulletin of Missionary Research* 12.3 (July 1988), pp. 119-29.

Bartlett, I.H., *The American Mind in the Mid-Nineteenth Century* (Arlington Heights, IL: Harlan Davidson, 2nd edn, 1982).

Bartling, V., 'Notes on Spirit-Baptism and Prophetic Utterance', *CTM* 39 (November 1968), pp. 708-14.

Bartling, W.J., 'The Congregation of Christ: A Charismatic Body. An Exegetical Study of I Corinthians 12', *CTM* 40 (January 1969), pp. 67-80.

Barton, F., 'No More Gifts? A Review Article', *Henceforth* 7.3 (Fall 1979), pp. 108-14.

Bauer, W., *Orthodoxy and Heresy in Earliest Christianity* (trans. D. Steinmetz; Philadelphia: Fortress Press, 1971).

Baum, G., 'Miracles', in *Man Becoming* (New York: Herder & Herder, 1970).

Baumgarten, A.I., 'Miracles and Halakah in Rabbinic Judaism', *JQR* 73 (January 1983), pp. 238-53.

Baxter, J.S., *Divine Healing for the Body* (Grand Rapids: Zondervan, 1979).

Baxter, R.E., *The Charismatic Gift of Tongues* (Grand Rapids: Kregel, 1981).

—*The Charismatic Gift of Tongues* (Grand Rapids: Kregel, 1981).

Beard, C.N., 'Gospel Proclamation in Word and Miracle' (MA thesis, Regent University Divinity School, 1992).

Beare, F.W., 'Speaking with Tongues: A Critical Survey of the New Testament Evidence', *JBL* 83 (August 1964), pp. 229-46.

Beasley-Murray, G.R., 'Jesus and the Spirit', in A. Descamps and R.P.A. de Halleux (eds.), *Mélanges bibliques in hommage au R.P. Béda Rigaux* (Gembloux: Editions J. Duculot, 1970), pp. 463-78.

Beason, S.H., 'The Relationship of Eschatology and Pneumatology in Representative New Testament Thought' (ThD dissertation, Southwestern Baptist Theological Seminary, 1964).

Becker, J., 'Wunder und Christologie: Zum literarkritischen und christologischen Problem der Wunder im Johannesevangelisum', *NTS* 16 (January 1970), pp. 130-48.

Behannon, W., 'Benjamin B. Warfield's Concept of Religious Authority' (ThD dissertation, Southwestern Baptist Theological Seminary, 1964).

Beker, J.C., 'Prophecy and the Spirit in the Apostolic Fathers' (PhD dissertation. University of Chicago, 1955).

—'ἀρραβών', *TDNT*, I, p. 475.

Beker, J.C., and J. Behm, 'γλῶσσα, ἐτερόγλωσσος', *TDNT*, I, pp. 719-27.

Bellshaw, W.G., 'The Confusion of Tongues', *BSac* 120 (April–June 1963), pp. 145-53.

Belval, N.J., *The Holy Spirit in St. Ambrose* (Rome: Officium Libri Catholici, 1971).

Benjamin, H.S., '*Pneuma* in John and Paul: A Comparative Study of the Term with Particular Reference to the Holy Spirit', *Biblical Theology Review* 6.1 (February 1976), pp. 27-48.

Benoit, P., *Jesus and the Gospel* (New York: Seabury, 1973).

Berkhof, H., *The Doctrine of the Holy Spirit* (Richmond, VA: John Knox Press, 1964).

Berkouwer, G., *The Providence of God* (trans. L.B. Smeeds; Grand Rapids: Eerdmans, 1952).

—*General Revelation* (Grand Rapids: Eerdmans, 1955).

Bertram, G., 'ἔργον, κτλ', *TDNT*, II, pp. 635-55.

—'θαῦμα, κτλ', *TDNT*, II, pp. 27-42.

Bertrams, H., *Das Wesen des Geistes nach der Anschauung des Apostels Paulus: Eine biblisch-theological Untersuchung* (Neutestamentliche Abhandlungen, 4; Münster: Aschendorff, 1913).

Best, E.E., 'Prophets and Preachers', *SJT* 12 (June 1959), pp. 129-50.

—'The Interpretation of Tongues', *SJT* 28.1 (1975), pp. 45-62.

—Paul's Apostolic Authority—?', *JSNT* 27 (June 1986), pp. 3-25.

Best, T.F., 'St Paul and the Decline of the Miraculous', *Encounter* 44 (Summer 1983), pp. 231-43.

Beyer, H.W., 'θεραπεία, θεραπεύω, θεράπων', *TDNT*, III, pp. 128-32.

Birnbaum, R., 'The Polemic on Miracles', *Judaism* 33 (Fall 1984), pp. 437-47.

Bittlinger, A., *Gifts and Graces: A Commentary on 1 Corinthians 12–14* (Grand Rapids: Eerdmans, 1967).

—'Der neutestamentliche charismatische Gottesdienst im Lichte der heutigen charismatischen Erneuerung der Kirche', in J. Panagopoulos (ed.), *Prophetic Vocation in the New Testament and Today* (Leiden: Brill, 1977), pp. 186-209.

Blackburn, B.L., 'Miracles and Miracle Stories', in J.B. Green, S. McKnight and I.H. Marshall (eds.), *Dictionary of Jesus and the Gospels* (Downers Grove, IL: Inter-Varsity Press, 1992).

Bloch, R., *Les prodiges dans l'antiquité classique* (Paris: Presses Universitaires de France, 1963).

Bokser, B.M., 'Wonder-Working and the Rabbinic Tradition: The Case of Hanina ben Dosa', *JSJ* 16 (June 1986), pp. 42-92.

Booth, J.L., 'The Purpose of Miracles' (ThD dissertation, Dallas Theological Seminary, 1965).

Borgen, P., 'Miracles of Healing in the New Testament', *StT* 35.2 (1981), pp. 91-106.

Boring, M.E., ' "What are we looking for?" Toward a Definition of the Term "Christian Prophet" ', in G.W. MacRae (ed.), *Society for Biblical Literature Seminar Papers 1973* (Missoula, MT: Scholars Press, 1973), II, pp. 142-54.

Bornkamm, G., *Das Ende des Gesetzes: Paulusstudien* (BEvT, 16; Munich: Chr. Kaiser Verlag, 1952).

Bornkamm, K., *Wunder und Zeugnis* (Tübingen: Mohr, 1968).

Bourke, M.M., 'The Miracle Stories of the Gospel', *Dunwoodie Review* 12.1 (1972), pp. 21-34.

Bouyer, L., 'Some Charismatic Manifestations in the History of the Church', in E. O'Connor (ed.), *Perspectives on Charismatic Renewal* (Notre Dame, IN: University of Notre Dame Press, 1975).

Bowlin, R., 'The Christian Prophets in the New Testament' (PhD dissertation, Vanderbilt University, 1958).

Boylan, W.E., 'Spirit and Kingdom: A Theology of Signs and Wonders' (MA thesis, Oral Roberts University, 1988).

Bradley, J.E., 'Miracles and Martyrdom in the Early Church: Some Theological and Ethical Implications', *Pneuma: The Journal of the Society for Pentecostal Studies* 13.1 (Spring 1991), pp. 65-82.

Brady, J.R., 'Do Miracles Authenticate the Messiah?', *Evangelical Review of Theology* 13.2 (April 1989), pp. 101-109.

Brann, N.L., 'The Proto-Protestant Assault on Church Magic: The "Errores Bohemanorum" according to the Abbot Trimethius (1462–1516)', *Journal of Religious History* 12 (June 1982), pp. 9-22.

Brennan, R.E., *The Seven Horns of the Lamb: A Study of the Gifts Based on Saint Thomas Aquina* (Milwaukee: Bruce, 1966).

Bresson, B.L., *Studies in Ecstasy* (New York: Vantage Press, 1966).

Brewer, E.C., *A Dictionary of Miracles: Imitative, Realistic and Dogmatic* (Philadelphia: J.B. Lippincott, 1966).

Bridge, D., *Signs and Wonders Today* (Downers Grove, IL: Inter-Varsity Press, 1985).

Bridge, D., and D. Phypers, *Spiritual Gifts and the Church* (Downers Grove, IL: Inter-Varsity Press, 1973).

Briggs, C., 'The Use of *ruach* in the Old Testament', *JBL* 19.2 (1900), pp. 132-45.

Britten, E., *Nineteenth Century Miracles* (New York: Arno Press, 1976).

Bron, B., *Das Wunder: Das theologische Wunderverständnis im Horizont des neuzeitlichen Natur- und Geschichtsbegriffs* (Göttingen: Vandenhoeck & Ruprecht, 2nd edn, 1979).

Brown, C., *Miracles and the Critical Mind* (Grand Rapids: Eerdmans, 1984).

—*That You May Believe: Miracles and Faith Then and Now* (Grand Rapids: Eerdmans, 1985).

—'The Other Half of the Gospel? (The Role of Miracles in the Contemporary Church)', *Christianity Today* 33 (April 1989), pp. 26-29.

Brown, D., *Understanding Pietism* (Grand Rapids: Eerdmans, 1978).

Brown, J., *Subject and Object in Modern Theology* (London: SCM Press, 1955).

Brown, R., 'Signs and Works', in *The Gospel According to John, I–XII* (AB, 29; Garden City, NY: Doubleday, 1967), pp. 525-32.

—'The Paraclete in the Fourth Gospel', *NTS* 13 (January 1967), pp. 113-32.

—'The Gospel Miracles', in *New Testament Essays* (Garden City, NY: Image Books, 1968).

Brown, S., 'Apostleship in the New Testament as an Historical and Theological Problem', *NTS* 30 (July 1984), pp. 474-80.

Bruce, F.F., 'The Holy Spirit in the Acts of the Apostles', *Int* 27 (April 1973), pp. 166-83.

—'The Holy Spirit in the Letter to the Galatians', in P. Elbert (ed.), *Essays on Apostolic Themes* (Peabody, MA: Hendrickson, 1985).

Brumback, C.A. *Suddenly . . . From Heaven* (Springfield, MO: Gospel Publishing House, 1961).

—*'What Meaneth This?' A Pentecostal Answer to a Pentecostal Question* (Springfield, MO: Gospel Publishing House, 1947).

Bruner, F.D., *A Theology of the Holy Spirit: The Pentecostal Experience and the New Testament Witness* (Grand Rapids: Eerdmans, 1970).

Büchsel, F., 'δῶρον, κτλ', *TDNT*, II, pp. 166-74.

—*Der Geist Gottes im neuen Testament* (Gütersloh: Bertelsmann, 1926).

Budgen, V., 'Prophecy in the New Testament—The Need for a Clear Test Case', *Reformation Today* 101 (1988), pp. 13-20; 102 (1988), pp. 19-28.

—*Charismatics and the Word of God: A Biblical and Historical Perspective on the Charismatic Movement* (Durham: Evangelical Press, enlarged edn, 1989).

Bultmann, R., 'καυχάομαι, κτλ', *TDNT*, III, pp. 645-54.

—*The Theology of the New Testament* (trans. K. Grobel; 2 vols.; New York: Charles Scribner's Sons, 1951).

—'The Question of Wonder', in R.W. Funk (ed.), *Faith and Understanding*, I (trans. L.P. Smith; London: SCM Press, 1969), pp. 247-61.

Bunn, J.T., 'Glossolalia in Historical Perspective', in W.E. Mills, *Speaking in Tongues: Let's Talk about It* (Waco, TX: Word Books, 1973), pp. 36-47.

Burdick, W., *Tongues: To Speak or Not to Speak* (Chicago: Moody Press, 1969).

Burge, G.M., *The Anointed Community: The Holy Spirit in the Johannine Tradition* (Grand Rapids: Eerdmans, 1987).

Burgess, S.M., 'Medieval Examples of Charismatic Piety in the Roman Catholic Church', in R.P. Spittler (ed.), *Perspectives on the New Pentecostalism* (Grand Rapids: Baker, 1976).

—*The Spirit and the Church: Antiquity* (Peabody, MA: Hendrickson, 1984).

Burgess, S.M., G.B. McGee and P. Alexander (eds.), *Dictionary of Pentecostal and Charismatic Movements* (Grand Rapids: Zondervan, 1988).

Burkill, T.A., 'The Notion of Miracle with Special Reference to St. Mark's Gospel', *ZNW* 50.1-2 (1959), pp. 33-48.

Burns, J.L., 'A Re-emphasis on the Purpose of Sign Gifts', *BSac* 132/527 (1975), pp. 242-49.

Burns, R.M., *The Great Debate on Miracles: From Joseph Glanvill to David Hume* (Lewisburg, PA: Bucknell University Press, 1982).

Burton, E. DeWitt, 'Appendix 17.1: *pneuma*', in *A Critical and Exegetical Commentary on the Epistle to the Galatians* (ICC; Edinburgh: T. & T. Clark, 1921), pp. 486-92.

Bushnell, H., *Nature and the Supernatural, As Together Constituting the One System of God* (New York: Charles Scribner's Sons, 1858).

Buswell, J.O., Jr, 'Miracle', in J.D. Douglas and M.C. Tenney (eds.), *New International Dictionary of the Bible* (Grand Rapids: Zondervan, 1987), pp. 660-62.

Bystrom, R.O., 'A Biblical Theology of B.B. Warfield: An Introduction to his Works' (MCS thesis, Regent College, 1974).

Caird, G.B., *The Apostolic Age* (London: Duckworth, 1955).

Cairns, D.S., *The Faith that Rebels: A Re-Examination of the Miracles of Jesus* (London: SCM Press, 3rd edn, 1929).

Callan, T., 'Prophecy and Ecstasy in Greco-Roman Religion and in 1 Corinthians', *NovT* 27 (April 1985), pp. 125-40.

Calvin, J., *John Calvin: Treatises against the Anabaptists and against the Libertines* (trans. and ed. B.W. Farley; Grand Rapids: Baker, 1982).

Campbell, T.C., 'The Doctrine of the Holy Spirit in the Theology of Athanasius', *SJT* 27 (November 1974), pp. 408-43.

—'Charismata in the Christian Communities of the Second Century', *Wesleyan Theological Journal* 17 (Fall 1982), pp. 7-25.

—'John Wesley and Conyers Middleton on Divine Intervention in History', *Church History* 55 (March 1986), pp. 39-49.

Campenhausen, H. von, *Ecclesiastical Authority and Spiritual Power in the Church of the First Four Centuries* (trans. J.A. Baker; London: A. & C. Black, 1969).

Carlston, C.E., 'The Question of Miracles', *ANQ* 12 (November 1971), pp. 99-107.

Carr, W., 'Towards a Contemporary Theology of the Holy Spirit', *SJT* 28.6 (1975), pp. 501-16.

Carroll, R.L., 'Glossolalia: Apostles to the Reformation', in W.H. Horton (ed.), *The Glossolalia Phenomenon* (Cleveland, TN: Pathway Press, 1966, pp. 69-94.

Carson, D.A., *Showing the Spirit: Theological Exposition of I Corinthians 12–14* (Grand Rapids: Baker, 1987).

Carter, C.W., *The Person and Ministry of the Holy Spirit: A Wesleyan Perspective* (Grand Rapids: Baker, 1974).

Castelot, J.J., SS, 'The Spirit of Prophecy: An Abiding Charism', *CBQ* 23 (April 1961), pp. 210-17.

Cave, C.H., 'The Obedience of Unclean Spirits', *NTS* 10 (October 1964), pp. 93-97.

Cave, J.D., 'An Investigation of the Place of Miracles in Protestant Christian Apologetics in the Twentieth Century' (ThD dissertation, Southwestern Baptist Theological Seminary, 1957).

Cavill, P., ' "Signs and Wonders" and the Venerable Bede', *EvQ* 88 (January 1988), pp. 31-42.

Chantry, W., *Signs of an Apostle: Observations on Pentecostalism, Old and New* (Edinburgh: Banner of Truth Press, 1973).

Chevallier, M.-A., *Esprit de Dieu, paroles d'hommes: Le rôle de l'esprit dans les ministères de la parole selon l'apôtre Paul* (Neuchatel: Delachaux & Niestlé, 1966).

Childers, J., 'Dunamis and the Continuation of the Kingdom of God in the Writings of Luke' (MA thesis, Trinity Evangelical Divinity School, 1969).

Codling, D.A., 'The Argument that the Revelatory Gifts of the Holy Spirit Ceased with the Closure of the Canon of Scripture' (ThM thesis, Westminster Theological Seminary, 1974).

Combrink, H.J.B., 'Die verhouding Pneuma-Dunamis', *Neotestamentica* 3.1 (1969), pp. 45-51.

Congar, Y.M.J., *Tradition and Traditions: An Historical and Theological Essay* (trans. M. Naseby and T. Rainborough; New York: Macmillan, 1967), pp. 107-37.

—*I Believe in the Holy Spirit* (3 vols.; New York: Seabury, 1983).

—*The Word and the Spirit* (trans. D. Smith; San Francisco: Harper & Row, 1986).

Conzelmann, H., and W. Zimmerli, 'χάρις, χαρίσμα, κτλ', *TDNT*, IX, pp. 372-406.

Cooke, R., *Do Miracles Then Continue?* (Hollidaysburg, PA: Manahath Press, 1981).

Coppes, L.J., *Whatever Happened to Biblical Tongues?* (Phillipsburg, NJ: Pilgrim Publishing, 1977).

Cothenet, E., 'Le Prophétisme dans le Nouveau Testament', in L. Pirot *et al.* (eds.), *Supplément au Dictionnaire de la Bible, Supplément 8* (Paris: Letouzey & Ané, 1972).

—'Les prophètes chrétiens comme exégètes charismatiques de l'Ecriture', in J. Panagopoulos (ed.), *Prophetic Vocation in the New Testament and Today* (Leiden: Brill, 1977), pp. 77-107.

Cottle, R.E., 'All Were Baptized (I Cor. 12.13)', *JETS* 17 (Spring 1974), pp. 75-80.

—'Tongues Shall Cease', *Pneuma* 1 (1979), pp. 43-49.

Countryman, L.W., 'How Many Baskets Full? The Value of Miracles in Mark', *CBQ* 47 (October 1985), pp. 643-55.

Court, J.M., 'The Philosophy of the Synoptic Miracles', *JETS* NS 23 (April 1972), pp. 1-15.

Craig, S.G., 'Benjamin B. Warfield', in *Biblical and Theological Studies* (Philadelphia: Presbyterian and Reformed Publishing, 1952).

Craig, W.L., 'Colin Brown, *Miracles and the Critical Mind*: A Review Article', *JETS* 27 (December 1984), pp. 473-85.

Criswell, W.A., *The Baptism, Filling and Gifts of the Holy Spirit* (Grand Rapids: Zondervan, 1973).

Crone, T.M., *Early Christian Prophecy: A Study of its Origin and Function* (Baltimore: St Mary's University Press, 1973).

Cullman, O., *Salvation in History* (trans. S.G. Sowers; New York: Harper & Row, 1967).

Cunningham, R., 'From Holiness to Healing: The Faith Cure in America, 1872–1892', *CH* 43 (December 1974), pp. 499-513.

Currie, S.D., ' "Speaking in Tongues": Evidence outside the New Testament Bearing on "Glossais Lalein" ', *Int* 19 (July 1965), pp. 274-94.

Custance, A.C., *Hidden Things of God's Revelation* (The Doorway Papers, 7; Grand Rapids: Zondervan, 1977).

Dallimore, A., *Forerunner of the Charismatic Movement: The Life of Edward Irving* (Chicago: Moody Press, 1983).

Dana, H.E., *The Holy Spirit in Acts* (Kansas City: Central Seminary Press, 1943).

Daniels, N., *Thomas Reid's Inquiry: The Geometry of Visibles and the Case for Realism* (New York: Burt Franklin, 1974).

Dautzenberg, G., 'Zum religionsgeschichtlichen Hintergrund der *diakrisis pneumaton* (1 Kor. 12.10)', *BZ* 15.1 (1971), pp. 93-104.

—'Botschaft und Bedeutung der urchristlichen Prophetie nach dem ersten Korintherbrief (2.6-16; 12-14)', in J. Panagopoulos (ed.), *Prophetic Vocation in the New Testament and Today* (Leiden: Brill, 1977), pp. 131-61.

Davies, J.G., 'Pentecost and Glossolalia', *JTS* 3 (October 1952), pp. 228-31.

Davies, R.E., *The Problem of Authority in the Continental Reformers* (London: Epworth Press, 1946).

Davies, W.E., *Paul and Rabbinic Judaism: Some Rabbinic Elements in Pauline Theology* (London: SPCK, 1970).

Davis, D.C., 'Princeton Inerrancy and the Nineteenth Century Philosophical Background of Contemporary Concerns', in J. Hannah (ed.), *Inerrancy and the Church* (Chicago: Moody Press, 1984), pp. 359-78.

Davison, J.E., 'Spiritual Gifts in the Roman Church: 1 Clement, Hermas and Justin Martyr' (PhD dissertation, University of Iowa, 1981).

Dayton, D., 'The Rise of the Evangelical Healing Movement in Nineteenth Century America', *Pneuma* 4.1 (Spring 1982), pp. 1-18.

Deere, J., 'Why Does God Do Miracles?', *Charisma* 18.2 (September 1992), pp. 30-36.

DeHaan, M.R., *Pentecost and After* (Grand Rapids: Zondervan, 1964).

DeHaan, R.W., *The Charismatic Controversy* (Grand Rapids: Zondervan, 1978).

Delling, G., 'τέλος, κτλ', *TDNT*, VIII, pp. 49-88.

—'Das Verständnis des Wunders im Neuen Testament', *ZST* 24 (1955), pp. 265-80.

—*Antike Wundertexte* (Berlin: de Gruyter, 2nd edn, 1960).

—'Botschaft und Wunder im Wirken Jesu', in H. Ristow and K. Matthiae (eds.), *Der geschichtliche Jesus und der kerygmatische Christus* (Berlin: de Gruyter, 1961), pp. 389-402.

DeMoor, L., 'John Calvin's View of Revelation', *EvQ* 3 (April 1931), pp. 172-92.

Denney, J., 'Holy Spirit', in J. Hastings (ed.), *Dictionary of Christ and the Gospels*, I (New York: Charles Scribner's Sons, 1906), pp. 731-44.

Dennis, E.B., 'The Duration of the Charismata: An Exegetical and Theological Study of 1 Corinthians 13.10 (MA thesis, CBN University, 1989).

Derrett, D., *Urchristliche Prophetie* (Stüttgart: Kohlhammer, 1975).

Dewar, L., *The Holy Spirit and Modern Thought* (London: Mowbrays, 1959).

Diamond, M.L., 'Miracles', in J.D. Griffin (ed.), *Philosophy of Religion and Theology* (Chambersburg, PA: American Academy of Religion, 1972).

Dillistone, F.W., 'The Biblical Doctrine of the Holy Spirit', *TTod* 3 (January 1947), pp. 486-97.

Dillow, J., *Speaking in Tongues: Seven Crucial Questions* (Grand Rapids: Zondervan, 1975).

DiOrio, R.A., *Signs and Wonders: Firsthand Experiences of Healing* (New York: Doubleday, 1987).

Dixon, L.E., 'Have the "Jewels of the Church" Been Found Again? The Irving-Darby Debate on Miraculous Gifts', *EJ* 5 (Spring 1987), pp. 78-92.

Dobbin, E.J., 'Towards a Theology of the Holy Spirit', *HeyJ* 17 (January 1976), pp. 5-19; (April 1976), pp. 129-49.

Dodd, C.H., 'Miracles in the Gospels', *ExpTim* 44 (August 1933), pp. 504-509.

—*The Bible Today* (New York: Macmillan, 1947).

Dollar, G.W., 'Church History and the Tongues Movement', *BSac* 120 (October–December 1963), pp. 309-11.

Dominy, B., 'Paul and Spiritual Gifts: Reflections on 1 Corinthians 12–14', *Southwestern Journal of Theology* 26 (Fall 1983), pp. 49-68.

Douglas, J., *The Criterion, or, Miracles Examined: With a View to Expose the Pretentions of Pagans and Papists; to Compare the Miraculous Powers Recorded in the New Testament, with those Said to Subsist in Later Times, and to Show the Great and Material Difference between them in Point of Evidence: from whence it Will Appear that the Former Must Be True and the Latter May Be False* (London: printed for A. Millar, 1745; microfiche, Louisville, KY: Lost Cause Press, 1968).

Dowey, E.A., *The Knowledge of God in Calvin's Theology* (New York: Columbia University Press, 1952).

Duggan, T.J., 'Thomas Reid's Theory of Sensation', *Philosophical Review* 69 (1960), pp. 90-100.

Duhm, H., *Die bösen Geister in Alten Testament* (Tübingen, Leipzig, 1904).

Duling, D.C., 'Kingdom of God, Kingdom of Heaven', *ABD*, IV, pp. 49-69.

Dulles, A., *A History of Apologetics* (Philadelphia: Westminster Press, 1971).

Dumais, M., 'Ministères, charismes et esprit dans l'oeuvre de Luc', *Eglise et théologie* 9 (October 1978), pp. 413-53.

Dumbrell, W.J., 'Spirit and Kingdom of God in the Old Testament', *RTR* 33 (January–April 1974), pp. 1-10.

Dunn, J.D.G., '2 Corinthians 3.17—"The Lord is the Spirit" ', *JTS* 21 (October 1970), pp. 309-20.

—'Spirit and Kingdom', *ExpTim* 82 (November 1970), pp. 36-40.

—'Rediscovering the Spirit', *ExpTim* 84 (October 1972), pp. 7-12; 84 (November 1972), pp. 40-44.

—'Spirit and Fire Baptism', *NovT* 14.2 (1972), pp. 81-92.

—*Jesus and the Spirit: A Study of the Religious and Charismatic Experience of Jesus and the First Christians as Reflected in the New Testament* (Philadelphia: Westminster Press, 1975).

—*Baptism in the Holy Spirit: A Re-Examination of the New Testament Teaching on the Gift of the Spirit in Relation to Pentecostalism Today* (Philadelphia: Westminster Press, 1977).

—'The Birth of a Metaphor: Baptized in the Spirit', *ExpTim* 89 (February 1978), pp. 134-38; (March 1978), pp. 173-75.

—'Models of Christian Community in the New Testament', in A. Bittlinger (ed.), *The Church is Charismatic: The World Council of Churches and the Charismatic Renewa* (Geneva: The World Council of Churches, 1981).

—'Rediscovering the Spirit, Part II', *ExpTim* 94 (October 1982), pp. 9-18.

Dunn, J.D.G., and G.H. Twelftree, 'Demon-Possession and Exorcism in the New Testament', *Churchman* 94.3 (1980), pp. 210-25.

DuPlessis, P.J., 'The Concept of *pneuma* in the Theology of Paul', *Neotestamentica* 3.1 (1969), pp. 9-20.

DuPont, J., 'La mission de Paul d'après Acts 26.13-23 et la mission des apôtres d'après Luc 24.44-49 et Actes 1.8', in M.D. Hooker and S.G. Wilson (eds.), *Paul and Paulinism: Studies in Honour of C.K. Barrett* (London: SPCK, 1982), pp. 290-99.

Duquoc, C., and C. Floristan (eds.), *Charisms in the Church* (New York: Seabury, 1978).

Durrwell, F.X., *The Holy Spirit of God: An Essay in Biblical Theology* (London: Chapman, 1986).

Edgar, T.R., *Miraculous Gifts: Are They for Today?* (Neptune, NJ: Loizeaux Brothers, 1983).

—'The Cessation of the Sign Gifts', *BSac* 145 (October–December 1988), pp. 371-86.

Edwards, O.C., Jr, 'The Exegesis of Acts 8.4-25 and its Implications for Confirmation and Glossolalia: A Review Article on Haenchen's Acts Commentary', *ATR* Supplementary Series 2 (September 1973), pp. 100-12.

Edwards, R.A., 'The Role of the Christian Prophet in Acts', in W.W. Gasque and R. P. Martin (eds.), *Apostolic History and the Gospel* (Exeter: Paternoster Press, 1970).

Egert, E., *The Holy Spirit in German Literature until the End of the Twelfth Century* (Paris: Mouton, 1973).

Eichholz, G., *Was heisst charismatische Gemeinde? (1 Kor. 12)* (Theologische Existenz Heute, 77; Munich: Chr. Kaiser Verlag, 1960).

Eichler, M., 'Charismatic Prophets and Charismatic Saviors (Anabaptist Leaders)', *Mennonite Quarterly Review* 55 (January 1981), pp. 45-61.

Eitrem, S., *Some Notes on the Demonology of the New Testament* (Symbolae Osloensis Supplement, 20; Oslo: Universitetsforlaget, 2nd edn, 1966).

Elbert, P., 'The Perfect Tense in Matthew 16.19 and the Three Charismata', *JETS* 17 (Summer 1974), pp. 149- 55.

—'Face to Face: Then or Now? An Exegesis of First Corinthians 13.8-13' (paper presented to the Society for Pentecostal Studies in Springfield, MO, December, 1977).

—'Calvin and Spiritual Gifts', *JETS* 22 (Spring 1979), pp. 235-56.

Ellis, E.E., 'The Role of the Christian Prophet in Acts', in W.W. Gasque and R.P. Martin (eds.), *Apostolic History and the Gospel* (Exeter: Paternoster Press, 1970).

—'Christ and the Spirit in 1 Corinthians', in B. Lindars and S. Smalley (eds.), *Christ and the Spirit in the New Testament.* (Cambridge: Cambridge University Press, 1973).

—' "Spiritual" Gifts in the Pauline Community', *NTS* 20 (January 1974), pp. 128-44.

—'Prophecy in the New Testament Church—and Today', in J. Panagopoulos (ed.), *Prophetic Vocation in the New Testament Church and Today* (Leiden: Brill, 1977), pp. 46-57.

—*Pauline Theology: Ministry and Society* (Grand Rapids: Eerdmans, 1989).

Engelsen, N.I.J., 'Glossolalia and Other Forms of Inspired Speech according to 1 Corinthians 12–14' (PhD dissertation, Yale University, 1970).

Ensley, E., *Sounds of Wonder: Speaking in Tongues in the Catholic Tradition* (New York: Paulist Press, 1977).

Epp, T.H., *The Use and Abuse of Tongues* (Lincoln, NE: Back to the Bible, 1963).

Erlandson, D.K., 'A New Look at Miracles', *Religious Studies* 13 (December 1977), pp. 417-28.

Ervin, H., *'These are Not Drunken As Ye Suppose . . . '* (Plainfield, NJ: Logos Publishers, 1968).

Estes, J.R., 'The Biblical Concept of Spiritual Gifts' (ThD dissertation, Southern Baptist Theological Seminary, 1967).

Evans, H.M., 'Tertullian: Pentecostal of Carthage', *Paraclete* 9.4 (Fall 1974), pp. 17-21.

—'Current Exegesis on the Kingdom of God', *Perspectives in Religious Studies* 14 (Spring 1987), pp. 67-77.

Ewert, D., *The Holy Spirit in the New Testament* (Scottdale, PA: Herald Press, 1983).

Falconer, R.A., 'The Holy Spirit in the Early Apostolic Age', *PRR* 11 (July 1900), pp. 438-60.

Falconer, R.A., 'The Holy Spirit in the Early Apostolic Age', *The PRR* 11 (July 1900), pp. 438-60.

Farmer, H.H., *The World and God: A Study of Prayer, Providence and Miracle in Christian Experience* (London: Nisbet, 1935).

Farnell, F.D., 'Is the Gift of Prophecy for Today?', *BSac* 149.595, 596; 150.597, 598 (July–September 1992, October–December 1992, January–March 1993, April–June 1993), pp. 277-303, 387-410.

Fascher, E., *Kritik am Wunder: Eine geschichtliche Skizze* (Stüttgart: Calwer Verlag, 1960).

Fee, G., 'Tongues—Least of the Gifts: Some Exegetical Observations on 1 Corinthians 12–14', *Pneuma* 2.2 (Fall 1980), pp. 3-14.

—*The First Epistle to the Corinthians* (NICNT; Grand Rapids: Eerdmans, 1987), pp. 4-20, 37-46, 641-52.

—'The Kingdom of God and the Church's Global Mission', in M.A. Dempster (ed.), *Called and Empowered* (Peabody, MA: Hendrickson, 1991).

Fenner, F., *Die Krankheit im Neuen Testament: Ein Religions- und Medizingeschichtliche Untersuchung* (UNT, 18; Leipzig: Hinrichs, 1930).

Fern, R.L., 'Hume's Critique of Miracles: An Irrelevant Triumph', *Religious Studies* 18 (September 1982), pp. 337-54.

Fitzmyer, J.A., 'Jesus in the Early Church through the Eyes of Luke–Acts', *Scripture Bulletin* 17 (1987), pp. 26-35.

Flender, H., *St Luke: Theologian of Redemptive History* (trans. R.H Fuller and I. Fuller; London: SPCK, 1967).

Floris, A.T., 'Two Fourth Century Witnesses on the Charismata', *Paraclete* 4.4 (Fall 1971), pp. 17-22.

—'Chrysostom and the Charismata', *Paraclete* 5.1 (Winter 1971), pp. 17-22.

Foerster, W., 'δαίμων, κτλ', *TDNT*, II, pp. 1-20.

Foerster, W., and G. Fohrer, 'σῴζω, σωτηρία, κτλ', *TDNT*, VII, pp. 965-1024.

Foord, D., 'Prophecy in the New Testament', *RTR* 31 (June–April 1972), pp. 10-25.

Force, J.E., 'Hume and the Relation of Science to Religion among Certain Members of the Royal Society', *Journal of the History of Ideas* 45 (October–December 1984), pp. 517-36.

Ford, J.M., 'The Spirit in the New Testament', in D. Callahan (ed.), *God, Jesus, and Spirit* (New York: Herder & Herder, 1969).

—'Toward a Theology of "Speaking in Tongues" ', *TS* 32 (March 1971), pp. 3-29.

Forster, A.H., 'The Meaning of Power for St Paul', *ATR* 32 (July 1950), pp. 179-85.

Forstman, H.J., *Word and Spirit: Calvin's Doctrine of Biblical Authority* (San Francisco: Stanford University Press, 1962).

Fortna, R.T., *The Gospel of Signs: A Reconstruction of the Narrative Source Underlying the Fourth Gospel* (SNTSMS, 11; Cambridge: Cambridge University Press, 1970).

Foster, F.H., 'The New Testament Miracles: An Investigation of Their Function', *American Journal of Theology* 12 (July 1908), pp. 369-91.

Foster, K.N., 'Discernment, the Powers and Spirit-Speaking' (PhD dissertation, Fuller Theological Seminary, School of World Mission, 1988).

Foubister, D.R., 'Healing in the Liturgy of the Post Apostolic Church', *SBT* 9 (October 1979), pp. 141-55.

Fowler, S., 'The Continuance of the Charismata', *EvQ* 45 (July–September 1973), pp. 172-183.

Fox, G., *Book of Miracles* (ed. H.J. Cadbury; New York: Octagon Books, 1973).

Fraiken, D., ' "Charismes et ministères" à la lumière de 1 Co 12–14', *Eglise et Théologie* 9 (October 1978), pp. 455-63.

Francis, P., 'The Holy Spirit: A Statistical Inquiry', *ExpTim* 96 (February 1985), pp. 136-37.

Franklin, L.D., 'Spiritual Gifts in Tertullian' (PhD dissertation, St Louis University, 1989).

Frazier, C.A. (ed.), *Faith Healing: Finger of God or Scientific Curiosity?* (Nashville: Thomas Nelson, 1973).

Frerichs, W.W., 'Joel 2.28-29 and Acts 2', *Dialogue* 23 (1984), pp. 93-96.

Fridrichsen, A., *The Problem of Miracle in Primitive Christianity* (trans. R.A. Harrisville and J.S. Hanson; Minneapolis: Augsburg, 1972).

—'Jesus' Kampf gegen die unreinen Geister', in A. Suhl (ed.), *Der Wunderbegriff im Neuen Testament* (Wege der Forschung, 295; Darmstadt: Wissenschaftliche Buchgesellschaft, 1980), pp. 248-65.

Friedrich, G. *et al.*, 'προφήτης, κτλ', *TDNT*, VI, pp. 781-862.

Frost, E., *Christian Healing: A Consideration of the Place of Spiritual Healing in the Church of Today in the Light of the Doctrine and Practice of the Ante-Nicene Church* (London: Mowbrays, 1954).

Fuchs, E., *Christus und der Geist bei Paulus: Eine biblisch-theologische Untersuchung* (UNT, 23; Leipzig: Hinrichs, 1932).

Fuhrmann, P.T., 'Calvin, the Expositor of Scripture', *Int* 6 (April 1952), pp. 188-209.

Fuller, D.P., 'Benjamin B. Warfield's View of Faith and History', *JETS* 11 (April 1968), pp. 75-83.

Fuller, R.H., *Interpreting the Miracles* (Philadelphia: Westminster Press, 1963).

—'Tongues in the New Testament', *American Church Quarterly* 3 (Fall 1963), pp. 162-68.

Fung, R.Y.K., 'Charismatic versus Organized Ministry? An Examination of an Alleged Antithesis', *EvQ* 52–53 (October–December 1980), pp. 195-214.

—'Ministry, Community and Spiritual Gifts', *EvQ* 56 (January 1984), pp. 3-20.

—'Function or Office? A Survey of the New Testament Evidence', *Evangelical Review of Theology* 8.1 (April 1984), pp. 16-39.

Furnish, V.P., 'Prophets, Apostles and Preachers: A Study of the Biblical Concept of Preaching', *Int* 17 (January 1963), pp. 48-60.

Gaebelein, A.C., *The Healing Question: An Examination of the Claims of Faith-Healing and Divine Healing Systems in the Light of Scriptures and History* (New York: Our Hope Publication Office, 1925).

Gaede, C.S., 'Glossolalia at Azuza Street: A Hidden Presupposition?', *WTJ* 51.1 (Spring 1989), pp. 77-92.

Gaffin, R.B., Jr, 'The Holy Spirit', *WTJ* 43.3 (Fall 1980), pp. 58-78.

—*Perspectives on Pentecost: Studies in New Testament Teaching on the Gifts of the Holy Spirit* (Grand Rapids: Baker, 1979).

Galloway, A.D., 'Recent Thinking on Christian Beliefs, III: The Holy Spirit in Recent Theology', *ExpTim* 88.4 (January 1977), pp. 100-103.

Gamble, R.C., '*Brevitas et Facilitas*: Toward an Understanding of Calvin's Hermeneutic', *WTJ* 47 (Spring 1985), pp. 1-17.

Garcia, A.L., 'Spiritual Gifts and the Work of the Kingdom', *Concordia Theological Quarterly* 49 (April–July 1985), pp. 149-60.

Gardiner, G.E., *The Corinthian Catastrophe* (Grand Rapids: Kregel, 1974).

Gatzweiler, K., *La conception paulinienne du miracle* (ALBO, 3.29; Leuven: Publications Universitaires, 1961).

Geisler, N.L., *Miracles and Modern Thought* (Grand Rapids: Zondervan, 1982).

—*Signs and Wonders* (Wheaton, IL: Tyndale House, 1988).

Gelpi, D.L., *The Divine Mother: A Trinitarian Theology of the Holy Spirit* (Washington, DC: University Press of America, 1984).

Gentry, K.L., *The Charismatic Gift of Prophecy—A Reformed Response to Wayne Grudem* (Memphis: Footstool Publications, 1989).

Gerlemann, G., 'Geist und Geistgaben im Alten Testament', in K. Galling (ed.), *Religion im Geschichte und Gegenwart*, II (7 vols.; Tübingen: Mohr, 3rd edn, 1957–65), pp. 1270-72.

Gerrish, B.A., 'Biblical Authority and the Continental Reformation', *SJT* 10 (December 1957), pp. 337-360.

Gerstner, J.H., 'Warfield's Case for Biblical Inerrancy', in J.W. Montgomery (ed.), *God's Inerrant Word* (Minneapolis: Bethany Fellowship, 1974).

Giesen, H., 'Der Heilige Geist als Ursprung und treibende Kraft des christlichen Lebens: Zu den Geistaussagen der Apostelgeschichte', *BK* 37.1 (1982), pp. 126-32.

Giles, K., 'Prophecy in the Bible and in the Church Today', *Interchange* 26 (1980), pp. 75-89.

—'Salvation in Lukan Theology (2): Salvation in the Book of Acts', *RTR* 42 (May–August 1982), pp. 45-59.

—'Apostles Before and After Paul', *Churchman* 96.3 (1985), pp. 241-56.

—*Patterns of Ministry among the First Christians* (Melbourne: Collins Dove, 1989).

Gillespie, T.W., 'Prophecy and Tongues: The Concept of Christian Prophecy in the Pauline Theology' (PhD dissertation, Claremont Graduate School and University Center, 1971).

—'The Pattern of Prophetic Speech in First Corinthians', *JBL* 97 (May 1978), pp. 74-95.

Gilsdorf, J., *The Puritan Apocalypse: New England Eschatology in the Seventeenth Century* (New York: Garland, 1989).

Glasswell, M.E., 'The Use of Miracles in the Markan Gospel', in C.F.D. Moule (ed.), *Miracles: Cambridge Studies in their Philosophy and History* (London: Mowbrays, 1965), pp. 149-163.

Gleason, R.W., 'Miracles and Contemporary Theology', *Thought* 37 (1962), pp. 12-34.

Glöel, J., *Der Heilige Geist in der Heilsverkündigung des Paulus: Eine biblisch-theologische Untersuchung* (Halle: Niemeyer, 1888).

Goppelt, L., *Apostolic and Post-Apostolic Times* (trans. R.A. Geulich; Grand Rapids: Baker, 1977).

—*Theology of the New Testament* (trans. J.E. Alsup; ed. J. Roloff; Grand Rapids: Eerdmans, 1981).

Goree, B.W., Jr, *The Cultural Bases of Montanism* (PhD dissertation, Baylor University, 1980).

Gowan, D.E., 'Salvation as Healing', *Ex Auditu: An Annual of the Frederick Neumann Symposium on Theological Interpretation of Scripture, Princeton Theological Seminary*, 5 (1989), pp. 1-19.

Graber, J.G., 'The Temporary Gifts of the Holy Spirit' (ThM thesis, Dallas Theological Seminary, 1947).

Grabner-Haider, A., *Paraklese und Eschatologie bie Paulus* (Münster: Aschendorff, 1967).

Grant, R.M., *Miracle and Natural Law in Graeco-Roman and Early Christian Thought* (Amsterdam: North Holland Publishing, 1952).

Grau, F., 'Der neutestamentliche Begriff *Charisma*: Seine Geschichte und seine Theologie' (DTheol dissertation, Ebehard-Karls-Universität, 1946).

Grave, S.A., *The Scottish Philosophy of Common Sense* (Oxford: Clarendon Press, 1960).

Graves, R.W., 'Tongues Shall Cease: A Critical Study of the Supposed Cessation of the Charismata', *Paraclete* 17.4 (Fall 1983), pp. 20-28.

—'Documenting Xenoglossy', *Paraclete* 21.2 (Spring 1987), pp. 27-30.

—*Praying in the Spirit* (Old Tappan, NJ: Chosen Books, 1987).

Green, M., *I Believe in the Holy Spirit* (Grand Rapids: Eerdmans, 1975).

Green, W.M., 'Glossolalia in the Second Century', *RQ* 16.3-4 (1973), pp. 231-39.

Greenspahn, F.E., 'Why Prophecy Ceased', *JBL* 108.1 (1989), pp. 37-49.

Greer, R.A., *The Fear of Freedom: A Study of Miracles in the Roman Imperial Church* (University Park, PA: The Pennsylvania State University Press, 1989).

Greeven, H., 'Propheten, Lehrer, Vorsteher bei Paulus', *ZNW* 44.1 (1952), pp. 1-43.

Grier, W.J. 'Benjamin Breckinridge Warfield', *Banner of Truth* 89 (February 1971), pp. 3-9.

Griffith-Thomas, W.R., *The Holy Spirit of God: Lectures on the L.P. Stone Foundation, Princeton Theological Seminary* (Grand Rapids: Eerdmans, 1963).

Griffiths, M.C., 'Today's Missionary, Yesterday's Apostle', *EMQ* 21 (April 1985), pp. 154-65.

Groh, D.E., 'Utterance and Exegesis: Biblical Interpretation in the Montanist Crisis', in D.E. Groh and R. Jewett (eds.), *The Living Text: Essays in Honor of Ernest W. Saunders* (Lanham, PA: The University Press of America, 1985), pp. 73-95.

Gromacki, R.G., *The Modern Tongues Movement* (Nutley, NJ: Presbyterian and Reformed Publishing, 1976).

Groot, A. de. *The Bible on Miracles* (trans. J.A. Roessen; De Pere, WI: St Norbert Abbey Press, 1966).

Gross, E.M., *Miracles, Demons and Spiritual Warfare: An Urgent Call for Discernment* (Grand Rapids: Baker, 1990).

Grudem, W., '1 Corinthians 14.20-26: Prophecy and Tongues as Signs of God's Attitude', *WTJ* 41 (Spring 1979), pp. 381-96.

—*The Gift of Prophecy in 1 Corinthians* (Washington, DC: The University Press of America, 1982).

—'Why Christians Can Still Prophesy', *Christianity Today* 32.16 (16 September 1988), pp. 31-35.

—*The Gift of Prophecy in the New Testament and Today* (East Westchester, IL: Crossway Books, 1988).

—'Does God Still Give Revelation Today?', *Charisma* 18.2 (September 1992), pp. 38-44.

Grundmann, W., 'δύναμαι, κτλ', *TDNT*, II, pp. 284-318.

—'ἰσχύω, κτλ', *TDNT*, III, pp. 397-402.

—*Der Begriff der Kraft in der neutestamentlichen Gedankenwelt* (BWANT, 4.8; Stüttgart: Kohlhammer, 1932).

—'Der Pfingstbericht der Apostelgeschichte in seinem theologischen Sinn', *Studia Evangelica* (1964), pp. 584-94.

Guillet, J., 'The Holy Spirit in Christ's Life', *Lumen Vitae* 28 (March 1973), pp. 31-40.

Gundry, R.H., ' "Ecstatic Utterance" (N.E.B.)?' *JTS* NS 17 (October 1966), pp. 299-307.

Gunkel, H., *The Influence of the Holy Spirit: The Popular View of the Apostolic Age and the Teaching of the Apostle Paul*, II (trans. R.A. Harrisville and P.A. Quanbeck; Philadelphia: Fortress Press, 1979).

Gustafson, R.A., *Authors of Confusion* (Tampa: Grace Publishing, 1971).

Gutbrod, K., *Die Wundergeschichten des Neuen Testaments: Dargestellt nach den ersten 3 Evangelisten* (Stüttgart: Calwer Verlag, 1967).

Guttmann, A., 'The Significance of Miracles for Talmudic Judaism', *HUCA* 20 (1947), pp. 363-406.

Guy, H.A., *New Testament Prophecy: Its Origin and Significance* (London: Epworth Press, 1947).

Haenchen, E., 'Faith and Miracle', *Studia Evangelica* 73 (1959), pp. 495-98.

Hahn, F., 'Charisms and Office', *TD* 29 (Fall 1981), pp. 239-43.

Hamilton, N.Q., *The Holy Spirit and Eschatology in Paul* (London: Oliver & Boyd, 1957).

Hanson, R.P.C., 'The Divinity of the Holy Spirit', *CQ* 1 (April 1969), pp. 298-306.

Hardon, J.A., 'The Miracle Narratives of the Acts of the Apostles', *CBQ* 16 (1954), pp. 303-18.

—'The Concept of Miracle from St Augustine to Modern Apologetics', *TS* 15 (June 1954), pp. 229-57.

Harnack, A., von, *Monasticism and the Confessions of St Augustine* (London: Williams & Norgate, 1901).

—*The Mission and Expansion of Christianity in the First Three Centuries* (trans. J. Moffat; 2 vols.; London: Williams & Norgate, 1908).

—*History of Dogma* (trans. N. Buchanan; 7 vols.; New York: Russell & Russell, 1958).

Harper, G.W., 'Renewal and Causality: Some Thoughts on a Conceptual Framework for a Charismatic Theology', *Journal of Ecumenical Studies* 24.1 (1987), pp. 93-103.

Harper, M., *The Healings of Jesus* (Downers Grove, IL: Inter-Varsity Press, 1986).

Harrell, D.E., Jr, *All Things Are Possible: The Healing and Charismatic Revivals in Modern America* (Bloomington, IN: Indiana University Press, 1975).

Harris, R.W., *Spoken by the Spirit: Documented Accounts of 'Other Tongues' from Arabic to Zulu* (Springfield, MO: Gospel Publishing House, 1973).

Harrisville, R.A., 'Speaking in Tongues—A Sign of Transcendence?', *Dialog* 13 (Winter 1974), pp. 11-18.

—'Speaking in Tongues: A Lexigraphical Study', *CBQ* 38 (January 1976), pp. 35-48.

Hasenhüttl, G., *Charisma: Ordnungsprinzip der Kirche* (Oekumenische Forschungen, 1; Basel: Herder, 1969).

Haspecker, J., 'Wunder im Alten Testament', *Theologische Akademie* 2.1 (1965), pp. 29-56.

Haughy, J.C. (ed.), *Theological Reflections on the Charismatic Renewal. Proceedings of the Chicago Conference, October 1-2, 1976* (Ann Arbor, MI: Servant Books, 1978).

Hawthorne, G.F., *The Presence and the Power: The Significance of the Holy Spirit in the Life and Ministry of Jesus* (Dallas: Word Books, 1991).

Hay, E.R., 'A Contranatural View of Miracle', *CJT* 13 (October 1967), pp. 266-80.

Haykin, M., 'Hanserd Knollys (ca 1599–1691) on the Gifts of the Spirit', *WTJ* 54 (Spring 1992), pp. 99-113.

Headlam, A.C., *The Miracles of the New Testament* (London: John Murray, 1914).

Hebert, A.J., *Raised from the Dead: True Stories of 400 Resurrection Miracles* (Rockford, IL: TAN Publications, 1986).

Heil, J.P., 'Significant Aspects of the Healing Miracles in Matthew', *CBQ* 41 (April 1979), pp. 274-87.

Heine, R.E., *Montanist Oracles and Testimonia* (Patristic Monograph Series, 14; Macon, GA: Mercer University Press, 1989).

Heitmann, C., and H. Mühlen (eds.), *Erfahrung und Theologie des Heiligen Geistes* (Munich: Kösel, 1974).

Held, H.J., 'Matthew as Interpreter of the Miracle Stories', in G. Bornkamm, G. Barth and H.J. Held, *Tradition and Interpretation in Matthew* (trans. P. Scott; Philadelphia: Westminster Press, 1963).

Helfmeyer, H.J., 'אות', *TDOT*, I, pp. 167-88.

Hemer, C.J., *The Book of Acts in the Setting of Hellenistic History* (ed. C.H. Gemph; Tübingen: Mohr [Paul Siebeck], 1989), pp. 415-43.

Hempel, J., *Heilung als Symbol und Wirklichkeit im biblischen Schrifttum* (Göttingen: Vandenhoeck & Ruprecht, 1958).

Hemphill, K.S., 'The Pauline Concept of Charisma' (PhD dissertation, Cambridge University, 1976).

—*Spiritual Gifts Empowering the New Testament Church* (Nashville: Broadman Press, 1988).

Hendricks, W.L., 'Glossolalia in the New Testament', in W.E. Mills (ed.), *Speaking in Tongues: Let's Talk About It* (Waco, TX: Word Books, 1973), pp. 48-60.

Hendry, G.S., *The Holy Spirit in Christian Theology* (Philadelphia: Westminster Press, 1956).

Hengel, M., *The Charismatic Leader and his Followers* (trans. J.C.G. Craig; ed. J. Riches; New York: Crossroad; Edinburgh: T. & T. Clark, 1981).

—*Between Jesus and Paul: Studies in the Earliest History of Christianity* (trans. J. Bowden; Philadelphia: Fortress Press, 1983).

Hengel, M., and R. Hengel, 'Die Heilungen Jesu und medizinisches Denken', in A. Suhl (ed.), *Der Wunderbegriff im Neuen Testament* (Wege der Forschung, 295; Darmstadt: Wissenschaftliche Buchgesellschaft, 1980).

Henry, C.F.H., *God, Revelation and Authority* (6 vols.; Waco, TX: Word Books, 1974).

Hermann, I., *Kurios und Pneuma: Studien zur Christologie der paulinischen Hauptbriefe* (SANT, 2; Munich: Kösel Verlag, 1961).

Heron, A.I.C., *The Holy Spirit* (Philadelphia: Westminster Press, 1983).

Hesse, M., 'Miracles and the Laws of Nature', in C.F.D. Moule (ed.), *Miracles: Cambridge Studies in their Philosophy and History* (London: Mowbrays, 1965), pp. 33-42.

Hiers, R.H., 'Satan, Demons and the Kingdom of God', *SJT* 27 (February 1974), pp. 35-47.

Hill, D., *Greek Words and Hebrew Meanings: Studies in the Semantics of Soteriological Terms* (SNTSMS, 5; Cambridge: Cambridge University Press, 1967), pp. 202-93.

—'Christian Prophets as Teachers or Instructors in the Church', in J. Panagopoulos (ed.), *Prophetic Vocation in the New Testament and Today* (NovTSup, 45; Leiden: Brill, 1977), pp. 108-130.

—*New Testament Prophecy* (Atlanta: John Knox, 1979).

Hillis, D.W. (ed.), *Tongues, Healing and You* (Grand Rapids: Baker, 1971).

—*Is the Whole Body a Tongue?* (Grand Rapids: Baker, 1974).

Hinson, E.G., 'A Brief History of Glossolalia', in F. Stagg, E.G. Hinson and W.E. Oates (eds.), *Glossolalia: Tongue Speaking in Biblical, Historical and Psychological Perspective* (Nashville, TN: Abingdon Press, 1967).

—'The Significance of Glossolalia in the History of Christianity', in W.E. Mills (ed.), *Speaking in Tongues, Let's Talk about It* (Waco, TX: Word Books, 1973).

Hocken, P. *et al.*, *New Heaven? New Earth?* (London: Darton, Longman & Todd, 1976).

Hodge, A.A., *Outlines of Theology* (New York: Robert Carter, 1868).

Hodge, C., *Systematic Theology* (New York: Charles Scribner, 1871–72).

Hodge, C.W., 'Christian Experience and Dogmatic Theology', *PTR* 8.1 (January 1910), pp. 1-43.

—'The Witness of the Holy Spirit to the Bible', *PTR* 11.1 (January 1913), pp. 41-84.

—'What is a Miracle?', *PTR* 14.2 (April 1916), pp. 202-64.

Hodges, Z.C., 'The Purpose of Tongues', *BSac* 120 (July–September 1963), pp. 226-33.

Hoefel, R.J., 'The Doctrine of Inspiration in the Writings of James Orr and B.B. Warfield: A Study in Contrasting Approaches to Scripture' (PhD dissertation, Fuller Theological Seminary, 1983).

—'B.B. Warfield and James Orr: A Study in Contrasting Approaches to Scripture', *Christian Scholar's Review* 16 (September 1986), pp. 40-52.

Hoehner, H.H., 'The Purpose of Tongues in 1 Corinthians 14.20-25', in D. Campbell (ed.), *Walvoord: A Tribute* (Chicago: Moody Press, 1982), pp. 53-66.

Hoekema, A!, *What About Tongues Speaking?* (Grand Rapids: Eerdmans, 1966).

—*Holy Spirit Baptism* (Grand Rapids: Eerdmans, 1971).

Hoeveler, J.D., Jr, *James McCosh and the Scottish Intellectual Tradition* (Princeton: Princeton University Press, 1981).

Hoffecker, W.A., *Piety and the Princeton Theologians: Archibald Alexander, Charles Hodge, and Benjamin Warfield* (Grand Rapids: Baker, 1981).

—'Benjamin B. Warfield', in D.F. Wells (ed.), *Reformed Theology in America: A History of its Modern Development* (Grand Rapids: Eerdmans, 1985).

Hoffman, R.J., ' "*Memeristai ho Christos*?" Anti-Enthusiast Polemic from Paul to Augustine', *Studia Theologica* 33.2 (1979), pp. 149-64.

Holdcroft, T.L., *The Holy Spirit: A Pentecostal Interpretation* (Springfield, MO: Gospel Publishing House, 1980).

Holland, R.F., 'The Miraculous', *American Philosophical Quarterly* 2 (1965), pp. 43-51.

Hollenweger, W.J., —*The Pentecostals: The Charismatic Movement in the Churches* (Minneapolis: Augsburg, 1972).

—*The Pentecostals* (trans. R.A. Wilson; Minneapolis: Augsburg, 1977).

—'After Twenty Years' Research on Pentecostalism', *Theology* 87 (November 1984), pp. 403-12.

Holtz, T., 'Das Kennzeichen des Geistes (1 Kor. 12.1-3)', *NTS* 18 (April 1972), pp. 365-76.

Horgan, T.D., 'Who Is the Holy Spirit? A Biblical Survey', *One in Christ* 25 (1989), pp. 322-32.

Horn, G.W., 'Holy Spirit', in *ABD*, III, pp. 260-80.

Horsely, R.A., ' "Like One of the Prophets of Old": Two Types of Popular Prophets at the Time of Jesus', *CBQ* 47 (July 1985), pp. 435-63.

Horton, S.M., *What the Bible Says about the Holy Spirit* (Springfield, MO: Gospel Publishing, 1976).

Hospers, G.H., *The Reformed Principle of Authority: The Scripture Principle of the Reformers Set Forth in the Light of Our Times* (Grand Rapids: The Reformed Press, 1924).

House, H.W., 'Tongues and the Mystery Religions of Corinth', *BSac* 140 (April–June 1983), pp. 134-50.

Houston, G., *Prophecy: A Gift for Today?* (Downers Grove, IL: Inter-Varsity Press, 1989).

Hove, A. van, *La Doctrine du Miracle chez Saint Thomas* (Paris: Wettern, Bruges, 1927).

Howard, J.G., 'The Doctrine of Permanent Spiritual Gifts' (ThD dissertation, Dallas Theological Seminary, 1967).

Hoyle, R.B., *The Holy Spirit in St Paul* (Garden City, NY: Doubleday, 1925).

Hull, J.E.H., *The Holy Spirit in the Acts of the Apostles* (London: Lutterworth Press, 1967).

Hull, J.M., *Hellenistic Magic and the Synoptic Tradition* (Naperville, IL: Allenson Book Co., 1974).

Hunter, H., 'Tongues-Speech: A Patristic Analysis', *JETS* 23 (June 1980), pp. 124-37.

—*Spirit Baptism* (Lanham, MD: The University Press of America, 1983).

Hurd, J.C., *The Origin of I Corinthians* (New York: Seabury, 1965).

Hurtado, L.W., 'The Function of Signs and Wonders in the Apostolic and Sub-Apostolic Period' (MA thesis, Trinity Evangelical Divinity School, 1967).

Hutchinson, W.R. *The Modernist Impulse in American Protestantism* (Cambridge, MA: Harvard University Press, 1976).

Iber, G., 'Zum Verstandnis von 1 Korinther 12,31', *ZNW* 41.1-2 (1963), pp. 43-52.

Inch, M., 'The Apologetic Use of "Sign" in the Fourth Gospel', *EvQ* 42 (January–March 1970), pp. 35-43.

—*Saga of the Spirit: A Biblical, Systematic, and Historical Theology of the Holy Spirit* (Grand Rapids: Baker, 1985).

Isaacs, M.E., *The Concept of Spirit: A Study of Pneuma in Hellenistic Judaism and its Bearing on the New Testament* (Heythrop Monographs, 1; London: Heythrop College, 1976).

Isbell, C.D., 'Glossolalia and Propheteialalia: A Study of 1 Corinthians 14', *Wesley Theological Journal* 10 (Spring 1975), pp. 15-22.

Jensen, P.F., 'Calvin, Charismatics and Miracles', *EvQ* 51 (July–September 1979), pp. 131-144.

Jeremias, J., *New Testament Theology: The Proclamation of Jesus* (trans. J. Bowden; New York: Charles Scribner's Sons, 1971).

Jervell, J., 'The Signs of an Apostle: Paul's Miracles', in *Essays on Luke–Acts and Early Christian History* (Minneapolis: Augsburg, 1984), pp. 77-95.

—'Sons of the Prophets: The Holy Spirit in the Acts of the Apostles', in *Essays on Luke–Acts and Early Christian History* (Minneapolis: Augsburg, 1984), pp. 96-121.

Jodock, D., 'The Impact of Cultural Change: Princeton Theology and Scriptural Authority Today', *Dialogue* 22 (Winter 1983), pp. 21-29.

Johanson, B.C., 'Tongues: A Sign for Unbelievers? A Structural and Exegetical Study of I Corinthians 14.20-25', *NTS* 25 (January 1979), pp. 180-203.

Johansson, N., 'I Corinthians 13 and I Corinthians 14', *NTS* 10 (April 1964), pp. 383-92.

Johnson, R.C., *Authority in Protestant Theology* (Philadelphia: Westminster Press, 1959).

Johnson, S.L., Jr, 'The Gift of Tongues and the Book of Acts', *BSac* 120 (October–December 1963), pp. 309-11.

Johnson, T.C., 'John Calvin and the Bible', *EvQ* 4 (July 1932), pp. 257-66.

Johnson, W.H., 'Miracles and History', *PTR* 8 (October 1910), pp. 529-59.

Johnston, G., *The Spirit-Paraclete in the Gospel of John* (Philadelphia: Fortress Press, 1970).

Jones, C., *A Guide to the Study of the Pentecostal Movement* (3 vols.; Metuchen, NJ: Scarecrow Press, 1983).

Jones, H., 'Are There Apostles Today?', *Foundations* 13 (1984), pp. 16-25.

Jones, P.R., '1 Corinthians 15.8: Paul the Last Apostle', *TynBul* 36 (1984), pp. 3-34.

Jooste, J.M., 'The Dynamic Characteristic of the Spirit of God—A Structure and Foundation for Pneumatology (DD dissertation, University of Pretoria, 1988).

Juaire, V., 'The Sign-Function of Miracles', *The Scotist* 16.1 (1960), pp. 36-47.

Judisch, D., *An Evaluation of Claims to the Charismatic Gifts* (Grand Rapids: Baker, 1978).

Jungkuntz, T., 'Secularization Theology, Charismatic Renewal, and Luther's Theology of the Cross', *Concordia Theological Monthly* 42 (January 1971), pp. 5-24.

Kalin, E.R., 'Inspired Community: A Glance at Canon History', *Concordia Theological Monthly* 43 (September 1971), pp. 541-49.

Kallas, J., *The Significance of the Synoptic Miracles* (London: SPCK, 1961).

—*Jesus and the Power of Satan* (Philadelphia: Westminster Press, 1968).

Käsemann, E., 'Wunder. Im NT', in K. Galling (ed.), *Religion im Geschichte und Gegenwart*. VI. *1835-1837* (7 vols.; Tübingen: Mohr, 3rd edn, 1957-65).

—*Essays on New Testament Themes* (trans. W.J. Montague; SBT, 41; London: SCM Press, 1964).

Keck, L.E., and J.L. Martyn, *Studies in Luke–Acts: Essays in Honor of Paul Schubert* (London: SPCK, 1968).

Kee, H.C., 'The Terminology of Mark's Exorcism Stories', *NTS* 14 (January 1968), pp. 232-46.

—'Aretalogy and Gospel', *JBL* 92 (September 1973), pp. 402-22.

—*Community of the New Age: Studies in Mark's Gospel* (Philadelphia: Westminster Press, 1977).

—*Miracle in the Early Christian World: A Study in Sociohistorical Method* (New Haven: Yale University Press, 1983).

Kelber, W., *The Kingdom in Mark: A New Place and a New Time* (Philadelphia: Fortress Press, 1974).

Keller, E., and M.-L. Keller, *Miracles in Dispute: A Continuing Debate* (trans. M. Kohl; Philadelphia: Fortress Press, 1969).

Kelly, A.J., 'The Gifts of the Spirit: Aquinas and the Modern Context', *The Thomist* 38 (April 1974), pp. 193-231.

Kelly, B.J., *The Seven Gifts* (New York: Sheed & Ward, 1942).

Kelly, J.N.D., *Early Christian Doctrines* (New York: Harper & Row, 1960).

Kelsey, D.H., *The Uses of Scripture in Recent Theology* (Philadelphia: Fortress Press, 1975).

Kelsey, M., *Healing and Christianity in Ancient Thought and Modern Times* (New York: Harper & Row, 1973).

Kerr, H.T., 'Faith of Our Fathers', *Princeton Seminary Bulletin* 43 (April 1950), pp. 13-17.

Kertelege, K., *Die Wunder Jesu im Markusevangelium: Ein redaktionsgeschichtliche Untersuchung* (SANT, 33; Munich: Kösel Verlag, 1970).

King-Farlow, J., 'Historical Insights on Miracles: Babbage, Hume, Aquinas', *International Journal of the Philosophy of Religion* 13.2 (1982), pp. 209-18.

Kinnaman, G.D., *And Signs Shall Follow: A Look at the Most Misunderstood Points of Charismatic Teaching* (Old Tappan, NJ: Fleming H. Revell, 1987).

Kittel, G., 'αἴνιγμα (ἔσοπτρον)', *TDNT*, I, pp. 178-80.

Klappert, B., 'Die Wunder Jesu im Neuen Testament', in *Das Ungewöhnliche: Wunder im Blick von Naturwissenschaft Theologie und Gemeinde* (Wuppertal: Aussaat-Bücherei, 45, 1969), pp. 25ff.

Klawiter, F.C., 'The New Prophecy in Early Christianity: The Origin, Nature and Development of Montanism, AD 165–220' (PhD dissertation, University of Chicago, 1975).

Kline, M.G., *The Structure of Biblical Authority* (Grand Rapids: Eerdmans, 1972).

Knight, H., 'The Old Testament Concept of Miracle', *SJT* 5 (December 1952), pp. 355-61.

Knox, R.A., *Enthusiasm: A Chapter in the History of Religion* (Oxford: Clarendon Press, 1962).

Koch, D.-A., *Die Bedeutung der Wundererzählungen für die Christologie des Markusevangeliums* (Berlin: de Gruyter, 1975).

Koch, K., *Speaking in Tongues and Divine Healing* (Des Plaines, IL: Regular Baptist Press, 1965).

—*The Strife of Tongues* (Grand Rapids: Kregel, 1969).

Koch, R., 'L'Aspect eschatologique de l'esprit du seigneur d'après Saint Paul', in *Studiorum Paulinorum Congressus Internationalis Catholicus*'(Rome: Pontifical Biblical Institute, 1961, 1963), pp. 131-41.

Kocher, M., 'Présupposés d'une pneumatologie charismatique', *Hokhma: Revue de Réflexion Théologique* 22 (1983), pp. 21-42; 23 (1983), pp. 49-60; 24 (1983), pp. 9-32.

Koenig, J., *Charismata: God's Gifts for God's People* (Philadelphia: Westminster Press, 1977).

—'From Mystery to Ministry: Paul as Interpreter of Charismatic Gifts', *USQR* 33 (Spring–Summer 1978), pp. 164-74.

Koenker, E.B., 'Some Charismatic Reforms in Western History', *International Catholic Review: Communio* 1 (Summer 1974), pp. 159-70.

Koole, J.L., *Gaven der Genezing* (Exegetica, 1.5; Delft: Van Keulen, 1953).

Krabbendam, H., 'B.B. Warfield vs. G.C. Berkhouwer on Scripture', in N. Geisler (ed.), *Inerrancy: The Extent of Biblical Authority* (Grand Rapids: Zondervan, 1980).

Kraft, C.H., *Christianity with Power: Your Worldview and Your Experience of the Supernatural* (Ann Arbor, MI: Servant Publications, 1989).

Kraft, H., 'Die altkirchliche Prophetie und die Entstehung des Montanismus', *TZ* 9 (July–August 1955), pp. 249-71.

—'Vom Ende der urchristlichen Prophetie', in J. Panagopoulos (ed.), *Prophetic Vocation in the New Testament and Today* (Leiden: Brill, 1977), pp. 162-85.

Kraus, C.N., 'The Principle of Authority in the Theology of B.B. Warfield, William Adams Brown, and Gerald Birney Smith' (PhD dissertation, Duke University, 1962).

Kreiser, B.R., *Miracles, Convulsions and Ecclesiastical Politics in Early Eighteenth Century Paris* (Princeton: Princeton University Press, 1978).

Kremer, J. *Pfingstbericht und Pfingstgeschehen* (Stüttgart: KBW, 1973).

Kselman, T.A., *Miracles and Prophecies in Nineteenth Century France* (New Brunswick, NJ: Rutgers University Press, 1983).

Kuhlmann, K., *I Believe in Miracles* (Old Tappan, NJ: Fleming H. Revell, 1969).

Kümmel, W.G., *The Theology of the New Testament* (Nashville: Abingdon Press, 1973).

Küng, H., 'The Charismatic Structure of the Church', in *The Church and Ecumenism* (New York: Paulist Press, 1965), pp. 41-61.

—'The Church as the Creation of the Spirit', in *The Church* (trans. Ray Ockenden and Rosaleen Ockenden; New York: Sheed & Ward, 1967), pp. 150-203.

Kuyper, A., *The Work of the Holy Spirit* (Grand Rapids: Eerdmans, 1956).

Kydd, R., 'Novatian's *De Trinitate*, 29: Evidence of the Charismatic?', *SJT* 30.4 (1977), pp. 313-18.

—'Origen and the Gifts of the Spirit', *Eglise et Théologie* 13 (January 1982), pp. 111-16.

—*Charismatic Gifts in the Early Church* (Peabody, MA: Hendrickson, 1984).

Labriolle, P. de (ed.), *Les sources de l'histoire du montanisme* (Fribourg: Librairie de l'Universite, 1913).

Ladd, G.E., 'The Holy Spirit in Galatians', in G. Hawthorne (ed.), *Current Issues in Biblical and Patristic Interpretation* (Grand Rapids: Eerdmans, 1975).

Lake, K., 'Note 9: The Holy Spirit', in *The Beginnings of Christianity*, V (Grand Rapids: Baker, 1965), pp. 96-111.

—'Note 10: The Gift of the Spirit on the Day of Pentecost', in *The Beginnings of Christianity*, V (Grand Rapids: Baker, 1965), pp. 111-121.

Lampe, G.W.H., *The Seal of the Spirit: A Study in the Doctrine of Baptism and Confirmation in the New Testament and the Fathers* (London: Longmans & Green, 1951).

—'The Holy Spirit in the Writings of St Luke', in D.E. Nineham (ed.), *Studies in the Gospels* (Oxford: Basil Blackwell, 1962).

—'Holy Spirit', *IDB*, II, pp. 626-38.

—'Miracles and Early Christian Apologetic', in C.F.D. Moule (ed.), *Miracles: Cambridge Studies in their Philosophy and History* (London: Mowbrays, 1965), pp. 203-18.

—'Miracles in the Acts of the Apostles', in C.F.D. Moule (ed.), *Miracles: Cambridge Studies in their Philosophy and History* (London: Mowbrays, 1965), pp. 163-78.

Lane, A.N.S., 'B.B. Warfield on the Humanity of Scripture', *VE* 14 (1987), pp. 77-94.

Langevin, P.E., 'La signification du miracle dans le message du Nouveau Testament', *ScEs* 27 (May–September 1975), pp. 161-86.

Langford, M.J., 'The Problem of "Meaning" of Miracle', *Religious Studies* 7 (March 1971), pp. 42-53.

Langton, E., *Essentials of Demonology: A Study of Jewish and Christian Doctrine: Its Origin and Development* (London: Epworth Press, 1949).

LaPorte, J., 'The Holy Spirit, Source of Life and Activity according to the Early Church', in E.D. O'Connor (ed.), *Perspectives on Charismatic Renewal* (South Bend, IN: University of Notre Dame Press, 1975).

Latourelle, R., 'Miracle and Revelation', in *Theology of Revelation* (New York: Alba House, 1967), pp. 389-405.

—*Miracles de Jèsus et thèologie du Miracle* (Montreal: Bellarmin, 1986).

Lauterburg, M., *Der Begriff des Charisma und seine Bedeutung für die praktische Theologie* (BFCT, 2.1; Gütersloh: Bertelsmann, 1898).

Lawton, J.S., *Miracles and Revelation* (New York: Association Press, 1960).

Lederle, H.I., *Treasures Old and New: Interpretations of 'Spirit Baptism' in the Charismatic Renewal Movement* (Peabody, MA: Hendrickson, 1988).

Lee, J.Y., 'Interpreting the Powers in Pauline Thought', *NovT* 12.1 (1970), pp. 54-69.

Lee-Pollard, D.A., 'Powerlessness as Power: A Key Emphasis in the Gospel of Mark', *SJT* 40.2 (1987), pp. 173-88.

Lehman, P.T., 'The Reformers' Use of the Bible', *TTod* 3 (October 1946), pp. 328-44.

Leivestad, R., *Christ the Conqueror* (London: SPCK, 1954).

—'Das Dogma von der prophetenlosen Zeit', *NTS* 19 (April 1973), pp. 288-99.

Letis, T.P., *Martin Luther and Charismatic Ecumenism* (Springfield, MO: Reformation Research Press, 1979).

Lewis, C.S., *Miracles: A Preliminary Study* (New York: Macmillan, 1947).

Lienhard, J.T., 'On "Discernment of Spirits" in the Early Church', *Theological Studies* 41 (September 1980), pp. 505-29.

Lightner, R.T., *Evangelical Theology: A Survey and Review* (Grand Rapids: Baker, 1986).

Lindars, B., 'Elijah, Elisha and the Gospel Miracles', in C.F.D. Moule (ed.), *Miracles: Cambridge Studies in their Philosophy and History* (London: Mowbrays, 1965), pp. 61-80.

Lindars, B., and S.S. Smalley (eds.), *Christ and the Spirit in the New Testament: In Honour of Charles Francis Digby Moule* (Cambridge: Cambridge University Press, 1973).

Lindblom, J., *Prophecy in Ancient Israel* (Philadelphia: Fortress Press, 1962).

—'Altchristlicher Prophetismus', in *Geschichte und Offenbarung* (Lund: Gleerup, 1968), pp. 162-205.

Lindsell, H., 'My Search for the Truth about the Holy Spirit', *Christian Life* (September 1983), pp. 29.

Linton, O., 'The Demand for a Sign from Heaven (Mk 8.11-12 and Parallels)', *StT* 19.1-2 (1965), pp. 112-29.

Livingstone, W.D., 'The Princeton Apologetic as Exemplified by the Work of B.B. Warfield and J. Gresham Machen: A Study in American Theology, 1880–1930' (PhD dissertation, Yale University, 1948).

Lloyd-Jones, M., *The Sovereign Spirit* (Wheaton, IL: Harold Shaw, 1985).

Loetscher, L.A., *The Broadening Church: A Study of Theological Issues in the Presbyterian Church since 1869* (Philadelphia: University of Pennsylvania Press, 1954).

Lofthouse, W.F., 'The Holy Spirit in the Acts and the Fourth Gospel', *ExpTim* 52 (June 1941), pp. 334-36.

Lohse, E., 'Miracles in the Fourth Gospel', in M. Hooker and C. Hickling (eds.), *What About the New Testament? Essays in Honour of Christopher Evans* (London: SCM Press, 1975), pp. 64-75.

Lombard, H.A., 'Charisma and Church Office', *Neotestamentica* 10.1 (1976), pp. 31-52.

Loos, H., van der, *The Miracles of Jesus* (NovTSup, 9; Leiden: Brill, 1966).

Lührmann, D., 'Jesus und seine Propheten: Gesprächsbeitrag', in J. Panagopoulos (ed.), *Prophetic Vocation in the New Testament and Today* (Leiden: Brill, 1977), pp. 210-17.

Lull, D.J., *The Spirit in Galatia: Paul's Interpretation of pneuma as Divine Power* (SBLDS, 49; Missoula, MT: Scholars Press, 1980).

MacArthur, J., *The Charismatics: A Doctrinal Perspective* (Grand Rapids: Zondervan, 1978).

MacArthur, J.F., Jr, *Charismatic Chaos* (Grand Rapids: Zondervan, 1992).

McCasland, S.V., *By the Finger of God: Demon Possession and Exorcism in Early Christianity in the Light of Modern Views of Mental Illness* (New York: Macmillan, 1951).

—'Miracle', *IDB*, III, pp. 392-402.

—'Signs and Wonders', *JBL* 76 (June 1957), pp. 149-52.

McCaslin, K., *What the Bible Says about Miracles* (Joplin, MO: College Press, MacDonald, W.G., 'Glossolalia in the New Testament', *Bulletin of the Evangelical Theological Society* 7 (Spring 1964), pp. 59-68.

McClanahan, J.S., Jr, 'Benjamin B. Warfield: Historian of Doctrine in Defense of Orthodoxy, 1881–1921' (PhD dissertation, Union Theological Seminary, 1988).

McDonnell, K., 'A Statement of the Theological Basis of the Catholic Charismatic Renewal', *Worship* 47 (December 1973), pp. 610-20.

—*Charismatic Renewal and the Churches* (New York: Seabury, 1976).

—*Presence, Power, Praise: Documents on the Charismatic Renewal* (3 vols.; Collegeville, MN: Liturgical Press, 1980).

—'The Determinative Doctrine of the Holy Spirit', *TTod* 39.2 (July 1982), pp. 142-61.

McGee, G.B (ed.), *Initial Evidence: Historical and Biblical Perspectives on the Pentecostal Doctrine of Spirit Baptism* (Peabody, MA: Hendrickson, 1991).

McGinn-Moorer, S.E., 'The New Prophecy of Asia Minor and the Rise of Ecclesiastical Patriarchy in Second Century Pauline Traditions' (PhD dissertation, Northwestern University, 1989).

MacGorman, J.W., 'Glossolalic Error and its Correction: 1 Corinthians 12–14', *RevExp* 80 (Summer 1983), pp. 389-400.

McIntyre, J., 'The Holy Spirit in Greek Patristic Thought', *SJT* 7 (December 1954), pp. 353-75.

MacKay, J.R., 'Benjamin B. Warfield—A Bibliography', *The Expositor* 8.24 (July 1922), pp. 26-44.

McKelvey, R.J., 'Christ the Cornerstone', *NTS* 8 (July 1961–62), pp. 352-59.

McNeill, J.T., *The History and Character of Calvinism* (New York: Oxford University Press, 1954).

—The Significance of the Word for Calvin', *CH* 28 (June 1959), pp. 131-46.

MacLeod, D., 'Has the Charismatic Age Ceased?', *Banner of Truth* 85 (1970), pp. 13-20.

—'Have Spiritual Gifts Ceased?', *The Outlook* 33.4 (April 1983), pp. 7-10.

Macleod, J., *Scottish Theology in Relation to Church History since the Reformation* (Edinburgh: The Publications Committee of the Free Church of Scotland, 1943).

MacMullen, R., 'Two Types of Conversions to Early Christianity', *Vigilae Christianae* 37.2 (1983), pp. 174-92.

McRae, J.R., '(to telion) in I Corinthians 13.10', *RQ* 14 (1971), pp. 168-83.

—'Charismata in the Second Century', in E. Livingstone (ed.), *Papers Presented to the Sixth International Conference on Patristic Studies* (*Studia Patristica*, 12.1; Berlin: Akademie Verlag, 1975), pp. 232-37.

Maier, W.A., 'Charismatic Renewal in the Lutheran Church: "Renewal in Missouri"', *Concordia Theological Quarterly* 53.1-2 (January–April, 1989), pp. 21-38.

Makarian, J.J., 'The Calvinistic Concept of the Biblical Revelation in the Theology of B.B. Warfield' (PhD dissertation, Drew University, 1963).

Malina, B.J., 'Jesus as a Charismatic Leader', *BTB* 14 (1984), pp. 55-62.

Mallone, G., *et al.*, *Those Controversial Gifts* (Downers Grove, IL: Inter-Varsity Press, 1983).

Maly, K., '1 Kor. 12.1-3, eine Regel zur Unterscheidung der Geister?', *BZ* NS 10 (1966), pp. 82-95.

—*Mündige Gemeinde: Untersuchungen zur pastoralen Führung des Apostels Paulus im 1 Korintherbrief* (Stüttgart: Katholisches Bibelwerk, 1967).

Mann, C.S., 'The Kingdom in Mark. A: Miracles', in *Mark* (AB, 27; Garden City, NY: Doubleday, 1986).

Mansfield, M.R., *Spirit and Gospel in Mark* (Peabody, MA: Hendrickson, 1987).

Marcus, J., 'Entering into the Kingly Power of God', *JBL* 107.4 (December 1988), pp. 663-75.

Mare, H., 'The Holy Spirit in the Apostolic Fathers', *Grace Journal* 13.2 (Spring 1972), pp. 3-12.

Mare, H.A., 'Prophet and Teacher in the New Testament Period', *Bulletin of the Evangelical Theological Society* 9 (Summer 1966), pp. 139-48.

Marsden, G.M., *The Evangelical Mind and the New School Presbyterian Experience* (New Haven: Yale University Press, 1970).

—*Fundamentalism and American Culture: The Shaping of Twentieth-Century American Evangelicalism* (New York: Oxford University Press, 1980).

Marshall, I.H., 'The Significance of Pentecost', *SJT* 30.4 (1977), pp. 347-69.

—'The Hope of a New Age: The Kingdom of God in the New Testament', *Themelios* 11.1 (September 1985), pp. 5-15.

Martin, G (ed.), *Scripture and the Charismatic Renewal: Proceedings of the Milwaukee Symposium, December 1–3, 1978* (Ann Arbor, MI: Servant Books, 1979).

Martin, I.J., 'Glossolalia in the Apostolic Church', *JBL* 63 (June 1944), pp. 123-30.

—'I Corinthians 13 Interpreted by its Context', *JBR* 18 (April 1950), pp. 101-105.

—*Glossolalia in the Apostolic Church: A Survey of Tongue Speech* (Berea, KY: Berea College Press, 1960).

Martin, R.P., *The Spirit and the Congregation* (Grand Rapids: Eerdmans, 1985).

—'Gifts, Spiritual', in *ADB*, II, pp. 1015-18.

May, H.F., *The Enlightenment in America* (New York: Oxford University Press, 1976).

Mayhue, R., *Divine Healing Today* (Chicago: Moody Press, 1983).
1988).

Meeter, J.E., and R. Nicole, *A Bibliography of Benjamin Breckinridge Warfield, 1851–1921* (Nutley, NJ: Presbyterian and Reformed Publishing, 1974).

Mehat, A., 'Saint Irenee et les Charismes', *Studia Patristica* 17.2 (1982), pp. 719-24.

Melinsky, M.A.H., *Healing Miracles: An Examination of the Place of Miracles in Christian Thought and Medical Practice* (London: Mowbrays, 1968).

Ménégoz, E., 'Der biblische Wunderbegriff', in A. Suhl (ed.), *Der Wunderbegriff im Neuen Testament* (Wege der Forschung, 295; Darmstadt: Wissenschaftliche Buchgesellschaft, 1980), pp. 39-79.

Menoud, P.-H., 'La signification du miracle selon le Nouveau Testament', *Revue d'Histoire et de Philosophie Religieuses* 28-29.3 (1948–49), pp. 173-92.

Mensching, G., *Das Wunder im Glauben und Aberglauben der Volker* (Leiden: Brill, 1957).

Mensching, G., W. Vollborn, E. Lohse and E. Käsemann, 'Wunder', in K. Galling (ed.), *Religion im Geschichte und Gegenwart*, VI (7 vols.; Tübingen: Mohr, 3rd edn, 1957–65).

Menzies, R.P., *The Development of Early Christian Pneumatology with Special Reference to Luke–Acts* (JSNTSup, 54; Sheffield: JSOT Press, 1991).

Menzies, W.W., 'The Holy Spirit in Christian Theology', in K.S. Kantzer and S.N. Gundry (eds.), *Perspectives on Evangelical Theology: Papers from the Thirtieth Annual Meeting of the Evangelical Theological Society* (Grand Rapids: Baker, 1979), pp. 67-79.

Merricks, W., *Edward Irving: Forgotten Giant* (East Peoria, IL: Scribe's Chamber Publications, 1983).

Metz, J.B., 'Wunder', in M. Buchberger (ed.), *Lexikon für Theologie und Kirche*, X (Freiburg: Herder, 1965), pp. 1251-65.

Meynell, H., 'Two Directions for Pneumatology', *Religious Studies Bulletin* 2.1 (1982), pp. 101-17.

Michaelis, W., 'κράτος, κτλ', *TDNT*, II, pp. 905-15.

Micklem, E.R., *Miracles and the New Psychology* (London: Oxford University Press, 1922).

Middleton, C., *A Free Inquiry into the Miraculous Powers which are supposed to have subsisted in the Christian church from the earliest ages through several successive centuries. By which it is shown that we have no sufficient reason to believe, upon the authority of the primitive fathers, that any such powers were continued to the church after the days of the Apostles* (London: R. Manby and H.S. Cox, 1749).

Miguens, E., '1 Cor. 13.8-13 Reconsidered', *CBQ* 37 (January 1975), pp. 76-97.

Miller, J.F., 'Is "Miracle" an Intelligible Notion?', *SJT* 20 (March 1967), pp. 25-36.

Miller, M.H., 'The Character of Miracles in Luke–Acts' (ThD dissertation, University of California, 1971).

Mills, W.E., *A Theological-Exegetical Approach to Glossolalia* (Lanham, MD: University Press of America, 1985).

—*Speaking in Tongues: A Guide to Research on Glossolalia* (Grand Rapids: Eerdmans, 1986).

Minear, P.S., *To Heal and To Reveal: The Prophetic Vocation According to St Luke* (New York: Seabury, 1976).

Moessner, D., 'Paul and the Pattern of the Prophet Like Moses in Acts', in *Society of Biblical Literature Seminar Papers 22* (Missoula, MT: Scholars Press, 1983), pp. 203-12.

Moltmann, J., *The Church in the Power of the Spirit: A Contribution to Messianic Ecclesiology* (trans. M. Kohl; New York: Harper & Row, 1977).

Monden, L., *Signs and Wonders: A Study of the Miraculous Element in Religion* (New York: Desclée, 1966).

Montague, G.T., 'Baptism in the Spirit and Speaking in Tongues: A Biblical Appraisal', *TD* 21 (Winter 1973), pp. 342-60.

—*The Spirit and His Gifts* (New York: Paulist Press, 1974).

—*The Holy Spirit: Growth of a Biblical Tradition* (New York: Paulist Press, 1976).

Moody, D., 'Charismatic and Official Ministries', *Int* 19 (April 1965), pp. 168-81.

—*Spirit of the Living God: Biblical Concepts Interpreted in Context* (Philadelphia: Westminster Press, 1968).

Morgan, E.S., *Visible Saints: The History of a Puritan Idea* (Ithaca, NY: Cornell University Press, 1963).

Morgan-Wynne, J.E., 'The Holy Spirit in the Christian Experience of Justin Martyr', *Vigilae Christianae* 38.2 (1984), pp. 172-77.

Morris, L.J., 'Miracles', in *The Gospel according to John* (NICNT; Grand Rapids: Eerdmans, 1971), pp. 684-91

Moule, C.F.D., 'The Vocabulary of Miracle', in C.F.D. Moule (ed.), *Miracles: Cambridge Studies in their Philosophy and History* (London: Mowbrays, 1965), pp. 238-38.

Moule, C.F.D (ed.), *Miracles: Cambridge Studies in their Philosophy and History* (London: Mowbrays; 1965).

Mowry, M.L., 'Charismatic Gifts in Paul', in M.M. Ward (ed.), *Biblical Studies in Contemporary Thought* (Burlington, VT: 1975), pp. 113-29.

Mühlen, H., *Der heilige Geist als Person: Beitrag zur Frage nach der dem heiligen Geiste eigentümlichen Funktion in der Trinität, bei der Inkarnation und im Gnadenbund* (Münsterische Beiträge zür Theologie, 26; Münster: Aschendorff, 1963).

—*A Charismatic Theology: Initiation in the Spirit* (New York: Paulist Press, 1978).

—'Charismatic Renewal: An Ecumenical Hope', *TD* 30 (Fall 1982), pp. 245-49.

Mulder, R.F., 'The Concept of Miracles' (PhD dissertation, Brown University, 1971).

Mullen, R.B., 'Horace Bushnell and the Question of Miracles', *CH* 58 (December 1989), pp. 460-73.

Müller, U.B., *Prophetie und Predigt in Neuen Testament* (Gütersloh: Gerd Mohn, 1975).

Munck, J., *Paul and the Salvation of Mankind* (trans. F. Clarke; London: SCM Press, 1959).

Munyon, T.L., 'Authority and Revelatory Gifts', *Paraclete* 22.2 (Spring 1988), pp. 1-4.

Murphy, E.F., *Spiritual Gifts and the Great Commission* (South Pasadena, CA: Mandate Press, 1975).

Murray, I. *et al* (eds.), 'Warfield Commemorative Issue, 1921–1971', *Banner of Truth* 89 (February 1971).

Murray, J.J., 'Have Miraculous Gifts Ceased?', *SBET* 3 (Autumn 1985), pp. 55-59.

Mussner, F., *The Miracles of Jesus: An Introduction* (trans. A. Wimmer; Notre Dame, IN: Notre Dame University Press, 1968).

Myers, J.M., and E.D. Freed, 'Is Paul also among the Prophets?', *Int* 20 (January 1966), pp. 40-53.

Neusner, J., *The Wonder-Working Lawyers of Talmudic Judaism: The Theory and Practice of Judaism in Its Formative Age* (New York: University Press of America, 1987).

Neve, L., *The Spirit of God in the Old Testament* (Tokyo: Seibunsha, 1972).

Newman, J.H., *Two Essays on Biblical and Ecclesiastical Miracles* (London: Longmans, Green & Co., 1892).

Nichols, T.L., 'Miracles as a Sign of the Good Creation' (PhD dissertation, Marquette University, 1987).

Nicol, W., *The Semeia in the Fourth Gospel: Tradition and Redaction* (NovTSup, 32; Leiden: Brill, 1972).

Nicole, R., 'The Inspiration of Scripture: B.B. Warfield and Dr. Dewey M. Beegle', *The Gordon Review* 8 (Winter 1964–65), pp. 93-109.

—'The Inspiration and Authority of Scripture: J.D.G. Dunn vs. B.B. Warfield', *Churchman* 97.3 (1983), pp. 198-215; 98.1 (1984), pp. 7-27.

Niesel, W., *The Theology of Calvin* (trans. H. Knight; Philadelphia: Westminster Press, 1956).

Noll, M.A., 'Warfield, Benjamin Breckinridge', in W.A. Elwell (ed.), *Evangelical Dictionary of Theology* (Grand Rapids: Baker, 1984).

Noll, M.A (ed.), *The Princeton Theology: Scripture, Science, and Theological Method from Archibald Alexander to Benjamin Warfield* (Grand Rapids: Baker, 1984).

Nolland, J., 'Grace as Power', *NovT* 28 (January 1986), pp. 26-31.

—'Luke's Use of *CHARIS*', *NTS* 32 (October 1986), pp. 614-20.

Nösgen, K.F., *Der Heilige Geist: Sein Wesen und die Art seines Wirkens* (2 vols.; Berlin: Trowitzsch und Sohn, 1905).

Nutall, G.F., *The Holy Spirit in Puritan Faith and Experience* (Oxford: Basil Blackwell, 1946).

O'Brèartuin, L.S., 'The Theology of Miracles (Aquinas)', *Ephemerides Carmeliticae* 20.1 (1969), pp. 3-51; 2 (1969), pp. 351-402.

O'Neill, J.C., *The Theology of Acts in its Historical Situation* (London: SPCK, 1961).

O'Reilly, L., *Word and Sign in the Acts of the Apostles: A Study in Lucan Theology* (Analecta Gregoriana, 243; Rome: Gregorian University, 1987).

Odegard, D., 'Miracles and Good Evidence', *Religious Studies* 18 (March 1982), pp. 37-46.

Oepke, A., 'ἰάομαι, κτλ', *TDNT*, III, pp. 194-215.

Oke, C.C., 'Paul's Method not a Demonstration but an Exhibition of the Spirit', *ExpTim* 67 (November 1955), pp. 35-36.

Opsahl, P.D (ed.), *The Holy Spirit in the Life of the Church from Biblical Times to the Present* (Minneapolis: Augsburg, 1978).

Osiek, C., 'Christian Prophecy: Once Upon a Time?', *Currents in Theology and Mission* 17 (August 1990), pp. 291-97.

Otto, R., 'The Kingdom of God and the Charismata', in *The Kingdom of God and the Son of Man* (trans. F.V. Filson and B.L. Woolf; London: Lutterworth Press, rev. edn, 1938), pp. 331-76.

Oudersluys, R.C., 'Charismatic Theology and the New Testament', *Reformed Review* 28.1 (1974), pp. 48-59.

—'The Purpose of Spiritual Gifts', *Reformed Review* 28 (Spring 1978), pp. 212-22.

Oulton, J.E.L. 'The Holy Spirit, Baptism, and Laying on of Hands in Acts', *ExpTim* 66 (May 1955), pp. 236-40.

Palma, A.D., 'The Holy Spirit in the Corporate Life of the Pauline Congregation' (ThD dissertation, Concordia Theological Seminary, 1974).

Panagopoulos, J., 'Die urchristliche Prophetie: Ihr Charakter und ihre Funktion', in J. Panagopoulos (ed.), *Prophetic Vocation in the New Testament and Today* (Leiden: Brill, 1977), pp. 1-32.

Parker, P., 'Early Christianity as a Religion of Healing', *St Luke Journal* 19 (March 1976), pp. 142-50.

Parratt, J.K., 'The Rebaptism of the Ephesian Disciples', *ExpTim* 79 (March 1968), pp. 182-83.

—'The Laying on of Hands in the New Testament', *ExpTim* 80 (April 1969), pp. 21-14.

—'The Witness of the Holy Spirit: Calvin, The Puritans, and St. Paul', *EvQ* 41 (July–September 1969), pp. 161-68.

—'The Holy Spirit and Baptism in the New Testament', *ExpTim* 82 (May 1971), pp. 231-35; (June 1971), pp. 266-71.

Parsons, M., 'Warfield and Scripture', *The Churchman* 91.3 (1977), pp. 198-220.

Patton, F.L., 'Benjamin Breckinridge Warfield: A Memorial Address', *PTR* 19 (July 1921), pp. 369-391.

Paulsen, H., 'Die bedeutung des montanismus für die herausbildung des kanons', *Vigiliae Christianae* 32 (March 1978), pp. 19-52.

Pearson, B.A., *The Pneumatikos-Psychikos Terminology in 1 Corinthians: A Study of the Theology of the Corinthian Opponents of Paul and its Relation to Gnosticism* (SBLDS, 12; Missoula, MT: Scholars Press, 1973).

Pentecost, J.D., *The Divine Comforter: The Person and Work of the Holy Spirit* (Chicago: Moody Press, 1975).

Perels, O., *Die Wunderüberlieferung der Synoptiker in ihrem Verhältnis zur Wortüberlieferung* (BWANT, 4.12; Stüttgart: Kohlhammer, 1934).

Perry, A.S., 'I Corinthians 13.12a: βλέπομεν γὰρ ἄρτι δι' ἐσόπτρου ἐν αἰνίγματι', *ExpTim* 58 (July 1946–1947), pp. 279.

Pesch, R., *Jesu ureigene Taten? Ein Betrag zur Wunderfrage* (Freiburg: Herder, 1970).

Peter, J.F., 'Warfield on the Scriptures', *RTR* 16 (October 1957), pp. 76-84.

Pfister, W., *Das Leben im Geist nach Paulus: Der Geist als Anfang und Vollendung des Christlichen Lebens* (Freiburg: Universitätsverlag, 1963).

Pfitzner, V.C., ' "Pneumatic" Apostleship: Apostle and Spirit in the Acts of the Apostles', in W. Haubeck and M. Bachmann (eds.), *Wort in der Zeit: Neutestamentliche Studien. Festgabe für Karl Heinrich Rengstorf* (Leiden: Brill, 1980).

Piepkorn, A.C., '*Charisma* in the New Testament and the Apostolic Church', *CTM* 42 (1967), pp. 369-89.

Piper, O.A.,'The Authority of the Bible', *TTod* 6 (July 1949–1950), pp. 159-73.

Pittenger, N., 'On Miracle', *ExpTim* 80 (January 1969), pp. 104-107; (February 1969), pp. 147-50.

Polhill, J.B., 'Perspectives on the Miracle Stories', *RevExp* 74 (Summer 1977), pp. 389-99.

Pont, G., *Les dons de l'Esprit Saint dans la pensée de saint Augustin* (Sierre: Editions Chateau Ravire, 1974).

Powell, C.H., *The Biblical Concept of Power* (London: Epworth Press, 1963).

Powell, D., 'Tertullianists and Cataphrygians', *Vigiliae Christianae* 29.1 (1975), pp. 33-54.

Power, D.N., 'Let the Sick Man Call', *HeyJ* 19 (July 1978), pp. 256-70.

Poythress, V.S., 'The Nature of Corinthian Glossolalia: Possible Options', *WTJ* 40 (Fall 1977), pp. 130-35.

Praeder, S.M., 'Miracle Worker and Missionary: Paul in the Acts of the Apostles', in *Society for Biblical Literature Seminar Papers 22* (Missoula, MT: Scholars Press, 1983).

—*Miracles in Christian Antiquity* (Philadelphia: Fortress Press, 1987).

Preisigke, F., 'Die Gotteskraft der frühchristlichen Zeit', in A. Suhl (ed.), *Der Wunderbegriff im Neuen Testament* (Wege der Forschung, 295; Darmstadt: Wissenschaftliche Buchgesellschaft, 1980), pp. 210-47.

Pringle-Pattison, A.S., *Scottish Philosophy: A Comparison of the Scottish and German Answers to Hume* (Edinburgh: W. Blackwood & Sons, 1885).

Pyle, H.F., *Truth about Tongues* (Denver: Accent Publications, 1973).

Quesnel, M., *Baptises dans l'Esprit: Bapteme et Esprit Saint dans les Actes des Apotres* (Paris: Cerf, 1985).

Rahner, K., *The Spirit in the Church* (New York: Crossroad, 1979).

Ramm, B., *The Witness of the Spirit: An Essay on the Contemporary Relevance of the Witness of the Spirit* (Grand Rapids: Eerdmans, 1959).

Ramsay, A.M., *The Charismatic Christ* (London: Dartman, Longman & Todd, 1976).

Ramsay, A.M., and L.-J. Suenens, *Come, Holy Spirit* (New York: Morehouse-Barlow, 1976).

Ramsey, I.T., *Miracles: An Exercise in Logical Mapwork* (Oxford: Oxford University Press, 1952).

Ramsey, I.T., *et al.*, *The Miracles and the Resurrection* (SPCK Theological Collections, 3; London: SPCK, 1964).

Recker, R., 'Satan: In Power or Dethroned?', *Calvin Theological Journal* 6 (November 1971), pp. 133-55.

Rees, T., *The Holy Spirit in Thought and Experience* (New York: Charles Scribner's Sons, 1915).

Reid, H.M.B., *The Holy Spirit and the Mystics* (London: Hodder & Stoughton, 1925).

Reid, J.K.S., *The Authority of Scripture: A Study of the Reformation and Post-Reformation Understanding of the Bible* (New York: Harper & Brothers, 1958).

Reid, L.R., ' "That Which is Perfect" in I Corinthians 13.10' (MDiv thesis, Grace Theological Seminary, 1978).

Reid, T., *Essays on the Active Powers of the Human Mind* (introduction by B. Brody; Cambridge, MA: MIT Press, 1969 [1785]).

—*Essays on the Intellectual Powers of the Mind* (introduction by B. Brody; Cambridge, MA: MIT Press, 1969 [1785]).

Reiling, J., *Hermas and Christian Prophecy: A Study of the Eleventh Mandate* (NovTSup, 37; Leiden: Brill, 1973).

—'Prophecy, Spirit and the Church', in J. Panagopoulos (ed.), *Prophetic Vocation in the New Testament and Today* (Leiden: Brill, 1977), pp. 58-76.

Reitzenstein, R., *Hellenistische Wundererzählungen* (Darmstadt: Wissenschaftliche Buchgesellschaft, 2nd edn, 1963).

Remus, H., 'Does Terminology Distinguish Early Christian from Pagan Miracles?', *JBL* 101.4 (December 1982), pp. 531-51.

—' "Magic or Miracle"? Some Second-Century Instances', *The Second Century: A Journal of Early Christian Studies* 2 (Fall 1982), pp. 127-56.

—*Pagan–Christian Conflict over Miracle in the Second Century* (Cambridge, MA: The Philadelphia Patristic Foundation, 1983).

—'Miracle, New Testament', *ADB*, IV, pp. 856-69.

Rengstorf, H., 'ἀποστέλλω, κτλ', *TDNT*, I, pp. 398-447.

—'δώδεκα, κτλ', *TDNT*, II, pp. 321-29.

—'σημεῖον, κτλ', *TDNT*, VII, pp. 200-69.

—'τέρας', *TDNT*, VIII, pp. 113-27.

Renner, R., *Die Wunder Jesu in Theologie und Unterricht* (Schauenburg: Lahr/Schwartzwald, 1966).

Reymond, R.L., *What About Continuing Revelations and Miracles in the Presbyterian Church Today? A Study of the Doctrine of the Sufficiency of Scripture* (Nutley, NJ: Presbyterian and Reformed Publishing, 1977).

Richards, P.H., 'The Nature of Miracle' (ThD dissertation, Union Theological Seminary, 1958).

Richardson, A., and W. Schweitzer (eds.), *Biblical Authority for Today* (Philadelphia: Westminster Press, 1951).

Richardson, A., *The Miracle Stories of the Gospels* (London: SCM Press, 1941).

—*An Introduction to the Theology of the New Testament* (New York: Harper & Row, 1958).

Ridderbos, H., *The Coming of the Kingdom* (ed. R.O. Zorn; trans. H. de Jongste; Philadelphia: Presbyterian and Reformed Publishing, 1962).

Riga, P., 'Signs of Glory: The Use of *semeion* in St John's Gospel', *Int* 17 (October 1963), pp. 402-24.

—*The Gifts of the Spirit* (Notre Dame, IN: Notre Dame Fides Publishers, 1974).

Rigaux, B., 'L'anticipation du salut eschatologique par l'Esprit', in S. Agourides, J.J. von Allmen *et al.*, *Foi et salut selon S. Paul* (AnBib, 42; Rome: Pontifical Biblical Institute, 1970), pp. 101-30.

Riley, M.D., 'An Examination of the Hebrew Concept of Miracle' (PhD dissertation, Southwestern Baptist Theological Seminary, 1981).

Ritter, A.M., *Charisma im Verständnis des Joannes Chrysostomes und seiner zeit* (Forschungen zur Kirchen- und Dogmengeschichte, 25; Göttingen: Vandenhoeck & Ruprecht, 1972).

Robeck, C.M., Jr, 'The Gift of Prophecy in Acts and Paul', *SBT* 4 (1974), pp. 15-35; 5 (1975), pp. 37-54.

—'The Gift of Prophecy and the All-Sufficiency of Scripture', *Paraclete* 13.1 (Winter 1979), pp. 27-31.

—'Montanism: A Problematic Spirit Movement', *Paraclete* 15.3 (Summer 1981), pp. 24-29.

—'Visions and Prophecy in the Writings of Cyprian', *Paraclete* 16.3 (Summer 1982), pp. 21-25.

—'The Role and Function of Prophetic Gifts for the Church at Carthage, AD 202–258' (PhD dissertation, Fuller Theological Seminary, 1985).

—'Canon, *Regulae Fidei*, and Continuing Revelation in the Early Church', in J.E. Bradley and R.A. Miller (eds.), *Church, Word, and Spirit: Historical and Theological Essays in Honor of Geoffry W. Bromiley* (Grand Rapids: Eerdmans, 1987).

Robeck, C.M., Jr (ed.), *Charismatic Experiences in History* (Peabody, MA: Hendrickson, 1985).

Roberts, P., 'A Sign: Christian or Pagan (I Corinthians 14.21-25)?', *ExpTim* 90 (April 1979), pp. 199-203.

Roberts, R.L., Jr, ' "That Which Is Perfect"—1 Cor. 13.10', *RQ* 3.4 (4th Quarter 1959), pp. 199-204.

Robertson, C.F. 'The Nature of New Testament Glossolalia' (ThD dissertation, Dallas Theological Seminary, 1975).

Robertson, O.P., 'Tongues: Sign of Covenantal Curse and Blessing', *WTJ* 38 (Fall 1975–76), pp. 43-53.

Robinson, D., 'The "Ordo Salutis" and the Charismatic Movement', *Churchman* 97.3 (1983), pp. 232-43.

Robinson, D.W.B., 'Charismata Versus Pneumatika: Paul's Method of Discussion', *RTR* 31 (May–August 1972), pp. 49-55.

Robinson, J.A.T., *The Body: A Study in Pauline Theology* (SBT, 5; London: SCM Press, 1952).

Robinson, J.M., *The Problem of History in Mark* (SBT, 21; London: SCM Press, 1957).

Roddy, A.J., *Though I Speak with Tongues* (Atascadero, CA: Scripture Research, 1974).

Rode, F., *Le miracle dans la controverse moderniste* (Paris: Beauchesne, 1965).

Rogers, C.L., Jr, 'The Gift of Tongues in the Post-Apostolic Church (AD. 100–400)', *BSac* 122 (April–June 1965), pp. 134-43.

Rogers, J.B., 'Van Til and Warfield on Scripture in the Westminster Confession', in E.R. Geehan (ed.), *Jerusalem and Athens* (Nutley, NJ: Presbyterian and Reformed Publishing, 1971).

Root, J.C., *Edward Irving: Man, Preacher, Prophet* (Boston: Sherman, French & Co., 1912).

Ross, J.P, 'Some Notes on Miracle in the Old Testament', in C.F.D. Moule (ed.), *Miracles: Cambridge Studies in their Philosophy and History* (London: Mowbrays, 1965), pp. 43-60.

Ruble, R., 'A Scriptural Evaluation of Tongues in Contemporary Theology' (ThD dissertation, Dallas Theological Seminary, 1964).

Runia, K., 'The "Gifts of the Spirit" ', *RTR* 29 (September–December 1970), pp. 82-94.

Russell, D.S. 'Appendix II: Spirit in Apocalyptic Literature', in *The Method and Message of Jewish Apocalyptic* (Philadelphia: Westminster Press, 1964), pp. 402-405.

Russell, W., 'The Anointing with the Holy Spirit in Luke–Acts', *TrinJ* NS 7 (Spring 1986), pp. 47-63.

—'The Holy Spirit's Ministry in the Fourth Gospel', *GTJ* 8 (Fall 1987), pp. 227-39.

Ruthven, J.M., 'On the Cessation of the Charismata', *Paraclete* 3.2 (Spring 1969), pp. 23-30; 3.3 (Summer 1969), pp. 21- 27; 3.4 (Autumn 1969), pp. 20-28.

Ryrie, C.C., *The Holy Spirit* (Chicago: Moody Press, 1965).

—*Balancing the Christian Life* (Chicago: Moody Press, 1969), pp. 163-68.

Saake, H., 'Paulus als Ekstatiker', *NovT* 15.2 (1973), pp. 153-60.

Sabourin, L., *The Divine Miracles Discussed and Defended* (Rome: Catholic Book Agency, 1977).

Sahas, D.J., 'The Formation of Later Islamic Doctrines as a Response to Byzantine Polemics: The Miracles of Muhammad', *GOTR* 27 (Summer–Fall 1982), pp. 307-24.

Sahlberg, C.-E., 'From Ecstasy to Enthusiasm: Some Trends in Scientific Attitude to the Pentecostal Movement', *Evangelical Review of Theology* 9 (January 1985), pp. 70-77.

Sala, H., 'An Investigation of the Baptism and Filling Work of the Holy Spirit in the New Testament as Related to the Pentecostal Doctrine of Initial Evidence' (PhD dissertation, Bob Jones University, 1966).

Sandeen, E.R., 'The Princeton Theology: One Source of Biblical Literalism in American Protestantism', *CH* 31 (September 1962), pp. 307-321.

Sanders, J.O., *The Holy Spirit and His Gifts* (Grand Rapids: Zondervan, 1970).

Sanders, J.T., 'First Corinthians 13: Its Interpretation Since the First World War', *Int* 20 (April 1966), pp. 159-87.

Sarles, K.L., 'An Appraisal of the Signs and Wonders Movement', *BSac* 145 (January–March 1988), pp. 57-84.

Sasse, H., 'Apostles, Prophets, Teachers', *RTR* 28 (January–April 1968), pp. 11-21.

Saunders, E.W., 'The Curative Power of the New Age', in *Jesus in the Gospels* (Englewood Cliffs, NJ: Prentice Hall, 1967), pp. 158-83.

Scharbert, J., 'Was versteht das Alte Testament unter Wunder?', *BK* 22.1 (1967), pp. 37-46.

Scharlemann, M.H., *Healing and Redemption* (St Louis: Concordia Press, 1965).

Schille, G., *Die urchristliche Wundertradition: Ein Beitrag zur Frage nach dem irdischen Jesus* (Arbeiten zur Theologie, 1.29; Stüttgart: Calwer Verlag, 1967).

Schlatter, A., *Der Glaube im Neuen Testament* (Stüttgart: Verlag der Vereinsbuchhandlung, 2nd edn, 1896).

—*Theology of the New Testament* (trans. J. Marsh; New York: Macmillan, 1955).

Schleier, H., *Principalities and Powers in the New Testament* (Quaestiones Disputae, 3; London: Burnes & Oates, 1961).

Schleperlem, W.E., *Die Montanismus und die phrygischen Kulte; ein religionsgeschichtliche Untersuchung* (trans. W. Bauer; Tübingen: Mohr, 1929).

Schlier, H., 'βέβαιος, βεβαιόω, βεβαίωσις', *TDNT*, I, pp. 598-600.

—'δάκτυλος', *TDNT*, II, p. 20.

Schlingensiepen, H., *Die Wunder des Neuen Testamentes: Wege und Abwege ihrer Deutung in der alten Kirche bis zur Mitte des fünften Jarhunderts* (BFCT, 2.28; Gütersloh: Bertelsmann, 1933).

Schlütz, K., *Isaias 11,2 (die sieben Gaben des Heiligen Geistes) in der ersten vier christlichen Jahrhunderten* (Alttestamentliche Abhandlungen, 11.4; Münster: Aschendorff, 1932).

Schmithals, W., *Gnosticism in Corinth* (trans. J.E. Steely; Nashville: Abingdon Press, 1971).

—*The Office of Apostle in the Early Church* (trans. J.E. Steely; New York: Abingdon Press, 1971).

Schnackenberg, R., *The Church in the New Testament* (New York: Herder & Herder, 1965).

—'Miracles in the New Testament and Modern Science', in *Present and Future: Modern Aspects of New Testament Theology* (Notre Dame: University of Notre Dame Press, 1966).

—'The Johannine Signs', in *The Gospel According to St John*, I (trans. K. Smith; New York: Herder & Herder, 1968), pp. 515-28.

—*God's Rule and Kingdom* (trans. J. Murray; New York: Herder & Herder, 1968).

—'Apostles before and during Paul's Time' (trans. M. Kwiran and W.W. Gasque), in W.W. Gasque and R.P. Martin (eds.), *Apostolic History and the Gospel* (Exeter: Paternoster Press, 1970).

Schnider, F., *Jesus der Prophet* (Göttingen: Vandenhoeck & Ruprecht, 1973).

Schogren, G.S., 'Will God Heal Us—A Re-Examination of James 5.14-16a', *EvQ* 61.2 (1989), pp. 99-108.

Schrage, W., 'Heil und Heilung im Neuen Testament', *EvT* 46.3 (May–June 1986), pp. 197-214.

Schreiner, J., 'Wirken des Geist Gottes in alttestamentlicher Sicht', *TGl* 81 (1991), pp. 3-51.

Schrenk, G., 'Geist und Enthusiasmus', in *Studien zu Paulus* (Zurich: Zwingli-Verlag, 1954), pp. 107-27.

Schubert, K., 'Wunderberichte und ihr Kerygma in der rabbinischen Tradition', *Kairos: Zeitschrift für Religionwissenschaft und Theologie* 24.1-2 (1982), pp. 31-37.

Schürmann, H., *Ursprung und Gestalt: Erörterungen und Besinnungen zum Neuen Testament* (Dusseldorf: Patmos, 1970).

Schutz, V.A., *Tongues and the Sign Gifts* (Grand Rapids: Grace Publications, n.d.).

Schütz, J.H., *Paul and the Anatomy of Apostolic Authority* (Cambridge: Cambridge University Press, 1975).

Schwarz, H., *Das Verständnis des Wunders bei Heim und Bultmann* (Arbeiten zur Theologie, 2.6; Stuttgart: Calwer Verlag, 1979).

Schweizer, E., 'The Spirit of Power: The Uniformity and Diversity of the Concept of the Holy Spirit in the New Testament' (trans. J. Bright and E. Debor), *Int* 6 (July 1952), pp. 259-78.

—'The Service of Worship: An Exposition of 1 Cor. 14', *Int* 13 (October 1959), pp. 400-408.

—*Church Order in the New Testament* (London: SCM Press, 1961).

—'Observance of the Law and Charismatic Activity in Matthew', *NTS* 16 (April 1969), pp. 213-30.

Schweizer, E., et al., 'πνεῦμα, κτλ', *TDNT*, VI, pp. 332-455.

Scofield, C.I., *The Holy Bible, Scofield Reference Edition* (New York: Oxford University Press, 1909).

—*The New Scofield Reference Bible* (New York: Oxford University Press, 1968).

—*Plain Papers on the Doctrine of the Holy Spirit* (Grand Rapids: Baker, 1974).

Scott, E.F., *The Spirit in the New Testament* (London: Hodder & Stoughton, 1923).

Scott, R.B.Y., 'Is Preaching Prophecy?', *CJT* 1 (April 1955), pp. 11-18.

Scroggs, R., 'The Exaltation of the Spirit by Some Early Christians', *JBL* 84 (December 1965), pp. 359-73.

—'Paul: *sophos* and *pneumatikos*', *NTS* 14 (October 1967–1968), pp. 33-55.

Seitz, O.J.F., 'The Commission of Prophets and "Apostles": A Re-examination of Mt. 23.34 with Lk. 11.49', *SE* IV (TU 102 [1968]), pp. 236-40.

Selwyn, E.C., *The Christian Prophets* (London: Macmillan, 1900).

Senior, D., 'The Miracles of Jesus', in R.E. Brown, J.A. Fitzmyer and R.E. Murphy (eds.), *The New Jerome Biblical Commentary* (New York: Prentice Hall, 1990), pp. 1369-73.

Serr, J., 'Les charisms dans la vie de l'église: témoignages patristiques', *Foi et Vie* 72.1 (1973), pp. 33-42.

Sesboüé, B., 'Bulletin de théologie dogmatique: pneumatologie', *Recherches de Science Religieuses* 76.1 (1988), pp. 115-28.

Seybold, K., and U.B. Müller, *Sickness and Healing* (trans. D.W. Stott; Nashville: Abingdon Press, 1981).

Sheils, W.J (ed.), *The Church and Healing* (Oxford: Basil Blackwell, 1982).

Shelton, J.B., *Mighty in Word and Deed: The Role of the Holy Spirit in Luke–Acts* (Peabody, MA: Hendrickson, 1991).

Shoemaker, W.R., 'The Use of *ruach* in the Old Testament, and of *pneuma* in the New Testament', *JBL* 23.1 (1904), pp. 13-65

Sider, R.J., 'The Historian, Miracles and the Post-Newtonian Man', *SJT* 25 (August 1972), pp. 309-19.

Siegmund, G. 'Theologie des Wunders', *TRev* 58 (1962), pp. 289-98.

Silva, M., 'Old Princeton, Westminster, and Inerrancy', *WTJ* 50 (Spring 1988), pp. 65-80.

Simpson, A.B., *The Holy Spirit or Power from on High* (2 vols.; Harrisburg, PA: Christian Publications, 1895).

—*The Gospel of Healing* (Harrisburg, PA: Christian Publications, 1915).

—*The Lord for the Body* (Harrisburg, PA: Christian Publications, 1925).

—*When the Comforter Came* (Harrisburg, PA: Christian Publications, n.d.).

Simundson, D.J., 'Health and Healing in the Bible', *WW* 2 (Fall 1982), pp. 330-38.

Sirks, G.J.,'The Cinderella of Theology: The Doctrine of the Holy Spirit', *HTR* 50 (April 1957), pp. 77-89.

Skinner, B., 'Is the Age of Miracles Past?', *Church Quarterly Review* 157 (October–December 1956), pp. 445-52.

Sloan, D., *The Scottish Enlightenment and the American College Ideal* (New York: Teachers' College Press, 1971).

Smalley, S.S. 'Spiritual Gifts and I Corinthians 1216', *JBL* 87 (December 1968), pp. 427-33.

—'Spirit, Kingdom and Prayer and Luke–Acts', *NovT* 15.1 (1973), pp. 59-71.

Smeaton, G., *The Doctrine of the Holy Spirit* (Edinburgh: T. & T. Clark, 1882).

Smedes, L.B., 'Of Miracles and Suffering', *The Reformed Journal* 39.2 (February 1989), pp. 14-21.

Smith, C.R., *Tongues in Biblical Perspective: A Summary of Biblical Conclusions Concerning Tongues* (Winona Lake, IN: BMH Books, rev. edn, 1973).

Smith, D.M., 'Glossolalia and Other Spiritual Gifts in a New Testament Perspective', *Int* 28 (July 1974), pp. 307-20.

Smith, G., 'Jewish, Christian and Pagan Views of Miracles under Flavian Emperors', in *Society of Biblical Literature Seminar Papers 20* (Missoula, MT: Scholars Press, 1981).

Smith, R.D., *Comparative Miracles* (St. Louis, MO: Herder, 1965).

Smylie, J.H., 'Testing the Spirit in the American Context: Great Awakenings, Pentecostalism and the Charismatic Movements', *Int* 33 (January 1979), pp. 32-46.

Snaith, N.H., *The Distinctive Ideas of the Old Testament* (New York: Schocken Books, 1964).

Snow, M.L., 'Conyers Middleton: Polemic Historian, 1683–1750' (PhD dissertation, Columbia University, 1970).

Snyder, H.A., 'The Church as Holy and Charismatic', *Wesleyan Theological Journal* 15 (Fall 1980), pp. 7-32.

—*Signs of the Spirit* (Grand Rapids: Zondervan, 1989).

Sontag, F., 'Should Theology Today Be Charismatic?', *JETS* 30 (June 1987), pp. 199-203.

Sörgel, P.M., 'From Legends to Lies: Protestant Attacks on Catholic Miracles in Later Reformation Germany', *Fides et Historia* 21 (June 1989), pp. 21-29.

Soyres, J. de, *Montanism and the Primitive Church: A Study in the Ecclesiastical History of the Second Century* (Lexington, KY: American Theological Library Association, 1965).

Speigl, J. von, 'Die Rolle der Wunder im vorkonstantinischen Christentum', *ZKT* 92.2 (1970), pp. 287-312.

Spittler, R.P., 'The Limits of Ecstasy: An Exegesis of 2 Corinthians 12.1-10', in G.F. Hawthorne (ed.), *Current Issues in Biblical and Patristic Interpretation* (Grand Rapids: Eerdmans, 1975), pp. 259-66.

Spittler, R.P (ed.), *Perspectives on the New Pentecostalism* (Grand Rapids: Baker, 1976).

Stagg, F.E. *et al.*, *Glossolalia: Tongue Speaking in Biblical, Historical, and Psychological Perspective* (Nashville: Abingdon Press, 1967).

Stalder, K., *Das Werk des Geistes in der Heiligung bei Paulus* (Zurich: EVZ Verlag, 1961).

Stam, J.E., 'Charismatic Theology in the Apostolic Tradition of Hippolytus', in G.F. Hawthorne (ed.), *Current Issues in Biblical and Patristic Interpretation* (Grand Rapids: Eerdmans, 1975).

Stanley, D., SJ, 'Salvation and Healing', *The Way* 10 (1970), pp. 298-317.

Starkey, L.M., *The Holy Spirit in the Church* (Nashville: Abingdon Press, 1965).

Steinmetz, D., 'Religious Ecstasy in Staupitz and the Young Luther', *The Sixteenth Century Journal* 11.1 (1980): pp. 23-37.

Stephanou, E.A., 'The Charismata in the Early Church Fathers', *GOTR* 21 (Summer 1976), pp. 125-46.

Stewart, J., 'On a Neglected Element in New Testament Theology', *SJT* 4 (1951), pp. 292-301.

Stibbs, A.M., and J.I. Packer, *The Spirit within You: The Church's Neglected Possession* (Grand Rapids: Baker, 1979).

Stolee, H.J., *Speaking in Tongues* (Minneapolis: Augsburg, 1963).

Stonehouse, N.B., 'Repentance, Baptism and the Gift of the Holy Spirit', in *Paul before the Areopagus* (Grand Rapids: Eerdmans, 1957), pp. 70-87.

Stott, J.R.W., *Baptism and Fullness: The Work of the Holy Spirit Today* (Downers Grove, IL: Inter-Varsity Press, 1976).

Strachan, G., *The Pentecostal Theology of Edward Irving* (London: Darton, Longman & Todd, 1973).

Strong, A.H., 'Miracles as Attesting Revelation', in *Systematic Theology* (Philadelphia: Judson Press, 1907).

Stronstad, R., 'The Holy Spirit in Luke–Acts', *Paraclete* 23.1 (Winter 1989), pp. 8-13; 23.2 (Spring 1989), pp. 18-26.

Suenens, L.J., *A New Pentecost?* (New York: Seabury, 1975).

Suhl, A (ed.), *Die Wunder Jesu: Ereignis und Uberlieferung* (Gütersloh: Gütersloher Verlagshaus, 1968).

Sullivan, F.A.,SJ, *Charisms and Charismatic Renewal: A Biblical and Theological Study* (Ann Arbor, MI: Servant Books, 1982).

Swails, J.W., *The Holy Spirit and the Messianic Age* (Franklin Springs, GA: Advocate Press, 1975).

Swanton, R., 'Warfield and Progressive Orthodoxy', *RTR* 23 (October 1964), pp. 74-87.

Sweet, J.M.P., 'A Sign for Unbelievers: Paul's Attitude toward Glossolalia', *NTS* 13 (April 1967), pp. 240-57.

Sweetman, L., Jr, 'The Gifts of the Spirit: A Study of Calvin's Comments on I Cor. 12.8-10, 28; Rom. 12.6-8; Eph. 4.11', in D.E. Holwerda (ed.), *Exploring the Heritage of John Calvin* (Grand Rapids: Baker, 1976).

Swete, H.B., *The Holy Spirit in the Ancient Church* (New York: Macmillan, 1912).

Swete, H.B., *The Holy Spirit in the New Testament* (New York: Macmillan, 1910).

—*The Holy Spirit in the Ancient Church* (New York: Macmillan, 1918).

Swindoll, C.R., *Tongues: An Answer to Charismatic Confusion* (Portland, OR: Multnomah Press, 1981).

Swineburn, R., *The Concept of Miracle* (London: Macmillan, 1970).

Synan, V.A., *The Holiness-Pentecostal Movement* (Grand Rapids: Eerdmans, 1972).

—*Aspects of Pentecostal-Charismatic Origins* (Plainfield, NJ: Logos, 1975).

—*In the Latter Days: The Outpouring of the Holy Spirit in the Twentieth Century* (Ann Arbor, MI: Servant Books, 1984).

Sywulka, P.E., 'The Contribution of Hebrews 2.3-4 to the Problem of Apostolic Miracles' (ThM thesis, Dallas Theological Seminary, 1967).

Tagawa, K., *Miracles et Evangile: La pensée de l' évangeliste Marc* (Etudes d'histoire et de philosophie religieuses, 62; Paris: Presses Universitaires de France, 1966).

Talbert, C.H., 'Paul's Understanding of the Holy Spirit: The Evidence of 1 Corinthians 12–14', in C.H. Talbert (ed.), *Perspectives on the New Testament: Essays in Honor of Frank Stagg* (Macon, GA: Mercer University Press, 1985), pp. 95-108.

Talbot, A.M.M., *Faith Healing in Late Byzantium: The Posthumous Miracles of the Patriarch Athanasios I of Constantinople by Theoktistos the Stoudite* (Brookline, MA: Hellenic College Press, 1983).

Talley, T., 'Healing: Sacrament or Charism?', *Worship* 46 (1972), pp. 518-27.

Tamkin, W., 'That Which Is Perfect: I Corinthians 13.10' (BD thesis, Grace Theological Seminary, 1949).

Tapeiner, D.A., 'Holy Spirit', *ISBE*, II, pp. 730-42.

Taylor, G.A., 'Miracles: Yes or No?', *PJ* 33.16 (14 August 1974), pp. 7-9.

Taylor, J.V., *The Go-Between God: The Holy Spirit and Christian Mission* (New York: Oxford University Press, 1979).

Taylor, V., *The Doctrine of the Holy Spirit* (London: Epworth Press, 1937).

Tennant, F.R., *Miracle and its Philosophical Presuppositions* (Cambridge: Cambridge University Press, 1925).

Thielicke, H., *A Theology of the Spirit* (ed. and trans. G.W. Bromiley; Grand Rapids: Eerdmans, 1982).

Thigpen, P., 'Did the Power of the Spirit Ever Leave the Church?', *Charisma* 18.2 (September 1992), pp. 20-29.

Thomas, G., 'The Cessation of the Extraordinary Gifts: Historical Evidence', *Banner of Truth* 118 (July–August 1973), pp. 17-21.

Thomas, K., *Religion and the Decline of Magic* (London: Weidenfeld & Nicolson, 1971).

Thomas, R., *Understanding Spiritual Gifts: The Christian's Special Gifts in Light of I Corinthians 12–14* (Chicago: Moody Press, 1978).

—'Prophecy Rediscovered? A Review of the Gift of Prophecy in the New Testament and Today (Wayne A. Grudem)', *BSac* 149/593 (January–March 1992), pp. 83-96.

Thomas, R.L., 'Tongues. . . Will Cease', *JETS* 17 (Spring 1974), pp. 81-89.

—'The Spiritual Gift of Prophecy in Rev. 22.18', *JETS* 32.2 (June 1989), pp. 201-216.

Thompson, J.M., *Miracles in the New Testament* (London: Arnold, 1911).

Tiede, D.L., *The Charismatic Figure as Miracle Worker* (SBLDS, 1; Missoula, MT: Scholars Press, 1972).

Tobias, R., 'Spirit Gifts in Lutheran Tradition', *Dialog* 13 (Winter 1974), pp. 19-24.

Torrance, T.F., 'Review of *Inspiration and Authority of the Bible*, by Benjamin B. Warfield', *SJT* 7 (March 1954), pp. 104-108.

Torrey, R.A., *Baptism with the Holy Spirit* (London: James Nisbet and Co., 1895).

—*The Person and Work of the Holy Spirit* (New York: Fleming H. Revell, 1910).

—*Divine Healing: Does God Perform Miracles Today?* (New York: Fleming H. Revell, 1924).

Toussaint, S.D., 'First Corinthians Thirteen and the Tongues Question', *BSac* 120 (October–December 1963), pp. 311-16.

Traub, G., 'Die Wunder im Neuen Testament', in A. Suhl (ed.), *Der Wunderbegriff im Neuen Testament* (Wege der Forschung, 295; Darmstadt: Wissenschaftliche Buchgesellschaft, 1980).

Trembath, K.R., *Evangelical Theories of Biblical Inspiration: A Review and Proposal* (New York: Oxford University Press, 1987).

Trevett, C., 'Prophecy and Anti-Episcopal Activity: A Third Error Combatted by Ignatius?', *Journal of Ecclesiastical History* 34 (January 1983), pp. 1-18.

Trigg, J.W., 'The Charismatic Intellectual: Origen's Understanding of Religious Leadership', *CH* 50 (March 1981), pp. 5-19.

Trites, A.A., 'Benjamin B. Warfield's View of the Authority of Scripture' (ThM Thesis, Princeton Theological Seminary, 1962).

Tugwell, S., *Did You Receive the Spirit?* (New York: Paulist Press, 1972).

—'Reflections on the Pentecostal Doctrine of "Baptism in the Holy Spirit"', *HeyJ* 14 (July 1972), pp. 268-81; 14 (October 1972), pp. 402-404.

—'The Gift of Tongues in the New Testament', *ExpTim* 84 (February 1973), pp. 137-40.

—*A New Heaven and a New Earth: An Encounter with Pentecostalism* (London: Darton, Longman & Todd, 1976).

Turner, M.M.B., 'The Significance of Spirit Endowment for Paul', *VE* 9 (1975), pp. 56-69.

—'The Concept of Receiving the Spirit in John's Gospel', *VE* 10 (1977), pp. 24-42.

—'The Significance of Receiving the Spirit in Luke–Acts: A Survey of Modern Scholarship', *TrinJ* NS 2 (Fall 1981), pp. 131-58.

—'Spiritual Gifts Then and Now', *VE* 12 (1985), pp. 7-64.

—'The Spirit and Power of Jesus' Miracles in the Lucan Conception', *NovT* 33.2 (April 1991), pp. 124-52.

—'The Spirit of Prophecy and the Power of Authoritative Preaching in Luke–Acts: A Question of Origins', *NTS* 38 (January 1992), pp. 66-88.

Turner, W.H., *Pentecost and Tongues* (Franklin Springs, GA: Advocate Press, 1968).

Twelftree, G., '*EI DE . . . EGO EKBALLO TA DAIMONA*', in D. Wenham and C. Blomberg (eds.), *The Miracles of Jesus* (Gospel Perspectives, 6; Sheffield: JSOT Press, 1986), pp. 361-400.

—*Christ Triumphant: Exorcism Then and Now* (London: Hodder & Stoughton, 1985).

Unger, M.F. *New Testament Teaching on Tongues* (Grand Rapids: Kregel, 1971).

—'Divine Healing', *BSac* 128 (July–September 1971), pp. 234-44.

—*The Baptism and Gifts of the Holy Spirit* (Chicago: Moody Press, 1974).

Unnik, W.C. van, 'A Formula Describing Prophecy', *NTS* 9 (January 1963), pp. 86-94.

—' "Den Geist löschet nicht aus" (I Thessalonicher v. 19)', *NovT* 10 (October 1968), pp. 255-69.

—'Jesus: Anathema or Kurios (I Cor. 12.3)', in B. Lindars and S. Smalley (eds.), *Christ and the Spirit in the New Testament* (Cambridge: Cambridge University Press, 1973).

Van Gorder, P., *Charismatic Confusion* (Grand Rapids: Radio Bible Class, 1972).

Van Til, C., Introduction to B.B. Warfield, *The Inspiration and Authority of the Bible* (Philadelphia: Presbyterian and Reformed Publishing, 1948).

Vander Stelt, J.D., *Philosophy and Scripture: A Study in Old Princeton and Westminster Theology* (Marlton, NJ: Mack, 1978).

Vander, L., *Are Tongues for Today? What the Bible Says About Sign Gifts* (Grand Rapids: Radio Bible Class, 1979).

Vermes, G., *Jesus the Jew: A Historian's Reading of the Gospels* (Philadelphia: Fortress Press, 1973).

Vielhauer, P., 'Prophecy', in *New Testament Apocrypha*, II (trans. R.M. Wilson (London: Lutterworth Press, 1965), pp. 601-607.

Vogt, N., 'Paranormal Healing and its Implications for the Concept of Miracles' (PhD dissertation, Fordham University, 1977).

Vögtl, A., 'The Miracles of Jesus against their Contemporary Background', in U.J. Schultz (ed.), *Jesus in his Times* (Philadelphia: Fortress Press, 1971).

Volz, P., *Der Geist Gottes und die verwandten Erscheinungen im Alten Testament und im anschliessenden Judentum* (Tübingen: Mohr [Paul Siebeck], 1910).

Vos, G., 'The Eschatological Aspect of the Pauline Concept of the Spirit', in *Biblical and Theological Studies* (New York: Charles Scribner's Sons, 1912), pp. 211-59.

Vriesen, T.C., 'Ruach Yahweh (Elohim) in the Old Testament', in *Biblical Essays* (Oudtestamentiese Werkgemeenskap in Suid-Afrika; Pretoria: Rege-Pers Baperk, 1966), pp. 50-61.

Wagner, C.P (ed.), *Signs and Wonders Today* (Altamonte Springs, FL: Creation House Publishers, expanded edn, 1987).

—*The Third Wave of the Holy Spirit* (Ann Arbor, MI: Servant Publishers, 1988).

Waldvogel, E.L., 'The "Overcoming Life": A Study of the Reformed Evangelical Origins of Pentecostalism' (PhD dissertation, Harvard University, 1977).

Walker, D.P., *Unclean Spirits: Possession and Exorcism in France and England in the Late Sixteenth and Early Seventeenth Centuries* (London: Scholars Press, 1981), pp. 66-70, 72-73.

—'The Cessation of Miracles', in I. Merkel and A.G. Debus (eds.), *Hermeticism and the Renaissance: Intellectual History and the Occult in Early Modern Europe* (Washington, DC: Folger Books, 1988), pp. 111-24.

Wallis, W.B., 'Benjamin B. Warfield: Didactic and Polemic Theologian', *Presbyterion: Covenant Seminary Review* 3 (Fall 1977), pp. 73-94.

Walt, B.J. van der, 'Thomas Aquinas' Idea about Wonders: A Critical Appraisal', in K. Rahner *et al* (eds.), *Dio e l'Eonomia della Salvezz* (Naples: Edizioni Domenicane Italiane, 1974), pp. 470-88.

Walvoord, J.F., *The Holy Spirit* (Grand Rapids: Zondervan, 1958).

—'Contemporary Issues in the Doctrine of the Spirit Today, Part IV: Spiritual Gifts Today', *BSac* 130 (October–December 1973), pp. 315-28.

—*The Holy Spirit at Work Today* (Lincoln, NE: Back to the Bible Broadcast, 1973).

—*The Holy Spirit: A Comprehensive Study of the Person and Work of the Holy Spirit* (Grand Rapids: Zondervan, 3rd edn, 1977).

—'The Holy Spirit and Spiritual Gifts', *BSac* 143 (April–June 1986), pp. 109-22.

Ward, B., ' "Signs and Wonders": Miracles in the Desert Tradition', *Studia Patristica* 2, pp. 539-43.

—*Miracles and the Medieval Mind: Theory, Record, and Event, 1000–1215* (Philadelphia: University of Pennsylvania Press, 1982).

Warfield B.B., 'The Spirit of God in the Old Testament', *PRR* 6.24 (October 1895), pp. 101-29.

—'Kikuyu, Clerical Veracity, and Miracles', *PTR* 12 (October 1914), pp. 529-85.

—*Counterfeit Miracles* (New York: Charles Scribner's Sons, 1918).

—'The Question of Miracles', *The Bible Student* 7 (March 1903), pp. 121-26; (April 1903), pp. 193-97; (May 1903), pp. 243-50; (June 1903), pp. 314-20, collected in *Selected Shorter Works of Benjamin B. Warfield* (ed. J.E. Meeter; Nutley, NJ: Presbyterian and Reformed Publishing, 1970, 1973).

—Introductory Note to A. Kuyper, *The Work of the Holy Spirit* (Grand Rapids: Eerdmans, 1979), pp. xxv-xxix.

—*Opuscula Warfieldii: Being Fugitive Pieces Published by Benjamin B. Warfield, 1880–1918* (15 vols.; Speer Library Archives, Princeton Theological Seminary).

—*Selected Shorter Works of Benjamin B. Warfield* (ed. J.E. Meeter; Nutley, NJ: Presbyterian and Reformed Publishing, 1970, 1973).

—*The Works of Benjamin B. Warfield* (ed. E.D. Warfield, W.P. Armstrong and C.W. Hodge; 10 vols.; Grand Rapids: Baker, 1981).

Watkin-Jones, H., *The Holy Spirit in the Medieval Church* (London: Epworth Press, 1922).

—*The Holy Spirit from Arminius to Wesley* (London: Epworth Press, 1929).

Webster, J., 'The Identity of the Holy Spirit', *Themelios* 9.1 (September 1983), pp. 4-7.

Wedderburn, A.J.M., 'Romans 8.26—Towards a Theology of Glossolalia?', *SJT* 28.4 (1975), pp. 368-77.

Weeden, T.J., Sr, *Mark: Traditions in Conflict* (Philadelphia: Fortress Press, 1971).

Weinel, H., *Die Wirkungen des Geistes und der Geister im nachapostolischen Zeitalter bis auf Irenäus* (Freiburg: Mohr, 1899).

Weinreich, O., 'Gebet und Wunder: Türöffnung im Wunder-, Prodigien-, und Zauberglauben der Antike, des Judentums und Christentums', in F. Focke (ed.),

Genethliakon Wilhelm Schmid (Tübingener Beiträge zur Altertumwissenschaft, 5; Stüttgart: Kohlhammer, 1929), pp. 200-464.

—*Antike Heilungswunder: Untersuchungen zum Wunderglauben der Griechen und Römer* (Berlin: de Gruyter, 1969).

Welliver, K.B., 'Pentecost and the Early Church: Patristic Interpretation of Acts 2' (PhD dissertation, Yale University, 1961).

Wendland, H.-D., 'Gesetz und Geist: Zum Problem des Schwärmertums bei Paulus', *Schriften des theologischen Konvents Augsburgischen Bekenntnisses* 6.1 (1952), pp. 38-54.

—'Das Wirken des Heligen Geistes in den Gläubigen nach Paulus', *TLZ* 77.8 (1952), pp. 457-70.

Wendland, J., *Miracles and Christianity* (trans. H.R. Mackintosh; London: Hodder & Stoughton, 1911).

Wendt, H.H., *Die Begriffe Fleische und Geist* (Gotha: Friedrich Andr. Perthes, 1878).

Wenham, D., 'Miracles Then and Now', *Themelios* 12 (September 1986), pp. 1-4.

Wenisch, B., *Geschichten oder Geschichte? Theologie des Wunders* (Salzburg: Verlag St Peter, 1981).

Wesley, J., —*A Letter to the Right Reverend the Lord Bishop of Gloucester, Occasioned by his Tract on the Office and Operations of the Holy Spirit* (Bristol: William Pine, 1763).

—'Letter to Dr. Conyers Middleton', in J. Telford (ed.), *The Letters of John Wesley*, II (London: Epworth Press, 1931), pp. 312-88.

—'Letter to Thomas Church', in J. Telford (ed.), *The Letters of John Wesley*, II (London: Epworth Press, 1931), pp. 252-62.

Westblade, D., 'Benjamin B. Warfield on Inspiration and Inerrancy', *SBT* 10 (April 1980), pp. 27-43.

Whitcomb, J.C., *Does God Want Christians to Perform Miracles Today?* (Winona Lake, IN: BMH Books, 1973).

White, R.F., 'Richard Gaffin and Wayne Grudem: A Comparison of Cessationist and Noncessationist Argumentation', *JETS* 35.2 (June 1992), pp. 173-81.

Whittacker, M. ' "Signs and Wonders": The Pagan Background', *SE* 5.2 (1968), pp. 155-58.

Wiebe, P.H. 'The Pentecostal Evidence Doctrine', *JETS* 27 (December 1984), pp. 465-72.

Wiers, J., 'Scottish Common Sense Realism in the Theology of B.B. Warfield' (unpublished paper, Trinity Evangelical Divinity School, June 1977).

Wiles, M.F., 'Miracles in the Early Church', in C.F.D. Moule (ed.), *Miracles: Cambridge Studies in their Philosophy and History* (London: Mowbrays, 1965).

Wilkinson, J., 'Healing in the Epistle of James', *SJT* 24 (August 1971), pp. 326-45.

—*Health and Healing: Studies in New Testament Principles and Practice* (Edinburgh: Handsel Press, 1980).

Willaert, B., 'De Heilige Geest, eschatologische gave in Christus', *Collationes Brugenses et Gandavanses* 3 (1957), pp. 145-60.

Williams, C., *The Descent of the Dove: A Short History of the Holy Spirit in the Church* (Grand Rapids: Eerdmans, 1939).

Williams, C.G., 'Glossolalia as a Religious Phenomenon: "Tongues" at Corinth and Pentecost', *Religion* 5 (Spring 1975), pp. 16-32.

—*Tongues of the Spirit* (Cardiff: University of Wales Press, 1981).

Williams, D.T., 'Salvation and Healing: Towards a Unified Theology', *Theologia Evangelica* 23 (June 1990), pp. 15-26.

Williams, G., and E. Waldvogel, 'A History of Speaking in Tongues and Related Gifts', in M.P. Hamilton (ed.), *The Charismatic Movement* (Grand Rapids: Eerdmans, 1975).

Williams, J., *The Holy Spirit: Lord and Life-Giver* (Neptune, NJ: Loizeaux Brothers, 1980).

Williams, J.R., *The Era of the Spirit* (Plainfield, NJ: Logos, 1971).

—'The Charismatic Movement and Reformed Theology' (unpublished paper, CBN University, Virginia Beach, VA, 1975).

—*The Gift of the Holy Spirit Today* (Plainfield, NJ: Logos, 1980).

—*Renewal Theology* (Grand Rapids: Zondervan, 1988).

Windisch, H., *The Spirit-Paraclete in the Fourth Gospel* (trans. J.W. Cox; Facet Books Biblical Series, 20; Philadelphia: Fortress Press, 1968).

Winn, A.C., 'Pneuma and Kerygma: A New Approach to the New Testament Doctrine of the Holy Spirit' (ThD dissertation, Union Theological Seminary, 1956).

Wolfson, H.A., *Philo* (Cambridge, MA: Harvard University Press, 1948).

Womack, D., *The Wellsprings of the Pentecostal Movement* (Springfield, MO: Gospel Publishing House, 1968).

Woodbridge, J.D., and R. Balmer, 'The Princetonians' Viewpoint of Biblical Authority: An Evaluation of Ernest Sandeen', in J.D. Woodbridge and D.A. Carson (eds.), *Scripture and Truth* (Grand Rapids: Zondervan, 1978).

Woods, G.F., 'The Evidential Value of the Biblical Miracles', in C.F.D. Moule (ed.), *Miracles: Cambridge Studies in their Philosophy and History* (London: Mowbrays, 1965), pp. 19-32.

Woolston, T., *A Discourse on the Miracles of Our Saviour* (London: published by the author, 6th edn, 1729).

Wright, C.J., *Miracle in History and in Modern Thought* (New York: Henry Holt, 1930).

Wright, D.F., 'Why Were the Montanists Condemned?', *Themelios* 2 (September 1976), pp. 15-22.

Wright, J., 'Discernment of Spirits in the New Testament', *Communio* 1 (Summer 1974), pp. 115-27.

Yates, J.E., *The Spirit and the Kingdom* (London: SPCK, 1963).

Young, J.E., ' "That Some Should Be Apostles" ', *EvQ* 48 (April–June 1976), pp. 96-104.

Young, R., 'Miracles and Epistemology', *Religious Studies* 8 (June 1972), pp. 115-26.

Young, W., 'Miracles in Church History', *The Churchman* 102.2 (1988), pp. 102-22.

Younger, P., 'A New Start toward a Doctrine of the Spirit', *CJT* 13 (April 1967), pp. 123-33.

Zakovitch, Y., 'Miracle, Old Testament', in *ADB*, IV, pp. 845-56.

Zeller, G.W., *God's Gift of Tongues: The Nature, Purpose and Duration of Tongues as Taught in the Bible* (Neptune, NJ: Loizeaux Brothers, 1978).

Zsindely, E., *Krankheit und Heilung im altern Pietismus* (Stüttgart: Zwingli-Verlag, 1962).

INDEXES

INDEX OF REFERENCES

INDEX OF NAMES